Religious Warfare in Europe,
1400–1536

Religious Warfare in Europe, 1400–1536

NORMAN HOUSLEY

OXFORD
UNIVERSITY PRESS

OXFORD

UNIVERSITY PRESS

Great Clarendon Street, Oxford OX2 6DP

Oxford University Press is a department of the University of Oxford.
It furthers the University's objective of excellence in research, scholarship,
and education by publishing worldwide in

Oxford New York

Auckland Bangkok Buenos Aires Cape Town Chennai
Dar es Salaam Delhi Hong Kong Istanbul Karachi Kolkata
Kuala Lumpur Madrid Melbourne Mexico City Mumbai Nairobi
São Paulo Shanghai Singapore Taipei Tokyo Toronto
and an associated company in Berlin

Oxford is a registered trade mark of Oxford University Press
in the UK and in certain other countries

Published in the United States
by Oxford University Press Inc., New York

British Library Cataloguing in Publication Data
Data available

Library of Congress Cataloging in Publication Data

Data available

ISBN 0-19-820811-1

1 3 5 7 9 10 8 6 4 2

Typeset in Ehrhardt
by SNP Best-set Typesetter Ltd., Hong Kong
Printed in Great Britain
on acid-free paper by
Biddles Ltd, Guildford and King's Lynn

Preface

CONSIDERING ITS MODEST LENGTH, this book has taken a disconcertingly long time to write. The idea for it came to me while I was finishing my general account of crusading in the late Middle Ages, *The Later Crusades, 1274–1580: From Lyons to Alcazar* (1992). What gave the project focus and direction, however, was my participation in two research groups in the 1990s: first, my membership of Philippe Contamine's team working on the volume on inter-state warfare and competition for the European Science Foundation programme 'The Origins of the Modern State in Europe', and secondly, my participation in Peter Schäfer's seminar on Messianism at the Institute for Advanced Study in Princeton in 1996. The intellectual stimulus offered by both groups proved invaluable; more generally, the months I was able to spend at the Institute in Princeton were tremendously useful because of the interdisciplinary contacts on which the Institute, quite rightly, prides itself. No less important have been the ideas I have encountered and tried out over the years at Jonathan Riley-Smith's Crusades seminar in Cambridge and London, at meetings in Richard Bonney's Centre for the History of Religious and Political Pluralism in Leicester, and at the Summer Meeting of the Ecclesiastical History Society at Warwick in 1998. Chapter 5 in particular benefited from outings at the Riley-Smith Crusades seminar, at the seminar on Medieval and Early Modern Warfare convened by the Department of War Studies at King's College London, and the 19th International Congress of Historical Studies which met at Oslo in August 2000.

Institutional support has been crucial. To the University of Leicester I owe a considerable debt of gratitude. It has been generous with both study leave and leave of absence, and it has financed a number of trips to use the British Library in London. The University Library's Inter-Library Loans Department has come up trumps on numerous occasions. The Leverhulme Trust awarded me a Fellowship which paid for six months leave of absence in 1996. The Arts and Humanities Research Board awarded me money which, together with study leave, gave me that elixir of joy for any academic, the full year free of teaching, in 2001–2. The British Academy kindly paid for me to go to the USA in 1996 and to Oslo in 2000. By appointing me a member of its School of Historical Studies in 1996, the Institute in Princeton enabled me to make use of not just its own superb Library, but also the Firestone Library at nearby Princeton University.

I am very grateful to Jonathan Riley-Smith for reading the entire book in draft. Finally, I must thank my wife Valerie and my children Simon and Sarah, for providing a family life where history is kept firmly in its place.

N.H.

Contents

Abbreviations

AHR	*American Historical Review*
CWE	*Collected Works of Erasmus* (Toronto: University of Toronto Press, 1974–)
CWMRE	[N. Housley], *Crusading and Warfare in Medieval and Renaissance Europe* (Aldershot: Ashgate, 2001)
CWSTM	*The Complete Works of St Thomas More* (New Haven: Yale University Press, 1963–)
EHR	*English Historical Review*
HZ	*Historische Zeitschrift*
JEH	*Journal of Ecclesiastical History*
JMH	*Journal of Medieval History*
LoB	Lawrence of Březová
LW	*Luther's Works*, 55 vols. (St Louis and Philadelphia: Concordia Publishing House and Fortress Press, 1958–67)
MH	*Monumenta Henricina*, 15 vols. (Coimbra: Comissão Executiva das Comemorações do Quinto Aniversário da Morte do Infante D. Henrique, 1960–74)
RHE	*Revue d'histoire ecclésiastique*
SCH	Studies in Church History
Setton, *PL*	K. M. Setton, *The Papacy and the Levant (1204–1571)*, 4 vols. (Philadelphia: American Philosophical Society, 1976–84)
TRHS	*Transactions of the Royal Historical Society*
UB	F. Palacký (ed.), *Urkundliche Beiträge zur Geschichte des Hussitenkrieges in den Jahren 1419–1436*, 2 vols. (Prague: Friedrich Tempsky, 1873)

CHAPTER ONE

The Subject: Religious Warfare in the Late Middle Ages and Early Reformation

1.1 THE STUDY OF RELIGIOUS WARFARE: APPROACHES AND PROBLEMS

Warfare and organized religious belief have been features of almost every human society in history, so an interaction between the two is never far from view. During the First World War, fought at a time when European society was relatively secularized, armies were exhorted to fight by a rhetoric which invoked God's aid for a national cause viewed as sacred. In the war's aftermath, the dead were remembered in annual celebrations cloaked in a liturgy and cultic ethos derived above all from religious traditions, while war memorials drew on an iconographic language which resonated with Christian values.[1] Both for public-spirited churchmen and rabble-rousers carried away by the nationalist excitement of the hour, and for communities devastated by losses on a hitherto unimaginable scale, religion provided invaluable terms of reference. The interaction between warfare and religion in an age before the massive changes wrought by the Enlightenment and the arrival of Mass Society was infinitely richer. In the Middle Ages and Early Modern period religious values did not simply provide terms of reference but a specific world-view which profoundly shaped the way contemporaries approached the practice of organized violence. In medieval Europe war was viewed as a means by which God's justice found expression, as a providential mechanism.[2] As Christine de Pisan put it in the early fifteenth century, 'warre & bataill whiche is made by iuste quarell is none other thing but

---

[1] W. J. Sheils (ed.), *The Church and War*, SCH 20 (Oxford: Blackwell, 1983); J. Winter, *Sites of Memory, Sites of Mourning: The Great War in European Cultural History* (Cambridge: Cambridge University Press, 1995). Amongst the more bizarre fruits of the excitement of 1914, Richard Sternfeld, a German Jew and Wagnerite who was also a distinguished historian of the Crusades, wrote a tract entitled 'Richard Wagner und der heilige deutsche Krieg': F. Spotts, *Bayreuth: A History of the Wagner Festival* (New Haven: Yale University Press, 1994), 155–6.

[2] J. T. Johnson, *Ideology, Reason and the Limitation of War: Religious and Secular Concepts 1200–1740* (Princeton: Princeton University Press, 1975), ch. 1 *passim*.

right execucion of iustyce, for to gyue the right there as it apperteyneth'.[3] Theologically, war had its place in God's purpose for mankind.

But it is clear that some wars were different. They were viewed by contemporaries as belonging not just to the sphere of providence but to a more intimate association with God's purpose. A divine mandate lay behind them: in the language used in Gratian's *Decretum*, they were *Deo auctore bella*, wars originated by God.[4] The armies which waged them were made up of God's warriors, chosen by him and showing themselves to be worthy of his favour, intervention, and rewards. In many cases opponents were demonized, labelled as God's enemies or as servants of the devil. This type of combat is best described as religious or holy warfare (*guerres de religion*, *Glaubenskriege*), signalling the direct and defining connection between the war and its religious aims and character.[5] Contemporaries wrote of the conflict being 'sanctified': for example, the English chronicler Thomas Walsingham used the phrase in relation to the crusade,[6] while the Hussite bishop Nicholas of Pelhřimov deployed it when referring to the defensive war waged by the Hussite coalition.[7] It should be noted that the sanctification of the war (*bellum* for Walsingham, *prelium* for Pelhřimov) did not necessarily entail that of the individual act of violence, normally termed the *effusio sanguinis*. The divine mandating of violence was not normally an excuse for indiscriminate butchery; indeed, the Taborites, who believed that they were waging their war in God's name, approached the conduct of their war with particular circumspection for that very reason. They practised an economy rather than a totality of violence.[8]

In European history the two most important series of religious wars were the Crusades and the Wars of Religion. Both have been subject to substantial historical revision in recent years and the methodology behind this book has been heavily influenced by the approaches and outcomes of that process of revision. In some respects the present study is an attempt to establish with greater clarity the relationship between the Crusades and the Wars of Religion. But before coming to that it is important to adopt a broader perspective and consider the various attempts which have been made hitherto to analyse religious warfare as a recurrent phenomenon in history.

The subject has attracted quite a lot of scholarly attention in recent years,

[3] Christine de Pisan, *The Book of Fayttes of Armes and of Chyvalrye*, ed. A. T. P. Byles (London: Oxford University Press for Early English Text Society, 1932), 10. The translation is by William Caxton, who printed the work in 1489.

[4] E.-D. Hehl, 'Was ist eigentlich ein Kreuzzug?', *HZ* 259 (1994), 297–336, at 308.

[5] On the issue of definition see the discussion in J. T. Johnson, *The Holy War Idea in Western and Islamic Traditions* (University Park: Pennsylvania State University Press, 1997), ch. 2, esp. 45.

[6] Thomas Walsingham, *Historia anglicana*, ed. H. T. Riley, 2 vols. (London: Rolls Series, 1863–4), ii. 71–2.

[7] F. M. Bartoš, 'Táborské bratrstvo let 1425–1426 na soudě svého biskupa Mikuláše z Pelhřimova', *Časopis Společnosti přátel starožitností českých v Praze*, 29 (1921), 102–22, at 114.

[8] Cf. Johnson, *Holy War Idea*, 45–6.

partly because of the role played by religion in the various wars which were generated by the break-up of Yugoslavia. Thus a collection of essays edited by Peter Herrmann in 1996 was entitled *Glaubenskriege in Vergangenheit und Gegenwart* and included an essay by Thomas Bremer dealing specifically with contemporary Yugoslavia.[9] Herrmann's collection was followed a year later by Peter Partner's *God of Battles: Holy Wars of Christianity and Islam*.[10] Partner's book was extremely fruitful. Its chief strength resides in his comparison of the Christian and Muslim practice of religious war; indeed, since he included chapters dealing with the Ancient Israelites, the Maccabean revolt, and the Zealots, all three of the great monotheistic religions are covered. Another strength is Partner's detailed knowledge and treatment of the persistence of the *jihad*, the Islamic war for the faith, in the period since *c*.1700, notably in struggles against the colonial powers in Africa and Asia. His comparative approach, and his brave decision to handle the *longue durée*, yielded many insights. He showed that Christian and Islamic religious war share a protean nature, which enabled them to revive in remarkably changed surroundings. In both cases religious war has been directed inwards against heretical groups, indeed in the case of Islam this type of *jihad* has perhaps been dominant over the centuries. During the Gulf War of 1991 both Saudi Arabia and Iraq secured declarations from their religious authorities (*'ulama*) to the effect that their war against each other was a *jihad*.[11] Less convincing was Partner's argument that the overall balance sheet of *jihad* has been fuller than Christian religious war in terms of 'internalized' struggle, holy war in a mainly moral sense. He pointed in particular to the writings of the Pakistani Islamic reformer Mawlana Abu'l-A'la Mawdudi (1903–79), who portrayed *jihad* as a form of moral and political activism in the context of modernization.[12] Yet this seems to ignore a good deal of crusading ideology, especially around 1200, as well as a rich seam of argumentation by humanists some three centuries later, not to speak of Loyola and other Counter-Reformation thinkers.[13] On the other hand, it is precisely the merit of Partner's approach that he invites disagreement and debate by setting out his argument in broad terms.

'The history of holy war, from the Biblical Hebrews to our own times, is a history of texts belonging to scriptural religions; it is also a history of human behaviour. The violence that men do, they seek to justify.'[14] This reference by Peter Partner to the important role played by Scripture within all the traditions which he examined serves as an introduction to a second approach towards the study of

---

[9] P. Herrmann (ed.), *Glaubenskriege in Vergangenheit und Gegenwart* (Göttingen: Vandenhoeck & Ruprecht, 1996). Thomas Bremer's essay is 'Religiöse Motive im jugoslawischen Konflikt der Gegenwart', 139–51.

[10] P. Partner, *God of Battles: Holy Wars of Christianity and Islam* (London: Harper Collins, 1997).

[11] Ibid. 260.   [12] Ibid. 234–6.

[13] See, e.g., C. T. Maier, 'Crisis, Liturgy and the Crusade in the Twelfth and Thirteenth Centuries', *JEH* 48 (1997), 628–57.

[14] Partner, *God of Battles*, p. xvi.

religious warfare. This is the analysis of particular texts as justifications or mandates for the conduct of violence in God's name. It is best represented by an article written by Michael Walzer, 'Exodus 32 and the Theory of Holy War: The History of a Citation'.[15] Exodus 32: 26–8 describes how Moses recruits the sons of Levi to carry out a ruthless programme of execution in the name of God.

Then Moses stood in the gate of the camp, and said 'Who is on the Lord's side? Come to me!' And all the sons of Levi gathered around him. He said to them, 'Thus says the Lord, the God of Israel, "Put your sword on your side, each of you! Go back and forth from gate to gate throughout the camp, and each of you kill your brother, your friend, and your neighbour."' The sons of Levi did as Moses commanded, and about three thousand of the people fell on that day.[16]

Walzer first pointed out that this was a highly unusual passage because God, acting through Moses, uses human agency to punish the wicked; at other times in Exodus and Numbers the agency is non-human, notably fire, plague, and serpents. This establishes the significance of the text for anyone interested in sacred violence.

Walzer then proceeded to set out the three main citations of the text. The first was by St Augustine, who used it to justify the persecution of the Donatists, arguing that the difference between the oppressive behaviour of Pharaoh and that of Moses, evidenced in Exodus 32: 26–8, lay precisely in motive, which in Moses' case was loving chastisement. The second citation was that of Aquinas. In contrast to Augustine, he saw the passage as dangerous, because of the interpretation which had been given to it by the radical reformers of the eleventh century. They had emphasized the duty of latter-day Levites, as men of God, to use violent means in order to purge the church of evil. For Aquinas this was an unacceptable invitation to disorder, and he countered this exegesis by arguing that this was Old Law and bore no relevance to the New Dispensation. Finally, there was Calvin's interpretation of the text. He returned to the Augustinian viewpoint that the text pointed the way for contemporary Christians to behave, but radicalized it substantially. The mediation of Moses, so important for Augustine, was superseded by the Protestant view of the elect being directly mandated by God, and the full grimness of the task which faced the new Levites was emphasized in terms of their having to kill their own brethren in God's service.[17]

[15] M. Walzer, 'Exodus 32 and the Theory of Holy War: The History of a Citation', *Harvard Theological Review*, 61 (1968), 1–14.

[16] For quotations from the Bible I use *New Revised Standard Version: Anglicized Edition* (Oxford: Oxford University Press, 1995).

[17] For a directly equivalent reading on the Catholic side see R. R. Harding, 'Revolution and Reform in the Holy League: Angers, Rennes, Nantes', *Journal of Modern History*, 53 (1981), 379–416, at 412–13; B. Diefendorf, *Beneath the Cross: Catholics and Huguenots in Sixteenth-Century Paris* (New York: Oxford University Press, 1991), 151.

Walzer's analysis of these exegetical changes was a true *tour de force*, and he performed the service of showing how rich the evolving dialectic between text and circumstance could be. As he put it, 'In these interpretations the three men reveal themselves and the special anxieties of their times . . . All three of them were forced to be biblical lawyers, but God's law in their hands was as different as men and ages could make it.'[18] All three views of Exodus 32: 26–8 were to find expression amongst the writings of men whose ideas will be considered in the following pages: indeed, in some ways the Augustinian, Thomist, and Calvinist interpretations of these three verses in Exodus formed the kernels of mainstream approaches towards the legitimate use of violence in God's name. But this is not to say that a similar approach could not prove as fruitful in the case of certain other passages of Scripture. Particularly interesting would be its application to the Book of Daniel, which Partner aptly described as 'a kind of meditation upon holy war, that purported to unveil secret things, and to predict the execution of divine judgement'.[19] An exception to the general failure to follow in Walzer's footsteps has been the attention given to the Book of Revelation, in the context of the recent proliferation of apocalyptic studies. Not surprisingly, this attention has resulted not in a demonstration of how rival interpretations have been forged, but in a general emphasis on how influential the imagery, arithmetic, and precise sequencing of events in Revelation were throughout the later Middle Ages and Early Modern period.[20]

Professional historians have not held a monopoly over interest in religious warfare. Present-day Christian authorities and thinkers have viewed it as a topic of concern. As part of its celebration of the Jubilee Year 2000 the Vatican issued an extraordinary document, 'Memory and Reconciliation: The Church and the Faults of the Past', which *inter alia* acknowledged guilt and sought forgiveness for the Catholic church's sponsorship and use of violence in the past. Naturally the Crusades and the Wars of Religion loomed large in the Vatican's view of how Christ's message of peace had been, in its eyes, drastically traduced.[21] Such interest in the church's historical track record has generated at least one study which felicitously combines a whole range of disciplines, notably theology, history, and sociology, in an attempt to answer its title's question, *Does Christianity Cause War?* (1997). David Martin's book, which originated as a series of lectures given at Oxford, forms a critique of Richard Dawkins's argument that religion has indeed caused wars. A certain tendency to dehistoricize is inevitable given

---

[18] 'Exodus 32', 14.

[19] Partner, *God of Battles*, 16. E. Marsch, *Biblische Prophetie und chronographische Dichtung. Stoff- und Wirkungsgeschichte der Vision des Propheten Daniel nach Dan. VII* (Berlin: Erich Schmidt Verlag, 1972), is useful on Daniel 7.

[20] R. K. Emmerson, *Antichrist in the Middle Ages: A Study in Medieval Apocalypticism, Art, and Literature* (Seattle: University of Washington Press, 1981); R. K. Emmerson and B. McGinn (eds.), *The Apocalypse in the Middle Ages* (Ithaca, NY: Cornell University Press, 1992).

[21] *Memory and Reconciliation: The Church and the Faults of the Past* (London: Catholic Truth Society, 2000).

the sheer breadth of Martin's approach, but it is compensated for by his virtuosity, his insights about the complex nature of communities, and his demonstration of how belief systems become absorbed into structures shaped by a multitude of other factors. In a chapter on semiotics, Martin referred to the inherently oxymoronic nature of Christianity, 'the first being last, the lord being servant, God becoming Man, strength achieved in weakness, and life saved in self-giving'. As he went on to remark, 'the primary oxymoron is the warfare of the cross and the whole armour of salvation. Christianity captured the language of war for the purpose of peace. But no victory of that kind is fully secure.'[22] Communities facing crises which could apparently only be resolved by violent means were able to exploit this without great difficulty. As we have seen, the exegetical traditions were already at hand or could be created for the occasion, and collective assurance came from a liturgy and sign language which were themselves pervaded by ambiguity.

Martin believed that the answer to his book's title question is in the negative because what appear to be religious wars turn out on close examination to involve communities which defined themselves largely in religious terms embarking on conflict because of the particular circumstances in which they found themselves. The key phase is 'markers of difference', which historically have centred for the most part around religion and ethnicity. Normally these do not generate conflict, but when such conflict occurs they are mobilized and may very easily be misread as the causation of the violence. Martin employed the contemporary example of Yugoslavia. The conflict between Serbia and Bosnia was clearly not at root a clash of Orthodox against Muslim: it sprang from the break-up of Yugoslavia. But religious markers, alongside ethnic ones, became dominant conduits of hostility during the war.[23] The situation was made more complicated by the historical tendency for most European national communities to be couched and defined in religious terms: 'Any Christian group, defending itself or, indeed, setting out on colonizing adventure, can be another Chosen and Elect People.'[24] Because of the belligerence running through European history like Ariadne's thread, this led to many wars being depicted in language borrowed from the Old Testament. But it need not have been so: the last example cited by Martin is Brazil, 'a society thoroughly animated by the presumption of a spiritual world but not on that account generating violence, either internally between faiths or externally'.[25]

Martin's whole argument is based on his conviction that there existed an 'irreducible core' of Christian belief, 'the original deposit of faith espoused by the obscure Galilean fraternity'. Manifestly it included the rejection of the sword, and the ambiguities which he saw as responsible for the later embrace of war came about when the church made its series of compromises with 'judges,

---

[22]   D. Martin, *Does Christianity Cause War?* (Oxford: Oxford University Press, 1997), 113.

[23]   Ibid. 15–20. There is a more extended examination of the situation in Yugoslavia in A. Hastings, *The Construction of Nationhood: Ethnicity, Religion and Nationalism* (Cambridge: Cambridge University Press, 1997), ch. 5. See also Bremer, 'Religiöse Motive'.

[24]   Martin, *Does Christianity Cause War?*, 150.   [25] Ibid. 219.

senators and consuls'.[26] The distinction plays a crucial role in enabling him to deny that what seem to be religious wars really merit that name. To anybody who believes that Christian history is that of the church, embodying Martin's 'original deposit' and subjecting it to the many tests of human development, the question in his title is much less easily answered. As we have seen, the Vatican, which naturally subscribes to the latter view, has abandoned any attempt to make such distinctions. Instead it has accepted that religious wars were waged, viewing this as a culpable aspect of Christian history, but arguing too that the positive features of the Catholic church's past produce a balance sheet which is overwhelmingly laudable. Whatever one's stance in this debate, David Martin's analysis of the causality of wars associated with religion remains highly relevant because of his concern to distinguish between the root causes of conflicts and the collective convictions and identities which have sustained the combatant powers. This concern has been shared by many historians and it is necessary to address their arguments.

In the first place, there have always been historians who have emphasized the economic or political causality of those wars which have involved religious values, rituals, or language. For such individuals, to designate certain conflicts as religious wars is to misconstrue a complex causal process and to place such conflicts within an artificial category. This argument would hold water if one were claiming that religious differences, goals, and perceptions were the *only* factors causing a particular war and shaping its course and outcome. But the days of such reductionism are long past. Again, Partner strikes the correct balance: 'There have been no holy wars fought for an exclusively idealistic motive, and the historiography that sets up purity of intention as a criterion for holy war is mistakenly moralistic in its methods.'[27] Natalie Zemon Davis made a similar point in the context of religious rioting: 'just as the prevalence of pillaging in a war does not prevent us from typing it as a holy war, so the prevalence of pillaging in a riot should not prevent us from seeing it as essentially religious.'[28] Indeed, the danger today lies much less in the offering of an exclusively religious interpretation of any war than of religious values being dismissed as camouflage or propaganda. No historian of the Crusades or the Wars of Religion now writing would exclude a whole range of political, economic, and social considerations from a study of those conflicts,[29] and the same applies to the warfare which we shall be examining in this study. For example, the finest recent account of the Hussite revolution, František Šmahel's *La Révolution hussite: une anomalie historique* (1985), has the great merit of surveying the whole complex of secular factors involved, including the temptation which a well-endowed Bohemian church posed to an impoverished lesser nobility, and the political reasons which persuaded the

---

[26] Ibid. 113–14.   [27] Partner, *God of Battles*, 309.

[28] N. Z. Davis, 'The Rites of Violence: Religious Riot in Sixteenth-Century France', *Past and Present*, 59 (1973), 51–91, at 65.

[29] See, e.g., M. P. Holt, *The French Wars of Religion, 1562–1629* (Cambridge: Cambridge University Press, 1995), 3.

country's magnates to sponsor religious reform. Šmahel amply demonstrated the links between these and many other factors, and the course and character taken by the Hussite wars. Yet this did not lead him to play down the importance of religious goals, and he reiterated their formative influence on the way the Hussites conducted their war.[30] Describing a particular conflict as a religious war is not an attempt to place it in an interpretative ghetto, but to throw fresh light on its character. It is justified if it enables us better to understand what occurred, through the techniques of comparative analysis.

This too, of course, goes beyond what some historians regard as sound practice. A good example resides in Tom Scott's major contribution towards the study of the German Peasants' War of 1524–5, 'Reformation and Peasants' War in Waldshut and Environs'.[31] The article forms a critique of the view that what brought townsmen and peasants into alliance during this war was their common subscription to Luther's revolutionary message. As Peter Blickle, chief proponent of this view, put it, 'what united the common project of peasants and townsmen was the gospel, or more precisely, the transformation of Reformation theology into a political theology'.[32] Looking closely at what happened in Waldshut and its region, Scott concluded that 'the complex pattern of Waldshut's relations with the peasants suggests that the origins of alliances between town and country in the Peasants' War and their contribution to its radicalization depended less upon the impact of an overriding extraneous ideology than upon the circumstances in which those alliances were formed'.[33] This argument found broader and brusquer expression in another article published a year later on the historiography of the war. Scott stated that he found it 'rather far-fetched to argue that burghers and peasants fought side-by-side in 1525 in the name of a *libertas christiana* based upon their shared commitment to the ideal of the Christian community'.[34] Others have disagreed, and there is an a priori rejection of the power of ideas in Scott's comment which is epistemological rather than evidential in character.[35] His conclusions about Waldshut command respect because of the solid archival sources which underpin them, and it may well be the case that the extraordinarily broad-based character of the German Peasants' War makes general conclusions as to the impact on it of religious

---

[30] F. Šmahel, *La Révolution hussite: une anomalie historique* (Paris: Presses Universitaires de France, 1985).

[31] T. Scott, 'Reformation and Peasants' War in Waldshut and Environs: A Structural Analysis', *Archiv für Reformationsgeschichte*, 69 (1978), 82–102, 70 (1979), 140–68.

[32] P. Blickle, *The Revolution of 1525: The German Peasants' War from a New Perspective*, trans. T. A. Brady Jr. and H. C. E. Midelfort, 2nd edn. (Baltimore: Johns Hopkins University Press, 1985), 115.

[33] Scott, 'Reformation and Peasants' War', 70 (1979), 168.

[34] T. Scott, 'The Peasants' War: A Historiographical Review', *Historical Journal*, 22 (1979), 693–720, 953–74, at 961.

[35] The same is true of J. Szűcs, 'Die Nation in historischer Sicht und der nationale Aspekt der Geschichte', in his *Nation und Geschichte. Studien*, trans. J. Kerekes et al. (Gyoma: Corvina Kiadó, 1981), 11–160.

ideas more than usually hazardous. Outside the special context of that conflict, however, there is a clear danger in insisting that only the closest and most detailed of studies can enable us to reconstruct what happened and why. The hegemony of the particular easily becomes the tyranny of the circumstantial.

It is worth emphasizing this general point about the nature of historical analysis because there is a trend in contemporary research to deny the existence of patterns, and to question attempts to formulate categories and types on that basis. A good example of the trend is Felipe Fernández-Armesto's *Millennium* (1995), an account of the past thousand years of world history. To attempt such a survey at all was an audacious undertaking, but it was made the more so by Fernández-Armesto's disarming avowal that he offered no patterns or interpretations. It was an approach which would have been unthinkable in the past when embarking on a survey of such ambitious scope. But for Fernández-Armesto, 'history is chaotic—a turbulence which happens at random or in which the causes are often in practice impossible to trace'. It was 'a mosaic made by a monkey'.[36] One distinguished historian has suggested that this disconcerting trend is the result of historians being influenced by chaos theory in the sciences.[37] Clearly this book would be impossible to write if I subscribed to the trend: on the contrary, I believe not only that there are patterns and developments to be established, but that it is one of the practising historian's tasks, and a particularly stimulating one, to identify and explain them.

This is not to deny that the task of elucidation is particularly challenging when we are dealing with religious belief. The latter is bound to raise problems of assessment and interpretation which are inherently different from those thrown up by political or economic history. Peter Russell's recent life of Prince Henry 'the Navigator' of Portugal illustrates the situation very well.[38] Throughout his adult life Henry was obsessed with crusading in Morocco, and Russell entirely avoids the trap, referred to earlier, of trying to explain it in terms of hoped-for economic gain. On the contrary, he shows that in material terms Portugal's (and Henry's) advantage lay overwhelmingly in the maintenance of peaceful relations with Morocco. How then to explain this obsession in a man who in almost all other aspects of his career was guided by hopes of material gain, and who was both cynical and opportunistic in his relations with his family and the popes? Russell gets around the problem by writing of two Henrys, the crusading hothead and the level-headed entrepreneur and administrator. He writes of Henry slipping into 'crusading mode', using 'Henry-speak', and putting on his 'crusader's rig'. This is engaging but it evades the problem of understanding Henry in full, a difficulty which Russell frankly accepts as insurmountable. The problem is deepened still

---

[36] F. Fernández-Armesto, *Millennium* (London: Bantam, 1995), 8, 10.

[37] D. H. Akenson, *God's Peoples: Covenant and Land in South Africa, Israel, and Ulster* (Ithaca, NY: Cornell University Press, 1992), 351–3.

[38] P. Russell, *Prince Henry 'the Navigator': A Life* (New Haven: Yale University Press, 2000).

further by the fact that Henry was undeniably capable of casuistry and dissimulation in pursuit of his crusading goals: this could easily cause us to question his motivation had Russell not so clearly ruled out the hope of gain.[39]

It may be suggested that the answer to this conundrum lies in taking a leaf out of David Martin's book and arguing that Henry's motivation was not so much religious as chivalric, that it derived from those codes of honour and fame onto which crusading had been grafted and which, in Henry's time, represented one of the key impulses behind the persistence of crusading's popularity.[40] This is a tempting approach to take, because it enables us to shift the explanation for his behaviour away from the hidden arena of Henry's psychological make-up and religious beliefs, into a more tangible and comprehensible world of knightly orders, courtly magnificence, battlefield heroics, and splendid tombs. But it remains an evasion. There is no substitute for considering seriously what rulers like Henry said about the religious goals of their wars, hard as it often is to sort the wheat of intent from the chaff of rhetoric and propaganda. It calls for empathy. In her study *Chivalry and Exploration 1298–1630*, Jennifer Goodman struck an important chord in this regard when she appealed for attempts to use the imagination in order to grasp the chivalric and crusading thinking of men like Henry the Navigator: 'The resurgence of old patterns—of feudal relationships, of cults of personal honor and vengeance, of holy wars—strikes the modern sceptic as inconceivable . . . All this territory of the mind cries out to be rediscovered.'[41]

As if trying to grasp the religious beliefs of individuals were not enough, we also face the problem of analysing the behaviour of groups. This may seem more difficult, but in fact there is a growing consensus on the validity of using such indicators as patterns of group activity, and the symbols and rites which are important to groups, as means of understanding their psychology.[42] There is also the possibility of comparative study, which has been attempted by a number of historians in the case of revolts, with stimulating results.[43] The best comparative

[39] Russell, *Prince Henry*, 21–2, 35, 50, 54, 72, 180, 190, 271, 294, 326, 361.

[40] See my *The Later Crusades, 1274–1580: From Lyons to Alcazar* (Oxford: Oxford University Press, 1992), 394–403.

[41] J. R. Goodman, *Chivalry and Exploration 1298–1630* (Woodbridge: Boydell, 1998), 24, and cf. her comments on 219.

[42] L. Millward, 'Social Psychology 2', in M. Eysenck (ed.), *Psychology: An Integrated Approach* (Harlow: Addison Wesley Longman, 1998), 356–406; M. A. Hogg and G. M. Vaughan, *Social Psychology*, 2nd edn. (Hemel Hempstead: Prentice Hall, 1998), 375–85. I am grateful to Anne Colley for drawing my attention to these studies. See also the comments in my 'Insurrection as Religious War, 1400–1536', *JMH* 25 (1999), 141–54, repr. in *CWMRE*, study VIII, at 152–3.

[43] See, e.g., F. G. Heymann, 'The Hussite Revolution and the German Peasants' War: An Historical Comparison', *Medievalia et humanistica*, NS 1 (1970), 141–59; F. Seibt, 'Tabor und die europäischen Revolutionen', *Bohemia: Jahrbuch des Collegium Carolinum*, 14 (1973), 33–42, repr. in F. Seibt, *Hussitenstudien: Personen, Ereignisse, Ideen einer frühen Revolution* (Munich: Oldenbourg, 1987), 175–84; F. Seibt, 'Die hussitische Revolution und der Deutsche Bauernkrieg', in P. Blickle (ed.), *Revolte und Revolution in Europa*, HZ NS suppl. vol. 4 (Munich: Oldenbourg, 1975), 47–61, repr. in Seibt,

analysis works toward the creation of types, an approach which has much to offer. For example, Gary Dickson has recently proposed six typical characteristics of religious revivalism in the Middle Ages, ranging from a concern with revitalizing orthodox religious culture, through to an attempt to create a specific context for that revitalization in a community which has been morally purified (most typically a monastic house or order, or a city).[44] As Dickson admits, he is building on the work of others, including Norman Cohn, whose *The Pursuit of the Millennium*, a study of popular millenarian movements in the Middle Ages, still exercises great influence nearly half a century after it was first published.[45] A striking feature of Cohn's study, and surely one reason for its enduring appeal, resides in its author's indefatigable search for patterns and trends in movements which at first sight seem extremely disparate. The methodology practised by Cohn and advocated by Dickson, analytical, comparative, and empathetic without being ingenuous, is broadly speaking that which will be applied to the insurrectionary armies with which, in part, this study is concerned.

The difficulties involved in analysing religious warfare are apparent: what are the potential gains? They are twofold. First, the range of military conflicts which we shall be investigating took place. Whether they were wars between communities which we now regard as states, insurrections taking place within those states, or conflicts fought between groups which formed along confessional lines of division, the significance of these activities is unquestionable.[46] Assessing as precisely as we may how religious programmes and values informed and shaped them will clarify them as historical events. Much the same applies to the backcloth of writing about religious warfare, favourable and critical, polemical and reflective, which as we shall see formed a constantly revealing commentary on events. We can hope to emerge with a fuller understanding of how far warfare in this period was permeated by religious conviction to the extent that combatants believed themselves to be God's warriors, acting at his command and, in the most explicit sense, implementing his purpose for his creation.

The second gain is more specific. As I remarked earlier, both the Crusades and the Wars of Religion have recently received a good deal of attention, and two of the major revisions are fundamental for this study. In the case of the Crusades, we are now much more conscious of their longevity. We have freed ourselves from the narrow definition of crusade which associated it exclusively with wars

---

Hussitenstudien, 217–28; P. Blickle, 'Peasant Revolts in the German Empire in the Late Middle Ages', *Social History*, 4 (1979), 223–39; P. Freedman, 'The German and Catalan Peasant Revolts', *AHR* 98 (1993), 39–54.

[44] G. Dickson, 'Revivalism as a Medieval Religious Genre', *JEH* 51 (2000), 473–96, esp. 491–3.

[45] N. Cohn, *The Pursuit of the Millennium: Revolutionary Millenarians and Mystical Anarchists of the Middle Ages*, rev. and expanded edn. (New York: Oxford University Press, 1970).

[46] Military activity which was organized and conducted by the religious Military Orders poses a separate set of methodological issues, and will not be considered in this book. For an overview, see A. Luttrell, 'The Military Orders, 1312–1798', in J. Riley-Smith, *The Oxford Illustrated History of the Crusades* (Oxford: Oxford University Press, 1995), 326–64.

fought to conquer or defend the Holy Land, wars which came to an end in 1291; and we have become aware of the persistence of crusading into at least the early sixteenth century.[47] It is a breakthrough of vital importance for this book. Historians of *mentalités* in the late Middle Ages and Renaissance had long acknowledged the persistence of the idea of crusade. Yvonne Labande-Mailfert wrote in 1975 that 'it would be impossible to exaggerate the diffusion of the idea of crusade in the West at the close of the fifteenth century; and the start of the sixteenth would signal a revival of these aspirations',[48] while Alain Milhou commented in 1983 that 'the history of the idea of crusade after the crusades themselves [sc. 1291 onwards] is that of the disintegration of the various elements which constituted it'.[49] Both are valid and telling comments but they do not go far enough. For it has now been established that, important as aspirations and ideas were, a great deal more was involved. A part of the background to all the conflicts which we shall examine was a concurrent pattern of crusade preaching, exhortations, and in some cases crusading activity. The key elements of crusading, vow, cross, and indulgence,[50] remained features of European religious and public life throughout the period studied in this book. Crusading, and religious war in the non-crusading sense, incessantly criss-crossed, producing an interaction which was much more fertile than it would have been had aspirations and ideas alone been at stake. Sometimes, as in Hussite Bohemia, they were in brutal conflict, producing the extraordinary result of several religious wars being simultaneously in operation. At other times, as in Portugal and Castile, a fruitful symbiosis took place, crusade forming, as it were, the 'cutting edge' of a broader surge of ideas generated by chivalric values, national feeling, and prophetic expectations. On at least one occasion, György Dózsa's revolt of 1514 in Hungary, a more complex interaction can be traced, one which involved both insurrection (as in Bohemia) and triumphalist orthodoxy (as in Iberia). What is certain is that a relationship existed throughout. Although the crusade retained institutional solidity through features which were now familiar, indeed scarcely changing, it was subject to some of the same pressures and developments which affected religious warfare in the broader sense.

As for the Wars of Religion, one of the most remarkable recent changes has been an acceptance of how fully the salient features of the confessional divide found expression in the habits of violence which they generated.[51] This applies

[47] Housley, *Later Crusades, passim.*

[48] Y. Labande-Mailfert, *Charles VIII et son milieu (1470–1498): La Jeunesse au pouvoir* (Paris: Klincksieck, 1975), 185.

[49] A. Milhou, *Colón y su mentalidad mesiánica en el ambiente franciscanista español* (Valladolid: Casa-Museo de Colón Seminario Americanista de la Universidad de Valladolid, 1983), 290.

[50] The term crusade will be used in this book when these elements are present. See J. Riley-Smith, *What Were the Crusades?* (London: Macmillan, 1977). C. Tyerman, *The Invention of the Crusades* (Basingstoke: Macmillan, 1998), 100–9, has useful comments on crusading in the 16th cent.

[51] See, e.g., B. Scribner, 'Preconditions of Tolerance and Intolerance in Sixteenth-Century Germany', in O. P. Grell and B. Scribner (eds.), *Tolerance and Intolerance in the European Reformation* (Cambridge: Cambridge University Press, 1996), 32–47.

in particular to the French Wars of Religion. It is now apparent that they were in the fullest sense holy wars, in which the actual violence perpetrated was regarded as sacred. Atrocities were committed by both sides during the Hussite wars and in the course of the perennial conflict waged on the Christian–Ottoman frontier in the Balkans, but they do not appear to have matched the intensity which was so striking a feature of the wars fought between Huguenots and Catholics in France.[52] This process of 'Putting Religion back into the Wars of Religion'[53] raises major questions, particularly in the light of the old view that warfare in the fifteenth century was largely emptied of any religious content. As we have seen in the discussion of Michael Walzer's article on Exodus 32: 26–8, there was no need for Europeans faced with this crisis in their religious affairs to 'reinvent the wheel' because leaders like John Calvin possessed the exegetical ability simply to revive a former interpretation of crucial scriptural texts and to strengthen it as they needed. And as David Martin showed, the very nature of Christianity's historical evolution played into their hands. But the question still arises as to whether they were breaking with a period in which religious warfare had been largely superseded, or whether Calvinists and Counter-Reformation Catholics were simply intensifying practices and sharpening modes of thinking which had never gone away. We shall see in the Conclusion that institutional continuities between the Crusades and the Wars of Religion can be located. That is interesting enough, and in the light of these recent historiographical trends it is not surprising. But the question is whether the continuity resides in more than the occasional direct borrowing or institutional resurrection. It is clear that with certain notable exceptions crusading exerted only a fraction of its former mass appeal by the early sixteenth century. But the existence of religious warfare in a broader sense raises profound questions. Was there ever a time between 1095 and 1648 when European society was free of religious warfare? Or do we have to accept that for more than half a millennium European Christians fought at least some of their wars in God's name?

1.2 THE CONTEXTS OF CONFLICT, C.1300–1536

It is important to start with the context, by surveying the range of key areas in which religion and warfare displayed a tendency to converge, and the circumstances in which that convergence became so marked that religious warfare resulted. The most natural place to begin is the range of borders where religious difference combined with disputes of a territorial or similar character to produce

---

[52] Though see below, Ch. 5.1, on the reputation of the Turks for cruelty, and note C. Heywood, 'The Frontier in Ottoman History: Old Ideas and New Myths', in D. Power and N. Standen (eds.), *Frontiers in Question: Eurasian Borderlands, 700–1700* (Basingstoke: Macmillan, 1999), 228–50, at 238–40.

[53] The title of a review article by Mack P. Holt: *French Historical Studies*, 18 (1993), 524–51. See also his *French Wars of Religion*, 3, 190–1.

belligerence.[54] The Mamluk conquest of the Holy Land in 1291 removed the most obvious such border, but others were by no means lacking in the late Middle Ages. In the eastern Mediterranean itself the rise of the Turkish Anatolian *beyliks*, especially those situated along the coast and exerting themselves in naval terms, brought a condition of sporadic warfare to the world of the Aegean sea lanes and the fragmented Catholic powers of the region. At the other end of the Mediterranean, the Nasrid emirate of Granada, the last remaining Islamic enclave in Iberia, shared a long border with the kingdom of Castile until the campaigns of Fernando and Isabella in 1482–92, which finally ended Muslim power in the peninsula. And in north-eastern Europe a vicious war persisted throughout almost the entire fourteenth century between the Teutonic Knights in Prussia and Livonia and their pagan neighbours in Lithuania.[55]

In the fifteenth century the situation changed dramatically in two respects. In the east, the rise of the Ottomans and their advance into the Balkans brought into being the first major land frontier between Christian and Muslim powers outside Iberia since the time of the crusader states in Palestine and Syria. The Catholic kingdom of Hungary was forced to maintain a militarized frontier in the south from the failure of Sultan Mehmed II to capture Belgrade in 1456, through to the fall of that city in 1521 and the disaster which ensued at Mohács in 1526. After these events the frontier moved northwards into Croatia and the Hungarian plain. This was the most significant border between faiths in the entire period. By contrast, the border in the Baltic region effectively vanished once Lithuania had been opened up for conversion in 1386. Hostilities with the Orthodox Russian principalities further east were not pursued with the consistency or brutality which had characterized the Teutonic Order's conflict with the Lithuanians.[56]

What, if any, generalizations may be made about a scenario with so many variations? By their very nature frontier relations highlight the problem of disentangling motives which was referred to earlier. Were wars waged over faith or over land, tribute, or booty? Did such conflicts break out because of underlying mistrust based on a negative perception of 'the infidel', or because of circumstances, such as thrusting ambition on one side or the simple breakdown of peace-keeping mechanisms? Several broad points can be made on the basis of research into the border zones outlined above. The first is that border societies proved able to accommodate dichotomies which in the past historians have tended to insist were irreconcilable. Religious warfare and *convivencia*, rejection and assimilation, were woven together into a composite social and cultural pattern. This

---

[54] See also my 'Frontier Societies and Crusading in the Late Middle Ages', *Mediterranean Historical Review*, 10 (1995), 104–19, repr. in *CWMRE*, study V.

[55] See relevant chapters in M. Jones (ed.), *The New Cambridge Medieval History*, vi: *c.1300–c.1415* (Cambridge: Cambridge University Press, 2000).

[56] Again, *The New Cambridge Medieval History* provides full treatment of all these areas. See C. Allmand (ed.), vol. vii: *c.1415–c.1500* (Cambridge: Cambridge University Press, 1998).

could produce a town like Dalmatian Senj, a pirate ('uskok') community which grew rapidly in the turmoil following Mohács, and came to form a vital link in the Croatian military frontier established by the Habsburgs. As Wendy Bracewell has shown, Senj embraced the paradox in full.[57] Although they never benefited from crusade privileges, the uskoks conducted their war against the Turks as a continual struggle in defence of the faith. In their own eyes they manned an *antemurale*, a bulwark or rampart of Christendom. The local clergy encouraged this viewpoint, blessing weapons, preaching exhortatory sermons, and displaying uskok standards and trophies in their churches. On one notable occasion the bishop of Senj actually took part in a campaign. 'This was a crusading creed, with military elements inextricably incorporated into religious life.'[58] It is telling that uskok activities were viewed as warfare on behalf of the faith even by Christian communities living under Ottoman rule and suffering, directly or indirectly, at the hands of the raiders, as well as by Dalmatian subjects of Venice who also incurred heavy losses from their attacks.[59]

The uskok view that war with Islam was natural and inevitable was far from unusual: it was shared, for example, by their eminent contemporary Francisco de Vitoria, the Salamanca legal commentator. Referring to Deuteronomy 20: 10–14, the terms of surrender which the Israelites were to offer to the inhabitants of any town which they besieged, Vitoria argued that 'in wars against the infidel . . . peace can never be hoped for on any terms; therefore the only remedy is to eliminate all of them who are capable of bearing arms against us, given that they are already guilty'. All captured infidel combatants should thus be killed and their women and children enslaved.[60] What is more striking is that the same Turks who as an enemy were demonized by the uskoks and their priests duelled with them on occasion in chivalric style,[61] celebrated common ties of kinship, and forged pacts of blood brotherhood (*pobratimstvo*) with individual uskoks. Turkish border raiders (*martoloses*) who defected to the Christians were welcomed into the uskok ranks once they had been baptized. Both sides embraced a common code of honour, a shared quest for renown, and a dread of shame. Most importantly, the need for booty to sustain Senj's economy was balanced by a mutual recognition that all-out war was in nobody's interests. 'The fundamental force that modified the inflexible opposition between uskok and Muslim implied by the ideal of holy war was that of local self-interest—whether it was primarily

---

[57] C. W. Bracewell, *The Uskoks of Senj: Piracy, Banditry, and Holy War in the Sixteenth-Century Adriatic* (Ithaca, NY: Cornell University Press, 1992), esp. chs. 6–7.

[58] Ibid. 159.   [59] Ibid. 218–19.

[60] Francisco de Vitoria, 'On the Law of War', in *Political Writings*, ed. and trans. A. Pagden and J. Lawrance (Cambridge: Cambridge University Press, 1991), 293–327, at 315, 318, 321.

[61] Duelling, which is antagonistic but depends on shared cultural values, epitomizes the paradox of rejection/assimilation. The fame earned by the leader of the Hungarian peasant crusade of 1514, György Dózsa, by killing a prominent Turkish opponent in a duel in February 1514 helped establish his eligibility to lead the crusade: M. D. Birnbaum, 'A Mock Calvary in 1514? The Dózsa-Passion', in G. E. Szőnyi (ed.), *European Iconography East and West* (Leiden: Brill, 1996), 91–108, at 93.

economic, as in the case of ransom agreements, or whether it rose more generally from a desire for a quieter life.'[62] The strength of Bracewell's interpretation resides in the fact that her appreciation of this pragmatic bedrock does not lead her to the viewpoint held by previous scholars that 'the uskoks' raiding activities were essentially devoid of ideological objectives'.[63]

One could say much more about Senj, but most of the evidence that Bracewell uses dates from the later sixteenth century and it therefore falls outside the scope of this book. In its broad outlines, however, there is little discrepancy between this portrait of relations between the faiths on the Dalmatian frontier, and the picture that has emerged of late of the border between Castile and Granada in the period leading up to 1482. Here too there existed an ideology of religious warfare, not that of *antemurale* but rather of pledged and overdue *Reconquista*. Yet there is evidence in plenty for both *convivencia* and acculturation, as well as mechanisms for moderating the inevitable outbreaks of hostility and for settling disputes peacefully. It is striking that in both cases the principle of 'good neighbourly behaviour' was referred to in the maintenance of peace.[64] Where the Senj model seems to break down is the frontier between Prussia and Lithuania, where the elements of contact, respect, and borrowing were fewer, and evidence for dehumanization and brutality more abundant. But even here, it has recently been shown, there were both intentions and means of controlling a violence which was mutually disadvantageous. Each side treated the other with grudging respect.[65]

In a sense, then, these frontiers display a collective application of what we might term the 'Henry the Navigator syndrome': a mixture of what seem to be irreconcilable ways of viewing and dealing with the enemy. We are naturally led to ask what circumstances on the Christian side could cause religious war to dominate. One such was clearly the relationship between the frontier and the 'interior'. At Senj, for example, the *antemurale* image was valuable in contesting incessant Venetian hostility to the uskoks' disruptive activities. The Venetians viewed the uskoks as no more than pirates: legally and politically it was useful to assert that they were, on the contrary, soldiers posted on one of Christendom's most exposed bulwarks. This sounds manipulative, but that would be to misread the subtle interplay of ideas which was occurring. The uskoks liked and promoted the idea that they were fighting a religious war; the papal court and the Habsburg authorities alike moulded this into dominant images such as the

[62] Bracewell, *Uskoks*, 182.

[63] P. Longworth, 'The Senj Uskoks Reconsidered', *Slavonic and East European Review*, 57 (1979), 348–68, at 365.

[64] Bracewell, *Uskoks*, 34; A. MacKay, 'The Ballad and the Frontier in Late Mediaeval Spain', *Bulletin of Hispanic Studies*, 53 (1976), 15–33, at 26–7.

[65] S. C. Rowell, *Lithuania Ascending: A Pagan Empire within East-Central Europe, 1295–1345* (Cambridge: Cambridge University Press, 1994), *passim*, esp. 261, 296; R. Mažeika, 'Of Cabbages and Knights: Trade and Trade Treaties with the Infidel on the Northern Frontier', *JMH* 20 (1994), 63–76.

propugnaculum adversus infideles, and the *antemurale Christianitatis*; and these images were in turn expounded to the uskoks by the resident lower clergy, enhancing their self-esteem and consolidating their group image.[66]

In the case of Granada, there was clearly a shifting relationship between the frontier authorities and communities on the one hand, and the Castilian crown and papacy on the other, based on perceptions of responsibilities and the control of resources. The adroit use of *Reconquista* ideology could secure valuable royal attention and money for what were at root regional needs, especially if the papacy could also be persuaded to grant crusading bulls. Prominent representatives of the frontier regions did not lack sophistication when it came to appealing for financial help. In 1471, for instance, the constable of Castile Miguel Lucas de Iranzo, writing to the pope on behalf of the frontier lands where he had established his own power-base, deployed language which would not have shamed a crusading oration by a contemporary Italian humanist: 'since for our part we are contributing all our possessions, our women, our children, our relatives, our freedom, our country, and in the end our very lives, other Christians should at least contribute a little money for the most sacred protection not of one individual, but of Christendom itself.'[67] On the other hand, too much outside attention, be it papal or royal, was unwelcome in a region which was used to looking after itself, especially if it was associated with the erosion of *convivencia* within the nation's religious culture, as it was in the period of the Fernandine conquest.[68]

The overall attitude of the 'political centre' therefore mattered greatly. Two contrasting examples will illustrate this. Before the emergence of the Ottoman Turks the initiative on the Latin side in the Aegean world (*Romania*) lay to a large extent with Venice. The city normally had much more to gain from trade and diplomacy than from belligerence. This was probably one important reason why the pronounced tendency towards *jihad* among the Anatolian *beyliks* did not have the effect of establishing an ethos of religious warfare in the region.[69] The main exception was formed by the series of Holy Leagues which were organized from 1334 onwards. Venice was as keen as anybody on gaining crusading privileges for these naval leagues but did not seek to go any further.[70] In much the same way, the republic had a good command of the rhetoric of crusade when it was forced into war with the Ottomans in the fifteenth century, but it was invariably sparing and

---

[66] Bracewell, *Uskoks*, 172. We shall return to this theme below, Ch. 4.3.

[67] *Hechos del condestable don Miguel Lucas de Iranzo (Crónica del siglo XV)*, ed. J. de M. Carriazo (Madrid: Espasa-Calpe, 1940), 475.

[68] T. F. Ruiz, 'Elite and Popular Culture in Late Fifteenth-Century Castilian Festivals: The Case of Jaen', in B. A. Hanawalt and K. L. Reyerson (eds.), *City and Spectacle in Medieval Europe* (Minneapolis: University of Minnesota Press, 1994), 296–318.

[69] E. A. Zachariadou, 'Holy War in the Aegean during the Fourteenth Century', in B. Arbel, B. Hamilton, and D. Jacoby (eds.), *Latins and Greeks in the Eastern Mediterranean after 1204* (London: Frank Cass, 1989), 212–25.

[70] Housley, *Later Crusades*, ch. 2 *passim*.

selective in the use which it made of it.[71] On the other hand, the Teutonic Knights missed no opportunity to accentuate their view that the struggle with the Lithuanians constituted a war on behalf of the faith. This was in line with the Order's history: it had always been bellicose in its approach towards paganism.[72] In both cases, of course, the attitude adopted sprang also from the nature of the frontier and the actual causes of conflict: but some formative role must be attributed to the traditions of the dominant political power and the *modus operandi* which its elite found most congenial.

One important reason why the Teutonic Knights took the uncompromising line they did on Lithuania was their hope of attracting volunteers for their war. Service at one or more of Christendom's *frontes guerrarum paganorum*, as *crucesignatus*, mercenary, or simple guest, was a central constituent of chivalric practice in the late Middle Ages. It has received a lot of attention in recent years, most impressively in the case of the *Preussenreisen*, the annual pattern of raids and full-scale campaigns into Lithuania which were organized by the Teutonic Order between about 1300 and 1413.[73] The *Reisen* were unique, and no other frontier managed to attract so many volunteers, a fair number of them repeatedly, over such a long stretch of time. Volunteers did make their way to Granada and Hospitaller Rhodes in the fourteenth century, and to Hungary and Rhodes in the fifteenth. Cyprus too was a popular venue, although it can rarely have offered the opportunity for fighting. Typically, military activity on these borders was combined with pilgrimage and sight-seeing, and in some cases with spying, diplomacy, and sexual adventures. The pattern continued, albeit much diminished, into the sixteenth century, when some volunteers fought for the Knights of St John at the siege of Malta in 1565.

This broad range of adventurous, essentially opportunistic combat raises interpretative problems which are not dissimilar to those thrown up by the warfare waged by the frontier communities which in most cases hosted the volunteers. This applies for example to the question of motivation: even sources written from a standpoint favourable to the Teutonic Order do not deny that volunteers went to Prussia to gain honour and fame as well as to 'spread Christianity' or 'defend the faith', and Werner Paravicini has described in rich detail the range of incentives put in place by the Teutonic Knights to make their guests' stay at Königsberg an enjoyable one.[74] But *au fond* it was the lure of fighting

---

[71] Setton, *PL* ii. 163–4, 367, 441; P. Preto, *Venezia e i Turchi* (Florence: Sansoni, 1975), 25–51.

[72] This emerged most clearly during the polemical dispute between the Order and Poland at the council of Constance. See, e.g., F. H. Russell, 'Paulus Vladimiri's Attack on the Just War: A Case Study in Legal Polemics', in B. Tierney and P. Linehan (eds.), *Authority and Power: Studies on Medieval Law and Government Presented to Walter Ullmann on his Seventieth Birthday* (Cambridge: Cambridge University Press, 1980), 237–54.

[73] The definitive study is W. Paravicini, *Die Preussenreisen des europäischen Adels*, 3 vols. (Sigmaringen: Jan Thorbecke, 1989 ff.). See also Rowell, *Lithuania Ascending*, and 'Baltic Europe', in Jones (ed.), *New Cambridge Medieval History*, vi. 699–734.

[74] Paravicini, *Die Preussenreisen*, i. 288–310.

pagani which attracted these men, and when the Lithuanians ceased being pagan the practice ended, at least once it became impracticable for the Order to conjure that unpalatable fact away any longer. Nowhere is the link between chivalry and warring against non-believers clearer than in the pre-eminence of being dubbed on such battlefields. Zurara, Henry the Navigator's biographer, imagined the prince anxiously reflecting at the taking of Ceuta in 1415 that he needed to kill some Moors: 'And for what glory will they be able to praise me on the day when I am made knight, if my sword has not been dipped to the hilt in the blood of the Infidels?'[75]

Like the uskoks, Henry (and Zurara) believed that 'the Infidels are our enemies by nature',[76] a viewpoint which was axiomatic among such chivalric enthusiasts. Yet it did not lead such men consistently to demonize their opponents to the extent of shunning their company. In this respect their ambivalence towards the enemy mirrored the attitudes of their host communities. In the case of the volunteers this was exemplified by Jean II le Maingre, better known as Boucicaut, who was appointed marshal of France in 1391. His reputation for seeking out combat against 'the Saracens' wherever and whenever he could was second to none. In one remarkable incident in 1403, when campaigning in Cyprus and facing a period of enforced idleness, Boucicaut looked around for an unbeliever to attack: 'he sought the advice of the knights of the land and the Genoese as to where they thought he might most conveniently carry out *une rese* against the enemies of the faith.'[77] This implacable antagonism towards unbelievers did not lead him to avoid their company. In the course of a lengthy perambulation of the Balkans and the eastern Mediterranean in 1388–9 Boucicaut enjoyed a stay of several weeks' duration at the court of Murad I: he even offered his services should the Ottoman sultan take the field against other Muslims.[78] But this did not make Boucicaut any less serious in his motivation when he took up arms against Murad's son Bayezid eight years later on the Nicopolis expedition.[79]

As is now commonplace, chivalry in the late Middle Ages was expressed in ways which to us appear incongruous, even eccentric. This can induce a scepticism which distorts our understanding, as occurred, notoriously, in Johan Huizinga's case.[80] This can be as misleading as the questioning of motivation discussed earlier, not least in respect of the association between chivalric endeavour and religious belief. It is hard not to be amused when reading that the Teutonic Order's famed Table of Honour (*Ehrentisch*) was set up in enemy territory in

---

[75] Gomes Eannes de Zurara, *Conquests and Discoveries of Henry the Navigator*, ed. V. de Castro e Almeida, trans. B. Miall (London: Allen & Unwin, 1936), 106.

[76] Ibid. 41.

[77] *Le Livre des fais du bon messire Jehan le Maingre, dit Bouciquaut, mareschal de France et gouverneur de Jennes*, ed. D. Lalande (Paris: Droz, 1985), 221.

[78] Ibid. 61–2.   [79] Ibid. 88–91.

[80] M. Keen, 'Huizinga, Kilgour and the Decline of Chivalry', *Medievalia et humanistica*, NS 8 (1977), 1–20.

1391, so that the Order's guests had to sit down to eat in armour for fear of enemy attack.[81] Incongruity easily generates suspicion of hypocrisy when Zurara informs us that Portuguese squires charged almost naked Africans wearing full armour and shouting 'Portugal and St James', 'for all the world as if they were about to engage the seasoned warriors of the armies of Morocco or Granada'.[82] But Peter Russell was right to warn us that in this instance such scepticism is an impediment to understanding either the motivation or the spirit in which the Portuguese discoveries and conquests were undertaken. Like the *Reisen*, these wars were shaped by religious belief; they fed on traditions of crusade and chivalry which remained highly attractive to contemporaries, irrespective of the other factors involved. And it was the genius of Henry the Navigator to tap into these traditions as a means of motivating his youthful assistants in their demanding task.[83]

The occasion and parameters for religious warfare at the frontiers of Christian Europe were provided by the existence and activities of an unbelieving enemy. The greatest threat to it lay not in *convivencia*, which could alternate with it without seriously damaging it, but in conversion, which fundamentally changed cross-border relations as well as putting paid to the flow of volunteers from the 'interior'. Behind labels like 'enemies of the cross' (*inimici crucis*) and 'the common foe of Christendom' ('enemigo común de la Cristianidad')[84] lay a concept of a Christian republic which could have bulwarks to be defended. Throughout the late Middle Ages, and especially after the Great Schism of 1378–1417, a strong sense prevailed of the inherent fragility of Catholic unity, of the danger of internal fissure being just as great as that of external assault. In July 1421, for example, King Sigismund of Hungary wrote to Cardinal Branda, who was organizing a new crusade against the Hussites, that he had not worked hard to reunite the church only to let the Hussites tear it apart again; and that there would be little point in staving off infidel Turkish attacks on Hungary only to lose Bohemia to heretics.[85]

This spatial republic had its temporal equivalent in the church militant, stretching through time and subject to the plans of God in the same way that the *respublica christiana* was subject to the *magisterium* of the papacy. Contemporary concern with eschatology, the constant unrolling of sacred history, provided a motor for religious war which was just as powerful as the defence of Christendom, and arguably more so.[86] The importance of eschatological

---

[81] Paravicini, *Die Preussenreisen*, i. 318.   [82] Russell, *Prince Henry*, 200.

[83] Ibid. 238, 363–4.

[84] See, e.g., J. Sánchez Montes, *Franceses, Protestantes, Turcos: Los Españoles ante la política internacional de Carlos V* (Madrid: Consejo Superior de Investigaciones Científicas, 1951), 101 n. 133.

[85] *UB* i, no. 127.

[86] For further exploration of some of the points made here see my study 'The Eschatological Imperative: Messianism and Holy War in Europe, 1260–1556', in P. Schäfer and M. R. Cohen (eds.), *Toward the Millennium: Messianic Expectations from the Bible to Waco* (Leiden: Brill, 1998), 123–50, repr. in *CWMRE*, study III.

awareness, focused on expectations of an imminent apocalypse, in the late Middle Ages and Early Modern period is now a recognized fact.[87] Indeed there have been few more radical shifts in recent years than historians' acceptance of just how constant and widespread were contemporaries' anxious attempts to 'read' the future in terms of Christ's Second Coming and his millennial rule. Jerome's famous 'curse' on millenarian speculation, and Augustine's interpretation of Revelation 20 as referring to the contemporary church, had long been abandoned; instead contemporaries engaged in repeated attempts to use the seductive figures and imagery found in books like Revelation, Daniel, and Isaiah to establish when the great drama of the Last Days would begin.[88]

The most important figure by far in this respect was Abbot Joachim of Fiore (*c*.1135–1202). It is hard to dispute the judgement of one leading commentator that 'The abbot of Fiore surely stood for a turning point in the history of European attitudes toward the future.'[89] Joachim's influence on apocalyptic thinking, and in particular on millenarian or chiliastic expectations, sprang from his division of human history into three stages (*status*), of which the third would be the millennial one, and from his pinpointing of the sixth age (*etas*) in the second *status* as the one in which the tribulations would take place which Revelation had long caused Christians to see as an essential preliminary to Christ's return.[90] From the early thirteenth century right through to the seventeenth, generation after generation of Joachites attempted to historicize the Last Days. The Book of Revelation provided them with some of the actors for this cosmic drama, including Antichrist, Gog, and Magog; while early Joachimist texts added some remarkable figures, notably an Angelic Pope (*pastor angelicus*) and a messianic Last Emperor. Together they made up an impressive list of dramatis personae.[91]

Apocalyptic thinking has normally adopted a pattern of crisis–judgement–vindication.[92] This was powerfully reinforced by the nature of the times, so the Joachimist agenda was bound to be one of war and revolution. The loss of the Holy Land, where the final defeat of Antichrist was to occur and Christ would return to his people, posed a dilemma which could only be solved by

---

[87] For example, it was one of three 'major themes' at the 19th International Congress of Historical Sciences held at Oslo in 2000: see A. Jolstad and M. Lunde (eds.), *Proceedings, 19th International Congress of Historical Sciences* (Oslo: University of Oslo, 2000), 53–81. For a short recent review see R. Rusconi, 'L'escatologia negli ultimi secoli del Medioevo', in A. Patschovsky and F. Šmahel (eds.), *Eschatologie und Hussitismus* (Prague: Historisches Institut, 1996), 7–24.

[88] R. E. Lerner, 'The Medieval Return to the Thousand-Year Sabbath', in Emmerson and McGinn (eds.), *Apocalypse*, 51–71.

[89] Ibid. 58.

[90] M. Reeves, 'The Originality and Influence of Joachim of Fiore', *Traditio*, 36 (1980), 269–316, forms the best introduction to this.

[91] The fundamental work remains M. Reeves, *The Influence of Prophecy in the Later Middle Ages: A Study in Joachimism* (Oxford: Oxford University Press, 1969).

[92] B. McGinn (ed.), *Visions of the End: Apocalyptic Traditions in the Middle Ages* (New York: Columbia University Press, 1998), pp. xvi–xvii. The new edn. of this invaluable collection of texts contains an updated bibliography.

incorporating within the programme of future events a great crusade to recover Jerusalem. Here the gentiles would be converted before Christ returned, fulfilling John 10: 16: 'So there will be one flock, one shepherd.' In this context it was difficult not to refer to actual crusade plans, and the Franciscan Jean de Roquetaillade (Johannes de Rupescissa), perhaps the fourteenth century's most original Joachite, conceived of his crusade in terms which strongly resemble what had recently been proposed.[93] More broadly, the triumphs achieved by Islam through both Mamluks and Ottomans forced Joachites to take full cognizance of these two powers. On the other hand, the lamentable condition of both the church and society at large made a deep-cutting process of internal purgation as fully a part of these prophetic expectations as the final triumph of the faith. To give a single example, in 1461 the German Carthusian Dionysius Ryckel wrote off the whole of the hierarchy, religious and secular, as irremediably oppressive and experienced visions of its severe chastisement at the hands of the Turks.[94] Chastisement and triumphalism, the church's near-destruction and its final success, formed twin poles for the apocalyptic electricity of Joachimism. Thus the pope could be viewed as *pastor angelicus* or as Antichrist; while the city of Rome, seat of both the papacy's *magisterium* and its much-criticized bureaucracy, was viewed in extraordinarily ambivalent ways, some seeing it as the New Jerusalem, others as a Babylon, whose total destruction was preordained and essential for the renewal of the true faith.[95]

Granted that violence in pursuit of God's ordained programme of events was inevitable, and that the timetable involved might be foretold with some accuracy, were such prophecies descriptive or prescriptive? There was obviously a big difference between working out that a particular ruler or pope was the Last Emperor or the *pastor angelicus*, of whom great things could be expected, and urging him on that basis to set an actual war in motion. A leading scholar of the subject, Robert Lerner, has argued powerfully that prophecies were normally consolatory rather than exhortatory. Lerner demonstrated how interpretation of one particular prophecy, that of the cedar of Lebanon, changed in the late Middle Ages. This was a good example of non-scriptural prophecy, its popularity residing partly in the fact that it contained something for virtually everyone: during the 1520s both Catholics and Lutherans found in the prophecy a reassuring response to the crises they both faced. Towards the end of a scholarly *tour de*

[93] Johannes de Rupescissa, *Liber secretorum eventuum*, ed. C. Morerod-Fattebert with an introduction by R. E. Lerner (Fribourg: Éditions Universitaires Fribourg Suisse, 1994), 167–8.

[94] C. Göllner, *Turcica*, 3 vols. (Bucharest: Editura Academiei Republicii Socialiste România, 1961–78), iii. 334–5.

[95] B. McGinn, 'Angel Pope and Papal Antichrist', *Church History*, 47 (1978), 155–73; M. Reeves (ed.), *Prophetic Rome in the High Renaissance Period* (Oxford: Oxford University Press, 1992); Milhou, *Colón*, 292–3, 328, 414–15; J. W. O'Malley, *Giles of Viterbo on Church and Reform: A Study in Renaissance Thought* (Leiden: Brill, 1968), 122–6, 133–5; id., *Praise and Blame in Renaissance Rome: Rhetoric, Doctrine and Reform in the Sacred Orators of the Papal Court, c.1450–1521* (Durham, NC: Duke University Press, 1979), 207 ff.

force which was not dissimilar to Walzer's analysis of the changing exegesis of Exodus 32, Lerner commented that 'Medieval chiliastic prophecies could, and usually did, have subversive implications, but such prophecies were rarely issued to encourage subversion . . . Medieval eschatological prophets hardly wrote as reformers or revolutionaries; their aim was to comprehend and make known God's plan without thinking that they or others could do anything to change it. Although they did not hesitate to express their prejudices and resentments, they did not mean to call for any human action other than "vigilance" and perseverance in Christian rectitude.'[96]

There are strong reasons to take issue with Lerner's view that eschatologists thought and behaved in this essentially fatalistic spirit. In general, there is the sheer popularity of this literature at all levels of society: Cola di Rienzo commented on this that 'if the prophecies of Merlin, Methodius, Policarp, Joachim and Cyril are the products of impure spirits or mere inventions, why are the church's pastors and prelates so willing to give them space in their libraries, in copies beautifully bound in silver?'[97] Taking this argument a stage further, it is hard to accept that such fascination was passive, rather than springing from the belief that human action would be legitimized and mobilized by the ability to 'read' God's will for his creation. There seems to be more inherent plausibility in Bernard McGinn's characterization of apocalypticism as 'a political rhetoric and a way of giving meaning to the world that has empowered individuals and groups to action'.[98] This is clearest in the case of prophecy and crusade. For example, a Joachimist prophecy about the imminent destruction of the Ottoman sultanate was used to counter defeatism in 1456, and stimulated recruitment for the crusade at Augsburg, Nürnberg, and Speyer.[99] And in the early sixteenth century Cardinal Bernardino López de Carvajal tried to use prophecy as a lever for action against the Turkish advance.[100]

Above all, the link between prophecy and crusade was emphasized when it came to calls for the recovery of Jerusalem. To a large extent this was because of the city's central place within apocalyptic thinking, but it was also due to the highly problematic nature of a recovery crusade as a military undertaking: it called for the mobilization of every argument which might help. Thus Giles of Viterbo, perhaps the best example in our period of a Joachite who was well placed to shape events, spoke in December 1507 of God's 'calling' to Pope Julius II through prophecies as well as current events to initiate a great crusade to win

---

[96] R. E. Lerner, *The Powers of Prophecy: The Cedar of Lebanon Vision from the Mongol Onslaught to the Dawn of the Enlightenment* (Berkeley and Los Angeles: University of California Press, 1983), 195–6.

[97] Johannes de Rupescissa, *Liber secretorum eventuum*, introd. 83.

[98] McGinn (ed.), *Visions of the End*, p. xix. Cf. L. Polizzotto, *The Elect Nation: The Savonarolan Movement in Florence 1494–1545* (Oxford: Oxford University Press, 1994), 205: 'in the context of apocalyptic expectations, some degree of consciously hortatory prophecy was inevitable.'

[99] Göllner, *Turcica*, iii. 335.

[100] N. H. Minnich, 'The Role of Prophecy in the Career of the Enigmatic Bernardino López de Carvajal', in Reeves (ed.), *Prophetic Rome*, 111–20; O'Malley, *Praise and Blame*, 235 n. 164.

back Jerusalem: 'Therefore act now, most blessed father. Behold with what voices, with what prophecies, with what noble deeds God calls on you.' Like Christopher Columbus, Giles placed much emphasis on the authority of Isaiah, whose chapter 60 seemed to link overseas discovery clearly with the recovery of Jerusalem.[101]

Even when urgency was much less apparent, prophecy was a handy argument to push a debate forward. A telling example from the very end of the period is Christopher St German's interpretation of Revelation 13: 18 to predict the imminent end of Islam and call for a crusade, in his *Salem and Bizance* (1533). This was not a Joachimist prophecy but a simple reading of the arithmetic in the verse, which famously runs: 'let anyone with understanding calculate the number of the beast, for it is the number of a person.' It was believed that Adam ('a person') had lived for 930 years, which was almost the same as the time which had passed since the birth of Muhammad (1533 minus 596 = 937 years). So the time had come for Islam, 'the beast', to end its reign. But for that actually to happen, St German noted, there must be an upsurge of enthusiasm for a crusade within the hearts of ordinary people, as in the past. If such an upsurge were to occur, as the author clearly hoped that it would, 'throughe grace', Scripture gave hope for the conversion of the infidels. 'And if there come such a desire in the hertes of the people: it were not vnlyke, but that they shulde haue the desire of theyr herte fulfilled, though other, whiche before them hadde lyke desire, had it not fulfilled, for the tyme was not yet come.' But 'I speake them not as prophecies, but as thynges, that as me semethe by reason of the sayde exposition, and by dyuers reasonable coniectures, are lykely to ensewe'.[102]

There is a second difficulty in assessing the impact of prophecy. Even if influence on events was aspired to by men like Giles of Viterbo, was it actually achieved? Marjorie Reeves, the pioneer of Joachimist studies in England, was well aware that 'the history of prophecy contains the delicate problem of the interplay between word and action',[103] in part because of the opposition which her advocacy of this largely new field of study encountered from historians belonging to the Gradgrind school. Reeves herself showed, and others have confirmed, that such an interplay did take place. When a particular policy had to be lobbied for, or to be 'sold' to a broader public, arguments based on eschato-

---

[101] 'Fulfillment of the Christian Golden Age under Pope Julius II: Text of a Discourse of Giles of Viterbo, 1507', ed. J. W. O'Malley, *Traditio*, 25 (1969), 265–338, repr. in *Rome and the Renaissance: Studies in Culture and Religion* (London: Variorum, 1981), study V, at 337; Milhou, *Colón*, 132–3. On Giles and the promotion of action see O'Malley, *Giles of Viterbo*, 181 ff.

[102] Christopher St German, 'Salem and Bizance', in *CWSTM* x, ed. J. Guy et al. (New Haven: Yale University Press, 1987), 323–92, at 384–7. There was a vogue for prophecies of an imminent crusade in England at this time: see A. Fox, 'Prophecies and Politics in the Reign of Henry VIII', in A. Fox and J. Guy (eds.), *Reassessing the Henrician Age: Humanism, Politics and Reform 1500–1550* (Oxford: Blackwell, 1986), 77–94.

[103] Reeves, *Influence of Prophecy*, 135.

logical readings were frequently invoked. And this of course is part of the problem. One factor lying behind Reeves's concern to demonstrate clear links between prophetic programmes and policies is the suspicion that rulers were likely to use Joachimist ideas as camouflage for goals which were actually rooted in dynastic or material interests. We thus return to the central problem of motivation which we have already approached from several other directions. In this case, it is looking increasingly likely that the answer lies less in establishing clear cases of influence, as Reeves tried to do, than in building up a plausible picture of an encompassing political culture in which prophecy held its place alongside other driving concerns and forces. The latter approach seems the way forward, for example, in dealing with the two most important instances of 'official messianism' in our period, Charles VIII of France and the Emperor Charles V. Both rulers pursued policies of aggrandizement which were associated not just with crusading objectives but also with a powerful reservoir of eschatological expectation largely based on historicized Joachimist readings of the Last Days. Geoffrey Parker has recently demonstrated how well such an approach works in the case of Philip II of Spain.[104]

We are on different terrain when eschatological programmes were tied not to governments and their ambitions, but to religious challenge and insurrection. Even Lerner was willing to acknowledge that an 'eschatological imperative' existed in the case of millenarian revolutionaries, citing the outstanding example of Tabor.[105] Lerner himself showed how a text written by Jean de Roquetaillade, the *Vade mecum* of 1356, was rewritten in Bohemia in 1422 with emphasis on its most violent passages. 'What would Rupescissa, the disciple of pacific St Francis, have thought had he known that half a century after his death his writings would help harvest in a faraway land the vintage of the grapes of wrath?'[106] After Tabor's heyday there was no comparable example of insurgents embracing a millenarian programme until the early sixteenth century. In Valencia the *Germanías* revolt produced one such case at Játiva in 1522, but this was occasioned by the fact that Joachimist ideas had taken a uniquely subversive direction in Iberia.[107] Elsewhere, social revolts were not distinguished by millenarian hopes, even when (as in Hungary in 1514) they took the form of religious wars for other reasons. Instead, apocalyptic thinking found a new outlet in the sectarian violence of the early Reformation period, most spectacularly in the Anabaptist seizure of power at Münster in 1534–5.

---

[104] 'Tudor England in the Messianic Vision of Philip II of Spain': Prothero Lecture of the Royal Historical Society, 2001. I am grateful to Prof. Parker for sending me the full text of his lecture.

[105] Lerner, *Powers of Prophecy*, 195 n. 17.

[106] R. E. Lerner, '"Popular Justice": Rupescissa in Hussite Bohemia', in Patschovsky and Šmahel (eds.), *Eschatologie und Hussitismus*, 39–51, quote at 49.

[107] S. T. Nalle, 'The Millennial Moment: Revolution and Radical Religion in Sixteenth-Century Spain', in Schäfer and Cohen (eds.), *Toward the Millennium*, 151–71.

The last area in which religious warfare found expression was that of national conflicts.[108] While the importance of eschatological preoccupations in this period is now generally accepted, the same cannot be said of the influence of national feeling. Traditionally, historians have detected a growth of national sentiment in the late Middle Ages, most frequently under the impact of war and its many demands. The Hundred Years War has long been the classic example.[109] Some, however, continue to be uneasy about such a generalization, perhaps above all about its political implications. They argue that the increasing consciousness of ethnic difference, expressed in references to national characteristics which had long become stereotypical, and the strident appeals to national solidarity issued by rulers, were separate trends of a cultural and political nature: they did not produce a 'middle ground' in which a community which was united ethnically, linguistically, and in certain cultural respects also felt itself to be a 'nation'. John Hale was an eloquent representative of this sceptical school of thought. 'The sentiment of nationhood was slow to evolve because it only rang true within a country as a whole at exceptional moments of danger from outside threats. Even then . . . rallying calls from the centre faded to whispers and eventually to silence as they slowly passed along unmade roads into regions with their own forms of speech and patterns of local loyalties.'[110] One recent advance lies in the perception that this is far from being an 'either/or' issue. Old views of a universal Christian community which by 1500 had fragmented into 'national' units are based on far too simplistic an analysis of how loyalties, either individual or collective, actually operated. Similarly, it is ingenuous to expect that feelings of national cohesiveness could ever be dissociated from the extraordinary growth of governmental power and demands. Bernard Guenée's telling comment on the situation in France, 'l'état a créé la nation',[111] could be applied to many other countries.

For our present purpose, it is not necessary to establish that national feeling was omnipresent in the late Middle Ages, that it affected all social classes,[112] that it was 'organic' as opposed to a construct, or even that it took precedence over the many other ties and loyalties which characterized society. What is undoubtedly the case is that at times the wars which were fought by 'national

---

[108] See my 'Pro deo et patria mori: Sanctified Patriotism in Europe, 1400–1600', in P. Contamine (ed.), War and Competition between States (Oxford: Oxford University Press, 2000), 221–48.

[109] See, e.g., C. Allmand, Henry V (London: Methuen, 1992), 404–25; more generally, R. Bean, 'War and the Birth of the Nation State', Journal of Economic History, 33 (1973), 203–21.

[110] J. Hale, The Civilization of Europe in the Renaissance (London: Fontana, 1993), 68. For sustained arguments along the same lines see the studies by J. Szűcs, 'Die Nation', passim; '"Nationalität" und "Nationalbewusstsein" in Mittelalter', in his Nation und Geschichte, 161–243.

[111] 'État et nation en France au moyen âge', Revue historique, 237 (1967), 17–30, at 27.

[112] In this respect the most important critique is by Ferenc Szakály, who has argued against the notion of peasant patriotism in Hungary: see his 'Das Bauerntum und die Kämpfe gegen die Türken bzw. gegen Habsburg in Ungarn im 16.–17. Jahrhundert', in G. Heckenast (ed.), Aus der Geschichte der ostmitteleuropäischen Bauernbewegungen im 16.–17. Jahrhundert (Budapest: Akadémiai Kiadó, 1977), 251–66.

communities', those states held together by an identity which went deeper than simple dynastic allegiance, were characterized by a heightened sense of emotional commitment which was expressed in religious terms. This phrasing looks like an evasion of the central issue, but the point is that as often as not the 'identity' at stake had a religious core. The reason has been well explained by Adrian Hastings in his study *The Construction of Nationhood*.[113] Hastings showed how religion played a decisive role in fashioning European nationhood, not least because of the attention paid by the church to the Old Testament. 'The whole concept of a 'Holy People', divinely chosen but enduring all the ups and downs of a confusing history, seems so very applicable to life nearer home.'[114] In this respect, he suggested, Christianity's embrace of the Hebrew scriptures had an effect which was not shared within Islam, where they did not enjoy the same status.[115]

Hastings was not alone in his perception of the important role played by Old Testament ideas in the way perceptions of nationhood were conceptualized. Donald Akenson commented that 'Every European nation at one time or another has had leaders or prophets who say that their country is chosen of God and is, in effect, the successor of the children of Israel, and that its citizens are living in a promised land.' Akenson, however, immediately qualified this remark by asserting that the concept rarely made any deep impact, notable exceptions being the three societies which he had singled out to study, namely Afrikaner South Africa, Israel, and Protestant Ulster.[116] Although Akenson himself did not say so, it might well be commented that none of these case studies was Catholic, and that a 'covenanting mentality', to borrow his phrase, could not take deep root in any country whose people owed allegiance to a universalist world-view. The fact is, however, that in the late Middle Ages it did, the result, as Adrian Hastings emphasized, being an ongoing tension between the exceptional and the universal, what Hastings termed 'a kind of focused universalism'.[117] The Catholic community was made up of individual peoples (*gentes*) which shaped their own religious identities around the special relationship which each believed itself to enjoy with God, while at the same time conscious of forming a part of the *respublica christiana*.

For obvious reasons, the tension was repeatedly on display in crusading history, perhaps above all in the period of crisis which followed the final loss of the Holy Land in 1291. For example, in his bull *Rex glorie* (1311), Pope Clement V walked a tightrope between Christian universalism and an acceptance of French exceptionalism: 'In the same way that the Israelites are known to have been granted the Lord's inheritance (*hereditas dominica*) by the choice of Heaven, to carry out the hidden wishes of God, so the kingdom of France has been selected as the Lord's special people, marked with the signs of honour, and chosen to

[113] Hastings, *Construction of Nationhood*, esp. ch. 8.   [114] Ibid. 197.   [115] Ibid. 201.
[116] Akenson, *God's Peoples*, 5.   [117] Hastings, *Construction of Nationhood*, 98.

carry out God's commands.'[118] The tension can be illustrated too in attempts to promote emigration to the Holy Land. Shortly after the First Crusade, Fulcher of Chartres described the new kingdom of Jerusalem in terms akin to a 'melting pot society', a place where people forgot the identities they had enjoyed in the west. In contrast, some two centuries later Peter Dubois accepted that the new wave of settlers needed to repopulate the Holy Land, once it had been recon-quered, would have to be given lands alongside their fellow-nationals, in order to prevent conflicts from breaking out.[119]

As we have seen, in *Rex glorie* Clement V came close to calling the kingdom of France the Holy Land in the west. Such an approach was fully in line with a broad-based tendency at the time to give France's crusading past pride of place in the evolving ideology of French kingship, a tendency which certainly brought rewards in terms of popular resonance but also entailed obligations which would weigh heavily on the shoulders of France's later kings.[120] After their initial wave of great successes in the Anglo-French war the English responded by staging a head-on challenge to their enemies' position: in Parliament in January 1377 Adam Houghton, Edward III's chancellor, asserted that military victory demon-strated that the English were God's Chosen People. It was their kingdom which was the true *heritage de Dieu*.[121] Six years later, when Bishop Henry Despenser led an English army to Flanders against the schismatic French troops who were garrisoning its towns, national pride and religious fervour briefly fused in a vigorous if crude assertion of English exceptionalism: as the archbishop of Canterbury, William Courtenay, commented in April 1383, 'the church cannot have peace without the realm, nor can the well-being of the realm be secured except through the church, and it is both meritorious to fight for the faith and fitting to fight for one's lord'. Despenser's expedition was legitimized as a cru-sade by the fact that it was launched in order to restore a Christian unity broken by the wilful wickedness of the enemy.[122] The tension between the exceptional and the universal could have found no better illustration.

---

[118]   See my 'Holy Land or Holy Lands? Palestine and the Catholic West in the Late Middle Ages and Renaissance', in R. N. Swanson (ed.), *The Holy Land, Holy Lands, and Christian History*, SCH 36 (Woodbridge: Boydell, 2000), 228–49, at 235.

[119]   Ibid. 241.

[120]   J. Strayer, 'France: The Holy Land, the Chosen People, and the Most Christian King', in T. K. Rabb and J. E. Seigel (eds.), *Action and Conviction in Early Modern Europe: Essays in Memory of E. H. Harbison* (Princeton: Princeton University Press, 1969), 3–16; C. Beaune, *The Birth of an Ideology: Myths and Sym-bols of Nation in Late-Medieval France*, trans. S. R. Huston, ed. F. L. Cheyette (Berkeley and Los Angeles: University of California Press, 1991), ch. 6; J. Krynen, *L'Empire du roi: Idées et croyances politiques en France XIIIe–Xve siècle* (Paris: Gallimard, 1993), 345–83.

[121]   *Rotuli parliamentorum*, 6 vols. (London, 1767–77), ii. 361–2. See also J. W. McKenna, 'How God Became an Englishman', in D. J. Guth and J. W. McKenna (eds.), *Tudor Rule and Revolution: Essays for G. R. Elton from his American Friends* (Cambridge: Cambridge University Press, 1982), 25–43, at 31–3; M. Wilks, 'Royal Patronage and Anti-Papalism from Ockham to Wyclif', in A. Hudson and M. Wilks (eds.), *From Ockham to Wyclif*, SCH, Subsidia 5 (Oxford: Blackwell, 1987), 135–63, at 148–50.

[122]   N. Housley, 'France, England, and the "National Crusade", 1302–1386', in G. Jondorf and D. N. Dumville (eds.), *France and the British Isles in the Middle Ages and Renaissance* (Woodbridge: Boydell, 1991), 183–201, repr. in *CWMRE*, study VII, with quote at 196.

By about 1400 sacred *patria* and national exceptionalism had become the main reference points for the conduct of religious warfare on behalf of God and country.[123] It was not difficult to portray a war fought in defence of the *patria* as a conflict for a God-given political, social, and religious order, comprising the nation's church, its saints, its laws, and its very language. As Michael Wilks expressed it in the case of England, 'Just as the Israelite had seen his physical occupation of the land of the covenant as the guarantee of his entitlement to salvation, so the right-thinking Englishman of the later fourteenth century came to picture himself as a *piers plowman*, the tiller of the soil of a landed church, a co-worker with Christ in the green fields of England.'[124] As Wilks's words show, this image was deeply rooted in the Old Testament, expressing Akenson's 'covenanting mentality'. But Christological themes were bound to intrude. The feeling persisted that a Chosen People would have a broader mission on behalf of Christ's church, typically entailing either the defence of the faith or the spreading of the gospel. The former found its most characteristic expression in the application of *antemurale* ideology to an entire national community, which seemed justifiable in a period in which the spread of government and its escalating fiscal demands made it possible to visualize an entire people shouldering the burden of sustaining the bulwark.

The best examples are Poland and Hungary. Paul Knoll and Angelo Tamborra showed that the idea of Poland functioning as Christendom's bulwark-state was formed in the mid-fourteenth century in the context of the kingdom's ambitions in the east, then revived in the fifteenth in response to the advance of the Turks.[125] But *antemurale* thinking seems to have exerted more of an impact in Hungary. Descriptions of Hungary as a form of bulwark date from the period immediately following the battle of Nicopolis (1396), and it naturally burgeoned after the Ottoman capture of Constantinople in 1453 and the relief of Belgrade in 1456. These events impressed on the minds of Hungarians and of Catholics generally the role which the country played, the image of Hungarians manning a national *antemurale* effectively purging their negative image as the descendants of pagan barbarians. By the early sixteenth century the theme had become a commonplace, finding expression, for example, at the diet of Rákos in 1505 and in István Werbőczy's compilation of Hungarian customary law, the *Tripartitum*, in 1517. It has been suggested that the *antemurale* image was so strongly embedded by this point that it far exceeded arguments based on patriotism in the exhortations made to garrison troops. But manning a bulwark was a form of exceptionalism: the disasters of the 1520s and 1530s were therefore interpreted in

---

[123] The classic study is E. H. Kantorowicz, '*Pro patria mori* in Medieval Political Thought', *AHR* 56 (1951), 472–92.

[124] Wilks, 'Royal Patronage', 151.

[125] P. Knoll, 'Poland as *Antemurale Christianitatis* in the Late Middle Ages', *Catholic Historical Review*, 60 (1974), 381–401; A. Tamborra, 'Problema turco e avamposto polacco fra Quattrocento e Cinquecento', in V. Branca and S. Graciotti (eds.), *Italia, Venezia e Polonia tra medio evo e età moderna* (Florence: Olschki, 1980), 531–49.

terms of the sins of the Hungarian people as a whole; the oppression of the peasantry by an exploitative yet negligent aristocracy was singled out as responsible by some commentators.[126] Once these had been purged by penance, the Hungarians would resume their rightful place as a Chosen People, who would expel the Turks from their *patria* and reconstitute the *antemurale* which their sinfulness had allowed the Turks to breach. János Varga summed up the whole sequence well: 'in this way sixteenth-century Hungary attained a consciousness of "exceptionalism", which was further fuelled by the bulwark-theme and provided the spiritual strength for the struggle against the Turks for another century.'[127]

Hungary in the sixteenth century thus entered a cycle of exceptionalism, catastrophic defeat, purgative penance, and renewal, which echoed the experience of medieval Castile in the *Reconquista*.[128] It is not surprising that the cycle mirrors the sequence usually predicted for apocalyptic events, since only a people purged of its sinfulness was fit to carry out God's eschatological plans. Castile itself exemplifies the alternative way of linking exceptionalism with the universalist theme, that of *dilatatio fidei*, the evangelization of pagan peoples by force of arms. And again, it is unsurprising that this beneficent triumphalism, a form of 'national messianism', was often portrayed in terms of the Joachimist programme, with its emphasis on the urgent need to realize John 10: 16 by bringing all the sheep into Christ's sheepfold.[129] It would become a dominant theme in Castilian national sentiment in the sixteenth century, in association with the defence of the Catholic faith from without and within.

Nothing better illustrates the way the twin poles of exceptionalism and universalism operated than the various migrations of Jerusalem. A sacred *patria* needed its own Jerusalem, and it is hardly surprising that on most occasions when the sanctification of the homeland took place, the association of its capital with Jerusalem was made. For example, Savonarola, the Ferrarese prophet and preacher who exercised control over Florence in 1494–8, proclaimed his adopted city to be a New Jerusalem, thereby adroitly associating Florentine civic patriotism (*campanilismo*) with his reforming zeal. But he also preached that the Florentines, once suitably purged of their sinfulness, would, like the Apostles, disseminate their message to the rest of the world, which would obligingly accept

---

[126] Göllner, *Turcica*, iii. 88.

[127] J. J. Varga, 'Europa und "Die Vormauer des Christentums". Die Entwicklungsgeschichte eines geflügelten Wortes', in B. Guthmüller and W. Kühlmann (eds.), *Europa und die Türken in der Renaissance* (Tübingen: Max Niemeyer, 2000), 55–63, with quote at 59. See also J. Jankovics, 'The Image of the Turks in Hungarian Renaissance Literature', ibid. 267–73; E. Fügedi, 'Two Kinds of Enemies—Two Kinds of Ideology: The Hungarian–Turkish Wars in the Fifteenth Century', in B. P. McGuire (ed.), *War and Peace in the Middle Ages* (Copenhagen: C. A. Reitzels Forlag, 1987), 146–60.

[128] P. Linehan, 'Religion, Nationalism and National Identity in Medieval Spain and Portugal', in S. Mews (ed.), *Religion and National Identity*, SCH 18 (Oxford: Blackwell, 1982), 161–99.

[129] J. L. Phelan, *The Millennial Kingdom of the Franciscans in the New World*, 2nd edn. (Berkeley and Los Angeles: University of California Press, 1970), esp. 5–28.

Florence's hegemony. And for Joachites like Savonarola, Jerusalem in Judaea retained its key eschatological role, so that city too could not be forgotten.[130] The complexity of the overall situation is best illustrated by reference to Castile. There was indeed in Castile 'a sacralized national geography', to use Alain Milhou's phrase, but it coexisted with a fascination with the 'real' Jerusalem which led Castilian Joachites to lay much emphasis on a crusade, to be initiated in Iberia, which would recover Jerusalem.[131] The 'Judaean Jerusalem' played a large role in the thinking of Columbus as well as in the approach of the early missionaries in the Americas. They considered their preaching to have an eschatological as well as a pastoral function: the baptism of these newly discovered *gentes* would form the prelude to the Last Days. Eventually, of course, creole society would break free from these restrictive eschatological parameters to assert its own identity. When it did so it was perhaps predictable that it would create its own sacred geography centring on its own, unique shrines.[132]

One of the European cities widely hailed as a New Jerusalem in the early fifteenth century was Prague. But Prague's standing, like that of Rome, differed radically according to the viewpoint of the observer. For moderate Hussites Prague was a *sacrosancta civitas*, as Jerome of Prague termed it in 1409. It was the illustrious capital of the 'most Christian' kingdom of *sacra Bohemia*, and it was also home to Hus's Bethlehem Chapel and the University of Prague, seedbeds of the reformed faith.[133] Its identification with Jerusalem was perhaps facilitated by the fact that Jan Milíč of Kroměříž, usually regarded as the first Czech reformer, had founded a community for repentant prostitutes in Prague which bore that name.[134] The Hussite song 'Arise, arise, great city of Prague' eulogized the city as Jerusalem, threatened by 'the king of Babylon'.[135] Jan Želivský preached that the Czechs had been blessed by God with the rediscovery of the gospel; from Prague they would spread the message of reform, evangelizing the rest of Christendom anew.[136] For Catholic Czechs the city had indeed once deserved the name of Jerusalem, 'on account of the most fair vision of peace which your hard work bestowed on the length and breadth of the kingdom'; but now that it was in the hands of the Hussites it had degenerated into the source of discord and

---

[130] D. Weinstein, *Savonarola and Florence: Prophecy and Patriotism in the Renaissance* (Princeton: Princeton University Press, 1970).

[131] Milhou, *Colón*, 287–434.

[132] Phelan, *Millennial Kingdom*; J. Lafaye, *Quetzalcóatl and Guadalupe: The Formation of Mexican National Consciousness 1531–1813*, trans. B. Keen (Chicago: University of Chicago Press, 1976).

[133] F. Šmahel, 'The Idea of the "Nation" in Hussite Bohemia', *Historica*, 16 (1969), 143–247, 17 (1969), 93–197, at 16 (1969), 173–8.

[134] T. A. Fudge, *The Magnificent Ride: The First Reformation in Hussite Bohemia* (Aldershot: Ashgate, 1998), 49–51, 189; Šmahel, 'Idea of the "Nation"', 17 (1969), 103. A. Molnár, 'L'Évolution de la théologie hussite', *Revue d'histoire et de philosophie religieuses*, 43 (1963), 133–71, at 136–40.

[135] Fudge, *Magnificent Ride*, 189 (text); Šmahel, 'Idea of the "Nation"', 17 (1969), 103.

[136] S. Bylina, 'Le Mouvement hussite devant les problèmes nationaux', in D. Loades and K. Walsh (eds.), *Faith and Identity: Christian Political Experience*, SCH, Subsidia 6 (Oxford: Blackwell, 1990), 57–67, at 63–4.

confusion.[137] And for the radical Taborites Prague was a New Babylon, inadequately reformed and still in thrall to the Catholic church. Like its namesake of old, 'it must be destroyed and consumed by the faithful'.[138] In the sermons which he wrote on the Apocalypse in *c.*1430, at a time when relations between the Hussite centre and left were becoming increasingly strained, Nicholas of Pelhřimov, the bishop of the Taborites, was particularly caustic about Prague. The Masters of its University had returned to 'papal ways' like dogs to their vomit. 'Many consider themselves to be Christians who are actually impious and murderous residents of Sodom, Gomorrah and Babylon.'[139]

These contrasting views of Prague reveal something of the confusion created by the interaction of national feeling centred around Old Testament ideas, eschatological programmes, and religious radicalism. To exert its fullest impact on warfare this interaction needed a revolutionary situation of precisely the type which Bohemia offered. And this makes Hussite Bohemia an excellent place to start a more in-depth analysis of the range of religious warfare which we have surveyed here.

---

[137] 'Litera de civitate Pragensi continens lamentationes de actis et factis quondam ab haereticis ibidem commissis', in K. Höfler (ed.), *Geschichtschreiber der husitischen Bewegung in Böhmen*, 2 vols. (Vienna: Kaiserl. Königl. Hof- und Staatsdruckerei, 1856–65), ii. 311–19, at 311.

[138] LoB, 'De gestis et variis accidentibus regni Boemiae 1414–1422', in Höfler (ed.), *Geschichtschreiber*, i. 321–527, at 435.

[139] Bartoš, 'Táborské bratrstvo', 111, 122, and see also 104, 121.

CHAPTER TWO

A Crucible of Religious Warfare: Bohemia during the Hussite Wars, 1400–1436

Hussite Bohemia was matched by no other part of Europe in the volume and range of military activity which was characterized by its initiators, participants, and apologists as religious in nature. The essential reason is clear enough. The religious reform movement in the Czech-speaking lands of the crown of Bohemia became identified, following Jan Hus's martyrdom at Constance in 1415, with a well-defined political community which had begun to view itself in national terms. When Sigismund of Luxemburg decided to attempt to impose his will on Bohemia by force, in 1420, the broad coalition of groups which embraced the reform movement resolved to use military means to defend what they construed as 'God's Law' (lex Dei). It is possible that the coalition would have cast this defence in terms of a religious war even had Sigismund's notorious invasion not been a crusade: but the Emperor-elect's agreement that it should take crusading form undoubtedly sharpened the feeling of his opponents that the conflict was sacred in character. Outside the Crusades themselves, there was no precedent in the Middle Ages for such a sustained and organized defence of religious doctrines against attack, nor was there to be a comparable case until the Reformation.[1]

In the Hussite wars one group of men fighting a religious war confronted another which held the same view: the wearers of the cross fought the defenders of the lay chalice.[2] This clash of sacred symbols was exceptional. For this reason alone the conflicts of the 1420s deserve our close attention. But the situation contained further layers of complexity. In the winter of 1419–20 southern

---

[1] The best introductions are J. Klassen, 'Hus, the Hussites and Bohemia', in Allmand (ed.), *New Cambridge Medieval History*, vii. 367–91; F. Seibt, 'Revolution und Hussitenkriege 1419–1436', in K. Bosl (ed.), *Handbuch der Geschichte der böhmischen Länder*, 4 vols. (Stuttgart, 1966–74), i. 444–536. The best concise analytical study is Šmahel, *La Révolution hussite*, while M. Lambert, *Medieval Heresy: Popular Movements from the Gregorian Reform to the Reformation*, 2nd edn. (Oxford: Blackwell, 1992), chs. 15–17, contextualizes Hussite beliefs well. Historiographical issues were reviewed by T. A. Fudge in 'The State of Hussite Historiography', *Mediaevistik*, 7 (1994), 93–117.

[2] Z. Drobná, *The Jena Codex: Hussite Pictorial Satire from the End of the Middle Ages*, trans. E. Wheeler (Prague: Odeon, 1970), 48.

Bohemia witnessed a wave of military activity driven by chiliastic conviction, focused above all on the new settlement at Hradiště, renamed Tabor. And when this chiliasm died down in the spring of 1420, Tabor remained a remarkably radical community, at first socially and long afterwards in terms of religious practice. The religious war which its warriors conducted on behalf of utraquism (communion in both kinds, *in utraque specie*) was more coloured by eschatological convictions than the war of defence waged by the Hussite centre, based at Prague and justified above all by its University Masters. It is not going too far to see Bohemia at this time as the battleground for four types of religious war: the war in defence of a purified set of religious beliefs associated with Prague, at heart cautious and inherently territorial; the more urgent and uncompromising form of combat waged by the Taborite and Orebite brotherhoods; the apocalyptic and purgative violence used by the chiliasts; and the crusading warfare represented by the expeditions with which the church tried, unsuccessfully, to suppress the Hussites. Add to this the fact that Bohemia in this period also produced one of the most passionate rejections of any form of religious war, voiced by Peter Chelčický, and the full spectrum of challenge and response is in place.

The Hussite wars are still a comparatively obscure subject in the English-speaking world, so before engaging with detail it may be useful briefly to outline their key events.[3] During the lengthy and tortuous negotiations which finally brought the conflict to an end, the Hussites repeatedly stressed that the military initiative (and hence the responsibility for the war which arose from it) had normally rested with the Catholics;[4] and it is true that the main thread in the pattern of warfare was made up of the sequence of crusades sent into Bohemia between 1420 and 1431. Historians have usually described five of these, although the numbering is problematic: the contemporary Catholic apologist Andrew of Regensburg, for example, merged the second and third crusades into a single enterprise.[5] The first of the crusades, however, was distinctive, not least because it was commanded by the Emperor-elect Sigismund in person. He hoped through this show of force to take possession of Prague, but the city was ably defended by Jan Žižka and, after suffering a defeat in battle outside the city on 1 November 1420, Sigismund had to withdraw from Bohemia.

From this point onwards Sigismund was preoccupied with the revival of the

---

[3]   For more detail see F. G. Heymann, 'The Crusades against the Hussites', in K. M. Setton (gen. ed.), *A History of the Crusades*, 2nd edn., 6 vols. (Madison: University of Wisconsin Press, 1969–90), iii. 586–646.

[4]   e.g. 'Z bratislavské schůzky krále Zikmunda s husitskými vůdci r. 1429', ed. F. M. Bartoš, *Časopis matice Moravské*, 49 (1925), 171–95, at 183; *Monumenta conciliorum generalium seculi decimi quinti*, 3 vols. (Vienna: Österreichische Akademie der Wissenschaften, 1857–86), i. 419.

[5]   N. Housley, 'Explaining Defeat: Andrew of Regensburg and the Hussite Crusades', in M. Balard et al. (eds.), *Dei gesta per Francos: Études sur les croisades dédiées à Jean Richard* (Aldershot: Ashgate, 2001), 87–95, at 89.

Ottoman threat to Hungary and had to hand over responsibility for subduing Bohemia to a series of lieutenants, electoral princes, and papal legates. The second crusade, launched late in the summer of 1421, was especially notable for its ecclesiastical direction. The papal legate Cardinal Branda of Castiglione and the archbishop–electors of Cologne, Trier, and Mainz played leading roles in the crusade's initiation, and all but the last named commanded troops in the field. Poor co–ordination and indecisiveness, failings which characterized all the crusades from this point onwards, brought early successes to nothing. At the same time it was apparent that Jan Žižka's tactical innovations, especially his improvised war wagons and use of field artillery, were paying dividends not only in terms of Hussite victories but also through the crushing impact which these had on crusader morale. As a result a third crusade launched in the autumn of 1422 was the least effective to date. A fourth crusade in 1427 and a fifth in 1431 were both routed with painful ease by the Hussites. These latter setbacks were all the greater because of the care and planning which went into them: the evidence of the *Reichstagsakten* shows that the imperial authorities had a sound grasp of what was going wrong and paid their opponents the compliment of trying to emulate their tactics and discipline.

These five crusades were massively destructive: raids carried out into neighbouring lands by the Hussites in the late 1420s and early 1430s brought welcome booty into Bohemia but the economic cost of the fighting remained substantial.[6] The crusaders were also uncommonly brutal; as in the Albigensian Crusade two centuries earlier, the Catholics' demonization of their enemy meant that the customary laws of war were ignored or suspended.[7] But the full complexity and impact of the warfare practised in Bohemia can only be grasped if two further forms of belligerence are taken into account. The first is the warfare which was almost constantly waged between the utraquists and the Catholics, both Czechs and neighbouring Germans: what contemporaries termed the *bellum cottidianum*. This too was brutal, and because it lacked the clear character of the crusading episodes, it appeared aimless; at such times it was natural to doubt the motivation of the combatants. Thus Heymann, reviewing the campaigning of Žižka's last year (1424), imagines contemporaries wondering: 'Had Žižka's holy war degenerated into mere revolutionary banditry?'[8] The second is the conflict which broke out between the Taborite and Orebite brotherhoods on the one hand, and the Hussite centre on the other, on occasions when the crusading threat abated. Its culmination was the battle of Lipany, on 30 May 1434, where

---

[6] On the economic impact of the warfare see R. C. Hoffmann, 'Warfare, Weather, and a Rural Economy: The Duchy of Wroclaw in the Mid-Fifteenth Century', *Viator*, 4 (1973), 273–305; Fudge, *Magnificent Ride*, 280–1.

[7] See, e.g., 'The Very Pretty Chronicle of John Žižka', trans. F. G. Heymann in his *John Žižka and the Hussite Revolution* (Princeton: Princeton University Press, 1955), 3–10, at 5, 7; Heymann, *John Žižka*, 102, 206, 274, 291; Heymann, 'Crusades', 597.

[8] Heymann, *John Žižka*, 401.

the radical field armies were defeated and the road to a settlement opened up which was based on a very limited reforming agenda. It was only when this settlement was reached, at Jihlava in 1436, that the wars came to an end, enabling Sigismund in August 1436 to enter peacefully the city which he had failed to take by force of arms sixteen years previously.[9]

Because it was a reforming movement, early Hussitism was not by its nature violent. Calls to arms were made by Jan Hus and Jakoubek of Stříbro in the years leading up to the crisis at Constance, but they were metaphorical rather than literal. In 1410, for example, Jakoubek defended Wyclif's works by referring to Ephesians 6: 12, 'For our struggle is not against enemies of blood and flesh, but against the rulers, against the authorities, against the cosmic powers of this present darkness, against the spiritual forces of evil in the heavenly places.' A struggle was indeed in progress, but it was not to be construed in terms of 'a material sword'.[10] The imprint of Waldensian pacifism was so strong that a doctrinaire rejection of the death penalty was amongst the articles condemned at the St Wenceslas synod of September 1418.[11] There were of course early instances of the use of violent means in the promotion of reform, and Kaminsky was surely correct in his suggestion that 'the spiritual battle against Antichrist, when worked out in terms of real people and real situations, must have tended to become a real battle, a clash of arms'.[12] The outstanding example was Jan Želivský's mobilization of his congregation to march on Prague's New Town Hall and defenestrate the anti-reform councillors there on 30 July 1419, an action which is now generally seen as calculated rather than spontaneous.[13] This was violence used to promote God's work, and it anticipated the iconoclastic riots of the early Reformation. But the overwhelming mood of the reformers at this point was peaceful. The main response to King Wenceslas IV's much-delayed clamp-down on utraquism in the summer of that year was the series of great open-air rallies on hill tops in southern Bohemia. The latter included the first, non-military Tabor near Nemějice. These gatherings were explicitly separatist and pacifist. As one Taborite song put it, 'Do not resist evil but go out to the mountain and here learn Truth.'[14]

'The time to wander with the pilgrim's staff is over. Now we shall have to march, sword in hand.' This remark by the leader of the Pilsen utraquists, Wenceslas Koranda, was made on 30 September 1419.[15] It brilliantly encapsulated the volte-face which occurred in Hussite thinking shortly after this point,

---

[9] Lambert, *Medieval Heresy*, 344–8.
[10] H. Kaminsky, *A History of the Hussite Revolution* (Berkeley and Los Angeles: University of California Press, 1967), 75–6, and cf. 73 on Hus's position.
[11] Ibid. 259–61: 'no-one may say that the death penalty is never to be inflicted' (260).
[12] Ibid. 168. Cf. similar comments by Lambert, *Medieval Heresy*, 329.
[13] Kaminsky, *History*, 278–96.
[14] Ibid. 286 and see n. 76 for a useful discussion of early Taborite pacifism.
[15] Heymann, *John Žižka*, 80: the chapter is entitled 'Pilgrim's Staff or Sword?'

without which the wars of the 1420s obviously could not have taken place. The causality of this *Wendepunkt* has long been a major concern of historians of the Hussite revolution in much the same way that the precise formation of the crusade idea has preoccupied historians of the First Crusade.[16] One of the things which complicates it is the multiplicity of strands of behaviour outlined earlier, which all originated at this time and were connected one with another. The violence of the millenarians arose from the belief that Christ's Second Coming was imminent: all true believers should make their way, not to the pilgrimage sites of 1419, but to five towns in west Bohemia held by the utraquists. Isaiah had prophesied in 19: 18 that they would be spared the wrath to come: 'On that day there will be five cities in the land of Egypt that speak the language of Canaan and swear allegiance to the Lord of hosts.' These towns were Pilsen, Saaz (Žatec), Louny, Slaný, and Klatovy. But more important in the long term were two radical communities: that at Hradec Králové, in eastern Bohemia, which was renamed Mount Horeb, and that at Hradiště, in southern Bohemia, named Tabor.

Tabor became the powerhouse of radical Hussitism, and hostile commentators within the Hussite coalition, such as the Prague town secretary and chronicler Lawrence of Březová, applied the name Taborites to all the chiliasts whose bloodthirsty activities they condemned. Lawrence wrote of the chiliasts perceiving themselves as angels sent by God to lead people to the hills where they would be saved on the Day of Wrath. He claimed that this role was exercised through coercion and brutality. The old order was no longer to be rejected but fought, and any Taborites who died 'would shortly return with the rest of the brothers to assist Christ in judging the enemies of God's Law and cleansing his temple'. Lawrence regarded them with horror, lamenting the fate of a land caught between the brutality of the crusaders on the one side and the chiliasts on the other: 'King Sigismund was an overt persecutor of the truth, but for their part the Taborites were more cruel: between them they lit the fires which reduced almost to nothing the noble and bountiful land of Bohemia.'[17] The duration of this chiliasm is difficult to pinpoint with precision because the passing of February 1420 without eschatological drama was accounted for in terms of a secret Second Coming: Christ would not make his return known until more vengeance had been exacted on his enemies. However, Taborite chiliasm had more or less run its course by the end of the year. The suppression of Martin Húska's heresy and the destruction of the Adamites in October 1421 showed that chiliasm had been thoroughly marginalized at Tabor.[18]

[16] e.g. F. Machilek, 'Heilserwartung und Revolution der Täboriten 1419/21', in K. Schnith (ed.), *Festiva Lanx: Studien zum mittelalterlichen Geistesleben Johannes Spörl dargebracht aus Anlass seines sechzigsten Geburtstages* (Munich: Salesianische Offizin, 1966), 67–94; A. Molnár, 'Non-violence et théologie de la révolution chez les Hussites du XVème siècle', *Lumière et vie*, 91 (1969), 33–46; T. A. Fudge, 'The Night of Antichrist: Popular Culture, Judgment and Revolution in Fifteenth-Century Bohemia', *Communio viatorum*, 37 (1995), 33–45.

[17] LoB, 'De gestis', 408–9, 411.   [18] Heymann, *John Žižka*, 258–64.

In its short lifetime it had made a deep impression, as militant chiliasm often does. We shall see that Catholics were always keen to demonize Tabor, but scarcely less hostile was the Hussite centre and right. Lawrence of Březová quoted the responses of the Prague University Masters to a list of chiliast beliefs. The latter included the enthusiastic embrace of violence in the cause of divine vengeance: 'Any one of the faithful is accursed who holds his sword back from the blood of the adversaries of Christ's Law, from personally pouring it out. Rather, each of the faithful ought to wash his hands in the blood of Christ's enemies, because blessed are all who return vengeance to the woeful daughter, just as she has done to us.' This sanctified violence, freed of all constraints, was condemned as 'heresy and tyrannical cruelty'.[19] The conservative John of Příbram claimed that the worst of the violence was the cynical response of the chiliast priests to the passing of the apocalyptic deadline, an attempt to defuse hostility by 'a new lie . . . to console the people', to the effect that the elect themselves should become God's avenging agents. This he linked with their repudiation of lordship: 'Now you will not pay rents to your lords any more, nor be subject to them, but will freely and undisturbedly possess their villages, fish-ponds, meadows, forests, and all their domains.'[20] This clearly tendentious reading has to be treated sceptically, but it probably contains some truth: because of the idea of a secret Second Coming, there was a transition from suspenseful adventism towards the outright abandonment of chiliasm, and it was characterized by the hacking out of regional seigneuries at both Tabor and Mount Horeb. This was much more easily achieved if appropriation and coercion were justified by the exercise of a general eschatological mandate.

Divested of its apocalyptic programme, Tabor remained a radical community within the Hussite coalition. This was of course largely true in terms of the religious beliefs and practices of the Taborites, which were irreconcilable with the much less radical approach taken at Prague: the differences between them could not be resolved and the tension residing at the heart of the coalition ended only with the clash at Lipany, which shattered Tabor's military hegemony. From the viewpoint of the warfare which it waged, however, Tabor was different in two other respects from the Hussite centre and right. First, eschatological currents were always more prominent at Tabor and featured in the way it fought, or at least, in the way its apologists thought that it should fight. Because it owed its very existence to the Hussite cause, Tabor was bound not just to identify itself more closely with the defence of the 'Law of God' than other towns where the utraquists had assumed control (including even Mount Horeb), but also to view its future as a community within an eschatological framework which was shaped by the progress of the reform. Secondly, Tabor cut across the social fabric of the rest of Bohemia. At its origins it famously practised communism, and while this

---

[19] McGinn (ed.), *Visions of the End*, 267.
[20] Ibid. 265–6. We shall return to this issue below, Ch. 4.1.

disappeared quite quickly alongside chiliasm, the community remained distinctively non-noble.[21] In its organization as well as in its tactics, Taborite warfare manifestly departed from medieval norms. The tendency of the Prague Masters to conceive of the war in terms of scholastic thinking on the role of the social orders did not fit conditions at Tabor.[22]

In practice neither of these prominent features of Tabor's nature and organization exercised as great an impact on Taborite warfare as one might expect. There were good reasons for this. In the early 1420s there was a danger that emphasizing eschatology would revive the chiliasm which had been painfully laid to rest. Thereafter, as Tabor became increasingly settled as a community, the reverse was the case: that eschatology would cease to register at all, and that the warfare which was being constantly waged would acquire a different tone and motivation. We shall see that this became the concern of the bishop of Tabor, Nicholas of Pelhřimov.[23] Without chiliasm, eschatology loses a lot of its power to electrify, unless there is an alternative source of excitement such as strong national feeling or a newly formulated sectarian belief. As for Tabor's social peculiarities, there was a danger that they would alienate the broad centre of the Hussite coalition, particularly if Catholic attempts to exploit them were to prove successful. The need to hold the coalition together meant that commonality of purpose had to be stressed: that the war being waged by Tabor was the same as that being fought by other utraquists, that they shared a common cause in the Four Articles, which stood for the 'Law of God'.[24] The constant claim of the Taborites was that they were fighting for God's Law: '[we are] campaigning for the divine law and fighting on its behalf.'[25] The temptation to stray into insurrectionary territory was thus resisted, but it is probable that it was not that strong in any case, since Tabor inherited the socially conservative features of Wyclif's theology alongside the ecclesiologically radical ones. Šmahel has argued convincingly that, outside the religious sphere, the Hussite programme had no revolutionary intent.[26] This has been misread in the past because the Catholic authorities at the time made great play of Tabor's alleged social radicalism in the hope of stirring into action secular leaders within Germany and beyond.[27]

The Hussite programme was a common cause of Czechs.[28] Founded amidst

---

[21] T. A. Fudge, ' "Neither Mine nor Thine": Communist Experiments in Hussite Bohemia', *Canadian Journal of History*, 33 (1998), 26–47; J. Klassen, 'The Disadvantaged and the Hussite Revolution', *International Review of Social History*, 35 (1990), 249–72.

[22] F. Seibt, *Hussitica: Zur Struktur einer Revolution* (Cologne: Böhlau, 1965), 16–57.

[23] Below, Ch. 6.1.   [24] Lambert, *Medieval Heresy*, 333–4.   [25] *UB* i, no. 509.

[26] Šmahel, *La Révolution hussite*, 71–2, 83, 127. See also his ' "Doctor evangelicus super omnes evangelistas": Wyclif's Fortune in Hussite Bohemia', *Bulletin of the Institute of Historical Research*, 43 (1970), 16–34, for Wyclif's influence on Hussite thinking.

[27] e.g. G. Holmes, 'Cardinal Beaufort and the Crusade against the Hussites', *EHR* 349 (1973), 721–50, at 725; *UB* ii, no. 789.

[28] For introductions to this issue see Bylina, 'Le Mouvement hussite'; Seibt, *Hussitica*, 58–124.

chiliastic excitement, and having nothing in common with the religious past of Bohemia, which it regarded as either misguided or irrelevant, one might expect Tabor to turn its back on any association of the Law of God with national feeling. Yet national identity was powerfully played on by Žižka during his time at Tabor (1420–3). On 12 September 1421 Žižka wrote to the people of Domažlice to encourage them to hold fast against a splinter group of the second crusade. He exhorted them to 'follow the example of the old Czechs who, their pikes firmly propped, defended not only God's cause but also their own'. Their opponents were 'enemies and destroyers of the Czech land'.[29] Žižka's biographer characterized this text as 'the most forceful and impressive of all [Žižka's] letters . . . a very telling testimony to Žižka's strong national feeling and to his consciousness of a national tradition'.[30] Heymann's emphasis on Žižka's national feeling has been criticized.[31] One should not read too much into one text, nor indeed forget that Žižka broke with Tabor in the summer of 1423. But the belief that not just the Taborites but all Czech utraquists formed an elect national group, charged with the defence and propagation of God's Law, was also voiced by Nicholas of Pelhřimov, whose identification with Tabor's ideology was much firmer and longer lasting than Žižka's.[32] In his *Chronicon Taboritarum*, for example, Nicholas recalled the preaching of the reformed faith 'in the illustrious kingdom of Bohemia', and described how the crusaders 'considered how they might best stifle this promising start and alongside it condemn and destroy the language of the Czech nation'.[33] It would probably not be going too far to describe Tabor's self-view as that of an elite or vanguard within a national coalition defined by God's choice of the Czechs as the restorers of his true faith.

As we saw in the previous chapter, one problem relating to 'sanctified patriotism' is the artificial nature of much medieval patriotism, taking artificial in its true and non-pejorative sense. All too readily it can be conjured up as a device, in order to mobilize support.[34] The problem is exemplified by Žižka's letter to Domažlice. The purpose of the letter was to inspire a *levée en masse*: 'Call the people together in the market place, so that all men, even the youngest and oldest, who are strong enough, may be up in arms at every hour of the day.'[35] Moreover, the town's allegiance was uncertain and the arrival of the crusaders might swing it back to the Catholic side. These circumstances easily explain the patriotic tone which Žižka adopted, in much the same way that they explain his reassurance that he would soon appear in person with support. Yet that tone would only have been worth adopting if it could be expected to have some effect.

---

[29]   Heymann, *John Žižka*, 488–9.   [30]   Ibid. 276.

[31]   Šmahel, 'Idea of the "Nation"', 17 (1969), 114.

[32]   H. Kaminsky, 'Nicholas of Pelhřimov's Tabor: An Adventure into the Eschaton', in Patschovsky and Šmahel (eds.), *Eschatologie und Hussitismus*, 139–67, at 147.

[33]   Nicholas of Pelhřimov and John of Lukavecz, 'Chronicon Taboritarum', in Höfler (ed.), *Geschichtschreiber*, ii. 475–820, at 476, 481.

[34]   Cf. Bylina, 'Le Mouvement hussite', 66.   [35]   Heymann, *John Žižka*, 488.

Šmahel may be correct in identifying two forms of national feeling, 'an instinctive nationalism' which embraced large sections of the population, and 'the ideological appropriation of national sentiment by certain learned men', but the fact remains that there were many bridges between the two.[36] The argument is frustratingly circular.

The situation becomes somewhat clearer when we come to consider the way the Hussite centre and right approached the defence of 'God's Law'. For here the 'national' cause was unquestionably prominent. In the first place, it was strongly present in the manifestos produced to encourage support for the Hussite coalition within Bohemia. In a detailed analysis of the early manifestos Karel Hruza followed Seibt's lead in emphasizing the importance of the impending crusade in the forging of a Hussite identity or cause: 'the menace of the crusade, the threat of annihilation, had greatly stimulated the self-consciousness of the Czech Hussites.'[37] In these conditions reservations about the precise nature of Czech national sentiment become largely irrelevant: defence of the *patria* in association with that of the 'Law of God' formed an overwhelmingly powerful motor.

Hruza's argument that the Hussite cause was 'incubated' by the crusade of 1420 is strengthened by his demonstration of how rapidly the 'national' theme was refined during the immediate lead-up to conflict in the spring of 1420. In a manifesto sent by Prague to all the Hussite communities on 3 April the tone was one of outrage at the actions of pope and Emperor-elect. This is by any standards an astonishing document. The Germans were described as 'our natural enemies', perennially hostile to the Czech language: they wanted to exterminate it in Bohemia, just as they already had in the Rhineland (*sic*), in Meissen, and in Prussia. The church was compared to a serpent, which had hatched an egg in the shape of the crusade, the 'cruel cross' recently raised 'with bloody hands' at Breslau against people whose only fault was their adherence to divine truth. 'Our stout ancestors', the 'old Czechs', and their love of country (*vlast*) were held up as examples for the defence of 'the golden and most Christian kingdom' of Bohemia against attack. The help of St Wenceslas, Bohemia's patron saint, was invoked.[38] Within two weeks a more sophisticated line of attack was being adopted. *Lingua*, *patria*, and *regnum*, associated yet distinct, were all brought into the equation, but the ground had to some extent shifted from rhetoric to law. In the first place, Sigismund's legitimacy was questioned, in so far as he had neither been chosen by the great lords of the realm nor crowned. And in the second, the wrongful accusation of heresy was highlighted. 'For that reason [the pope] has instructed his legate to distribute the cross as if we were heretics, to the great

[36] Šmahel, *La Révolution hussite*, 91–2, echoing his 'Idea of the "Nation"', 17 (1969), 192–3.

[37] K. Hruza, 'Die hussitischen Manifeste vom April 1420', *Deutsches Archiv für Erforschung des Mittelalters*, 53 (1997), 119–77, at 131, and cf. Seibt, *Hussitica*, 37.

[38] Hruza, 'Die hussitischen Manifeste', 162–6.

damage and detriment of the Czech tongue; a process which is contrary both to law and the [right] ordering of Christendom.'[39]

The more measured tone of the second of these manifestos recurs in the letter sent to Venice in July 1420 in an attempt to secure the republic's assistance in the form of an attack on Austrian lands. Prague was now under siege, and the letter began with a sonorous and quasi-humanist statement of the duty to defend one's *patria*:

Amidst the range of responsibilities facing us as individuals, by which the human race is oppressed and ground down, one above all embraces all the claims to grace, and that is our duty towards our country. The most noble have always loved their country and have sacrificed belongings, bodies, sweet life itself, in glorious combat to ensure its safety. They are fortunate, since their illustrious death earns them an undying place in the memories of their descendants. On the other hand, those who neglect their country, disgraced, banished and unworthy, are forgotten as soon as they perish.[40]

Sigismund was characterized as the enemy of the 'crown and most Christian kingdom of Bohemia' and the foe of the Czech language, as shown by his misdeeds from the council of Constance onwards. As one would expect, the atrocities committed by the crusaders were given much attention, and these were attributed to Sigismund's resolve totally to annihilate the Czech language, 'to wipe out and lay waste to the whole language'. But the legal aspect of the situation, the fact that Sigismund had no constitutional right to act as he did and that the Hussites were unjustly accused of heresy, was emphasized, together with the real reason for Sigismund's Bohemian programme, which was his hope of securing imperial coronation by pleasing the pope.[41] Similar chords were sounded in a manifesto sent 'to each and every adherent of the Christian faith' in February 1421. Sigismund and the papal legate, Ferdinand of Lucena, had acted both unjustly and wickedly, and their crusaders had committed appalling atrocities against the Czechs solely on the grounds of national hatred: 'our simple country-folk they seized in their hovels and on the roads, making off with their belongings and killing them without mercy out of raw hatred for the tongue they spoke. They burnt them alive in their houses and grabbed little children from the arms of their grieving mothers. They spared nobody they could get near, be they unwarlike, young, old, or suckling women. All they subjected to cruel death and blood-red massacre.'[42]

Such manifestos were far from being alone in placing the national theme centre stage. Repeatedly from late 1419 onwards the threat posed to the Czech lan-

---

[39] Hruza, 'Die hussitischen Manifeste', 166–77, with quote at 170. For nomenclature see J. Prochno, 'Terra Bohemiae, Regnum Bohemiae, Corona Bohemiae', in M. Hellmann (ed.), *Corona Regni: Studien über die Krone als Symbol des Staates im späteren Mittelalter* (Weimar: Hermann Böhlaus Nachfolger, 1961), 198–224.

[40] *UB* i, no. 37, at p. 39.   [41] Ibid., no. 37.   [42] Ibid. ii. 487–94, at p. 489.

guage was emphasized. Thus in October 1419 the Prague authorities defined the goals of a broad-based alliance as 'securing the freedom of God's Law, defending the honour of our kingdom and language, and repudiating the vicious charge of heresy cast against us and the kingdom of Bohemia'.[43] In July 1420 the defence of the city of Prague was described as 'protecting God's Law and the honour of our language'.[44] Archbishop Conrad of Prague adhered to the Four Articles in April 1421 'in order to increase divine praise and honour, free God's invincible truth, protect the honour of our language, and pursue the common good'.[45] Rewards granted to Hynek of Waldstein (Kolstein) in June 1421 were justified 'by reason of his services in spreading divine law, to ourselves, and to the whole language of the Czechs'.[46] And in September 1424 Prague banned all citizens who had supported Sigismund, 'forgetful of their own honour and of that of their representatives, in defending God's Law and the honour of our language'.[47]

For the author of the 'Very Pretty Chronicle of John Žižka', writing towards the end of the wars, the conflict was ethnic in nature. The pope declared a crusade not against the followers of Jan Hus but against the Czechs, 'and he gave indulgences, whosoever slew such a Czech or took his life this way or the other, that he that did this was rid of all sin and punishment'. Czechs and Germans fought savagely, 'and above all the Germans sought the lives of the Czechs, and the Czechs of the Germans'.[48] This was an exaggeration, but there are signs that the papal *curia* played into its opponents' hands, sacrificing discretion in the hope of stepping up recruitment for the crusades. The first crusade bull, of March 1420, was directed against 'Wyclifites and Hussites' and avoided any political or national references. But the one sent to Cardinal Branda in April 1421 referred to 'Wyclifites and Hussites, and other heretics and unbelievers . . . infesting the whole of the kingdom of Bohemia and its adjacent regions . . . and striving to wipe out the Catholic faith, above all in the German nation'.[49]

Lawrence of Březová's narrative account of the early stage of the war gives the clearest indications that defence of the *patria*, with all its attendant associations of historical prowess and ancestral honour, invigorated the protection of the *lex Dei*. The national theme is strong in Lawrence's whole account of the warfare, although it might be more accurate to define it as a 'regnal' theme, which was more than tinged by Prague *campanilismo*.[50] For Lawrence the defence of Bohemia and the Law of God were synonymous, simply because in the minds of the crusaders themselves the two had become fused into a single object of destruction. His attitude is encapsulated in his description of Sigismund's siege camp of 1420:

[43] Ibid. i, no. 4.   [44] Ibid., no. 39.   [45] Ibid., no. 78.   [46] Ibid., no. 120.
[47] Ibid., no. 309.   [48] 'Very Pretty Chronicle', 5.   [49] *UB* i, nos. 12, 74.
[50] See F. Seibt, 'Communitas primogenita. Zur Prager Hegemonialpolitik in der hussitischen Revolution', *Historisches Jahrbuch*, 81 (1962), 80–100, repr. in Seibt, *Hussitenstudien*, 61–77; F. Seibt, 'Vom Vítkov bis zum Vyšehrad. Der Kampf um die böhmische Krone 1420 im Licht der Prager Propaganda', *Historisches Jahrbuch*, 94 (1974), 89–117, repr. in Seibt, *Hussitenstudien*, 185–207.

From day to day, many people of every type flocked to the camp's site on account of the wicked crusade which the pope had declared against the Czechs, and in particular against supporters of the lay chalice. By capturing the illustrious and splendid city of Prague and thereby annulling and preventing the sharing of the chalice, they hoped to obtain the indulgence from pain and guilt, which their priests had promised them, albeit falsely, as a means of exciting them to destroy the faithful Czechs of both sexes.[51]

To drive home his point, Lawrence went on to remark that the crusaders burnt any Czech who fell into their hands, unless their Catholic Czech allies could rescue him first, 'even if he had never taken communion in both kinds'.[52]

In this way the scene was set for an account of the defence of Prague against overwhelming odds which assumed the dimensions of a religious epic, in which God watched over and protected his faithful Czechs against the inhuman forces of Antichrist. In Bylina's words, 'Contemporaries envisaged the elevation of the Czech nation as God's Chosen People, and of Czech soil as the place to which Christ would return.'[53] Following the successful defence of the Vítkov against the crusaders on 14 July, 'The soldiers of Prague knelt down in the Hospital field, gave thanks to God, and sang "Te Deum" in loud voices, because he gave them this victory over their enemies, not indeed through their strength, which was so small, but by a miracle.'[54] It was a 'victory sent from above', a 'miraculous triumph over the enemy'.[55] A similar exultation in divine assistance characterized Lawrence's description of the battle of the Vyšehrad on 1 November 1420, the last big encounter with Sigismund's ill-fated 'coronation crusade'. Prague's defenders faltered in the face of the Moravian attack, but 'my lord of *Crussina* [Hynek Krušina of Lichtenburg, the Hussite commander] saw this and yelled in a loud voice "Good brothers, turn back, act today as mighty warriors in Christ's war, because this war is God's, not ours. You will witness the Lord God placing all his enemies, and ours, in our hands". Before he had even finished these words, somebody shouted: "Look, the enemy are fleeing, they are in flight!" All then rushed forward, drove the enemy from the entrenchments and put them to flight.'[56] Even the slaughter of the Moravian nobility which followed this reversal of fortunes proved to be grist to the national mill: Sigismund was viciously sparing the lives of his German and Hungarian followers while allowing his Moravian ones to be killed, thereby denuding the lands of the Bohemian crown of its nobility.[57] Lawrence of Březová's lament for the fall of the 'flower of Moravian chivalry' on this occasion is a reminder of the way the Hussite centre embraced traditional social values and norms, as is his description of Hussite dubbings on the eve of battle in 1421: 'following a short address by the priests everybody sank to the earth and offered up devout prayers to God; rising from

---

[51] LoB, 'De gestis', 374.   [52] Ibid. 375.   [53] Bylina, 'Le Mouvement hussite', 63.
[54] LoB, 'De gestis', 378; Heymann, *John Žižka*, 136–47.   [55] LoB, 'De gestis', 379.
[56] Ibid. 421; Heymann, *John Žižka*, 176–9.   [57] LoB, 'De gestis', 422.

prayer, they created a number of new knights, to inspire them to be bolder in defending the truth.'[58]

Anybody reading such sources as Lawrence's chronicle, his ecstatic poem celebrating the crushing of the last crusade at Domažlice in 1431,[59] or Jan Žižka's remarkable battle song, 'You who are the warriors of God',[60] could be forgiven for thinking that the Hussites encountered no problems or tensions in waging war in defence of their beliefs. In reality this was far from being the case. One reason for exercising critical care in judging the credibility of Lawrence's more extravagant passages is our knowledge that assembling a military defence of shared Hussite interests was imperilled not just by deep-rooted disagreements on how to interpret the Law of God, but also by scarcely less fundamental doubts on the part of many Hussites about the validity of conducting any form of war. The winter and spring of 1419–20 were remarkable because at the very moment when adventists grouped in the five cities of salvation were practising what Kaminsky has termed 'the total warfare called for by chiliast military doctrine',[61] there occurred at Prague a wide-ranging debate about the legitimacy of combat. The debate has survived not just in outline form but also in much of its detail. Particularly well represented are the views of Jakoubek of Stříbro. He was the most distinguished thinker of the Hussite centre,[62] and the single most important legatee of Hus's own approach.[63]

Jakoubek's twofold task was to refute the scriptural basis for the adventists' activity, and to work out the justification for a defence of the Hussite cause against the impending crusade. His problem was that the chief argument used to demolish the adventist position, the denial of their literal interpretation of Scripture, also worked against the assumption of arms against Sigismund, since the whole emphasis of the New Testament was on *arma spiritualia* rather than *arma carnalia*. As we saw earlier, Ephesians 6: 12 put it in a nutshell. The quandary may be viewed in a text which Jakoubek penned in early 1420, refuting adventist prophecies.[64] The key passages used to underpin adventist flight theory were Jeremiah 51: 6 ('Flee from the midst of Babylon'), and Isaiah 19: 18 and Luke 19: 17–19, both referring to the cities of salvation. But these passages were not to be taken as referring to actual flight or to real cities. As Origen and 'the great and faithful Augustine' had made clear, 'Babylon' was a state of mind

---

[58] Ibid. 526. See also Heymann, *John Žižka*, 305; F. M. Bartoš, *The Hussite Revolution 1424–1437*, Engl. edn. by J. M. Klassen (Boulder, Colo.: East European Monographs, 1986), 104, for dubbings in the field after successes in 1421 and 1433.

[59] LoB, 'Carmen insignis corone Boemie', in Höfler (ed.), *Geschichtschreiber*, i. 596–620. See also Šmahel, 'Idea of the "Nation"', 17 (1969), 130–1.

[60] Heymann, *John Žižka*, 497–8.   [61] Kaminsky, *History*, 367.

[62] Kaminsky, ibid. 314, described him as 'the Prague master who was closest to enjoying a national, pan-Hussite prestige'.

[63] The eight texts were edited by Kaminsky, 'The Treatises of MS o 13 on Adventism, Chiliasm and Warfare', in his *History*, 517–50.

[64] Ibid. 519–22.

rather than a geographical location, and 'wherever he resides in the material sense, the just man lives in the spiritual Jerusalem and not in the spiritual Babylon'. The just man who died rather than consent to evil would be saved irrespective of whether he lived 'in Prague or in Písek or in Pilsen'.[65]

Prophecies, Jakoubek argued, abounded in Scripture and to seize on a literal interpretation of any single one to advocate a particular course of action was to encourage disorder and disillusionment. One man prophesies that Sigismund is the king of Babylon and will descend on Bohemia and destroy Prague, which is Babylon; while another prophesies that this will not happen. Who is to be believed? The only safe approach for the priesthood is to set aside such presumption, live according to the gospel, and exhort the laity to abandon their sinfulness. At the present time the laity were being whipped up by their priests into taking up arms, which generated murder and hatred, contrary to New Testament exhortations to bear wrongs patiently. Both Scripture and the example of the early church pointed to the repudiation of *arma carnalia*: 'The way of the evangelical priest is therefore to encourage evangelical warfare in God's cause, in accordance with the Gospels and in a Catholic manner, with spiritual weapons, following the example of the early church of Christ's Apostles.'[66] This was a doctrine of non-resistance and had it been followed the Hussite wars would have been short indeed.

Jakoubek's escape route from this quandary lay in Romans 13. 'However, I concede that wars may be fought lawfully by the greater secular powers, as it says in Romans 13 [: 1–6], to whom the sword is entrusted for the punishment of the wicked.' The dangers nonetheless were great, unless the *potestates sublimiores* waged war in accordance with certain specific conditions: 'in the first place, the cause for which the war is waged, must be the cause of God; secondly [there must be] right intention; thirdly, [there must exist] a God-given inspiration to wage war in this way, that which David used to have when he waged war in God's cause; and fourthly, the charity of the combatant must be so strong that he is willing to cease fighting as soon as his opponent is ready to accept that he is in the wrong.' Jakoubek thus established grounds on which the Hussite centre could legitimately wage war in defence of religious beliefs which associated such *arma carnalia* with Babylon. To re-emphasize the importance of Romans 13, he ended with a renewed attack on the presumptuousness which he believed lay at the root of the adventist fallacy: 'Let nobody audaciously presume that he possesses a divine inspiration to wage war in this way just because of erroneous and counterfeit fantasies, leading him to stir the people up to assault somebody and shed their blood in an irregular manner.'[67]

Neither Jakoubek's demolition of the adventist position nor his advocacy of a religious war based on scholastic theology coupled with traditional just war the-

---

[65] 'Treatises', 520.   [66] Ibid. 521.   [67] Ibid. 522.

ory went uncriticized. The Taborite Master John of Jičín took issue with Jakoubek's views on the spiritual Babylon and the latter wrote a long letter in reply which has survived in two separate versions.[68] Jakoubek clung to his view that a spiritual interpretation was not just the more valid one but also the safest in terms of guiding the laity. For example, Matthew 24: 16 stated that at a critical point in history, foretold by Daniel, 'those in Judaea must flee to the mountains'. Since everybody accepted that 'those in Judaea' should be construed not as the inhabitants of Judaea but as the faithful, why should the exhortation to flight be taken literally? It was crucial not to confuse the laity because 'confusion is rather close to desperation'. The role of the priesthood was to provide guidance, not to bring about upheaval as the chiliasts had done. 'What is more deserving of belief by every [Christian] wayfarer than that the faithful will be saved who live in accordance with Gospel precepts, in faith, hope, and charity until their lives' end, and who refuse to engage in evil as their conscience guides them, continuing in this fashion until they die, at God's will, wholly irrespective of their dwelling place, be it city, castle, town, field, road, village or forest?'[69]

In this plea for stable and reformed communities of utraquist belief there lay an agenda which was implicitly conservative in social as well as in religious terms; indeed it is hard to disentangle Jakoubek's criticism of the chiliast position from a disapproval of Tabor's growing puritanism. This emerges most clearly in the longer version of his reply to John of Jičín, in which he took issue with John's 'either or' approach towards the notion of Babylon, which lay at the root of flight theory. Jakoubek cited Matthew 15: 11, a powerful anti-separatist text: 'It is not what goes into the mouth that defiles a person, but it is what comes out of the mouth that defiles.' Accordingly he denied that the righteous must abandon communities where 'Babylonish' values prevailed: 'the good, the just and the holy can dwell in the midst of the wicked of Babylon and make use in a good and holy manner of those same things which the Babylonians use wickedly and profanely.' The implication was that the priesthood carried the responsibility for combating such values through their example and preaching. Amongst the chiliasts, by contrast, the laity were being encouraged by dubious scriptural exegesis and priestly exhortation to abandon their accustomed manual labour. They seized arms, killed, and lived off the possessions of their neighbours. Priests who formerly had preached against any form of bloodshed now embraced it, and people wondered how this volte-face had come about.[70]

Jakoubek's horror at the behaviour of the Taborite priests found expression in another tract in which he forthrightly labelled them 'men of violence' (*percussores*).[71] They had responded to his citation of Romans 12: 19 (God's reservation of vengeance to himself) by referring to the Books of the Maccabees, which they said should be read aloud to the people for encouragement. For Jakoubek this

---

[68] Ibid. 530–4, 534–44.   [69] Ibid. 533.   [70] Ibid. 543–4.   [71] Ibid. 528–30.

was an 'imperfect way of fighting', the expression of a dispensation which had been superseded by that of grace and love. Combat now should be spiritual, as laid down in Ephesians 6: 10–18, 'following in this the Lord Jesus Christ and his Apostles and martyrs, and the other saints, true soldiers of Christ, on the road which is royal and secure'.[72] It was Matthew 5: 10, not Maccabees, which should be expounded by evangelical priests: 'Blessed are those who are persecuted for righteousness' sake, for theirs is the kingdom of heaven', a preparation for martyrdom rather than battle. Closely mirroring the approach which he took towards Babylon, Jakoubek argued vigorously that the Maccabees' *carnalia bella* were a precedent for the Hussites' predicament only figuratively. To follow them literally was to usher in 'anger, sedition, and violent acts, culminating in the shedding of blood'. There was always the danger that individuals would avenge their own injuries 'under the pretext of God's cause and God's injury', that they would be driven not by God's cause but by the devil.

Jakoubek sailed very close to the pacifist wind in this tract, and his grudging permission for a war of defence was given only at the cost of denigrating the secular powers: 'This way, which indeed is imperfect, is permitted and conceded to the greater powers because of their own imperfection.'[73] In yet another tract he addressed himself specifically to 'the twofold way and road of waging war in God's cause'.[74] The first, and by far the superior way, was that of 'our captain of war (*noster dux belli*) the Lord Jesus, and his Apostles and martyrs who in this imitated their lord, and the rest of the saints who followed him'.[75] This was the way of suffering, and it was bolstered by a barrage of scriptural references including two which had always played a key role in crusading apologetics, Matthew 10: 37–8 and Luke 14: 26–7, Christ's demand that his disciples should 'take up the cross and follow me'. To see such passages occurring in this context is to be reminded of the sheer plasticity of the *via crucis*. Similarly, in a curious inverted prophecy of the Hussite female warriors whose courage would soon astonish the crusaders, Jakoubek commented that even women who engaged in this *via bellandi* would triumph over the enemy, 'because they fight not with the strength of their body but with the power of their faith'.[76] Priests above all must fight in this way, and as if to confound the Taborites' reliance on Maccabees, Jakoubek cited 1 Maccabees 5: 67, in which battling priests fall in action 'for they went out to battle unwisely'.[77]

Jakoubek found it hard to be so eloquent on the 'second way of fighting in God's cause', immediately stating that it is one 'in which there resides more danger to salvation'. Romans 13: 1–7 and 1 Peter 2: 14 ('governors [are] sent by [God] to punish those who do wrong and to praise those who do right') established the legitimacy of a war conducted by the 'greater powers', but it must be waged in

---

[72] 'Treatises', 528–9.   [73] Ibid. 528.   [74] Ibid. 525–8.
[75] Ibid. 525.   [76] Ibid. 526.   [77] Ibid. 527.

accordance with the conditions which we have already noted. It was supremely perilous because in practice it was virtually impossible to sustain a fitting spirit of charity towards the enemy. That it might be mandated by direct revelation Jakoubek found hard to believe, 'since such wars [in the Old Testament] were fought in common and by certain revelation, which nowadays is not accustomed to happen; it can come about, but it is unusual'.[78] Almost as if he realized how severe his message was, Jakoubek tempered it, though only slightly, at the end. 'You can see that I do not altogether deny this second way of waging war, which can be done by people possessing the authority, but not by evangelical priests; and the first way remains more perfect and secure.'[79]

But the times called for rather more enthusiasm for the 'second way of fighting'. In perhaps the most revealing of all these tracts, Jakoubek of Stříbro joined forces with another of the most revered Hussite leaders, Master Christian of Prachatice, to arbitrate in a polemic which had arisen between two priests, Nicholas and Wenceslas, 'in a public arena', over a number of issues thrown up by the defence of utraquism early in 1420.[80] There could scarcely be clearer evidence both of the resonances of this debate, what Kaminsky termed 'a real contest for the Hussite mind',[81] and of the role assigned to the University Masters in establishing a common position. Christian and Jakoubek revealed that they had taken the advice of other Masters before giving their responses on four matters. One was to affirm that a woman who had embraced the Hussite cause might leave her husband if he stopped her hearing the word of God and receiving communion. A second was a further rebuttal of adventist flight theory, on grounds now familiar to us. The third and fourth directly addressed the issue of the armed defence of God's Law.

At first it looks as if the line of argument replicates the severe stance taken by Jakoubek on other occasions. Yes, it is the duty of secular lords to defend God's Law with the material sword, on the basis of Romans 13: 4 and 1 Peter 2: 14. No, 'subject communities of believers' may not do so if the secular powers prove remiss, because Christ's way was that of patient endurance of suffering, and fighting could not be reconciled with charity. Scripture, Augustine, and canon law (in the shape of Gratian's Causa 23) agreed that 'it is not permitted to any member of the populace to incite wars'. Then comes a dramatic change:

We concede that secular lords may resist God and his law to such an extent that God himself removes their power, and then it would be licit for communities summoned by God for this work (*communitatibus a deo ad hoc opus admissis*) to defend Gospel truth in fact rather than metaphor, provided they keep order and do so according to Christ's law. And what moves them must be divine inspiration or a certain revelation, or at least evidence which is quite unmistakable.[82]

---

[78] Ibid. 528.   [79] Ibid. 528.   [80] Ibid. 544–7.
[81] Kaminsky, *History*, 323.   [82] 'Treatises', 545–6.

The caveats swiftly follow. Nobody should undertake this course of action 'audaciously and precipitately'; it was better to work for justice in other ways than through overthrowing lordship, if the latter showed any signs of mending its ways; above all, the way of suffering was inherently superior.[83]

Nonetheless, the softening of stance is unmistakable. Faced with an intransigent Sigismund, the Hussite community could both depose him and defend God's Law against him.[84] The line of thinking adopted by Jakoubek was clearly reflected in the way the Prague civic authorities depicted their defence of the city in 1420, a conceptualization which yoked together the duty of each individual to defend God's Law with the delegation of the 'secular arm' to the city and its allies: 'the defence of the truth of the Gospel in the face of every evil, and against all who attack us when we advocate it, is enjoined on everybody, both through the duty of the Gospel calling and through the investing in us of the secular arm: we must resist [Sigismund] to the end as a tyrant and as a most cruel Antichrist'.[85]

Resistance theory had emerged and with it the legitimacy of taking up arms to defend the *causa Dei*, despite the perils attending it. These perils are treated in the last of the tracts, *Bellandi materiam*, which was probably written by the most conservative of the Hussite ideologists, John of Příbram, in the spring or summer of 1420.[86] The classic conditions of a just war are expounded, 'just vindication' (*iusta vendicacio*), 'licit authorization', and 'right intention'; but the emphasis is firmly laid on the last of these, 'which principally and finally makes a way legitimate'. The reason is immediately apparent, 'it is essential that the cause which is being fought for, or which ought to be fought for, should be God's justice and not material goods'. In fact, the author of this text remarks, the only cause for which one should fight is one in which death will constitute martyrdom: 'For nobody should expose themselves to war, which brings the danger of death, except for a cause in which the fallen will be martyrs'.[87] This extreme statement derives from the author's anxiety that the armed defence of the *causa Dei* will degenerate into civil war, from which Bohemia will emerge weakened and a prey to foreign invasion. 'What could be more foolish than for the Czech people to fight among themselves, without reasonable cause, for material gain? Once that gain is acquired and one's neighbour slain, a foreign nation will subjugate everybody.'[88] The Czechs had more than enough enemies who were just waiting for such an opportunity. There is a strong sense of patriotism in this tract, but it focuses on a territorial concept of 'Czechness' which includes the Catholics and therefore cuts across the emerging idea of a Hussite national iden-

---

[83] 'Treatises', 546.
[84] Kaminsky, *History*, 323, argued that this was an application of Wyclif's doctrine that mortal sin barred a man from exercising political authority, but this is not supported by the wording.
[85] LoB, 'De gestis', 384.   [86] 'Treatises', 547–50.   [87] Ibid. 547.   [88] Ibid. 548.

tity. Civil war was especially unchristian if those guilty of fratricide were fighting for money rather than conviction, and God would punish those who used his Law as camouflage for attacks on *simplices*.[89]

There was a significant though curious alliance of interests between the neo-Waldensian Jakoubek and the politically conservative author of *Bellandi materiam*. Repugnance at the excesses of the chiliasts, the difficulty of reconciling literal combat with Christ's teaching, and anxiety about the effects on the kingdom of Bohemia of validating a war between Catholic and Hussite Czechs were powerful factors acting as a brake on Hussite religious war. What therefore created the exuberant sentiments which are so characteristic of sources like Lawrence of Březová's narrative account of the war? One is tempted to say events, or more precisely two series of events. The effect of the invasion of 1420 we have already noted, in the manifestos issued from Prague and in Lawrence's own epic treatment of the siege of the city. The effect on intellectuals was not necessarily decisive: the pacifist Peter Chelčický recorded conversations during the siege in which Jakoubek of Stříbro made it clear that he still saw his 'second way' as fraught with perils, even though he realized the foolishness (and perhaps also the ingratitude) of openly questioning the validity of the armed defence.[90] But the convictions of ordinary Hussites were undoubtedly strengthened, as they enjoyed a series of victories against crusaders whose brutal behaviour confirmed that they were agents of Antichrist.[91]

The defence of Prague in 1420 was, however, only the first in an extraordinary sequence of military successes which culminated with the crushing of the fifth crusade in 1431. Just as the success of the First Crusade in capturing Jerusalem in 1099 confirmed the crusading message, so the series of Hussite victories confirmed their religious war: this was their *Deus vult*. The evidence for this lies above all in their manifestos and in their defence of their position during the negotiations which took place with their opponents. In the manifesto of February 1421 the achievement of the Hussites in driving off the first crusade was highlighted:

[Ferdinand of Lucena] busied himself calling together innumerable people from more than thirty kingdoms and provinces, well-equipped with weapons, but in manners and behaviour insolent in the extreme and totally unworthy of Christ's name, including many who were natural enemies of this undefeated kingdom. Like Gog and Magog facing the Lamb, [they confronted] Joseph's tiny flock, wholly naked, unskilled in warfare and the use of arms, lacking any human assistance in the shape of arms, horses, and soldiers, trusting only in the help of the Highest. And through him it happily triumphed over this huge and celebrated army of kings and princes, and triumphs yet.[92]

[89] Ibid. 549.   [90] Kaminsky, *History*, 392.
[91] J. Durdík, *Hussitisches Heerwesen* (Berlin: Deutscher Militärverlag, 1961), 77–85.
[92] *UB* ii. 487–94, at 489.

The classic example is the opening address given on behalf of the Hussites at the meeting at Bratislava in the spring of 1429. The speaker was Peter Payne, the English Hussite.[93] His speech embraced themes which we have already witnessed playing an important role in forging Hussite self-identity. A number of Payne's emphases made clear his alignment with the radicals, especially his belief in the imminence of the Last Days, his identification of the church as the Whore of Babylon (Revelation 17: 3–6), and his perception of the Hussites not just as the persecuted elect, the few who would be saved from the destruction to come, but also as society's impotent and humble (1 Corinthians 1: 26–8). On the other hand, several references to Bohemia as the 'most Christian kingdom', and an impassioned lament for the devastation of the entire country by the ravages of war, would have endeared Payne to the more conservative, territorial groups within the coalition. Near the start of the speech Christ himself is audaciously 'nationalized' by being described as 'the unconquered knight and warrior of Prague'. Jakoubek of Stříbro's metaphorical *noster dux belli*, the Christ who conquered by suffering the cross and who summoned his followers to do the same, had been metamorphosed into a ferocious Czech warrior, scourge of the men who wore that cross on their clothing.

More striking than either Payne's eschatological and radical leanings, or his references to Czech national feeling, however, is the sheer self-confidence of his address. Delivered not long after the defeat of the fourth crusade in 1427, Payne's speech reflects a movement at the very height of its military reputation. Taking as his theme 'above all things truth is victor' (1 Esdras 3: 12), he brazenly exulted in the victories of the Hussite armies. 'We do not attribute our victories to ourselves but to God their creator, whose truth we, albeit unworthily, defend against your assaults. He is our witness, he who holds up heaven and earth, that we are not waging this war on our own account, nor do we resist you out of self-esteem or hope of profit, or any other audacious cause.'[94] The advance in Hussite thinking in the years which had passed since the start of the war is undeniable. The religious wars of the Old Testament, prudently set aside as irrelevant nine years previously by Jakoubek of Stříbro, are here woven into a tapestry of divine approbation and support: the Hussites are the modern Israelites, their champions the new Gideons.[95] Even more remarkable are the Bernardine cadences in which the position of the all-conquering Hussites is contrasted with that of their miserable foes: 'Happy are they who suffer for Christ, unhappy you who persecute Christ. Happy are they who fall for Christ's sake, unhappy you who fight for the devil and perish more miserably than beasts. Happy are they who, whether

---

[93] 'Z bratislavské schůzky', *passim*. For the context see Bartoš, *Hussite Revolution*, 41–4.

[94] 'Z bratislavské schůzky', 187–8.

[95] An approach reflected in Aeneas Sylvius Piccolomini's *Historia bohemica* (Frankfurt: Christophorus Olffen, 1687), ch. 47: 'Theutones per circuitum habitantes, alios Philistaeos, alios Idumaeos, Moabitasque vocabant. Bohemiam terram promissionis esse dicebant.'

they stand or fall, deserve success and victorious triumph, unhappy you who, whether you stand or fall, hasten to hell, and, even if you are victorious with spear and sword, will still lie prostrate beneath your sin and evil-doing.'[96]

Recent history, like sacred history, provided Payne with ammunition. The cross worn by the crusaders was that of Antichrist, the proof lying in Sigismund's career: when he fought against the Turks he was victorious, but now, fighting against God's truth, he loses every time. 'Do you not wonder at it, that on so many occasions your armies, ten times ours in size and equipment, turn their backs in blind confusion and flee at the hands of a handful of peasants, defeated, prostrated, ashamed?' Exaggerating somewhat, he pointed out that these latter defeats were at the hands of *villani*: 'an unheard-of miracle, o king'.[97] The words of St Paul in 1 Corinthians 1: 26–28 had thus been realized.[98] The power of God had been clearly and repeatedly manifested and it was impossible to defeat it. 'Nobody has or ever can overcome God and his truth, so it is in vain, o mortal king, that you set out with your worldly princes to destroy a truth which is inextinguishable and immortal, and which has God both as its author and as its defender.'[99] Sigismund's only escape from his dilemma was to recognize that the church's blandishments were those of Antichrist, and to embrace the truth of the Four Articles, thereby winning the loyalty of his Bohemian subjects.[100]

No less triumphalist than Payne was Nicholas of Pelhřimov, bishop of the Taborites, in the sermon cycle on Revelation which he wrote *c.* 1430.[101] Nicholas undoubtedly had his concerns about the progress of events. He was angry that the Hussite centre seemed willing to settle for no more than the lay chalice, and fearful about what he perceived as the growing materialism of Taborite society.[102] The success of Hussite arms over the past decade, nonetheless, filled Nicholas with the conviction that the defence of the *lex Dei* constituted a holy war. 'On several occasions now our opponents have been thrown into confusion. Many times they thought that they could dispose of Hus and the Hussites as easily as they did at Constance . . . but God scattered them and confused them and will continue to do so on account of his incomprehensible glory.' Christ himself fought alongside the Hussites and sent his angels to shield them.[103] In 1430 the Taborite leaders dispatched a manifesto throughout Europe in which the same self-confidence was abundantly present, accompanied by fury that the Catholic authorities were still denying the Hussites a public debate on their beliefs. Those

---

[96] 'Z bratislavské schůzky', 187.   [97] Ibid.
[98] Ibid. 181–2. At the very point when Payne cited it, this text was playing a major role in the theological scrutiny of Joan of Arc. See D. A. Fraioli, *Joan of Arc: The Early Debate* (Woodbridge: Boydell, 2000), 37, 90–1, 113.
[99] 'Z bratislavské schůzky', 186.   [100] Ibid. 188.
[101] Kaminsky, 'Nicholas of Pelhřimov's Tabor', *passim*.
[102] Bartoš, 'Táborské bratrstvo', 104, 111, 121–2; see below, Ch. 6.1.
[103] Bartoš, 'Táborské bratrstvo', 120–1.

who listened to the pope were foolish because the history of the past ten years showed clearly on whose side God was fighting.

And if you decree nothing other than [fresh] wars against us, then we will call to our aid God and his truth, and we will defend it until death. We will not be alarmed by the excommunication or the curses of the pope or the cardinals or the bishops. For we know that the pope is not God, as he makes himself out to be, by cursing and excommunicating when he wants to, and blessing when he wants to. Because he has been cursing and excommunicating us for many years now and God in his grace has not stopped coming to our assistance.[104]

Essentially the same points were made in a general Hussite manifesto sent out in July 1431, at the time of the Eger talks. Readers were asked to consider whether the actions of the popes, including the preaching of 'the bloody cross', showed them to be worthy of occupying Peter's see. 'And if, as they propose, they invade our kingdom with their great and mighty armies, with the intention of bringing about its wholesale destruction, as is claimed, then we will place our trust in the virtue of the Highest, whose cause we are pursuing, and we will drive away force with force, just as all laws and all rights permit.'[105]

Such expressions of defiance were courageous, and in February 1432 an assembly of the French clergy at Bourges was prepared to give some credence to the argument that the constant defeat of the crusaders was divine punishment for 'the monstrous behaviour of the clergy and people'.[106] The fact remained however that, as Bartoš remarked, the Bratislava meeting was the first step on the road towards the settlement of the dispute by negotiation seven years later at Jihlava.[107] Jakoubek of Stříbro, the great conciliator between Prague and Tabor, died in August 1429. With hindsight it is apparent that the Hussite movement's conservative wing was bound to listen to the warnings and promises of skilled negotiators like Nicholas of Cusa in much the same way that Payne had imagined King Sigismund being seduced by the pope's offers. Once their demand for discussion of beliefs had been grudgingly met, the Hussites were vulnerable to the charge that they no longer had a just cause for war: As Gilles Charlier, the dean of Cambrai, put it, 'In what way can the cause be just when we offer you peace, when we strive to lead you back into the bosom of mother church?' They had after all long boasted that 'Truth conquers', and for that no arms were needed.[108] Hussite religious war, the offspring of Catholic antagonism, could not long survive the movement towards conciliation any more than the Teutonic Order's

---

[104] J. Prokeš, 'Táborské manifesty z r. 1430 a 1431. Přispěvek k politice Prokopa Velikého', *Časopis matice Moravské*, 52 (1928), 21 n. 1.

[105] *UB* ii, no. 751, at p. 231.   [106] Ibid. ii, no. 793, at p. 273.

[107] Bartoš, *Hussite Revolution*, 40.

[108] *Monumenta conciliorum generalium*, i. 420–1. It is hard not to admire the skill with which Gilles Charlier turned their own arguments against the Hussite envoys at Basle.

Reisen could survive the conversion of the Lithuanians. For this reason Lawrence of Březová's remarkable 'Song of the illustrious crown of Bohemia', written for the celebrations which followed the crushing of the fifth crusade at Domažlice in 1431, was a kind of swan song for 'Hussite nationalism', whose blend of religious conviction, patriotic passion, and eschatological mission was inherently volatile. After the failure of this final attempt at coercion, the way was clear for a full-scale civil war to break out between the Hussites themselves: the next big battle was Lipany.

How can one best assess the character of Hussite religious war? Two obvious ways suggest themselves. One is by comparing it with other examples of religious warfare which occurred at the time. The obvious comparison to bring to bear is the Anglo-French war. That conflict produced, in the *Gesta Henrici Quinti*, one of the most remarkable medieval expressions of national messianism. For the anonymous author of the *Gesta*, as for the monarch whose words he claimed to be reporting, the English were unquestionably the elect of God. 'These I have here with me are God's people . . . [and] the Almighty, with these His humble few, is able to overcome the opposing arrogance of the French . . . as if to say, He can if he wishes.'[109] Their all-conquering king was God's chosen champion. 'O God of warriors, England is indebted to Thee—England whom Thou hast graced with a prince of such great felicity and devotion.'[110] Their almost incredible victory at Agincourt was crystal-clear proof of divine backing, and their French opponents were stubborn for refusing to recognize the judgement of God on their wickedness. 'O God, why does this wretched and stiff-necked nation not obey these divine sentences, so many and so terrible, to which, by a vengeance most clearly made manifest, obedience is demanded of them?'[111]

The *Gesta Henrici Quinti* was no eccentric anomaly: its author was a royal chaplain and Christopher Allmand demonstrated that a number of other texts composed during Henry V's reign, including poems, sermons, and speeches delivered at the opening of Parliament, concurred with his exalted views.[112] In December 1420, for example, Chancellor Langley informed Parliament that 'we English have very special cause and reason to honour and thank Almighty God for the high grace, victory, and success which he has shown to the king our sovereign'.[113] Even as late as 1425 God could still be claimed as a supporter of the English war effort: 'since the death of [Henry V], God has delivered a number of castles, walled towns, and other fortified places, to the lordship [of Henry VI], so it could be shown that the Lord's hand has fought for him.'[114] The theme of English election, first propounded in the wake of Edward III's great victories,

---

[109] *Gesta Henrici Quinti*, ed. and trans. F. Taylor and J. S. Roskell (Oxford: Oxford University Press, 1975), 78–9.
[110] Ibid. 154–5.   [111] Ibid. 124–5.   [112] Allmand, *Henry V*, ch. 19 *passim*.
[113] *Rotuli parliamentorum*, iv. 123.   [114] Ibid. 265.

thus attained its medieval zenith during the short-lived but spectacular French war conducted by Henry V.[115]

The counterpart on the French side was, of course, the even more meteoric career of Joan of Arc. It is a truism to say that Joan, with her voices, her sword sent by God, and her banner inscribed with religious imagery, elevated Charles VII's cause to the level of a religious war.[116] Perhaps the strongest impact was on her opponents. In a letter of protest to Charles VII the duke of Bedford, still basking in Henrican triumphalism, voiced the indignation of a man who held that God's backing would be manifested in military success.[117] The French had long ceased to enjoy such success, and Charles VII's secretary Alain Chartier conducted a painful but frank enquiry into the theological meaning of this just a few years before Joan appeared on the scene.[118] With Joan's own victories, of course, this began to change, and in his assessment of Joan's mission, written in 1429, Jacques Gelu expressed the hope that the elect people of France had now been chastised enough for their sins and would be restored to divine favour:

God took pity on the people of Israel after many afflictions, and chose it as his own. So we cannot fail to believe that the kingdom of France, which has always remained steadfast in faith, and which has now been punished enough for its misdeeds, returning to God in penitence, will be deemed by divine majesty to be worthy of help; indeed, as we noted above, the very subject we are handling [i.e. Joan's appearance] shows that God's clemency is inclined towards justice and mercy for his king and people, and that his forgiveness is being extended.[119]

A more jubilant note was struck in Christine de Pisan's *Ditié de Jehanne d'Arc*, the poem which she wrote in midsummer 1429 to celebrate Joan at the height of her successes.[120] God's intervention in the war through the person of Joan was direct, dramatic, and unmistakable. His covenant with the French royal house had been renewed: 'O what honour divine proof has bestowed on the crown of France. For by the graces which [God] grants to it he shows how much he approves of it, and that he finds more faith in the royal house than anywhere else.'[121] The turn-around in French fortunes had come about *par divine mission*.[122] In it God's providence was manifest, as was his singling out of Charles VII for an agenda of great deeds. Joan was 'the Maid sent by God, in whom the Holy Spirit

---

[115] McKenna, 'How God Became an Englishman', 35–7.

[116] e.g. M. G. A. Vale, *Charles VII* (London: Eyre Methuen, 1974), 55.

[117] J. Quicherat (ed.), *Procès de condamnation et de réhabilitation de Jeanne d'Arc dite la Pucelle*, 5 vols. (Paris: Jules Renouard, 1841–9), iv. 382–6.

[118] See below, Ch. 6.1.

[119] P. Lanéry d'Arc (ed.), *Mémoires et consultations en faveur de Jeanne d'Arc* (Paris: Alphonse Picard, 1889), 576. See also Fraioli, *Joan of Arc*, 87–102.

[120] Christine de Pisan, *Ditié de Jehanne d'Arc*, ed. A. J. Kennedy and K. Varty (Oxford: Society for the Study of Mediaeval Languages and Literature, 1977). See also Fraioli, *Joan of Arc*, 103–25.

[121] *Ditié*, 30, *huitain* 12.   [122] Ibid., *huitain* 10.

has placed his great grace, and who has received the gift of great largesse from on high'.[123] The justice of the French cause was thus validated, and, addressing French men-at-arms, Christine exhorted them to fight with confidence in the expectation of divine rewards. 'Be constant, for I swear to you that you will receive glory and praise in Heaven! I dare to say that he who fights for the right will gain Paradise.'[124] As for the English, Christine addressed them in tones which readily explain Bedford's indignation: 'Blind people! Do you not see that God's hand is at work here. Do you want to fight against God?'[125]

Yet there was to be no straightforward exchange of roles. The Valois reconquest was prolonged and arduous, interrupted by aristocratic rebellion, and conducted by a man who singularly lacked Henry V's messianic character.[126] One of Joan's most famous claims was that anybody who waged war against the kingdom of France waged war against Jesus Christ himself.[127] As Joseph Strayer remarked, this was in one sense no more than a statement of official royal ideology stretching back more than a century, with links to the chain of thought to which Clement V had given expression in *Rex glorie* in 1311.[128] Deborah Fraioli has recently emphasized how important it was to legitimize Joan in terms of this ideology: 'Joan's mission was able to be seamlessly integrated with France's belief in its own sacred dynasticism.'[129] But if this ideology established that every war waged by the king of France was *ex officio* religious in character (like every war fought by the Byzantine Emperor),[130] it by no means followed that the combatants were driven by religious zeal. Only in special circumstances, like those created by Joan in 1429, did this occur. When it did, eschatological expectations began to be voiced, most notably in the form of 'Last Emperor' prophecies, which nurtured hopes of expansion and conquest abroad. It is striking that even the embattled Charles VII was viewed at least twice as a possible 'Last Emperor': by Christine de Pisan in the *Ditié de Jehanne d'Arc*, and by an otherwise unknown Jean du Bois in 1445.[131]

This is not to dismiss the *Gesta Henrici Quinti* or the sources praising Joan. Themes of national election, the use of a rhetoric drawing heavily on Old Testament warfare, the emphatically providential reading which was given to success and failure, added up to much more than *topoi* or propagandistic devices. But they do not compare with the remarkable fervour visible in so many of the sources for the Hussite wars. More interestingly, the relative ease with which the

---

[123] Ibid. 32, *huitain* 22.   [124] Ibid. 35, *huitain* 38.   [125] Ibid. 37, *huitain* 47.
[126] Vale, *Charles VII*, 70–162.
[127] 'Tous ceux qui guerroient audit saint royaume de France, guerroient contre le roy Jhesus': Quicherat (ed.), *Procès de condamnation*, v. 127.
[128] Strayer, 'France: The Holy Land', 15–16.   [129] Fraioli, *Joan of Arc*, 2.
[130] G. T. Dennis, 'Defenders of the Christian People: Holy War in Byzantium', in A. E. Laiou and R. P. Mottahedeh (eds.), *The Crusades from the Perspective of Byzantium and the Muslim World* (Washington: Dumbarton Oaks Research Library and Collection, 2001), 31–9, at 34.
[131] *Ditié*, 36, *huitain* 43; N. Valois, 'Conseils et prédictions adressés à Charles VII, en 1445 par un certain Jean du Bois', *Annuaire-Bulletin de la Société de l'Histoire de France*, 46 (1909), 201–38.

English brought into service national messianism under the direction of a pious king pursuing a just cause highlights the remarkable achievement of the Hussites in 1420. For they faced circumstances which were almost diametrically opposed to those which prevailed in Henry V's England. In their case a heterogeneous coalition with deep religious differences, whose chief ideologists harboured strongly Waldensian leanings, managed to wage a war in defence of the Law of God against a man whom many of the combatants had until very recently been prepared to accept as their king.

This brings us back to the issue of the crusade. The fact that Hussite religious war was waged against crusaders provides the second obvious reference point in assessing its character. It may be argued that the only way to forge the necessary degree of utraquist unity in the face of the crusade, given the extraordinary obstacles to that unity, was to create a kind of 'counter-crusade'. Religious conviction was therefore emphasized and carried onto the battlefield in the form of totems, above all the chalice and veneration for the martyred Hus, precisely in order to drive away threatening differences. Ironically, Hussite religious war would then be the product of disunity in much the same way that the crusade was, since Sigismund's consent to its use lay as much as anything else in his inability to mobilize the support of the German electoral princes by constitutional means.

This is an argument to be used with care. There are no lack of Hussite references to the crusade against them, and as we would expect they are all characterized by a mixture of indignation and scorn. We have already witnessed the depiction of the crusade as a 'serpent's egg' in the manifesto of April 1420, and the reference to the crusaders' cross as the cross of Antichrist in Payne's 1429 Bratislava speech.[132] The Hussites liked to point out that the cross worn by their opponents was 'not the cross of Christ, which knows not how to oppress the innocent and destroy the very people who cherish it, but the impious cross of Antichrist'.[133] Ferdinand of Lucena, the first of the series of papal legates dispatched to invigorate the Catholic cause, 'incendiary and begetter of wickedness', was 'the messenger not of Christ, the sole author of peace and salvation, but of Antichrist, who like Behemoth rejoices in weapons and shields of metal, and glories and grows in blood, murder, pestilence, and the oppression of the holy innocents'. At Breslau 'he did not shun from raising the cross with bloody hands'.[134] In their response to the Catholic orators at Basle in 1433, the Hussite barons complained of the 'bloody cross . . . [preached] against us as if we were heretics',[135] while Prokop the Bald, the Taborite leader, furiously denied that the Hussites had started the war: 'The highest, who knows all, is aware that it was your side which unleashed the war, raising the bloody cross against us, as noted

---

[132] Above, at nn. 38, 97.   [133] *UB* i, no. 37, p. 40.
[134] Ibid. ii. 487–94, at 489.   [135] *Monumenta conciliorum generalium*, i. 415.

above, without any fault on our side, devastating the kingdom of Bohemia inhu-
manly with sword and fire.'[136]

The indulgences enjoyed by the crusaders received similar treatment. In 1421
the Prague authorities condemned them as 'most wicked indulgences'.[137]
Lawrence of Březová described the crusaders of 1421 as 'a wicked and impious
people, who were not inclined to mercy by the sighs of women, their floods of
tears, or the pleas of little children. Thanks to the sins of the Czechs[138] they perpetrated every kind of wickedness at their disposal, and blithely blasphemed as
they did so, believing that through so many heinous deeds they were serving God
and would earn an indulgence for their sins.'[139] The Taborite manifesto which
was sent out in 1430 was sarcastic in its description of the crusade indulgences
which had so often been preached:

Do not allow yourselves ever again to be foolishly seduced in this way by their false indulgence: stay at home with your goods, wives, and children. Let the pope at Rome come
to visit us in person with all his cardinals and bishops and priests. Let them fight against
us and earn for themselves the absolution of sins, the grace and indulgence, which they
are preaching to you. God knows they need them. And with the help of Almighty God
we'll give them all the indulgences they ask for.[140]

It is important to remember too that the first in the sequence of crises leading to
the Hussite wars occurred in 1412 when the preaching in Prague of Pope John
XXIII's crusade indulgences against King Ladislas of Naples provoked a storm
of indignation amongst the reformers.[141]

Clearly the crusade, as manifested in the apparatus of cross and indulgence
which was confronted and fought by the Hussites in Bohemia, was not something that could directly influence their response. Does the same apply to crusading ideas and attitudes in a less specific sense? Alain Milhou certainly thought
so. For him, the Hussite radicals formed 'a good example of the "national re-
modelling" of the crusade ideal into a struggle against the powerful in the church
and in the world'.[142] There does seem to be an uncanny similarity to crusading
ideas and rhetoric in many Hussite pronouncements; it is almost as if they echo
what was being said and written by their own enemies. In manifestos, songs,
narrative accounts, letters, and speeches crusading themes appear and reappear:

[136] Ibid. 419.   [137] *UB* ii. 487–94, at 489.
[138] 'Peccatis Boemorum exigentibus': Lawrence is not excusing the wickedness of the crusaders but
explaining why God allowed their evildoing to take place.
[139] LoB, 'De gestis', 525.
[140] Prokes, 'Táborské manifesty', 20, and cf. Bartoš, *Hussite Revolution*, 55–6.
[141] Lambert, *Medieval Heresy*, 304–6. For the bulls, which are standard ones for the time, see J. Ersil
(ed.), *Acta summorum pontificum res gestas Bohemicas aevi praehussitici et hussitici illustrantia*, 2 vols.
(Prague: Academia h.e. in Aedibus Academiae Scientiarum Bohemoslovacae, 1980), i, nos. 604–7.
[142] Milhou, *Colón*, 295–6.

that the Hussites are fighting for God's cause, that they are Christ's warriors, and that those who die will be saved. Angels protected the Hussites just as they had the crusaders and before them the Israelites.[143] There was the same connection between Old Testament conflicts and contemporary events, so that a battle scene in the Bible could be illustrated with a battle clearly taking place during the Hussite wars, while King David could be depicted as a Hussite warrior.[144] When the Hussite centre fought the radicals, the conflict was described as 'ark against ark'.[145] At times God's intervention took dramatic form. During an encounter between Žižka and the Catholic Czechs at Sudoměř on 25 March 1420 a sudden darkening of the sky which worked to the Taborites' advantage was perceived as miraculous.[146] A similar occasion was the routing of the second crusade at Žatec in October 1421, as narrated by Lawrence of Březová:

But before King Sigismund had hastened back to his army from Hungary, where he was at the time, the weeping, cries, and wailing of the women, maids, and widows reached the ears of the lord Jesus, bringing down God's wrath and his just vindication upon the whole enemy army. For in an astonishing way, and without human intervention, Almighty God made these wicked people flee. On 2 October, through the working of divine providence, tents located throughout the army burst into flame. Something like a yellow column appeared above the tents, moving from one to another, and wherever the column stood, fire consumed the tents. Everybody took to flight, leaving their belongings behind and barely able to save their own skins. When the people of Žatec saw this, they chased them for some miles, killing several hundred, taking many others into captivity, and praising with immense joy the glory of a God who in this way scattered their enemies and the persecutors of his truth.[147]

And Hussite Bohemia, 'the golden and most Christian kingdom', provides one of the most striking examples in our period of a *translatio terre sancte*. Milhou was particularly struck by the way the Hussites furnished their embattled *patria* with a transcendental status: 'The Jerusalem of the crusades was far indeed from the preoccupations of the Taborites, so far that they never aspired to organize a crusade . . . Instead the kingdom of those fighting against Antichrist was converted into a new Palestine.'[148]

The problem is that such 'crusading' features in the conduct and projection of Hussite religious war do not need to be explained by reference to the crusade. What looks like borrowing could easily derive from a common scriptural patrimony: Hussite thinkers could pillage the Bible as easily as could Catholic apologists. Developmental parallels exist but they could be no more than that. For

---

[143] Bartoš, 'Táborské bratrstvo', 121; P. Rousset, *Les Origines et les caractères de la Première Croisade* (Neuchâtel: Baconnière, 1945), 93.
[144] Fudge, *Magnificent Ride*, 232–3.
[145] Ibid. 115 and n. 161. Heymann used the phrase as a chapter title in *John Žižka*, ch. 24.
[146] Heymann, *John Žižka*, 93–4.   [147] LoB, 'De gestis', 496. See also Heymann, 'Crusades', 602.
[148] Milhou, *Colón*, 296.

example, we have noted that Hussite religious war evolved from a background of penitential pilgrimage just as crusading did, but that seems to have been pure coincidence. And as we saw in the previous chapter, national messianism coupled with a tendency to sanctify the *patria* were broad-based features of this period. They applied as much to Bohemia as to anywhere else. The University of Prague was a centre of great prestige and Bohemia generally was fully within the mainstream of European intellectual development. The influence of crusading, in the *specific* sense of the crusades which were waged against the utraquists, therefore cannot be proven. All we can say is that, placed under extraordinary military pressure which took the form of a series of crusades, the Hussites, from ideologists and commanders to rank-and-file soldiers, waged a prolonged religious war on behalf of God's Law. They responded to their enemies with military techniques which were so innovative, and so effectively managed by men like Jan Žižka and Prokop the Bald, that their religious war achieved a success which eluded most crusaders, both in Bohemia and elsewhere. But the brilliance of that military response could not disguise the fact that the 'Hussite nation' which staged it contained fissures which in the end caused its downfall.

CHAPTER THREE

The Christian Commonwealth of Europe, 1436–1536

In the preceding chapter we witnessed developments occurring over a short period of time and within a comparatively small geographical area. These tight parameters of time and space are major factors behind the interest of Hussite Bohemia for the student of religious war. They enable us to establish personal links between theoreticians like Jakoubek of Stříbro and Peter Chelčický, and ascertain the direct impact of their ideas upon the actions of fighting men. No similar example occurred in the hundred years following the Jihlava Accord of 1436. Relevant ideas and activity exist in abundance, but working out patterns and trends presents formidable difficulties. To some extent the teasing out of these patterns and trends can wait until the analytical chapters which follow: but it is essential first to pinpoint the principal theatres of combat within which religious war operated. And in doing so it makes sense to divide the survey in two, because it would be foolish to deny the unique significance of the early Reformation.[1]

3.1 THE COMMONWEALTH CHALLENGED, 1436–1517

Arguably the greatest force shaping religious war in this period was the re-emergence of the Ottoman Turks as an expansionist power. The events narrated in Chapter 2 occurred during the hiatus in the Ottoman advance into Europe which resulted from Tamerlane's devastating victory at Ankara in 1402. The encroachments of Mehmed I and the early campaigns of Murad II were of great concern to Hungary and Venice, but they were in essence frontier struggles, and they seem to have exerted little impact on countries further to the west. By the late 1430s, however, the Ottomans had fully recovered from Tamerlane's assault and they once more began to pose a serious threat to eastern Europe, and a potential one to the Catholic heartlands. Thus the organization of a crusade, which played comparatively little role at the council of Constance (1414–18), became

---

[1] For general accounts of this period see Allmand (ed.), *New Cambridge Medieval History*, vii; T. A. Brady et al. (eds.), *Handbook of European History, 1400–1600*, 2 vols. (Grand Rapids, Mich.: William B. Eerdsmans, 1996).

much more important at the councils of Basle (1431–49) and Ferrara-Florence (1438–45). In 1444 the Turks crushed a Hungarian crusading army at Varna. Sultan Mehmed II, who came to the throne in 1451, focused his attention from the start on Byzantine Constantinople and captured the city in May 1453.[2] Thereafter the Turkish appetite and capacity for conquest could be missed by nobody. For more than a century the Turks would have an enormous bearing on European political, religious, and cultural life. Above all, they influenced thinking about religious war.

The most obvious effect which the Ottoman Turks had on the mental world of Catholics came about through the attempts made by virtually every pope of the period to initiate a general military response which would assume crusading form. The impact of preaching, financial measures, and rhetoric was profound: the crusade was effectively confirmed as the dominant expression of Catholic religious war. Without the Turks this probably would not have happened. Following the conversion of the Lithuanians in the 1380s the Baltic crusades were coming to an end and warfare against the Mamluks and the Moors of Granada had died down to the level of raids, destructive but intermittent in nature. The exception was Portugal, where chivalric values, including crusading against non-believers, enjoyed a remarkable resurgence early in the fifteenth century due very largely, it would appear, to the influence which Philippa of Lancaster exerted on her sons.[3] But the disasters in the south-eastern Balkans came close to giving crusading a renewed lease of life in broader stretches of Europe. This development was much assisted by two prominent groups of individuals who, for very different reasons, found much to admire in the crusade. James Hankins has written of 'the curious preoccupation of humanists with crusading in the second half of the fifteenth century', noting that the 'well over four hundred surviving literary compositions, short and long, written by at least fifty different humanists' during the reign of Sultan Mehmed II (1451–81) together form a corpus of material which is 'at least equal to all the surviving crusading literature of the High Middle Ages put together'. It is apparent both from Hankins's work and from that of others that the Italian humanists in particular made important contributions to crusading ideology.[4] At the same time that they

[2] These events are well reviewed by Setton, *PL* ii. 1–137; C. Imber, *The Ottoman Empire 1300–1481* (Istanbul: Isis, 1990), 55–159.

[3] Russell, *Prince Henry*, 13–58. See also C. Erdmann, 'Der Kreuzzugsgedanke in Portugal', *Hz* 141 (1930), 23–53.

[4] J. Hankins, 'Renaissance Crusaders: Humanist Crusade Literature in the Age of Mehmed II', *Dumbarton Oaks Papers*, 49 (1995), 111–207, at 112, 117. Also important is the work of Nancy Bisaha and Margaret Meserve, to both of whom I am indebted for bibliographic references. See M. Meserve, 'Medieval Sources for Renaissance Theories on the Origins of the Ottoman Turks', in Guthmüller and Kühlmann (eds.), *Europa und die Türken*, 409–36; N. Bisaha, ' "New Barbarian" or Worthy Adversary? Humanist Constructs of the Ottoman Turks in Fifteenth-Century Italy', in D. R. Blanks and M. Frassetto (eds.), *Western Views of Islam in Medieval and Early Modern Europe: Perception of Other* (Basingstoke: Macmillan, 1999), 185–205.

did this, the Franciscan Observants were undertaking preaching campaigns on behalf of papal crusading projects which aroused considerable (though short-lived) interest and enthusiasm. Men like Giovanni da Capistrano, Angelo Carletti da Chivasso, and Bartolomeo da Colle were worthy successors to the mendicant preachers of the thirteenth century.[5]

It is a commonplace that, with some notable exceptions, the efforts of popes, orators, and preachers to inspire and organize a general crusade against the Turks met with a lacklustre response.[6] The dialectic between peace 'at home' and war 'abroad', though still central to European diplomatic relations, in practice secured neither.[7] But it is all too easy to misinterpret this and, as a result, to undervalue the importance of the overall resurgence of crusading in this period. Clearly the papacy was no longer capable of mobilizing military activity on a large scale; the failure of Pius II's congress at Mantua demonstrated this very clearly, not least to the pope himself.[8] But this does not mean that the strenuous efforts of the papal and ecclesiastical apparatus to move hearts and minds did not have an effect in the localities. To give just one example, Claudius Sieber-Lehmann has demonstrated the impact on Switzerland in the form of preaching and collection for the crusade, the widespread appeal of indulgences, the provision of care for refugees from the east, the anxious dissemination of news of Ottoman advances and the celebration of Christian successes, the casting of bells whose daily clanging at noon formed a constant alert to the Turkish threat, and the celebration of the Feast of the Transfiguration as another reminder of the Ottoman menace.[9] The impact exerted was clearly powerful, but on many occasions different from what was planned. In fact the crusade in this period can best be viewed as a starter motor or conduit for other religious or social forces which were latent and whose dynamism it helped to release or, once released, to channel. Depending to a very large degree on local conditions, these forces could be primarily fissive or cohesive in their effect.[10]

We can observe the consequences clearly in two very different contexts, and at opposite ends of the Christian commonwealth, in Hungary and Castile. During

---

[5] M. Viora, 'Angelo Carletti da Chivasso e la crociata contro i Turchi del 1480–81', *Studi francescani*, NS 22 (1925), 319–40; M. Arosio, 'Bartolomeo da Colle (1421–1484): Predicatore dell'Osservanza francescana e dantista minore', in *Gli ordini mendicanti in Val d'Elsa* (Castelfiorentino: Società Storica della Valdelsa, 1999), 73–189, at 97–114. I am grateful to Prof. Arosio for sending me a copy of his study.

[6] Setton, *PL* ii–iii *passim*. Setton focused his attention on activity at the highest levels and rarely considered the actual preaching of the crusade and its consequences.

[7] D. Mertens, 'Europäische Friede und Türkenkrieg im Spätmittelalter', in H. Duchhardt (ed.), *Zwischenstaatliche Friedenswahrung in Mittelalter und Früher Neuzeit* (Cologne: Böhlau, 1991), 45–90.

[8] J. Helmrath, 'Pius II und die Türken', in Guthmüller and Kühlmann (eds.), *Europa und die Türken*, 79–137; Setton, *PL* ii. 200–70.

[9] C. Sieber-Lehmann, '"Teutsche Nation" und Eidgenossenschaft. Der Zusammenhang zwischen Türkenkrieg und Burgunderkriegen', *HZ* 253 (1991), 561–602, at 573–91.

[10] Cf. F.-R. Erkens, 'Einleitung', in F.-R. Erkens (ed.), *Europa und die osmanische Expansion im ausgehenden Mittelalter* (*Zeitschrift für historische Forschung*, suppl. vol. 20) (Berlin: Duncker & Humblot, 1997), 7–12, at 10.

the years immediately before 1453 Hungary was already taking its position as a leading 'bulwark of Christendom', and the extraordinary successes of János Hunyadi were celebrated in the west as an inspirational example which other Catholic states should follow.[11] But for all its attractiveness and resonance, the bulwark image was misleading. Monarchical authority within Hungary was challenged by a powerful nobility, in particular by a group of magnates who associated vigorous defensive measures with the undercutting of their own position.[12] The nobility failed to act as the bulwark's principal props: this was one reason why Hunyadi himself had to cultivate the bulwark image in order to secure outside help. In 1456 Mehmed II led a vast army to besiege Belgrade, the most important fortress in southern Hungary. It was the most vulnerable part of the *antemurale*; to vary the metaphor, the door or key giving access to Hungary and beyond it to all of Christendom.[13] King Ladislas V fled to Vienna, and without the national mobilization which the crisis demanded even Hunyadi proposed abandoning Belgrade. It was an army made up mainly of peasant crusaders, recruited and led by the Franciscan Giovanni da Capistrano, which drove the sultan back from the city in heavy fighting on 21–2 July. Giovanni's achievement in recruiting *crucesignati* and motivating them in the field was the first clear sign of the Observants' ability to breathe new life into the crusading message, especially when it was preached *in extremis*.[14]

As one historian put it, 'the crusades in eastern Europe, including Hungary, were above all peasant enterprises'.[15] This was possible due to the practice of levying peasants into royal armies, which went back to the late fourteenth century.[16] On the other hand, given prevailing attitudes towards social obligations, expecting peasants not only to serve in defence of the *patria* but to do so without any support or leadership from their lords could hardly be regarded as acceptable.[17] In a letter written on 3 July 1456, even Giovanni da Capistrano expressed his disgust at the inactivity of the king and lords, predicting that unless they

---

[11] J. Held, *Hunyadi: Legend and Reality* (Boulder, Colo.: East European Monographs, 1985), 80–134.

[12] P. Engel, *The Realm of St Stephen: A History of Medieval Hungary, 895–1526*, trans. T. Pálosfalvi, ed. A. Ayton (London: I. B. Tauris, 2001), chs. 17–20, esp. 338–44; Held, *Hunyadi*, 17–41; J. M. Bak, 'Politics, Society and Defense in Medieval and Early Modern Hungary', in J. M. Bak and B. K. Király (eds.), *From Hunyadi to Rákóczi: War and Society in Late Medieval and Early Modern Hungary* (New York: Brooklyn College Press, 1982), 1–22; J. M. Bak, 'The Price of War and Peace in Late Medieval Hungary', in B. P. McGuire (ed.), *War and Peace in the Middle Ages* (Copenhagen: Reitzels, 1987), 161–78.

[13] Giovanni da Tagliacozzo, 'Relatio de victoria Belgradensi', in *Annales Minorum*, 3rd edn. by J. M. Fonseca (Quaracchi: Tipografia Barbèra-Alfani e Venturi, 1931–), xii. 750–96, at 753, 777.

[14] J. Hofer, 'Der Sieger von Belgrad 1456', *Historisches Jahrbuch*, 51 (1931), 163–212; Held, *Hunyadi*, 155–69 (stressing Hunyadi's contribution); Setton, *PL* ii. 172–83.

[15] G. Barta, 'Der ungarische Bauernkrieg vom Jahre 1514', in Heckenast (ed.), *Aus der Geschichte*, 63–9, at 63.

[16] J. Held, 'Peasants in Arms, 1437–1438 & 1456', in Bak and Király (eds.), *From Hunyadi to Rákóczi*, 81–101.

[17] J. M. Bak, 'Delinquent Lords and Forsaken Serfs: Thoughts on War and Society during the Crisis of Feudalism', in S. B. Vardy (ed.), *Society in Change: Studies in Honour of Bela K. Király* (Boulder, Colo.: East European Monographs, 1983), 291–304.

came to fight Mehmed II at Belgrade, the sultan would before long be paying them a visit in their own homes: 'because the present time is not one for slumbering and wallowing in idleness, and the hour has struck to awake from sleep'.[18] It is not surprising that the preacher's followers felt just as strongly if not more so. When noble contingents began to arrive at Belgrade in the immediate aftermath of the great victory, they created an atmosphere of considerable friction. After an earlier success the crusaders had burned piles of booty seized from the Turks, 'so that they would not be carried off by the rich (*potentiores*), who had not been present';[19] the incident is revealing of what could be expected of the nobility. Some crusaders now boasted openly that the victory was owed solely to their charismatic leader and Jesus Christ, whose name they had used as a mantra-cum-battle cry throughout the fighting. The kingdom's barons, they proclaimed, had played no part in the success: 'The crusaders had it publicly proclaimed on the morrow of victory, that the triumph which God had bestowed on them on the previous day had not been due to the work or labour of any single baron of the kingdom of Hungary, but had come about solely through the virtue of the most holy name of Jesus Christ and of his most sacred Cross, and through the merits and hard work of our most blessed father, Brother Giovanni da Capistrano.' This was little more than the truth but it was still a highly provocative thing to say. Giovanni himself appeared with all speed on the scene, reproved the ringleaders and imposed silence on everybody.[20]

Contrary to their hopes of capitalizing on the victory by advancing southwards and regaining land lost earlier, Giovanni da Capistrano and János Hunyadi together decided that this 'popular disturbance' (*commotio in populo*) made it imperative to disband the peasant army forthwith. Their swift action lost the strategic initiative (to the anger of the legate Juan da Carvajal), but it brought the crusade to a peaceful conclusion. 'Then the crusaders received licence to depart, and a blessing, from the most blessed father, acting as their captain. They all returned home joyfully, astounded and marvelling at the things which God had brought about through the ministry and offices of the most blessed father. In this way the crusade came to a close.'[21] But it is clear that violence, and quite possibly rebellion, was narrowly averted. Giovanni da Tagliacozzo recorded how he had indiscreetly pressed his superior Fr. Paolo on the issue of 'why the barons of Hungary had not appeared at a time when [the realm] faced such a serious crisis'. Paolo's reply adroitly turned the troubling circumstances to the advantage of Giovanni da Capistrano: this was God's design, to make it impossible for the victory to be ascribed to anybody but Giovanni. 'So all the Hungarians agree that

---

[18] L. Thallóczy and H. Antal (eds.), *Codex diplomaticus partium regno Hungariae adnexarum II* (Budapest: Magyar Tudományos Akadémia, 1907), 465–7.

[19] Giovanni da Tagliacozzo, 'Relatio', 762. Older editions of the text omitted certain important passages which were reproduced in this edition.

[20] Ibid. 793.   [21] Ibid. 794.

our blessed father was the liberator of the entire kingdom.'[22] This ingenious answer, cited by Giovanni da Tagliacozzo as part of his programme of countering Giovanni da Capistrano's denigrators, was handy because 'the kingdom's liberator' was a foreign friar, an outsider with no political axe to grind and no dynastic interests to pursue. Awkward questions about political and social responsibilities could be shelved.

Such questions could not however be avoided forever; they were bound to be posed again once Ottoman pressure was renewed. The bulwark metaphor, so dominant in the discourse of crusading, encouraged them. For if, as Juan da Carvajal wrote to Sforza of Milan in April 1456, Hungary was Christendom's bulwark and Belgrade the key to Hungary's defence, it was hard to avoid asking the question what the Hungarians themselves, and a fortiori their political and social elite, were doing about it.[23] The problem was epitomized in 1 Maccabees 3: 17–22, which Giovanni da Capistrano quoted in 1456 when confronted with the weakness of his forces.[24] Verses 18–19 consoled the crusaders, as they had so many of their predecessors, with the reflection that 'in the sight of Heaven there is no difference between saving by many or by few. It is not on the size of the army that victory in battle depends, but strength comes from Heaven'. But verse 21 ('we fight for our lives and our laws') was a clear reference to the mobilization of a national community, and in particular the professional fighting cadres, the baronial *banderia*, who at Belgrade were conspicuously absent.

This emphasis on responsibility increased steadily as the princes of Europe made it clear that they were not prepared to respond with energy to the Ottoman threat or the papal appeals which it generated. Their failure became a recurrent theme of Pope Pius II in the painful years following the congress of Mantua.[25] There was rarely a Giovanni da Capistrano on hand and embattled regions and communities found that they had to man the pumps themselves. In the decades that followed 1456 there were several striking instances of the inhabitants of Christendom's threatened border lands in the south-east resorting to measures of self help against the Turks as freelance Turkish raiding parties (the *akinjis*) penetrated deep into lands subject to the Habsburgs. These measures were occasioned by the failure of the traditional social hierarchy to provide defence, and they all too readily spilled over into threats to social order. For a time these took only written form. Carl Göllner noted that pamphlets such as the *Bittschrift der Landschaft Krain* (1475) included the ineffectual defence against the Turks and the financial abuses associated with it among the mounting grievances of the 'Common Man'.[26] After 1456 the first clear link between anti-Turkish defence and rebellion seems to have occurred in Upper Styria in 1478, when the leaders of the local peasant league (*Bund*) formed against Turkish raiders denounced

---

[22] Ibid. 795.   [23] Thallóczy and Antal (eds.), *Codex diplomaticus*, 462–4.
[24] Giovanni da Tagliacozzo, 'Relatio', 783.   [25] Setton, *PL* ii. 231–70.
[26] Göllner, *Turcica*, iii. 55.

fifty-three noblemen who were allegedly acting as guides to the Turks (a significant accusation), and renounced the payment of taxes and tolls to Emperor and landlords.[27]

The message was clear: when a society was already bitterly divided along political and social lines, the Ottoman impact could broaden rather than narrow these dangerous fissures. In such circumstances the preaching of a crusade could become akin to lighting a fuse to a powder keg of pent-up fury, since the patriotic cause was preached as Christ's own and the functional failure of society's leaders was perceived as a betrayal of the Saviour himself. This was precisely what took place in Hungary in 1514 in the Dózsa rebellion.[28] The immediate background to the uprising provided almost a guarantee of trouble. Hungary's market towns (*oppida*) were teeming with unemployed herdsmen (*Heiducken*) thanks to a recent economic slump. In the autumn of 1512 the king, Wladislas II Jagiello, suffered heavy military losses to the Ottoman pasha of Bosnia and in June 1513 he begged Rome for money, in the twin forms of a papal grant and the preaching of crusade indulgences to raise cash. But for various reasons the new pope, Leo X, preferred to try raising an actual crusading army, a task which he entrusted to the archbishop of Esztergom, Tamás Bakócz. This highly ambitious prelate had recently been defeated by Leo in the competition for the papacy, and he viewed a successful crusade as the means of restoring his reputation. He therefore set about his task with great energy. Initial preaching by the secular clergy proved ineffective, so in April 1514 Bakócz entrusted the preaching to the Franciscan Observants, who carried out the job with much greater zeal. An army about 15,000 strong assembled near Pest and a minor nobleman called György Dózsa Székely was appointed as its commander. Large concentrations of crusaders had formed elsewhere in Hungary, totalling about 50,000 men.

Dózsa marched southwards from the Pest encampment on 10 May and just five days later Archbishop Bakócz called off the preaching of his crusade on the grounds that noble property was being attacked and nobles killed at the behest of the preachers. On 22 May a full-scale military encounter occurred at Várad, in which a force of nobles was routed by the crusaders. We can reconstruct with reasonable clarity what had happened to divert the crusade from its intention to fight the Turks. As in 1456, the nobility failed to take the field themselves, or to provide the *crucesignati* with leadership or assistance of any kind. What made

---

[27] Jakob Unrest, *Österreichische Chronik*, ed. K. Grossmann, Monumenta Germaniae Historica, Scriptores rerum germanicarum, NS 11 (Weimar: Hermann Böhlaus Nachfolger, 1957), 90–101. See also Bak, 'Delinquent Lords', 298–9.

[28] For the next four paragraphs, see my 'Crusading as Social Revolt: The Hungarian Peasant Uprising of 1514', *JEH* 49 (1998), 1–28, repr. in *CWMRE*, study XVII; P. Gunst, 'Der ungarische Bauernaufstand von 1514', in Blickle (ed.), *Revolte und Revolution*, 62–83; J. Szűcs, 'Die Ideologie des Bauernkrieges', in his *Nation und Geschichte. Studien*, trans. J. Kerekes et al. (Gyoma: Corvina Kiadó, 1981), 329–78; P. Freedman, 'The Hungarian Peasant Revolt of 1514', in V. Rajsp (ed.), *Grafenauerjev Zbornik* (Ljubljana: Znanstvenoraziskovalni Center SAZU, 1996), 433–46.

this more infuriating was the fact that since the death of King Matthias I Corvinus in 1490 the magnates had taken over the collection of taxes levied for the maintenance of the kingdom's perimeter fortresses; by siphoning off these proceeds to their private uses they had contributed to the military crisis in the south which made the crusade necessary. In 1514, moreover, their response to the crusade was even more negative than in 1456. They attempted to impede preaching because it would rob them of their labour force during the summer months. A violent response to this on the part of the crusaders was justified and maybe encouraged by the same Franciscan Observants who played the key role in preaching the expedition. Quite possibly the Observants, who accompanied the peasant hosts into the field, were even more audacious and preached that the cause of Christ was one of liberation from seigneurial oppression as well as the defence of home and hearth from the infidel.[29]

Two aspects of the situation in 1514 are particularly striking. One is that the uprising, far from being viewed as a deflection from or even a necessary but discrete preliminary to anti-Ottoman activities, was fitted into a broad ideological context which encompassed the latter. In the so-called Cegléd proclamation, written by Dózsa himself between 28 May and 6 June, the nobles were lambasted as *infideles*.[30] In the circumstances, such terminology cannot have been coincidental. The line of thinking visible in embryonic form in 1456, and taking clearer shape in Inner Austria in 1478, had now crystallized: the nobles were demonized, associated with the Turkish foe. The other striking feature is the remarkably buoyant *esprit de corps* that Dózsa's *cruciferi* enjoyed, 'a form of community spirit' as one scholar put it,[31] which derived specifically from their status as crusaders. This they continued to celebrate even after they had been violently denounced by church and state.[32] The Dózsa uprising is therefore a unique example of a 'crusade-revolt', in which not just the form but the psychology of crusade animated a major attempt to overthrow a social order which had become so corrupted that it was perceived to have merged with the enemy and to be standing in the way of God's purpose.

By the autumn of 1514 Dózsa's uprising had been suppressed and its leader executed in a fashion so peculiarly savage that it can be read as proof of the alarm experienced by the authorities at what had taken place.[33] So far as we can tell, Dózsa's social programme, which he created amidst the turmoil of events, was to replicate across Hungary the relatively egalitarian conditions with which he was familiar from his native Székely community in eastern Transylvania.[34] As in the

---

[29] P. Freedman, *Images of the Medieval Peasant* (Stanford, Calif.: Stanford University Press, 1999), 279–80.

[30] A. Fekete Nagy et al. (eds.), *Monumenta rusticorum in Hungaria rebellium anno MDXIV* (Budapest: Akadémiai Kiadó, 1979), no. 79.

[31] Barta, 'Der ungarische Bauernkrieg', 65, and cf. 67.

[32] Housley, 'Crusading as Social Revolt', 12–24.

[33] Birnbaum, 'A Mock Calvary in 1514?', *passim*.   [34] Szűcs, 'Die Ideologie', 362–9.

early days of Tabor, the 1514 uprising therefore gives us a link between religious belief and the use of violence to bring about far-reaching economic and social change. But there the similarity ends. At Tabor the religious core was revolutionary: the proclamation of the *lex Dei* as the sole authority which should steer Christian behaviour, a return to the stark liturgical practices of the apostolic church, above all an explicit chiliasm. Amongst Dózsa's crusaders, by contrast, religious belief was highly orthodox. Despite the assertions of some historians, for whom no peasant uprising is complete without its chiliastic programme,[35] chiliasm is absent from the sources for their thinking. Hussite influence is possible but at best unproven. Papal, and for that matter royal, authority was accepted and salvation through works, especially indulgences, was embraced. It is true that in the excitement of the moment the *cruciferi*, or more likely their Franciscan mentors, gave traditional Catholic doctrine some extraordinary twists, including the proclamation that indulgences, like secular property, could be inherited.[36] But for the most part this was a distinctly conservative revolt in religious terms. The high clergy were attacked as landowners rather than as churchmen and no particular hostility was displayed towards monastic houses, which had been the case with the Taborites.[37]

In this respect the uprising which is most comparable to the Dózsa rebellion is the Pilgrimage of Grace in 1536. At first sight such a comparison seems far-fetched. The Dózsa rebellion was after all a civil conflict which gave rise to astonishing brutality on both sides, while the pilgrimage was more of a demonstration than a war. The Catholic protesters of 1536 issued nothing akin to the bloodthirsty Cegléd manifesto of 1514.[38] And the uprising of 1514 was a social revolt, while that of 1536 was occasioned predominantly by royal policy. But in both cases there was a strong conviction that the established order was seriously out of kilter. In Hungary in 1514 this conviction focused on the failure of the nobility to provide the military leadership which was its primary function and the justification for its status; in England in 1536 the focus was on the unprecedented royal assault on the church, with its dire implications for 'the society of orders'. As Michael Bush has put it, 'The policies and actions of the government were found intolerable because of the contempt they expressed for the basic components of this social theory: the royal family, the nobility, the clergy and the commonalty.'[39] Recently, Bush reiterated the point that the pilgrimage, like other risings of the commons in England, was in essence a defence of a society arranged into distinct orders: 'The essential purpose of a rising of

---

[35] Notably Szűcs, ibid. 359.   [36] Fekete Nagy et al. (eds.), *Monumenta rusticorum*, no. 49.

[37] 'Very Pretty Chronicle', 6; Housley, 'Crusading as Social Revolt', 22.

[38] Though the priest at Croft did use precisely the same threat against people who declined to go on the pilgrimage that Dózsa deployed in the Cegléd manifesto: Fekete Nagy et al. (eds.), *Monumenta rusticorum*, no. 49; C. S. L. Davies, 'The Pilgrimage of Grace Reconsidered', *Past and Present*, 41 (1968), 54–75, at 69.

[39] M. Bush, *The Pilgrimage of Grace: A Study of the Rebel Armies of October 1536* (Manchester: Manchester University Press, 1996), 103.

the commons was to denote that the body politic was out of joint.'[40] In both 1514 and 1536, too, traditional religion furnished channels along which resentment and opposition could be directed, those of crusade and pilgrimage. Hence, as C. S. L. Davies pointed out, the importance of the pilgrims' oath and marching song: they provided something akin to the cohesion which Dózsa's *cruciferi* acquired from the cross which they sported on their clothing and followed on their banners.[41]

The problem was of course that pilgrimage was an inherently peaceful activity. This was demonstrated clearly by the *débâcle* of 1536, but Aske's failure had been interestingly anticipated sixty years previously in a very different context. This was the movement sparked off by the arrest of Hans Böhm, the enigmatic Drummer of Niklashausen. In the spring of 1476 Böhm became famous overnight through his vision of the Virgin at Niklashausen, a village near Würzburg in the Tauber valley. The influx of many thousands of mainly lower-class pilgrims to worship at the new shrine and hear Böhm speak created a dangerous situation when Böhm began preaching resistance to oppressive lordship. In early July insurrection appeared imminent and the bishop of Würzburg, who was the most important regional lord, had Böhm arrested by a troop of horsemen. Several thousand of his devotees marched on the bishop's castle at Würzburg to effect his release. They had few weapons, a point which deeply impressed one commentator, the historian Johannes Trithemius: 'they placed their entire hope and confidence not in arms and machines of war, of which they possessed scarcely any, but in the merits of sanctity of their beloved Hans.'[42] Instead they carried hundreds of giant candles from the shrine church: this was a demonstration rather than an army. Consequently, while the force appeared dangerous enough, when it tried to storm the walls of Würzburg a single discharge of artillery proved sufficient to rout it. For all the fears of the authorities, the movement in favour of Böhm died away without further incident. Tellingly, pilgrimages to the shrine at Niklashausen continued until the church was dismantled early in 1477.[43]

It is the fears of the royal authorities which point up the contrast between the situation in England in 1536 and that in Hungary in 1514. One of the most striking pieces of evidence left by the Pilgrimage of Grace is the series of questions which Thomas Cromwell himself wrote down to be posed of Thomas, Lord

---

[40] M. Bush, 'The Risings of the Commons in England, 1381–1549', in J. Denton (ed.), *Orders and Hierarchies in Late Medieval and Renaissance Europe* (Manchester: Manchester University Press, 1999), 109–25.

[41] C. S. L. Davies, 'Popular Religion and the Pilgrimage of Grace', in A. Fletcher and J. Stevenson (eds.), *Order and Disorder in Early Modern England* (Cambridge: Cambridge University Press, 1985), 58–91, at 75–8.

[42] K. Arnold, *Niklashausen 1476: Quellen und Untersuchungen zur sozialreligiösen Bewegung des Hans Behem und zur Agrarstruktur eines spätmittelalterlichen Dorfes* (Baden-Baden: Verlag Valentin Koerner, 1980), 271.

[43] Ibid., *passim*; Cohn, *Pursuit*, 226–33.

Darcy, castellan at Pontefract, when the latter was interrogated after the suppression of the pilgrimage on suspicion of treachery because he had effectively surrendered the fortress. Cromwell's suspicions had been aroused by the fact that after the castle's hand-over to the rebels on 20 October Darcy, noting that the Durham contingent of pilgrims wore badges showing the Five Wounds of Christ, had allegedly 'remembered' that there was a cache of Five Wounds badges left over from his crusade to Seville in 1511. Cromwell's questions make it clear that he was above all concerned that the pilgrimage could have been transmuted into a crusade, or crusade-revolt, by the handing out of these badges traditionally associated with the crusade. Out of fifteen questions which were to be posed to Darcy concerning the provenance and use of the badges, three specifically addressed this issue:

74. Item, was it not to thentent ye wold haue made the souldiours to beleve that they shuld feight in the defence of the faith of Chist, and to thentent they shuld not feare to die in that cause? 82. Item, d(i)d not you make [the badges, rather than finding them] for the setting for(th) (of) th(e) saide insurrection of Yorkeshire, for the animating of the sould(io)urs (that they might thin)kin that they had a iuste cause to fight in pretend(in)g their rebellion to be for the defence of the (faith) of Christ? 87. Item, whether it was not declared to them wiche ware those badges that they were Christes souldiours, and that when they loked vppon their badges of v woundes of Christ, they shuld think that their cause was for the defence of Christes faith and his churche?[44]

This was precisely what Dózsa's *cruciferi* had believed twenty-two years previously. Whether or not Cromwell had heard of events in far-off Hungary, he was certainly aware of recent plotting by the Aragonese party to synchronize a domestic revolt with a Habsburg invasion of England. A few years later such an invasion would be promoted explicitly as a crusade.[45]

In the previous chapter we saw that the movement from pilgrimage to the armed defence of the *lex Dei* was a fundamental one ideologically for the radical Hussites because it signalled a switch from separatist flight to engagement.[46] But as Cromwell anticipated in 1536, the same movement could be a shift in gear rather than a radical change of direction. When they occupied Pontefract Castle, Aske's followers were not fleeing into the hills in anticipation of the Last Days, but marching south to make their grievances known. It has been suggested that the various hosts were internally well disciplined because those constituting them were familiar with militia mustering techniques.[47] It would not take much

---

[44] M. Bateson (ed.), 'Aske's Examination', *EHR* 5 (1890), 550–73, at 555.
[45] C. Tyerman, *England and the Crusades 1095–1588* (Chicago: University of Chicago Press, 1988), 343–4, 362–6.
[46] Above, Ch. 2, at nn. 15–16.
[47] Bush, *Pilgrimage of Grace*, 422: 'it would seem that the pilgrim hosts were genuine armies, not civilian rabbles.'

to alter their mood: the symbols of crusade might have been enough in themselves without any need to bring to bear the full apparatus of preaching which the Hungarians had experienced in 1514. It was a question of mood rather than one of basic thinking, and mood changes could be swift, especially if powerful symbols associated with the defence of the faith were brought to bear. Almost certainly this was in Darcy's mind when he distributed the Five Wounds badges: he had been involved in Habsburg crusade plotting two years previously and while Aske himself eschewed violence, other leaders of the pilgrimage, such as Lords Lumley and Latimer and Sir Robert Constable, were more bellicose in their approach.[48] C. S. L. Davies suggested that in 1536 'prolonged religious fighting could (and probably would) have produced a vigorous, crusading catholicism'.[49] Maybe even Hans Böhm's would-be rescuers in 1476 would have undergone a similar transformation, given the training and leadership which there was no time to provide.

With the Pilgrimage of Grace we have strayed into the early Reformation, but it is important to consolidate the point made so dramatically by the Dózsa rebellion and presaged by earlier events in east-central Europe: that traditional, indeed conservative, patterns of religious thinking and behaviour could function as stimuli and conduits for insurrection as readily as innovative ones had a century earlier in Bohemia. What brought the two together in all these cases was a deep-rooted sense of grievance and disappointment on the part of the ruled. Within a kingdom like Hungary, suffering from a deep-rooted dislocation of monarchical authority and exposed to ferocious external pressure, the revival of the crusade introduced disruptive forces on a massive scale. Contemporaries knew this: Bakócz and probably Leo X were aware that they were playing with fire in 1514.[50] Turning to Castile, we see the opposite scenario. Here too there was unrest and insurgency,[51] but the dominant pattern which emerged by c.1500 was one of rulers and ruled united by a view of their common destiny within the overall Catholic community. In the local context this was naturally a cohesive movement: in brief, it stood for national unity in the service of a royal messianism. But precisely in these terms it also represented a challenge to the broader Catholic commonwealth, because such exceptionalism implied superiority. It was an attitude which would be encapsulated in Philip II's reputed remark that 'religion is too serious a matter to be left to the pope'.[52] To that extent it was divisive, albeit much less obviously divisive than insurrectionary movements.

Royal, and increasingly national messianism were commonplace in Europe in the later fifteenth and early sixteenth centuries. As we saw in Chapter 1, even

---

[48] Tyerman, *England and the Crusades*, 360, 363.
[49] Davies, 'Pilgrimage of Grace', 74. Cf. Bush, *Pilgrimage of Grace*, 119.
[50] See Barta, 'Der ungarische Bauernkrieg', 64, for the reception of the crusade proposal in Hungary.
[51] Usefully emphasized by T. F. Ruiz, *Spanish Society, 1400–1600* (Harlow: Longman, 2001), 163–207.
[52] J. H. Elliott, *Imperial Spain 1469–1716* (London: Edward Arnold, 1963), 223.

Hungary, with all its internal divisions, gave rise to a national self-image which incorporated the theme of the embattled bulwark which its rulers promoted so assiduously in their relations with the papacy.[53] But it would be hard to sustain the claim that any other region matched the remarkable vigour with which national feeling in Castile came to be associated with the defence and expansion of the faith. The seedbed for this was the final phase of the *Reconquista*, in which the revivified crusade played a major role through the preaching of the 'bula de la cruzada'.[54] It would be wrong to place too much emphasis on 1453, because even before that date there was a revival of interest in crusading in Castile. This was partly because of outbursts of crusading enthusiasm at the frontier, and partly because Castile responded to Portugal's military expansion into Morocco and colonization of the Atlantic Islands by advancing its own territorial claims and the crusading agenda which went with them. But the main reason was periodic warfare between the Castilian crown and Granada, such as the conflict which punctuated the 1430s, producing a victory of reasonable importance at La Higueruela in 1431.[55]

The result was that although the *Reconquista* had made very few territorial gains in nearly a century, Castile's ambassador at the council of Basle in 1434, Alonso of Cartagena, the learned and highly able *converso* bishop of Burgos, was able to make use of it when he asserted his king's precedence over Henry VI of England. 'When kings enjoy equal status', Alonso argued, 'primacy has to be accorded to the one who is actually engaged in God's war (*en acto de guerra de Dios*) . . . My lord the king of Castile is continuously making war against the pagans and the unbelievers, and as a consequence he is fully occupied in divine war (*guerra divinal*) by decree of the supreme emperor who is God.'[56] Even after the fall of Constantinople and the increasing emphasis which was placed on the Ottoman threat, the Iberian monarchies insisted on equivalence. They were largely successful, albeit sometimes at the price of agreeing that a fixed proportion of the financial proceeds of crusade preaching should be set aside for the war against the Turks. Successive waves of preaching and negotiations for a major crusade against the Ottomans had the effect of stimulating demands for the same bulls to be granted, *mutatis mutandis*, for Iberia. Castile's petitions for crusade bulls in relation to Granada were regularly accompanied by demands by the Portuguese for bulls in favour of its African conquests.[57]

---

[53] See above, Ch. 1, at nn. 125–6.
[54] Housley, *Later Crusades*, 291–304; J. Goñi Gaztambide, *Historia de la Bula de la cruzada en España* (Vitoria: Editorial del Seminario, 1958), *passim*.
[55] Goñi Gaztambide, *Historia*, 353–4, 647–50; Russell, *Prince Henry*, 164–5; 221–3; L. Suárez Fernández, *Juan II y la frontera de Granada* (Valladolid: Universidad de Valladolid, Consejo Superior de Investigaciones Científicas, 1954).
[56] Milhou, *Colón*, 355 n. 804. See also Sánchez Montes, *Franceses, Protestantes, Turcos*, 38–42.
[57] E. Benito Ruano, 'Granada o Constantinopla', *Hispania*, 60 (1960), 267–314; A. Echevarria, *The Fortress of Faith: The Attitude towards Muslims in Fifteenth-Century Spain* (Leiden: Brill, 1999), 19–20 and ch. 1 *passim*.

Goñi Gaztambide and de Witte long ago established beyond a doubt the solidity of this ideological and institutional link between events in the western Mediterranean and Atlantic archipelagos, and those taking place in the east.[58] There was a startling contrast between the failure experienced by the papacy in its attempts to promote a crusade against the Ottomans, and the extraordinary success of Castile's momentous war with Granada in 1482–92. The contrast is illuminating in terms of the circumstances which could still make crusading an effective mechanism even at the close of the fifteenth century. What is important here, however, is the way in which the victories of 1482–92, gained through a revival of the crusade, stimulated an already deep-set pattern of eschatological thinking in Castile, tying it firmly to a royal messianism which was now free to pursue objectives outside the peninsula. Castilian patriotic feeling, engendered within the ideological framework of *Reconquista*, increasingly found its keenest expression in the conviction that the monarchy's wars outside Iberia also were being fought on behalf of the faith.

Much of this was due to the importation of Joachimist patterns of eschatological thinking, which found some of their most receptive audiences in Iberia. It is impossible now to pinpoint with precision the respective roles of the crusade and Joachimism. Milhou speculated that the Catholic Monarchs, Fernando of Aragon and Isabella of Castile, encouraged Joachimist programmes because these enabled them to 'tap into' crusading resources; but it is equally possible that a susceptibility to crusading themes caused leading figures to embrace Joachimism.[59] It is clear that the two sets of ideas largely complemented and reinforced each other, because Joachimism in Iberia was so popular both with elite groups and in society at large. Recent research, especially that of Martin Aurell, has established the importance of the Catalan-Aragonese federation as the main route of entry into Iberia of Joachimism, occurring around 1300.[60] Spiritual Franciscans fleeing from papal persecution found a warm welcome at the royal court, where prophecy enjoyed an exceptional vogue. The Spirituals identified themselves as the Joachimist *viri spirituales* and thus staked a claim to the programme's third *status*, effectively excluding the secular clergy. But they

[58] Goñi Gaztambide, *Historia*, chs. 12–14; C.-M. de Witte, 'Les Bulles pontificales et l'expansion portugaise au XVe siècle', *RHE* 48 (1953), 683–718, 49 (1954), 438–61, 51 (1956), 413–53, 809–36, 53 (1958), 5–46, 443–71.

[59] A. Milhou, 'La Chauve-souris, le Nouveau David et le roi caché (trois images de l'empereur des derniers temps dans le monde ibérique: XIIIe–XVIIe s.)', *Mélanges de la Casa de Velásquez*, 18 (1982), 61–78, at 71.

[60] M. Aurell, 'Eschatologie, spiritualité et politique dans la confédération catalano-aragonaise (1282–1412)', in *Fin du monde et signes des temps: Visionnaires et prophètes en France méridionale (fin XIIIe–début XVe siècle)*, Cahiers de Fanjeaux 27 (Toulouse: Privat, 1992), 191–235; M. Aurell, 'Prophétie et messianisme politique: La Péninsule ibérique au miroir du *Liber Ostensor* de Jean de Roquetaillade', in A. Vauchez (ed.), *Les Textes prophétiques et la prophétie en Occident (XIIe–XVIe siècle)*, Mélanges de l'École Française de Rome 102 (Rome: École Française de Rome, 1990), 317–61. See also Milhou, *Colón*, 372–3; Milhou, 'La Chauve-souris', *passim*.

also pinpointed the key role to be played by messianic individuals. Two of these, the 'New David' and the *Encubierto* ('the concealed one'), were to exert a fascination for centuries to come. They would reform the church, recapture Jerusalem, where they would rebuild the Holy House (*Casa santa*),[61] convert the infidels and Jews, and inaugurate a universal reign of millennial justice.

In Iberian Joachimism the *Encubierto* was often (though not invariably) a popular leader, usually emerging during a rebellion, such as the *Germanías* revolt of 1522 when Játiva was taken over by an anonymous *Encubierto* who instituted an egalitarian social regime.[62] One particularly violent Joachimist text was Johan Alamany's *La venguda de Antichrist*, which dated from the first half of the fifteenth century but achieved a remarkable revival when it was republished at Valencia in November 1520 during the revolt of the *Germanías*. *La venguda de Antichrist* envisaged action on all fronts: the *Encubierto* would place himself at the head of an army of the poor which would annihilate the exploitative rich as well as the Jews and Moors in Spain, then proceed east to recover Jerusalem, defeat Antichrist, and inaugurate the new millennium. For Alamany, unusually, the New David was to be the Joachimist *pastor angelicus*.[63] The role of New David was much more suited to a monarch, stripped of course of any socially redistributive programme and usually expressed in terms of universal monarchy. The entire cluster of associations, including the curious 'bat' (*vespertilio*) which may have originated at Valencia, found most vigorous expression in relation to Fernando of Aragon: eleven prophecies centred around the king between 1473 and 1516.[64]

During the Trastámara period these ideas and roles crossed over into Castile, although they only really burgeoned there after 1482.[65] Since it was in the New World that Castile made its deepest mark in this period, it is not surprising that it is in relation to the American discoveries that the entire complex of ideas made up of royal and national messianism has been most fully researched and its consequences evoked. In his masterly study of Columbus' mentality Alain Milhou exposed the lineaments of scriptural exegesis and Joachimist prognosis which led the discoverer to access and share the expectations of many Castilians of his time. As Milhou showed, the interest of Columbus' ideas resides precisely in their lack of originality: he was an inspired synthesizer and his writings display attitudes and hopes which were deeply rooted in Iberia and still evolving: ideologically Columbus was situated 'at the mid point in a long trajectory'.[66] The dis-

[61] For the *Casa santa*, see A. MacKay, 'Religion, Culture, and Ideology on the Late Medieval Castilian–Granadan Frontier', in R. Bartlett and A. MacKay (eds.), *Medieval Frontier Societies* (Oxford: Oxford University Press, 1989), 217–43, at 242.

[62] Nalle, 'The Millennial Moment', *passim*; R. García Cárcel, *Las Germanías de Valencia* (Barcelona: Ediciones Península, 1975), 132–9.

[63] Milhou, *Colón*, 302–11; Milhou, 'La Chauve-souris', 69–70.

[64] Milhou, *Colón*, 381, 391–4; A. I. Carrasco Manchado, 'Propaganda política en los panegíricos poéticos de los reyes católicos: una aproximación', *Anuario de estudios medievales*, 25 (1995), 517–43.

[65] Milhou, *Colón*, 349–50, 387.   [66] Ibid. 426.

coverer's obsession with the recovery of the city of Jerusalem can only be under-stood within the context of the central place which it held within the Iberian Joachimist tradition. Here it had been placed by Arnau de Vilanova in a resonant phrase in his prophecy *Vae mundo in centum annis* (*c.*1300): 'and there will be a desert in [that] land until the New David arrives to repair the tower of Zion.'[67] But Arnau's prophecy only enjoyed the success it did because his audience was ready for it. This was partly because of the 'Spanish complex', the sense of in-jured pride that due to the circumstances of the *Reconquista* Spain had been under-represented in the Palestine crusades.[68] The migration of Joachimist ideas into the Americas was traced by John Phelan in his account of the first phase of Spanish conquest and settlement in the Indies. He demonstrated their profound impact on the activities of the early Franciscan missionaries. When they began their preaching they shared a strong conviction that theirs was the last major work of conversion to be undertaken before the Last Days.[69] More re-cently, Anthony Pagden has pointed out that eschatological strains of thinking had their place even amongst the *conquistadores*.[70] There now remains no sound case for denying that westwards exploration, conquest, and conversion were all driven, amongst other things, by eschatological hopes.

But it is in the activities of the Spanish monarchy in the Old World that royal messianism left its richest traces. It becomes apparent that from the time of the Catholic Monarchs onwards Spanish rulers were pulled eastwards not just by power politics, territorial ambitions, and dynastic claims, but also by messianic hopes. In particular, there could be no escape from Jerusalem: for all the attempts which had been made to relocate the holy city metaphorically, the actual town in Judaea continued to exert a magnetic attraction due to its sheer eschatological significance. 'The conquest of Jerusalem was an idea cherished by the Spaniards, in fact it became a constant obsession.'[71] Sánchez Montes may have exaggerated somewhat, but there is much evidence for the existence around 1500 of beliefs akin to that expressed after the fall of Setenil in 1484: 'They will wipe out the Moorish faith (*la morisma*) from top to bottom, and gain the Holy House (*la Casa santa*) just as it was foretold, placing on the Holy Sepulchre their royal standard of the Crusade (*surreal pendón cruzado*).'[72] Of the eleven Fernandine prophecies

---

[67] Milhou, 'La Chauve-souris', 68.

[68] Milhou, *Colón*, 356; A. Meyuhas Ginio, 'Rêves de croisade contre les Sarrasins dans la Castile du XVe siècle (Alonso de Espina, *Fortalitium fidei*)', *Revue de l'histoire des religions*, 212 (1995), 145–74, esp. 155.

[69] Phelan, *Millennial Kingdom*, 23.

[70] A. Pagden, 'Identity Formation in Spanish America', in N. Canny and A. Pagden (eds.), *Colonial Identity in the Atlantic World, 1500–1800* (Princeton: Princeton University Press, 1987), 51–93, at 52; A. Pagden, *Lords of All the World: Ideologies of Empire in Spain, Britain and France c.1500–c.1800* (New Haven: Yale University Press, 1995), 74.

[71] Sánchez Montes, *Franceses, Protestantes, Turcos*, 108.

[72] P. M. Cátedra, *La historiografía en verso en la época de los reyes católicos: Juan Barba y su Consolatoria de Castilla* (Salamanca: University of Salamanca, 1989), 76. Cf. Milhou, *Colón*, 170.

referred to above, all but one incorporated the conquest of Jerusalem.[73] Prophecy after prophecy caused Fernando to take eschatology into account in the formulation of state policy. During his expansion into North Africa prophetic undercurrents were especially resonant. According to Sandoval, the king refused to contemplate his imminent demise in 1516 because he had been assured by the *beata* of Barco de Ávila that he would not die until he had recovered Jerusalem.[74]

The Emperor Charles V was of course heir to these Iberian prophecies: 'This is our Great Caesar | He will conquer all | In person he will travel | As far as Calvary's hall.'[75] But Charles's election to the Empire in 1519 brought with it other ideological baggage with quite different roots which injected further expectancy. In her classic study of Joachimism Marjorie Reeves stressed that Charles's baptismal name, his power, and the variety of his dynastic origins made him seem ideally equipped to occupy the combined role of Second Charlemagne and Last Emperor. At critical points in his career, among them the election itself, the battle of Pavia in 1525, the sack of Rome in 1527, and the Tunis expedition of 1535, the convergence of action and prognostication generated enormous excitement.[76] John Headley too has written of 'possibly the most unique public intoxication ever experienced in the Western development'. It influenced amongst others the imperial chancellor Gattinara, who was well aware of Joachimist prophetic programmes and evinced a full-blown imperial messianism which Headley aptly compared with that of Dante two centuries previously.[77] But it was another of Charles's leading advisers, his secretary Alfonso de Valdés, who gave voice to the most explicit and remarkable messianic outburst in the wake of the great victory at Pavia:

It seems that God, by a miracle, has granted the Emperor this victory so that he may not only defend Christendom and resist the power of the Turk . . . but that . . . he may also seek out the Turks and Moors on their own lands and, exalting our holy Catholic faith as his ancestors did, recover the empire of Constantinople and the holy mansion of Jerusalem which for our sins they hold in their possession. Thus it may come about, as is prophesied by many, that under the rule of this most Christian prince, the whole world may receive our holy Catholic faith and the words of our Redeemer may be fulfilled: 'let there be one sheepfold and one shepherd'.[78]

---

[73] Milhou, *Colón*, 391–4.

[74] Sánchez Montes, *Franceses, Protestantes, Turcos*, 99; MacKay, 'Religion, Culture, and Ideology', 242–3.

[75] Göllner, *Turcica*, iii. 99.   [76] Reeves, *Influence of Prophecy*, 359–74.

[77] J. M. Headley, 'Rhetoric and Reality: Messianic, Humanist, and Civilian Themes in the Imperial Ethos of Gattinara', in Reeves (ed.), *Prophetic Rome*, 241–69, esp. 252 (quote), 267.

[78] Sánchez Montes, *Franceses, Protestantes, Turcos*, 105 and cf. the comment by Charles V quoted on 108–9. I have used the translation by A. Terry, 'War and Literature in Sixteenth-Century Spain', in J. R. Mulryne and M. Shewring (eds.), *War, Literature and the Arts in Sixteenth-Century Europe* (Basingstoke: Macmillan, 1989), 101–18, at 101. For post-Pavia euphoria see also A. Redondo, 'Mesianismo y re-

Fernando of Aragon and Charles V fought some of their bitterest wars in Italy. At first sight the peninsula looks like an exceptionally unlikely arena in which to locate messianic expectations and religious warfare. For some contemporaries, and for many historians since, the links established between the Italian wars and expectations, prophetic or otherwise, of a great crusade against the Turks, are classic signs of the invention of propaganda as a device in the hands of ambitious and demanding statesmen. Machiavelli was in no doubt that Fernando 'made use of religion' as 'a cloak' not just when he attacked Muslims in Granada and North Africa, but also in his Italian and French wars.[79] By this reading, when he proclaimed his invasion of Italy in 1494 to be the first step in a crusading enterprise, Charles VIII of France was setting an example which virtually every combatant in the following decades copied and refined with cynical ingenuity.[80] Recently, however, historians have been made more aware of the huge corpus of prophecies and prophetic interpretations of contemporary happenings that survives from this period; and they have become more inclined to situate both an awareness of the Ottoman menace and a sense of eschatological urgency within contemporaries' perspective on the Italian conflicts.[81] This makes eminent sense, for it is increasingly apparent that the excitement so visible in sources from Iberia and imperial circles was pan-European in nature, and that the decades around 1500 were amongst the most eschatologically charged in all Christian history. The Joachimist background to the Italian ambitions of Charles VIII makes it hard to believe that the French king and his immediate entourage were simply indulging in a manipulative exercise in propaganda when they depicted their invasion as a revival of the ancient Guelf cause.[82] And Italy itself was a hotbed of messianic expectations.[83] These expectations found a place in various political contexts. Giles of Viterbo, renowned preacher and general of the Augustinian Order, was singled out by Marjorie Reeves as a prime example of the role which Joachimist ideas played at the highest levels of church politics in the years either side of 1500.[84] Giles was eclectic in his search for a messianic leader: at different times he looked towards Pope Julius II, the king of Portugal, and Charles V to play the dominant role. His eulogy of the Emperor in his study of the Cabala, *Scechina*, was as enthusiastic as Alfonso de Valdés's

formismo en Castilla a raíz de la batalla de Pavía: El *Memorial* de don Beltrán de Guevara dirigido a Carlos V (1525)', in C. Iglesias et al. (eds.), *Homenaje a José Antonio Maravall*, 3 vols. (Madrid: Centro de Investigaciones Sociológicas, 1985), iii. 237–57.

[79] Niccolò Machiavelli, *The Prince*, ch. 21, ed. and trans. Q. Skinner and R. Price (Cambridge: Cambridge University Press, 1988), 76–7.

[80] e.g. Tyerman, *Invention*, 95.

[81] The essays in Reeves (ed.), *Prophetic Rome*, form an excellent example of this.

[82] Labande-Mailfert, *Charles VIII*, is balanced on this issue.

[83] See Ottavia Niccoli's classic study, *Prophecy and People in Renaissance Italy*, trans. L. G. Cochrane (Princeton: Princeton University Press, 1990).

[84] Reeves, *Influence of Prophecy*, 267–71. On Giles see *Dizionario biografico degli Italiani* (Rome: Istituto della Enciclopedia Italiana, 1960–), xlii. 341–53, with full bibliographical references.

outpouring of 1525. For Giles Charles V was the new Moses, David, and Caesar combined.[85]

Particularly striking was Savonarolan Florence (1494–8). As Donald Weinstein showed, the Ferrarese preacher cleverly grafted his prophetic insights onto civic republican traditions of thought. The Savonarolan programme enjoyed the impact which it did precisely because it combined Joachimist prophecy, with a particular emphasis on penitence, with an appeal to Florentine patriotism (*campanilismo*) which at times was quite blatant.[86] In sermon after sermon Savonarola assured the Florentines that if they would only repent of their sins and make themselves worthy of God's choice, the republic's bound-aries would know no limits: other peoples would clamour to be governed by them and even the Turks would be inspired to embrace the Christian faith.[87] Practical-ities were not considered: God would supply all the arms, horses, and money which were needed.[88] Florence was the New Jerusalem, 'the city of God',[89] and in March 1496, in a ceremony which bordered on the hysterical, Savonarola announced to the Florentines that Christ was their King. 'O Florence, in you is fulfilled the prophecy of Zaccaria: "Be exultant, daughter of Zion, behold your gentle king comes to you seated on an ass." '[90] Other words which he used at this extraordinary service demonstrated the inherent tension between national messianism and universality: 'Florence, this is the king of the universe, he who has willed to become your special king.'[91]

These swirling currents of eschatological and patriotic excitement are increasingly being accorded their due significance in terms of the politics and culture of the time. As Ottavia Niccoli has written, prophecy in particular was 'a unifying sign connecting nature to religion and religion to politics and co-ordinating all the scattered shreds of a culture'.[92] But it would be erroneous to expect the same translation of ideas into the practice of war which we have seen occurring, or being anticipated by the anxious authorities, in the case of insur-rectionist movements. In the first place, the messianic aspirations of such rulers as Fernando of Aragon, Charles VIII, and the Emperor Charles V made comparatively little difference to the ways they financed and recruited their armies, except in those cases where they were linked to the formal mechanisms of the crusade. But if the glimpses which we can catch of an intrusion of messianic ideas into the recruitment halls and camps are infrequent, they are also

[85] Giles of Viterbo, *Scechina e libellus de litteris Hebraicis*, ed. F. Secret, 2 vols. (Rome: Centro Inter-nazionale di Studi Umanistici, 1959), i. 69, 160–1, 233, ii. 281.

[86] Weinstein, *Savonarola and Florence, passim*.

[87] e.g. Fra Girolamo Savonarola, *Prediche italiane ai Fiorentini*, ed. F. Cognasso and R. Palmarocchi, 4 vols. (Perugia: 'La Nuova Italia' Editrice, 1930–5), iii/2. 188.

[88] Ibid., ii. 189.

[89] Ibid., iii/1. 126–7; Fra Girolamo Savonarola, *Prediche sopra Aggeo*, ed. L. Firpo (Rome, 1965), 340–1.

[90] Savonarola, *Prediche italiane*, iii/2. 365.   [91] Ibid. 370.

[92] Niccoli, *Prophecy and People*, p. xvi.

revealing. In several telling passages in his anti-war tracts Erasmus criticized the contemporary practice of priests preaching in a bellicose fashion in camp, of soldiers being assured that if they fell for God and king they would go to heaven, and of armies following the banner of the cross in quasi-crusading fashion: 'the cross fights the cross and Christ makes war on Christ', as he put it in *Querela pacis* in 1517.[93] In the early 1520s the Milanese kept such a banner marked with the cross in their cathedral, to be carried into battle against the French.[94]

Spanish examples are not hard to find. At the start of his study of Columbus' thought world, Alain Milhou devoted several pages to a reconstruction of the religious ideas and values of the discoverer's contemporary, the Aragonese nobleman Martín Martínez de Ampiés. He was a trained soldier and fought against the French in the Perpignan campaign of 1495; but he was also a man of letters and a devout Catholic. He translated Bernhard von Breydenbach's immensely popular *Peregrinatio in Terram Sanctam* and wrote a *Libro del Anticristo* and a Mariological treatise, the *Triumpho de Maria*. Milhou concluded that Ampiés's career and beliefs bring together a number of themes, which were soon to become so important that Milhou's list merits reproduction in full:

Harmony between arms, letters, and devotion; pride in the new-found might of a unified Spain whose monarchs, acting as Christendom's champions, could expunge the Spanish complex of failing to take part in the eastern crusades; fear about the imminent end of the world; curiosity about Jerusalem, unknown lands and peoples, the global struggle against Islam and the place of the Jews in salvation history; respect for Rome and the papacy; the influence of the Franciscans; and devotion for Mary.[95]

This was a rich agenda, but at its heart was precisely the sort of conflation of religion, patriotism, and war which Erasmus found so objectionable; it was exemplified at the battle of Ravenna in 1512, when the Spanish captain Pedro de Luján exhorted his troops to take no account of the enemy's superior numbers because God fought for Spain.[96]

Milhou's point in writing his mini-biography of Martín Martínez de Ampiés was that Columbus' ideas, which have often been regarded as eccentric, were in fact far from being unrepresentative of his age. It would be going much further to claim that Ampiés was typical of his fellow-nobles in Aragon, let alone in other Iberian states. The situation facing those who did share Ampiés's distinctive outlook was in any case complicated after 1519, when their king was elected as Holy Roman Emperor. Quite apart from the fact that the election altered Charles's

[93] Desiderius Erasmus, 'Querela pacis', trans. B. Radice, ed. A. H. T. Levi, in *CWE* xxvii. 289–322, at 309.

[94] Niccoli, *Prophecy and People*, 112.   [95] Milhou, *Colón*, 13–29, with quote at 29.

[96] J. M. Doussinague, *La política internacional de Fernando el Católico* (Madrid: Espasa-Calpe, 1944), 28.

political agenda in a manner which was bound to concern his Iberian subjects, it also somewhat detached him from the peninsula's messianic traditions.[97] The Emperor's Tunis expedition of 1535 was a case in point. It was accompanied by an outburst of messianic enthusiasm, stimulated undoubtedly to some extent by the fact that it was preached as a crusade; but the celebration of this success was framed in imperial rather than Iberian terms. It was 'the last offensive undertaking of a Roman Emperor at the head of a European army against the unbelievers: to that extent the Imperial ideology of the late Middle Ages enjoyed a final, short-lived awakening'.[98] Charles V's apologists were sophisticated enough to come up with answers to this quandary: faced with the need to mobilize Castilian resources to defend Habsburg interests in Hungary, they confronted the Valladolid Cortes of 1527 with an elaborate version of Castile's messianic mission which Juan Sánchez Montes viewed as a milestone in ideological formulation. No other Christian nation, the Cortes was informed, possessed either Castile's strength or its roll call of historic achievements on behalf of the faith: they must rise to the challenge of the hour.[99] As the Benedictine chronicler Gonzalo Arredondo y Alvarado put it in the following year, Castile was 'the invincible defender of the faith' against all its foes, spiritual and corporeal.[100] Nonetheless, it was only after the accession of Philip II in 1555 that Spanish 'national messianism' found its richest expression. Within a generation, as we shall see in the conclusion, its trajectory had reached such a point that career soldiers could leave evidence of their firm belief that they had fought for God as well as for king and country.

In the light of contemporary excitement about Charles V's messianic role, it is ironic that some of the most telling evidence for the mobilization of popular enthusiasm based on religious excitement of this kind relates to the republic of Florence during the siege of the city by Charles's own army in 1530. The followers of Savonarola, or *piagnoni* as they were called, looked to Christ, given kingship over Florence in 1496, to save his city; and on 24 February Christ's monarchy was celebrated in the consecration of a special standard. As the Venetian ambassador, Carlo Capello, wrote in a dispatch:

On the 24th by decree of the Council of 80 [Benedetto da Foiano] preached in the Great Council on this subject, and blessed a standard which bore the image of our lord Jesus Christ. He presented it to the standard-bearer, exhorting the entire city that when all other means of preserving their freedom failed, they should unfurl it and march out to

[97]   Sánchez Montes, *Franceses, Protestantes, Turcos, passim.*
[98]   H. Duchhardt, 'Das Tunisunternehmen Karls V. 1535', *Mitteilungen des österreichischen Staatsarchivs*, 37 (1984), 35–72, with quote at 62–3. See also Sánchez Montes, *Franceses, Protestantes, Turcos*, 93–8.
[99]   F. de Laiglesia (ed.), *Estudios históricos (1515–19)*, 3 vols. (Madrid: Imprenta Clásica Española, 1918–19), i. 371–80. See also Sánchez Montes, *Franceses, Protestantes, Turcos*, 121–3.
[100]   Pagden, *Lords of All the World*, 42, 223.

meet their enemies, in the sure belief that just as they had once chosen his Majesty as their protector and king, so they could trust in all certainty that they would conquer beneath his standard.

As Capello went on to remark, this gesture was accompanied by a programme of processions, fasting, and communion, 'in such a way that it is not easy to judge which is the greater, the constancy of their spirits in defending [the city], or the hope which they show of enjoying the most certain salvation in divine Majesty, abandoned though they are by everybody else'.[101] Indeed the city's *gonfaloniere*, Francesco Ferrucci, lauded as 'the new Gideon', made rhetorical use of this last point, emphasizing that although they faced the combined power of pope and Emperor, they need not fear, because Christ was fighting for them.[102] Coinage struck during the siege bore the inscription 'Jesus King of Florence'.[103] *Piagnoni* referred back to Savonarola's own preaching, 'which they called prophecies', to the effect that 'when the city was at its last gasp, and no other remedy existed, and no human agency could do anything on its behalf, then at the last hour, and not beforehand, angels bearing swords would be despatched from heaven to its walls, to effect its relief in miraculous fashion'. Nor, remarked the sceptical historian Benedetto Varchi, was it only the uninformed and foolish who gave credence to this idea: nobles and the educated also believed it, and it was preached in the Dominican churches of San Marco and Santa Maria Novella.[104]

It is apparent that a remarkable atmosphere existed in Florence during this siege, not least because contemporaries perceived it as the last chance to save the city for republicanism. 'With the conviction that Florence was in God's care went the belief that her enemies were His, and that the Florentines were thus engaged upon a holy war against the forces of evil.'[105] But we should be careful not to read too much into it. It was not reproduced elsewhere in the context of national or civic messianism: rather, the closest parallel, which we shall encounter at the end of this chapter, is with the outstanding example of sectarian messianism. The formidable growth of state power, and the will and ability of rulers to project images of authority in order to mobilize public support for their policy, pose interpretative problems of a high order. The infiltration of Europe's leading courts by a humanist culture which revitalized old-established

[101] E. Alberi (ed.), *Relazioni degli ambasciatori veneti al Senato*, ser. 2, vol. i (Florence: Società Editrice Fiorentina, 1839), 275–6.
[102] Benedetto Varchi, *Storia fiorentina* (Cologne: Pietro Martello, 1721), 406.
[103] C. Roth, *The Last Florentine Republic* (London: Methuen, 1925), 298.
[104] Varchi, *Storia fiorentina*, 401–2.
[105] Polizzotto, *The Elect Nation*, 374–85, with quote at 379–80. Cf. Roth, *The Last Florentine Republic*, 203: 'The atmosphere was that of a revivalist camp.' For evidence that the atmosphere was not created solely by the siege itself, see L. Polizzotto, 'Prophecy, Politics and History in Early Sixteenth-Century Florence: The Admonitory Letters of Francesco d'Antonio de' Ricci', in P. Denley and C. Edam (eds.), *Florence and Italy: Renaissance Studies in Honour of Nicolai Rubinstein* (London: Committee for Medieval Studies, Westfield College, 1988), 107–31, at 113–14, 123–6.

religious expectations with classical values means that the images projected were at times remarkably sophisticated. To dismiss these images as propaganda is indeed, as Milhou commented, reductionist,[106] but it would be naive to ignore the fact that rulers appreciated their value. Both messianism and the draping of forthright appeals to patriotism in sacred clothes were useful instruments in the arduous task of persuading subjects to provide the all-important financial support for warfare. For example, in 1486 Don Rodrigo Ponce de León, a commander in the Granada war, dispatched to the Castilian nobility a commentary on prophecies of St John and St Isidore which purported to show that Fernando was the *Encubierto* and the New David. 'I say this, my lords, because all of you, in person and with all your might, and right cheerful hearts, should serve and assist such a noble king to wipe out all the Moors and heretics, in honour of the holy Catholic faith. And know this for certain, that you will have no other *Encubierto* than the kings of Aragon, one or two or more as it pleases God. And they and their sons and lineages will rule over the world until its end.'[107]

Of course neither this, nor the fact that the projection was made so much easier by the diffusion of printing, means that subjects actually were persuaded, especially where expansionist policies were concerned. The debate which took place at the Avis court in the 1430s over the pros and cons of invading Morocco shows that members of the dynasty and the aristocracy nurtured no illusions about the likely response of the population at large.[108] Charles VIII's invasion of Italy in 1494 was initiated in the teeth of a wave of opposition based on the costs involved, the hazards of the campaign, the disruption of trade, and the domestic instability which the king's absence would cause.[109] And Milhou showed that when the major towns of Castile responded to the king's proposal for a crusade to capture Tunis in 1511, they made it clear that the recent conquest of Bougie represented the limit of their patience with Fernando's African ambitions.[110] This last example demonstrates that subjects were fully capable of subscribing to an ideology such as royal messianism without signing up for the financial costs which they knew it would entail.[111] It seems likely that the members of the Valladolid Cortes of 1527 felt much the same, especially as they were being asked for pay for the defence of far-off Hungary. In other words, except at times of particular excitement, arguments based on crusading tradition, prophecy, national

---

[106] Milhou, *Colón*, 170, and cf. his remarks in 'La Chauve-souris', 63.

[107] Quoted in Milhou, *Colón*, 237–8.   [108] Russell, *Prince Henry*, 135–66.

[109] Labande-Mailfert, *Charles VIII*, 219–31.

[110] A. Milhou, 'Propaganda mesiánica y opinión pública: Las reacciones de las ciudades del reino de Castilla frente al proyecto fernandino de cruzada (1510–11)', in Iglesias et al. (eds.), *Homenaje a José Antonio Maravall*, iii. 51–62.

[111] Milhou, *Colón*, 324 n. 733, pointed out that previous historians like Doussinague had taken for granted that there existed 'una pulsión profunda' within Castilian society for Maghribian expansion, without strong evidence for it. Cf. Milhou, 'Propaganda mesiánica', 56, and for similar sentiments expressed at the Cortes in the last years of Philip II's reign, G. Parker, *Philip II* (London: Hutchinson, 1979), 184.

pride, and the demands of chivalry were like chess pieces in the ongoing dialogue between rulers and ruled about their mutual obligations: important as they were, they could rarely win the game alone.

If this sounds calculating, it is as well to bear in mind the balance struck by Milhou: 'a readiness to believe, above all when it came to the crusade and universal monarchy, was perfectly compatible with *maquiavelismo*.'[112] In this regard Fernando of Aragon made a revealing comment in a letter to the viceroy of Naples in May 1510 on the subject of the Tunis expedition which he was planning. It was important, the king wrote, to maintain that the fleet being assembled was intended to fight against the Moors, 'as indeed it will be if [the French] do not get in the way'.[113] It is therefore salutary to remain sceptical, without reverting to the dismissive tendency which the sheer volume of unearthed evidence in this field has now rendered unacceptable. Again and again the hegemoniacal ambitions of Europe's rulers were couched and projected in terms of elevated religious designs. This is far from saying that the conflicts which resulted were religious wars. What it does mean, however, is that the portrayal of warfare in terms of religious hopes and concerns continued to occur to a marked degree: enough so, indeed, to attract the disapproval of Erasmus and the grudging admiration of Machiavelli.[114]

3.2 THE COMMONWEALTH DIVIDED, 1517–1536

The relationship between warfare and religious belief around 1500 was complex and volatile. It was bound to become yet more so once existing patterns of social insurrection, eschatological expectation, and patriotic excitement were interwoven with the sectarian strife generated by the early Reformation. It is logical to start our survey of these years with Luther, whose views on the legality of war and the circumstances in which violence might be used in the furtherance or defence of religious ends have obviously been accorded much attention.[115] As Luther's contemporaries complained, the reformer's opinions were far from straightforward. It is helpful to start with the views which he expressed on the defence of Christian lands against the Ottoman Turks, focusing on 'On War against the Turk' (*Vom Kriege wider die Türken*, 1529), his most mature and

[112] Milhou, *Colón*, 340.
[113] Doussinague, *La política internacional*, 616–17: 'So color que es para la guerra de los moros, como en verdad lo será si él no lo estorva.' See also Milhou, 'Propaganda mesiánica', 61.
[114] As so often with Machiavelli, it is not entirely clear whether he approves of Fernando of Aragon or not: Machiavelli, *The Prince*, ch. 21, pp. 76–7.
[115] M. Brecht, 'Luther und die Türken', in Guthmüller and Kühlmann (eds.), *Europa und die Türken*, 9–27; R. Mau, 'Luthers Stellung zu den Türken', in H. Junghans (ed.), *Leben und Werk Martin Luthers von 1526 bis 1546*, 2 vols. (Göttingen: Vandenhoeck & Ruprecht, 1983), i. 647–62, ii. 956–66. Both refer to the voluminous older literature.

detailed treatment of the issue.[116] His denial of the papacy's *magisterium* and his rejection of salvation through works naturally caused him to repudiate the crusade. In a number of colourful passages Luther pursued the theme that papal indulgences and taxes raised for the crusade were symptomatic of the corruption of the papal office: 'Think of all the heartbreak and misery that have been caused by the *cruciata*, by the indulgences, and by crusade taxes. With these Christians have been stirred up to fight the Turk when they ought to have been fighting the devil and unbelief with word and with prayer.'[117] The disastrous history of the church's involvement in warfare proved the foolishness of defying Paul's clear injunction in Ephesians 6: 12 that the Christian's struggle should be spiritual rather than material. The battles of Mohács and Pavia (where papal troops had fought alongside the French) were but the most recent examples of this. Indeed, 'if I were a soldier and saw a priest's banner in the field, or a banner of the cross, even though it was a crucifix, I should run as though the devil were chasing me'.[118]

But to say that there was no such thing as a Christian war was not to deny Christians the right to take up arms when their lands and families were subject to Ottoman attack. In such circumstances Luther's political thinking caused him to look to the secular authorities to take a clear lead: 'If the banner of Emperor Charles or of a prince is in the field, then let everyone run boldly and gladly to the banner to which his allegiance is sworn.'[119] In a providential world, moreover, armies needed God's support, so it was crucial that soldiers fight in a just manner and in a spirit of repentance. If they did this they had a better chance of success, and those who died would be saved: not because they had fought in a religious war, but because they were justified by their faith. Luther was under no illusions about the latter point, but 'it does not matter if the entire crowd is not good, provided only that the head and some of the chief men are upright'.[120] The army's activities must be preceded and accompanied by repentance and prayer, for 'if the Turk's god, the devil, is not beaten first, there is reason to fear that the Turk will not be so easy to beat'.[121]

'On War against the Turk' is a coherent statement and it generated a consistent Lutheran approach towards the defence of Germany. The essential features of the latter were encapsulated in a pamphlet by Johannes Brenz published at Wittenberg in 1537 in anticipation of a Turkish invasion of Germany. Although heavily eschatological, based on a reading of the prophet Daniel's dream in Daniel 7: 1–27, Brenz's tract was both careful and precise:

The preachers are also obligated earnestly to exhort the Emperor and princes [of Germany] to perform their appointed task—to resist the Turk with the sword. The rulers should not worry about the possibility that the Turk's might may be greater than

---

[116] Martin Luther, 'On War against the Turk', trans. C. M. Jacobs, in *LW* xlvi. 155–205.
[117] Ibid. 186, and cf. 164, 201.   [118] Ibid. 168.
[119] Ibid. 169.   [120] Ibid. 193.   [121] Ibid. 170.

their own; instead, they should obey God's command and precept, confidently believing that He will help them to combat the murderous Turks. And the subjects are duty-bound to assist their lords, thus safeguarding themselves, their wives, and their children. Such obedience is a good, holy work; if anyone perish while performing it, he should not doubt that he dies in obedience to God; and if otherwise he truly believes in Christ, he will certainly attain eternal bliss.[122]

The fact that this approach resembled the Catholic crusade in a number of key respects, notably in its emphasis on repentance and prayer, enabled Lutheran communities to work alongside their confessional foes at times of crisis.[123]

To a large extent Luther had cleared the ground with an earlier work, 'Whether Soldiers, Too, Can Be Saved' (*Ob Kriegesleute auch in seligem Stande sein können*, 1526), which emanated from discussions with a leading soldier, Assa von Kram.[124] Starting from his customary stance of Augustinian pessimism, Luther linked the military profession to the need for political authority, citing as proof of its legitimacy Luke 3: 14, Christ's instructions to some soldiers who requested his guidance. No soldier need fear damnation on account of his calling, but neither could he expect salvation to come through it: 'no one is saved as a soldier but only as a Christian.'[125] With considerable care Luther fashioned a pre-battle exhortation appropriate to a pious Protestant soldier: it emphasized the justice of the cause; obedience to a prince; humility before God; and confidence in God's mercy.[126] Doubtless one reason why Luther exercised this care was the fact that he had been taken to task a year earlier for expressing himself rather loosely about soldiers who suppressed the peasants rebelling throughout the Empire. 'Thus, anyone who is killed on the side of the rulers may be a true martyr in the eyes of God, if he fights with the kind of conscience I have just described, for he acts in obedience to God's word.'[127] This caused Luther's critics to declare (to use Luther's own inimitable language), 'God help us. Luther forgot himself that time! Before he taught that a man must obtain grace and salvation by faith alone, and not by works, and here he ascribes salvation not only to works, but even to the heinous work of bloodshed! The Rhine is on fire at last!'[128] The reformer was quick to clarify the situation.[129]

---

[122] J. W. Bohnstedt, 'The Infidel Scourge of God: The Turkish Menace as Seen by German Pamphleteers of the Reformation Era', *Transactions of the American Philosophical Society*, NS 58 (1968), 1–58, at 46–7. The year 1537 was a very fruitful one for pamphlet literature about the Turks: Göllner, *Turcica*, i. 282–95, with Brenz on 284–5.

[123] Luther's mature stance is well summarized in a letter to Duke Joachim of Brandenburg in August 1532: Martin Luther, 'Letters', ed. and trans. G. G. Krödel and H. T. Lehmann, *LW* xlviii–l, iii. 68–71, no. 252.

[124] Martin Luther, 'Whether Soldiers, Too, Can Be Saved', trans. C. M. Jacobs, in *LW* xlvi. 87–137.

[125] Ibid. 135, and see also 95–7.   [126] Ibid. 132–3.

[127] Martin Luther, 'Against the Robbing and Murdering Hordes of Peasants', trans. C. M. Jacobs, in *LW* xlvi. 45–55, at 53.

[128] Martin Luther, 'An Open Letter on the Harsh Book against the Peasants', trans. C. M. Jacobs, in *LW* xlvi. 57–85, at 82–3.

[129] Luther, 'Whether Soldiers, Too, Can Be Saved', 135.

Protestant soldiers could therefore march, alongside Catholics if need be, under the imperial banners in self-defence against the Turks. But could they take up arms against those same Catholics when the latter were acting under Charles V's orders? Here lay Luther's greatest dilemma. It has been carefully analysed, particularly in relation to the years 1529–31, between the second diet of Speyer and the formation of the Schmalkaldic League. An attempt to suppress Lutheranism through force of arms seemed imminent and its founder was constantly looked to for guidance. For a number of reasons Luther found it agonizingly difficult to sanction resistance to Charles V. He saw no way to reconcile it with Romans 13: 1–7, Paul's solemn injunction to obey the civil powers 'for there is no authority except from God, and those authorities that exist have been instituted by God'; he hated the prospect of having to join forces with the south German and Swiss Protestants; and he was unwilling to weaken Charles V's defence of the Empire against the Turks.[130] For a long time Luther clung to a simple faith in God's providential protection against Catholic military action. But a turning point came in 'Dr Martin Luther's Warning to his Dear German People' (*Warnunge D. Martini Luther, An seine lieben Deudschen*), written during the autumn of 1530.[131] It was his indignant response to the *Confutatio pontificia*, the uncompromising Catholic reply to the Augsburg Confession. Luther now declared that 'if war breaks out, which God forbid, I will not reprove those who defend themselves against the murderous and bloodthirsty papists, nor let anyone else rebuke them as being seditious, but I will accept their action and let it pass as self-defense'.[132] The tone of the document was far from bellicose: Luther dreaded a war against the Emperor and his chief intention was to dissuade the latter's subjects from responding to a call to arms, rather than actively sanctioning or organizing defence against them.

In 1532 Charles V conceded the members of the Schmalkaldic League a measure of security with the Peace of Nürnberg, and Luther died on the eve of the first major confessional conflict, the Schmalkaldic War of 1546–7. So far what we have viewed the reformer advocating can best be described as a variant of the classical Christian just war, to be waged in the right frame of mind so that God would support it. A providential world-view thus ensured that the Hussite concern that their war must be waged in an appropriate way returned to the agenda of this new group of reformers: ends and means must match. The Hussite analogy is important because several passages in the 'Warning' indicate lines of thinking which Luther might well have pursued if the anticipated attack had materialized. Particularly striking is one section in which Luther predicted that

---

[130] See the review of Luther's position in Q. Skinner, *The Foundations of Modern Political Thought*, 2 vols. (Cambridge: Cambridge University Press, 1978), ii. 194–202, though he pays insufficient attention to the impact of the Turks on Luther's thinking.

[131] Martin Luther, 'Dr Martin Luther's Warning to his Dear German People, 1531', trans. M. H. Bertram, in *LW* xlvii. 3–55.

[132] Ibid. 19.

the Catholic armies would suffer crushing defeats 'as we Germans did when we ventured to break the peace with St [*sic*] John Huss and fought against the Bohemians'. For 'God can easily raise up a Judas Maccabeus (even if my followers and I sit by quietly and suffer) who will smash Antiochus with his army and teach him real warfare'. Luther did not attach any identity to these warriors selected by God: his emphasis was entirely on the fact that the Catholics would be waging war with a bad conscience, as the German crusaders supposedly had during the Hussite wars, and would prove easy pickings for enemies who were fuelled by religious conviction. 'Let him who does not know what it means to wage war with a bad conscience and a despondent heart try it now. If the papists wage war, he will experience it, just as our ancestors did in a similar situation against the Bohemians and Žižka.'[133]

In a later passage Luther used language of remarkable force: 'he who fights and contends against the gospel necessarily fights simultaneously against God, against Jesus Christ, against the Holy Spirit, against the precious blood of Christ, against his death, against God's word, against all the articles of faith, against all the sacraments, against all the doctrines which are given, confirmed, and preserved by the gospel . . . in brief, against all angels and saints, against heaven and earth and all creatures.'[134] It is surely not going too far to say that these emotional phrases give an indication of the rhetoric which would have been mobilized in the event of a Catholic offensive in the 1530s, just as it had been in Bohemia in the 1420s. What was required was a switch from the language of religious condemnation to that of religious motivation. In this respect Luther's own comparison of the Protestant situation with the Hussite one is highly instructive. Faced with a similar challenge from Sigismund, the Hussite centre had moved from a position of paralysis, first to the acceptance of a war of justified defence, and then to the belief that their successful defence of both *patria* and *lex Dei* was God-given in nature. Like the Hussites, Luther was essentially reactive and much preferred to negotiate; but his confidence in the reformed faith which he had created led him to trust in God's support. And Luther, like the Hussites, was fascinated by eschatology. We shall see that this led him into extremely interesting formulations of the eschatological roles of the pope and the Turks. In this he was not alone. As two recent commentators have put it, 'the value of being able to claim that [the reformers] were the godly troops of Christ fighting the ungodly soldiers of the papacy—Antichrist in Rome—in the last eschatological battle portrayed in the books of Daniel and Revelation can . . . hardly be overestimated'.[135]

Despite their rejection of both the theology and the apparatus of crusade, the reformed faiths could therefore, like Hussitism before them, embrace religious

---

[133] Ibid. 17–18.   [134] Ibid. 35.

[135] A. Cunningham and O. P. Grell, *The Four Horsemen of the Apocalypse: Religion, War, Famine and Death in Reformation Europe* (Cambridge: Cambridge University Press, 2000), 20.

warfare. Luther's own 'righteous war' required a strong emotional charge to give it the characteristics of religious war. In the course of time that charge was to derive from two sources: eschatological conviction and patriotic zeal. In the short term the role of eschatological conviction was manifested most clearly in the careers of the radical theologians Thomas Müntzer and Melchior Hoffman, who controversially tied it to the concept of an elect group mandated with the destruction of the godless. Like Luther, both men were enormously attracted by the example of the Hussites. In 1521 Müntzer hoped that the contemporary Czechs, legatees of 'the dear and saintly warrior John Hus', would be the front-line troops of the radical Reformation,[136] while for Hoffman the Hussite defence of the *lex Dei* had been the prime example in recent times of an elect group executing God's justice.[137] Patriotic zeal, on the other hand, is most clearly visible in Zwingli's approach, in which the basic concept of the justified war in defence of the reformed faith was lifted to a higher plane by the idea of the embattled community of the elect. This was already evident in his 'A Godly Warning to the Confederates of Schwyz' (*Ein göttliche Vermahnung an die Eidgenossen zu Schwyz*, May 1522).[138] Written in response to the heavy losses sustained by the Swiss at the battle of Bicocca on 27 April, the tract was an attempt to bring about a total withdrawal from the Italian wars, on the basis that Swiss blood should not be shed for reasons of money. Erasmian distaste for war runs alongside a fiery patriotism: when the Swiss fought for freedom rather than cash God supported them as he had the Israelites.[139] With such comparisons Zwingli accessed an ebullient vernacular tradition of celebrating Swiss victories as proof of God's support. The analogy with the Israelites dated back at least as far as the victory at Murten in 1476, and in 1495 another Swiss patriot had written: 'O God stand at their side; | And Mary, maid so pure; | The noble Swiss will fight; | In justice they'll endure.'[140] Songs like this one bring to mind the popular celebration of Hussite successes, and there can be no doubt of the enormous potential here once the defence of the gospel and national community were fully joined. Conversely, remembering that the Catholic/Hussite divide had plunged Bohemia into civil war, it was fortunate for the Swiss that the Kappel wars of 1529–31 between Protestants and Catholics were ended before relations became too bitter.

As for Luther, the most severe test of his personal position occurred in 1524–5

---

[136]   *The Collected Works of Thomas Müntzer*, ed. and trans. P. Matheson (Edinburgh: T. & T. Clark, 1988), 352–79, with quote at 362.

[137]   J. M. Stayer, *Anabaptists and the Sword* (Lawrence, Kan.: Coronado Press, 1972), 218. See also his 'Melchior Hoffman and the Sword', *Mennonite Quarterly Review*, 45 (1971), 265–77.

[138]   Ulrich Zwingli, 'Eine göttliche Vermahnung an die Eidgenossen zu Schwyz', in *Huldreich Zwinglis sämtliche Werke*, vol. i (Munich: Kraus Reprint, 1981), 155–88.

[139]   Ibid. 170–2.

[140]   R. von Liliencron (ed.), *Die historischen Volkslieder der Deutschen vom 13. bis 16. Jahrhundert*, 4 vols. (Leipzig: Königliche Akademie der Wissenschaften, 1865–9; repr. Hildesheim, 1966), i, no. 80, ii, nos. 144, 197.

when the German-speaking lands were convulsed by the Peasants' War, or Rebellion of the Common Man (*gemeiner Mann*).[141] The Peasants' War has a number of features in common with the Dózsa rebellion a decade earlier, most importantly the same complaint that functional lordship had collapsed. Discontent was voiced about the failure of the German authorities to take action against the Turks: the author of one satire written just before the rebellion commented with heavy sarcasm that there was no need to fear a Turkish invasion because taxes raised for the purpose of defending Germany had been invested in 'more than thirty feasts . . . to say nothing of foot races, tournaments, sledding parties, fancy dress balls, and other such vital preparations'.[142] But the charge of negligence did not play the major role which it had done in Hungary, presumably because Hungary itself was still in place as Christendom's bulwark: quite possibly things would have been different had the Peasants' War occurred after the disastrous Hungarian defeat at Mohács in 1526. Instead, the charge of oppression was more general. As one of the Twelve Articles of the Swabian peasants expressed it in relation to death taxes, 'The very ones who should be guarding and protecting our goods have skinned and trimmed us of them instead.'[143] As we saw in Chapter 1, perhaps the most important single characteristic of the rebellion was its regionalism. Uprisings occurred across the length and breadth of the Empire, with particularly violent outbreaks in Thuringia, Franconia, Swabia, Alsace, and the Tyrol. Links existed or were forged between these regional bands (*Haufen*) but both causality and progress varied greatly. What the uprisings had in common was the fact that they all expressed a range of economic and legal grievances against the landowning class, accompanied by demands that the reformed faith should be freely preached.[144]

The part which religion played in this great insurrection has been debated from many angles. The most substantial contributions have come from two German scholars, Günther Franz and Peter Blickle. In his classic study Franz pinpointed the importance of evangelical preaching in confirming that social revolt in the Empire could be based on Divine Law (*göttliches Recht*). Previous rebellions, notably the series of *Bundschuh* revolts, had expressed their goals by reference to Scripture, but there had been a tendency also to place the emphasis on infringements of customary law (*altes Recht*).[145] Blickle placed the importance of this breakthrough within its full historical setting by revealing the extent to

---

[141] Scott, 'The Peasants' War: A Historiographical Review', is an excellent introduction to the historiography.

[142] G. Strauss (ed.), *Manifestations of Discontent in Germany on the Eve of the Reformation* (Bloomington: Indiana University Press, 1971), 178.

[143] Blickle, *The Revolution of 1525*, 200.

[144] T. Scott and B. Scribner (eds. and trans.), *The German Peasants' War: A History in Documents* (Atlantic Highlands, NJ: Humanities Press International, 1991), 'Introduction', 19–53, and nos. 1–10.

[145] G. Franz, *Der deutsche Bauernkrieg*, 10th edn. (Darmstadt: Wissenschaftliche Buchgesellschaft, 1975). See also his 'Zur Geschichte des Bundschuhs', *Zeitschrift für die Geschichte des Oberrheins*, NS 47 (1934), 1–23.

which the Peasants' War constituted a general crisis of authority in the Holy Roman Empire. The whole of the existing order in the Empire, tenurial, political, and ecclesiastical, was challenged by the 'biblicism' which Protestant preaching had unleashed. *Sola scriptura* provided the reference point, both methodological and justificatory, for the questioning of all forms of lordship. As Otto Brunfels put it in 1524, 'Urban, secular and imperial laws should be modified according to the laws of Scripture and the love of one's neighbour.'[146] There was a new self-confidence about such comments which makes them qualitatively different from earlier attacks on social injustice (especially serfdom) as irreconcilable with Scripture and patristic tradition.[147]

One can certainly accept therefore that the Peasants' War was *about* religion, amongst other things, and that the ferment of ideas created by events since 1517 helped to generate much of the excitement which is so apparent in the sources. It is striking how often the rebels emphasized that they were first and foremost Christians.[148] But this is not the same thing as saying that it was a religious war.[149] Its leaders placed great emphasis on the righteousness of their cause and stressed that their followers should behave in a godly way, as befitted the reason they had taken up arms. But there are no signs that the combatants saw themselves as acting in response to a divine mandate, that they portrayed themselves as God's elect, or that they were driven by chiliastic ambitions. Indeed, one of Peter Blickle's most valuable contributions to the scholarship of the subject has been to demonstrate how far the revolt was rooted in well-established forms of peasant co-operation, the *Gemeinden*. These communities acted as the basic building blocks in the whole structure of the revolt: *Gemeinden* were grouped into *Haufen*, and several *Haufen* came together to form a regional *Bund*.[150] It was always unlikely that a movement which sprang from such conservative roots, and built them into its own *modus operandi*, would develop either a self-perception or a programme as radical as that of the early Taborites, or of the Hungarian *cruciferi* of 1514. Rather, the clearest comparison is with the Pilgrimage of Grace, which, though it embraced diametrically opposite religious beliefs, displayed analogous organizational features and a similar restraint in its activities.

For in the light of the increasingly oppressive nature of lordship which forms the background to the peasants' rebellion, their approach towards their oppo-

---

[146] Quoted in H. J. Cohn, 'Anticlericalism in the German Peasants' War 1525', *Past and Present*, 83 (1979), 3–31, at 9.

[147] To this extent I disagree with Paul Freedman's argument that the moral condemnation of serfdom was not radically changed by Reformation theology: 'The German and Catalan Peasant Revolts', 47, 51–2. See also his *Images of the Medieval Peasant*, 280–6.

[148] e.g. *The Collected Works of Thomas Müntzer*, 147–8, 152–3; Scott and Scribner (eds. and trans.), *The German Peasants' War*, no. 36.

[149] As argued by H. A. Oberman, 'The Gospel of Social Unrest: 450 Years after the So-Called "German Peasants' War" of 1525', *Harvard Theological Review*, 69 (1976), 103–29.

[150] This is well explained in B. Scribner, 'Communities and the Nature of Power', in B. Scribner (ed.), *Germany: A New Social and Economic History*, i: *1450–1630* (London: Arnold, 1996), 291–325.

nents was astonishingly restrained. One of the most recent historians of the revolt, James Stayer, has characterized the uprising's opening stage as more like a general strike than a rebellion.[151] When the Christian Union was formed in Upper Swabia in March 1525, the language with which its adherents announced its formation to their enemies bordered on the apologetic:

We poor folk inform your graces that the worthy commons of this land has allied itself in a Christian union, to the praise of Almighty God, for the promotion of the holy Gospel and Word of God, and as succour for divine law, and to nobody's annoyance or vexation, with the assurance that we are not opposed to whatever we are obliged by spiritual and secular authorities to perform according to divine law. If anyone complains of us to your graces or if we are slandered by anyone, whoever they are, now or in the future, because of this Christian union, we will demand nothing other than divine law; and it is our intention to do violence to no one.[152]

The massacre of nobles carried out at Weinsberg in April 1525 was exceptional, and the tenor of both the articles of grievance and the military activities of the insurgents forms a remarkable contrast with the brutality practised by both sides in the Dózsa revolt, especially the grisly practice of impaling. Blickle has emphasized that this behavioural restraint featured amongst the range of reasons for the failure of the rebellion; godly law liberated but it did not guide. 'Godly law, as the peasants at that point understood it, provided no basis for aggressive, implacable, militarily disciplined actions against the nobles and prelates.'[153] The denunciation of the revolt by Luther was of course particularly painful, but no major evangelical preacher came out in support of the rebels. 'The godly law remained silent because no one spelled it out. It lost its authority because it did not solve the crisis, and it lost its explosive power because the military and political leaders . . . did not know how to exploit it to produce a new political order.'[154]

If it is only recently that these features of the Peasants' War have been properly appreciated, it is partly because of the way Thomas Müntzer's role in the revolt has been re-evaluated. Müntzer reached the peak of his popularity in the former DDR, whose scholars gave him pride of place in their pantheon of harbingers of socialism, and depicted him as the leading theologian of the Peasants' War.[155] Müntzer's angry intolerance of religious corruption and social injustice was accompanied by a conviction that God would not tolerate them, and that he would use the righteous and downtrodden as the instruments of his

---

[151] J. M. Stayer, *The German Peasants' War and Anabaptist Community of Goods* (Montreal: McGill-Queen's University Press, 1991), 21.

[152] Scott and Scribner (eds. and trans.), *The German Peasants' War*, no. 30, and cf. nos. 31–2.

[153] Blickle, *The Revolution of 1525*, 98.   [154] Ibid. 99–100.

[155] T. Scott, 'From Polemic to Sobriety: Thomas Müntzer in Recent Research', *JEH* 39 (1988), 557–72. See also Scott's biography, *Thomas Müntzer: Theology and Revolution in the German Reformation* (Basingstoke: Macmillan, 1989).

wrath. 'For God cannot desert his elect, although at times he may appear to do so, but he will carry out his vengeance at the appointed time.'[156] Müntzer was convinced by his own experiences and by scriptural exegesis that God's vengeance was imminent, the main signs being the radical Reformation and the outbreak of the Peasants' War. For this reason he threw in his lot with the rebels, undergoing capture after the battle of Frankenhausen in May 1525 and execution soon afterwards. The more balanced assessment of recent years emphasizes that he was only ever important within the Thuringian theatre of the war, and views his social radicalism in a more pragmatic framework. For example, although in July 1524 he stressed that feudal dues must continue to be paid once a new covenant had been forged between rulers and ruled, ten months later he was justifying the pillaging carried out by the rebels. Quite simply, circumstances had changed: in July 1524 Müntzer still hoped to effect major change with the assistance of the Lutheran princes and their administrators, who included his correspondent John Zeiss, while in May 1525 he stood alongside the rebels.[157] Apart from such tactical shifts in his thinking, there is also the vexed question of Müntzer's language. His surviving writings reveal a torrent of ideas couched in German which is at once mystical and earthy, allusive and direct, peculiarly defiant of analysis and even at times of translation. He was a many-sided individual. Peter Matheson has pointed to evidence that he was a revered pastor, yet some of his letters are as abusive as anything written in the early Reformation.[158]

As in the case of other individuals, notably Erasmus and More, we have to be careful not to let the fascination of Müntzer's ideas and language lead us to exaggerate the importance of his views and their contemporary impact. It seems likely, for example, that the less celebrated Michael Gaismair and Melchior Hoffman had more immediate impact than Müntzer. Gaismair, who like Müntzer called for the merciless extermination of the godless, was the leader of the revolt in the Tyrol, while Hoffman was read and much admired by his fellow-Anabaptists.[159] That said, Müntzer remains a figure of some importance in this study for several reasons. First, his conviction that violent change must occur because of his reading of eschatological signs makes him one of the most significant contributors to the European chiliastic tradition. In part this flows from a paradox. For Müntzer's theology placed exceptional emphasis on the achievement of grace through suffering: in effect, each Christian must experience spiritual crucifixion.[160] This led him to take up extreme positions, commenting for example

---

[156]   *The Collected Works of Thomas Müntzer*, 91.   [157]   Ibid. 102, 151.
[158]   Ibid., pp. x–xiii, 162–5.
[159]   K. Deppermann, *Melchior Hoffman: Social Unrest and Apocalyptic Visions in the Age of Reformation*, trans. M. Wren, ed. B. Drewery (Edinburgh: T & T. Clark, 1987); W. Klaassen, *Michael Gaismair Revolutionary and Reformer* (Leiden: Brill, 1978).
[160]   A point well made by T. Nipperdey, 'Theology and Revolution in Thomas Müntzer', in J. M. Stayer and W. O. Packull (eds.), *The Anabaptists and Thomas Müntzer* (Dubuque, Ia.: Kendall/Hunt, 1980), 105–17, at 109.

in 1524 that 'even if you have already devoured all the books of the Bible you still must suffer the sharp edge of the plough-share'.[161] His letter 'to the persecuted Christians of Sangerhausen' (*c*.20 July 1524) has much in common with More's *Dialogue of Comfort against Tribulation* in its earnest exhortation to patience and faith.[162] It is necessary to explain why this did not lead Müntzer to adopt a pacifist position. Secondly, the gulf between Müntzer's revolutionary agenda and his own lack of status and resources drove him to explore a series of options for engineering change. His search for instruments of God's justice was conducted in circumstances of great personal difficulty and distress between 1521 and 1525.[163] More so than Savonarola, Müntzer's case illustrates Machiavelli's dismissal of the 'unarmed prophet' as an ineffectual figure in the world of power politics.[164]

Prophets could however find themselves holding real power, and nine years after Müntzer's execution this occurred in Münster in Westphalia when Jan Matthys, the Anabaptist prophet from Haarlem, was welcomed to a city which his fellow-sectarians had succeeded in taking over. The Anabaptist regime at Münster, which was finally overthrown after a long siege by the bishop of Münster in the summer of 1535, forms by far the strongest impact which the sectarians of the Reformation's first generation exerted on religious warfare.[165] For Münster was a powerful and well-known city, consisting of about 10,000 people at the time of the Anabaptist seizure of power. The fact that it could fall into the hands of sectarians at all was remarkable, and due to the convergence of a number of factors, including the division of power in the town council between Lutherans and Catholics, the incompetence of the prince-bishop, Franz von Waldeck, and a highly effective wave of Anabaptist proselytizing at the end of 1533. The winning of hegemony within the town council in February 1534 was consolidated by an influx of Anabaptists from Holland, attracted by the prospect of sharing the rich city's wealth and awaiting there the Last Days, which Matthys predicted to be imminent.

Münster invites comparison with two other urban chiliastic regimes. One, as I have already noted, is Savonarolan Florence, particularly during the imperialist siege of the city which had taken place just a few years previously. This is instructive because the Anabaptists based their regime not on civic *campanilismo* combined with Joachimist expectations of the end, but on sectarian exclusiveness fired by chiliasm. Like Florence, Münster was a New Jerusalem, but only Anabaptists were the New Israelites.[166] Non-Anabaptists were expelled in pitiable circumstances in February 1534, following the rejection of Matthys's

---

[161] *The Collected Works of Thomas Müntzer*, 199.   [162] Ibid. 86–91.
[163] Scott, *Thomas Müntzer*, 30–175.   [164] *The Prince*, ch. 6, p. 21.
[165] There are numerous studies on Anabaptist Münster, but for the English-speaking reader the best recent account is A. Arthur, *The Tailor-King: The Rise and Fall of the Anabaptist Kingdom of Münster* (New York: St Martin's Press, 1999).
[166] See, e.g., *Hermanni A. Kerssenbroch Anabaptistici Furoris Monasterium inclitam Westphaliae metropolim evertentis historica narratio*, ed. H. Detmer (Münster: Theissing, 1899), 508–9.

extraordinary proposal that they should all be massacred.[167] The other interesting comparison is of course with early Tabor. Anabaptist Münster rivalled Tabor in the fervour with which the Last Days were awaited, as well as in the ingenuity with which the failure of Christ to reappear was explained away.[168]

At Münster Melchior Hoffman's theology of apocalyptic violence was taken to its extreme. Hoffman was never able to accept that the elect should themselves take up the sword: even in his most developed prophecies, in which the New Jerusalem of Strasburg was besieged by Charles V, the Anabaptists were to act only as auxiliaries while others fought.[169] But the Münster Anabaptists went further. The transition from pilgrimage to warfare discussed earlier had its equivalent in their belief that their seizure of power ushered in a new age in history, in which New Testament quietism was superseded. Their apocalyptic fury received a lavish commentary on paper in the writings of the regime's chief apologist, the preacher Berndt Rothmann, especially in his *Von der Wracke* of late 1534: 'There may be those who think that God himself will come down from heaven with his angels to avenge himself on the godless, and who confidently wait for it. No, dear brother. He will come, that is true. But the vengeance must first be carried out by God's servants who will properly repay the unrighteous godless as God has commanded them.'[170] The circumstances of the siege of Münster meant that this purgative bellicosity found limited expression in reality. The Anabaptists were told that they would be relieved by an army of their fellow-elect, the 144,000 saved of Revelation 14: 1, who would fan out from Münster to overrun the world. A thousand copies of *Von der Wracke* were smuggled out of Münster in the hope of inciting insurrection elsewhere.

It was probably from Rothmann's tracts that Erasmus' correspondents received their detailed knowledge of the Münster Anabaptists' ideology. Writing from Düsseldorf shortly after the city's fall, Conrad Heresbach passed on an account of their beliefs, including the violent strain of their apocalypticism: 'In such ways it is proper for this new people of Israel to attack, savage, damage, and in the end totally wipe out the Moabites, Philistines, and Midianites; for the sword of vengeance has been assigned to them, with this new Joshua at their head.'[171] Particularly strenuous efforts at raising support for the uprising were invested in Holland, but there was an effective governmental backlash and the many thousands who responded there were prevented from mobilizing fully. As

---

[167] See, e.g., *Hermanni A. Kerssenbroch Anabaptistici Furoris Monasterium inclitam Westphaliae metropolim evertentis historica narratio*, 632–3.

[168] Housley, 'The Eschatological Imperative', 142–7.

[169] Deppermann, *Melchior Hoffman*, 257–60.

[170] W. Klaassen (ed.), *Anabaptism in Outline: Selected Primary Sources* (Kitchener: Herald Press, 1981), 335. Full text in *Die Schriften Bernhard Rothmanns*, ed. R. Stupperich (Münster: Aschendorffsche Verlagsbuchhandlung, 1970), 284–97.

[171] *Opus epistolarum Des. Erasmi Roterodami*, ed. P. S. Allen et al., 11 vols. (Oxford: Oxford University Press, 1906–47), xi. 166, no. 3031a.

it was, the remarkable skill and courage with which the Münster Anabaptists conducted their defence demonstrated their powerful sense of conviction as well as their military prowess. Typically, it was through treachery that the city eventually fell.

Like the early Taborites, the Münster Anabaptists practised community of goods. As if determined to scandalize contemporaries as much as possible, they also embraced polygamy, which was introduced in July 1534. By this point Matthys had died and his protégé Jan Bockelson (Jan van Leyden, Heresbach's 'new Joshua') had seized power in the city. Bockelson transformed the government of the besieged city. In September he proclaimed it a kingdom and himself took the title of king as a New David. A former play-actor, Bockelson's regime of terror included many features which were intended for dramatic effect. But it would be a mistake to write off Bockelson's 'kingdom of Münster' as a bizarre aberration. Norman Cohn was not pandering to sensationalism when he accorded Anabaptist Münster lavish attention at the close of his seminal study of chiliasm, for it represents probably the most important, as well as one of the best-documented, chiliastic regimes within the entire European tradition.[172] Given the logic of chiliasts, most of Bockelson's actions make sense. We shall see that even polygamy has been explained within the context of making the regime work more effectively.

When Münster fell in June 1535 a sequence of events in early Reformation history effectively played itself out. Conservative reformers, in particular Luther, had formulated views on warfare which enabled them to assist in the defence of the Empire against the Turks and, if necessary, defend themselves against future Catholic attack. Meanwhile the radicals, especially Müntzer and the Münster Anabaptists, had gone so far as to sanctify programmes of violence as an inherently purgative process based on a belief in Christ's imminent return. This had taken almost two decades. The Hussites had made much the same journey in less than a year, but for them circumstances were very different. The evangelical reform movement was more broadly based and its theological underpinnings were more complex. It should be added that the response by the forces of church and state was more varied in the case of the Reformation. There was nothing so straightforward as Sigismund's crusade of 1420, which played such a key role in concentrating the minds of the Hussites on the issue of how to defend the *lex Dei*. Münster changed a good deal: there is a sense in which it was the early Reformation's Lipany. The radical sectarians never again won control of a major city within which they enjoyed virtual carte blanche to impose their views on the reordering of society, together with the need to work out their stance on the use of force in Christ's name. Within the Anabaptist movement, the shock

---

[172] Cohn, *Pursuit*, 252–80. J. M. Stayer, 'Christianity in One City: Anabaptist Münster, 1534–35', in H. J. Hillerbrand (ed.), *Radical Tendencies in the Reformation: Divergent Perspectives* (Kirksville, Mo.: Sixteenth Century Journal Publishers, 1988), 117–34, is particularly good on Bockelson's regime.

of events at Münster was traumatic and lasting. The hope of generating renewed holy war was pursued in the late 1530s, notably by Jan van Batenburg, but the horror stories associated with Bockelson's kingdom were disseminated widely in broadsheets and they proved enough to establish the hegemony of the separatist, pacifist wing, associated above all with Menno Simons.[173]

There is thus a logic to halting in the mid-1530s, and it is reinforced by other events which occurred at this time. We have already seen that the Pilgrimage of Grace, in 1536, brings within the scope of the analysis a great Catholic reaction to the Reformation; this we can compare with those insurrections which derived from evangelical preaching. The same year witnessed the formulation of the Franco-Ottoman Capitulations at Istanbul, a landmark in the integration of the sultanate into European diplomatic affairs.[174] And two key thinkers died at this time. In 1536 the death of Erasmus removed from European public life the man who more than any other had espoused a religious faith purged of all associations with violence, especially violence which was allegedly being perpetrated at God's command. For Erasmus news of the events at Münster only confirmed the extreme pessimism which overcame him towards the end of his life.[175] In July 1535, just a fortnight after the exultant bishop of Münster rode into his recaptured city, Thomas More was beheaded in London. We shall see in Chapter 5 that More espoused a view of the devout Catholic's approach towards the exercise of power which managed, albeit with some difficulty, to reconcile piety with violence. Many remarkable developments lay in the near future, including the Schmalkaldic Wars (1546–55), the French Wars of Religion (1562 onwards), and the group of conflicts associated with the Catholic Reformation. In different ways, however, all constituted new departures in which thinking and practices were developing as second stages from the ferment of ideas on religious warfare created by the remarkable generation of Erasmus, More, Müntzer, and Rothmann.

---

[173] Stayer, *Anabaptists and the Sword*, 284–321.
[174] Setton, *PL* iii. 400–1.
[175] *Opus epistolarum Des. Erasmi*, xi. 33, 39, 79, nos. 2961, 2965, 3000.

CHAPTER FOUR

The Assembling of Authority: Scripture, Messianic Individuals, and Symbols

Amongst the evidence for the Dózsa peasant rebellion of 1514 is a short pamphlet (*Flugschrift*) entitled 'A great miracle which took place through the cross which a cardinal handed out throughout the land of Hungary against the Turks'. The pamphlet was very popular and survived in several imprints. The 'great miracle' (*gross wundertzaychen*) of the title occurred in May 1514. The papal legate Tamás Bakócz had responded to the initial assaults committed against nobles and their property by ordering the *crucesignati* to disperse to their homes. Nobody was to associate with them under threat of punishment. In their main camp near Pest several thousand of the *crucesignati* were called on to decide for themselves whether to obey the legate's injunction or to disobey him, and through him confront the church's hierarchy, by continuing with the crusade. They would make this choice by assembling under one of two banners on which the crucifix was prominently displayed. At first the banner standing for dispersal attracted the vast majority of the volunteers. But then the crucifix on the banner fell off, not once, but three times in succession. This miraculous intervention persuaded the peasants to continue with the crusade, 'so those who had [formerly] wished to return home changed their minds. They all resolved to stand or fall together, and it was the will of all that they be allowed to proceed.'[1]

The incident is not hard to interpret. Generically, it belongs to the pattern of portents and visions whose role in contemporary Italy was analysed by Ottavia Niccoli. But there was a pointed significance about the tumbling crucifix which made it different from most of Niccoli's examples. On the whole, one of the attractions of such portents as the visions of a phantom host at Verdello, which occurred in 1517, was their openness to a wide range of interpretations.[2] Faced with the abrupt withdrawal of the mediating authorization of the church's hierarchy, the Hungarians needed a direct mandate from above, and they received

[1] Fekete Nagy et al. (eds.), *Monumenta rusticorum*, no. 227, and cf. no. 200. See also Göllner, *Turcica*, i. 57–9, iii. 345, 349.
[2] Niccoli, *Prophecy and People*, 65–6, 79, 84–5.

one in a manner which no bearer of Christ's cross could fail to understand. As the crusade proceeded, other ways of dealing with the problem posed by Archbishop Bakócz were devized. These included an emphasis on group solidarity and the distinction which the crusaders drew between their continuing allegiance to king and their wholesale repudiation of noble authority.[3] But the miracle of the crucifix sufficed for the moment: it resolved the crisis at Pest and so enabled the crusade to continue.

The incident at Pest establishes the relevance of any discussion of authority in relation to the conduct of a war which was perceived as divinely mandated. Far from being abstract or academic, the issue was a central concern for participants. If it could not be clearly shown that they acted in God's name and for his purpose, the entire war lost its validity. Naturally the search for authority was keenest when rebellion was also involved, because in such cases the religious mandate had the job of providing cohesion for the revolt as well as dealing with the arguments thrown up by the affronted 'powers that be'. In addition to Dózsa's crusaders, the two best examples are therefore the Hussites and the German rebels of 1524–5. We have seen that in Prague during the winter of 1419–20 a sophisticated debate about the validity and mode of conduct of a war of resistance against Sigismund took place at the same time that an extreme millenarian position was being adopted in the Taborite and Orebite communities. The Hussite centre eventually emerged unaffected by chiliastic ideas, but however conservative it was socially, the association of a religious cause with a political one meant that the manifestos disseminated in the early 1420s were bound to be of a markedly radical nature.[4] By contrast, the disastrous outcome of the German rebellion of 1524–5 flowed in part from its leaders' inability to persuade a single mainstream Protestant theologian to back their actions. Unless they went down the chiliastic road, they therefore found themselves acting on a dangerously insubstantial basis, that of 'God's Law' as set out and related to existing social realities in a series of manifestos. This relative poverty of ideas cannot be compared with military or political considerations in explaining the ultimate defeat of the revolt, but it is striking that this, by far the biggest of the three rebellions, was the weakest in terms of self-projection.[5]

The issue of authority in relation to religious war could never be entirely straightforward, even when the theological premises and the mediating structures were both firmly in place. In these respects the crusade may appear to be clarity itself, yet human nature demanded that both premises and structures receive the stamp of divine approval conferred by military success. Crusading history provides much evidence of the anguish and soul-searching which resulted when this failed to occur. For example, in 1432 an assembly of French clergy con-

---

[3] Housley, 'Crusading as Social Revolt', 12–24.   [4] Šmahel, *La Révolution hussite, passim.*
[5] R. Kolb, 'The Theologians and the Peasants: Conservative Evangelical Reactions to the German Peasants' Revolt', *Archiv für Reformationsgeschichte*, 69 (1978), 103–31.

vened by Charles VII at Bourges set out the paradox of the recurrent defeats inflicted on the crusading armies in Bohemia. Certainly the wars were just in so far as the Hussites were convicted heretics; but failure showed that they did not enjoy the support of God, who was 'inscrutable in his judgements'.[6] A much fuller commentary on the Catholic dilemma resides in the writings of the Bavarian apologist Andrew of Regensburg. Andrew lived in a city which not only hosted some of the Reichstags where the Hussite crisis was debated, but also acted as an important military assembly point; so his view of events was well informed. He set himself the task of explaining the humiliating defeats in Bohemia, using a range of arguments and examples drawn from theology, Scripture, and history; but at the end of the day he found the paradox impossible to resolve intellectually and had to fall back on faith. Significantly, in doing so he drew on the precedent of Otto of Freising's commentary on the disastrous Second Crusade.[7]

Conversely, as we saw in Chapter 2, the military successes achieved by the Hussite coalition over the invading crusaders were just as important as any number of arguments advanced by the Prague academics in convincing the Czechs that God stood by them. A major theme in Peter Payne's speech in defence of the Hussite position at the Bratislava meeting in April 1429 was that whereas Sigismund had enjoyed success in his wars against the Turks, he had repeatedly failed to crush the Hussites with force.[8] Clearly the sanction of crusade was not enough in itself, nor was it necessary to bestow legitimacy. All things being equal, however, the exponents of a crusade had a good deal in their favour when it came to conceptualizing where they stood: papal authority, indulgences and penitential practice in general, the cross as an unmistakable symbol of commitment to the *negotium Christi*, were all very familiar. Dózsa's rebels clung to them, albeit somewhat selectively, even after their crusade had formally been cancelled and they themselves had been outlawed. Others could not, or did not wish to do so. The purpose of this chapter is to investigate the means by which the identification of a military venture with God's will and purpose was demonstrated and expressed in such circumstances. Where could authority be located, and how could its sanction best be proved and depicted in order to sustain conviction and keep morale high?

4.1 TEXTS

God's will was expressed in holy writ, and the role of certain key texts and their exegesis was therefore crucial. More than in the Islamic tradition of holy war, scriptural explication played a major role throughout the history of religious

---

[6] *UB* ii. 273, no. 793. [7] Housley, 'Explaining Defeat', *passim*.
[8] 'Z bratislavské schůzky', 187.

warfare in Christian communities, not least because the texts themselves were so malleable in nature. As David Martin put it, 'Islam does not need to reinterpret the eschatological text "Compel them to come in" when it is perfectly able to deliver that message without equivocation. In Islam the *double entendre* of Christianity is rendered otiose.'[9] As we observed in Chapter 1, Michael Walzer's analysis of the very different ways in which Exodus 32 was interpreted from Augustine to Calvin could be replicated in the case of a large number of major biblical passages relating to war. The plasticity of such texts is not in question: what we need to address is the role of changing circumstances in making certain texts more valuable than others. Granted that it is no longer acceptable to deny historicity in the exegesis of major texts, is it any more reasonable to adopt the 'instrumentalist' position which relegates those texts to the status of camouflage for a stance which was taken up for political, social, or economic reasons?[10]

First and foremost there is chiliasm, the anxious expectation of a millenarian age of bliss to be enjoyed only by God's chosen few, and ushered in by their destruction of the wicked. Timing and mandate both had to be addressed: how could it be known that Christ's return was imminent, and what was the warrant for preceding his return with bloodshed? For the first issue the most important text was naturally Revelation, with the emphasis lying on the identification of the various protagonists. But scarcely less revered were the Old Testament prophets such as Daniel. Daniel 7, in which the prophet dreamed of four great beasts which symbolized four earthly monarchies, was a favourite of the Habsburgs: Jorg Breu the Younger painted a dishevelled-looking Daniel expounding it to an attentive Charles V while imperial troops fought their opponents in the background.[11] But Daniel 2: 31–45 received no less attention than Daniel 7.[12] These verses describe the prophet's interpretation of Nebuchadnezzar's dream about a monstrous image in terms of a succession of five earthly kingdoms, culminating at verse 44 with the prophecy that following the destruction of the fifth kingdom, 'the God of heaven will set up a kingdom that shall never be destroyed, nor shall this kingdom be left to another people'.

The chapter was the subject of one of the most famous sermons preached during the Reformation, when Müntzer interpreted it before Duke John of Saxony and his Lutheran son John Frederick at Allstedt in July 1524.[13] Before

[9] Martin, *Does Christianity Cause War?*, 198 and cf. 112–13.

[10] For example, Deppermann, *Melchior Hoffman*, 340, comes close to adopting this approach when he comments that 'No one can say how many "pacifist" Anabaptists would have taken up arms if an uprising in one of the Dutch towns had had anything like the success of that in Münster.'

[11] M. Tanner, *The Last Descendant of Aeneas: The Hapsburgs and the Mythic Image of the Emperor* (New Haven: Yale University Press, 1993), 144–5.

[12] U. Andermann, 'Geschichtsdeutung und Prophetie. Krisenerfahrung und -bewältigung am Beispiel der osmanischen Expansion im Spätmittelalter und in der Reformationszeit', in Guthmüller and Kühlmann (eds.), *Europa und die Türken*, 29–54, at 40–1.

[13] *The Collected Works of Thomas Müntzer*, 226–52.

coming to Daniel and the dream Müntzer surveyed the degeneration of Christianity since the early church, comparing the 'wretched, ruinous condition of the poor Christian Church' in his day with that of Israel as described by 'the good prophets Isaiah, Jeremiah, Ezekiel, and the others'. He took issue with the assertion of mainstream theologians that the predictions of the Old Testament prophets could not be 'read'. On the contrary, Müntzer asserted, 'this text of Daniel . . . is as clear as the bright sun'. The first four kingdoms could be identified as those of the Babylonians, the Medes and Persians, the Greeks, and the Romans. As for the fifth, its mixture of iron and clay clearly pointed to the Catholic church, eager to use the coercive power of the sword to suppress dissent but frustrated by 'the vain schemings of hypocrisy, which swarms and slithers over the face of the whole earth'. With the Reformation the church's power was already challenged, 'and the work of ending the fifth Empire of the world is now in full swing'.

Daniel 2 was an important text also for those addressing the second issue associated with chiliasm: that of how, and by whom, the job of physical destruction was to be achieved. Daniel had foretold the smashing of Nebuchadnezzar's great image by a stone which was not fashioned by human hands (Daniel 2: 45). For those chiliasts who rejected the use of violence, the key point was that the stone was not made by human hands. This revealed that the job of destruction should be left to God, acting perhaps through the Turks. For activists, on the other hand, the stone was a metaphor for God's agents in bringing down the corrupt fifth kingdom and ushering in the Golden Age. For Müntzer the obvious identification was with the forces of the radical Reformation. He cited Psalm 44 and 1 Chronicles 14: 11 as proof that God acted through his chosen agents: 'they [sc. the Israelites] did not win the land by the sword, but by the power of God, but the sword was the means used, just as eating and drinking is a means for us to stay alive. Hence the sword, too, is necessary to eliminate the godless.'[14] The divine mandate to kill the godless was clear from such varied texts as Deuteronomy 13: 5 ('You shall purge the evil from your midst'), Exodus 22: 18 ('You shall not permit a female sorcerer to live'), and Romans 13: 4 ('The authority does not bear the sword in vain. It is the servant of God to execute wrath on the evildoer').

As for the question of agency, the Allstedt sermon of July 1524 is fascinating in part because it shows Müntzer at a point of transition. He still hoped that the Lutheran princes would act in accordance with Pauline doctrine as God's servants, but he was fully prepared to threaten them with deposition, should they refuse to institute radical religious change. Then the sword would pass to those prepared to carry out God's will, 'the poor laity and the peasants', as foretold by Daniel 7: 27: 'The kingship and dominion and the greatness of the kingdoms under the whole heaven shall be given to the people of the holy ones of the Most High.' A particularly striking feature of this sermon is Müntzer's use of Romans

---

[14] Ibid. 250.

13: 4. A text which so easily became an injunction to obedience was for him a lever on the Lutheran princes. Those who failed to use the sword to carry out God's will would forfeit it.

Despite these warnings, which interestingly do not seem to have offended Duke John and John Frederick, the Allstedt sermon is relatively restrained as a summons to war. It is instructive to compare it with one of Müntzer's most famous letters, in which he called his former parishioners at Allstedt to arms in late April 1525.[15] The context was the burgeoning revolt of the Common Man, and the language bordered on the hysterical: 'Go to it, go to it, while the fire is hot! Don't let your sword grow cold, don't let it hang down limply! Hammer away ding-dong on the anvils of Nimrod, cast down their tower to the ground!'[16] The scriptural underpinning is essentially what it had been some months previously in the sermon at Allstedt: 'The whole business', Müntzer conveniently explained, 'can be read up in Matthew 24, Ezekiel 34, Daniel 7, Ezra 16, Revelation 6, and all these texts are explained by Romans 13.' For the most part these are chiliastic references, which is not surprising given that Müntzer's belief in the imminence of a radical transformation had strengthened during the intervening months. The most interesting citation is that of Romans 13, showing that even at this moment of crisis Müntzer's mind was on the problem of how God's will was to be translated into practice. Ezekiel 34, with its forthright condemnation of the bad shepherds, was quoted several times by Müntzer in his last letters, as he came to associate religious with social change.[17]

In the case of Müntzer's contemporary Melchior Hoffman, a much more significant development of ideas may be viewed. Indeed, if we add to Hoffman's own views the writings of his follower Berndt Rothmann, the chief theologian of the kingdom of Münster, we can see a movement in three stages. Hoffman's biographer Klaus Deppermann showed that Hoffman had a clear perception of the imminent Second Coming by 1525. Alarmed by the iconoclasm which he had witnessed in Livonia, and by the outbreak of the Peasants' War, he adhered to a passive view of human agency: 'For Christ does not shine forth where there is malice, hatred, division, anger or rebellion; the sun has set there and there is no light.'[18] But it was in his exegesis of Daniel 12, published in 1526, that his views were set out at length. This was a complex scenario for the apocalypse most notable for the precise timing accorded to the two phases of events, an overall timing of seven years derived from figures in Daniel 12 and Revelation 11 and 12. In neither phase were the elect themselves to take up arms. Even in the second phase, when they would be persecuted by two hostile rulers (Duke George of Saxony and King Sigismund of Poland), and assailed by the forces of Gog and Magog, they were to rely on favourable rulers, in true Lutheran style, for protection.[19]

[15] *The Collected Works of Thomas Müntzer*, 140–2.
[16] Ibid. 142.   [17] Ibid. 142, 156, 157 and n. 1212, 158–9.
[18] Deppermann, *Melchior Hoffman*, 62.   [19] Ibid. 72–8.

Between 1529 and 1533 Hoffman gradually adopted a more radical stance on the coming apocalypse. In the first place, his reading became still more specific: the city of Strasburg, where he had taken up residence in June 1529, was designated as the New Jerusalem. It would have to be defended against a siege conducted by Charles V. 'God is telling us that in the utmost extremity she [sc. Strasburg] should raise the banner of divine justice, namely the eternal son of righteousness. This must first be proclaimed here.'[20] Following the repulse of the Emperor, the 144,000 apostolic messengers of Revelation 14: 3 would go out from Strasburg to establish a millennial kingdom which would last until the delayed Last Judgement. Although the Anabaptists, the elect, were now identified with Strasburg and promised the earth as the reward for their suffering, they were still not to fight themselves. The most they could do during the imperial siege of Strasburg was auxiliary tasks such as digging trenches and carrying out guard duty.[21] What had led Hoffman to develop his views? It may have been the Turkish failure at Vienna in 1529, which caused him to doubt that the Ottomans were powerful enough to act as God's agent in breaking the back of the corrupt regime. More importantly, he had become convinced that the 'Strasburg prophets', who included the extraordinary visionaries Lienhard and Ursula Jost, were channels of God's will and that the Anabaptists should inherit and rule over the purged earth while awaiting Christ's return.

The third stage in the development of Hoffman's ideas occurred at Münster. Here Hoffman's template was given a decisive twist by a combination of eschatological ripening, political success, and military pressure. Although Hoffman himself had revised his eschatological timetable, there was a wave of apocalyptic expectation in the Netherlands in the autumn and winter of 1533–4 which brought about many conversions to Anabaptism. The Anabaptist seizure of Münster led Berndt Rothmann to devise his own eschatological schema. Rothmann was no mean theologian: he was respected by the early reformers and his chief works on behalf of the Anabaptist regime at Münster, *Restitution* and *Von der Wracke* (both 1534), were exegetically sophisticated treatments of eschatology.[22] As we saw in Chapter 3, both works were smuggled out of Münster during the siege to try to persuade fellow-Anabaptists of a Hoffmanite persuasion to come to relieve the city; so Rothmann had to tackle the issue of timing head on. He candidly admitted his own volte-face: 'around the time we were baptized we all laid down our weapons and prepared ourselves as a sacrifice. It was our opinion that it would not be proper to resist the godless except in accepting suffering, and death itself, with patience.'[23] But this view had changed

---

[20] Klaasen (ed.), *Anabaptism in Outline*, 329.

[21] Deppermann, *Melchior Hoffman*, 262, draws an interesting comparison with the cathar *perfecti* and *credentes*.

[22] *Die Schriften Bernhard Rothmanns*, *passim*. See also J. M. Stayer, 'The Münsterite Rationalization of Bernhard Rothmann', *Journal of the History of Ideas*, 28 (1967), 179–92; M. Brecht, 'Die Theologie Bernhard Rothmanns', *Jahrbuch für Westfälische Kirchengeschichte*, 78 (1985), 49–82.

[23] Quoted by Stayer, 'The Münsterite Rationalization of Bernhard Rothmann', 180.

when the Münster Anabaptists perceived themselves to stand at a critical point and time in sacred history. Rothmann's eschatological schema was a clever combination of Joachimism and Daniel 2.[24] The Reformation proved that the corrupt fourth kingdom described by Daniel, that of the Romans, had been over-thrown and the third *status* had begun. What James Stayer termed 'a speculative numerology' drawn from God's punishment of Israel in 1 Kings 17 and the Babylonian captivity was deployed to confirm this reading, but it was unques-tionably the sheer sense of urgency provoked by the Reformation and the seizure of power at Münster which instilled conviction in Rothmann and, we can assume, his fellow-believers within the city. 'Such knowledge could belong only to the last days.'[25]

Not only were scriptural injunctions towards passive suffering related to the second *status* and now redundant, but the millennial theocracy's defenders bore the responsibility of acting as God's purgative agents. Christ would not return until his enemies had been killed. The defence of Münster itself was only the be-ginning. 'It has pleased [the Lord] that we and all true Christians should not now limit ourselves to fending off the power of the godless through the sword. He also wants to give the sword into the hand of his people to take revenge on every-thing that is unjust and bad throughout the entire world.'[26] Rothmann empha-sized the importance of the prophets Isaiah, Jeremiah, Ezekiel, and Daniel in outlining his view of the arrival of the millenarian age.[27] In the overturning of Hoffman's views about the non-violent role of the elect, perhaps the two most important texts were Ezekiel 9 and Revelation 7. Both texts signalled the all-important role of baptism in distinguishing the elect from the doomed. In Ezekiel 9 the prophet foretold God's vengeance on the people of Jerusalem, car-ried out by six men with 'slaughter weapons' who proved to be pitiless in their work. The only people spared were those who lamented the sinfulness of the age, and these were marked on the forehead by a scribe who preceded the execution squad. In Revelation 7 God's four avenging angels similarly spared those who were marked on their foreheads. The number spared, 144,000, was viewed as highly significant at Münster: during the siege discussion took place as to how this number could be accommodated when they arrived in the New Jerusalem, preparatory to their conquest of the world.[28]

A century before Müntzer, Hoffman, and Rothmann sought scriptural an-swers to these central questions of timing and mandate, it is possible to observe the Taborite chiliasts confronting the same issues. Like the radical reformers, they read the signs of the times as indicating the onset of the Last Days and the imminent return of Christ. But their initial response, during the eventful winter of 1419–20, was flight from evil. There were more than enough scriptural ex-

[24] Deppermann, *Melchior Hoffman*, 342–8.
[25] Stayer, 'The Münsterite Rationalization of Bernhard Rothmann', 187.   [26] Ibid. 192.
[27] *Die Schriften Bernhard Rothmanns*, 355.   [28] Stayer, *Anabaptists and the Sword*, 265.

hortations to the elect that they should distance themselves physically from those who were soon to be subjected to God's wrath. Isaiah 52: 11 ('Depart, depart, go out from there! Touch no unclean thing'), Revelation 18: 4 (' "Come out of her, my people, so that you do not take part in her sins, and so that you do not share in her plagues" '), and Jeremiah 51: 6 ('Flee from the midst of Babylon, save your lives, each of you! Do not perish because of her guilt, for this is the time of the Lord's vengeance'), were amongst the passages cited in adventist letters. Other texts were more specific. Amos 9: 10 warned of the fate awaiting those who were laggardly, Matthew 19: 29 sanctioned the abandonment of family and hearth, and, above all, Isaiah 19: 18 pointed to five cities as places of refuge for the elect.[29] The transition from this mood of anxious fatalism to one of holy war conducted against the godless was crucial to the development of Tabor. We have already seen that it remains highly problematic.[30]

To start with, it is striking that the same books of Scripture were used to support the change: Matthew 24: 6 ('And you will hear of wars and rumours of wars'), Isaiah 30: 32 ('battling with brandished arm [the Lord] will fight with him'), and Revelation 17: 14 ('they will make war on the Lamb, and the Lamb will conquer them') were amongst the passages cited in support of what Kaminsky termed 'a new, adventist theory of warfare sanctioned by the requirements of the Day of Wrath'.[31] At first sight this looks like clear evidence for the mere instrumentality of Scripture. It was said at the time by Peter Chelčický, and has been repeated since by Marxist historians, that the very foundation of the military Tabor at Hradiště established a new centre of power which was bound to fight wars.[32] Given Tabor's origins in the ferment of 1419, it was also predictable that initially these conflicts would be couched in chiliastic ideology. From this viewpoint, the Taborite reinterpretation of the meaning of the stone in Daniel 2 was straightforward: they simply turned a few pages of their bibles to find verses which enabled them to switch from flight to persecution. But this would be unwarrantedly cynical, and a closer look at some of the sources reveals a more satisfying explanation for the volte-face.

A key passage was Matthew 24: 28, 'Wherever the corpse is, there the vultures will gather.' The corpse or body was Christ's, and given the Hussites' close identification with the eucharist, the association between the *congregatio fidelium* and godly warfare which the verse can be seen as establishing was bound to strike a chord once Tabor was built. With the elect assembled, there was an ineluctable tendency to turn to warfare given that the chiliastic engine was still running. In adventist terms, the circle was squared through the ingenious argument that Christ had already returned secretly, in accordance with 1 Thessalonians 5: 2,

---

[29] Kaminsky, *History*, 311–16; Machilek, 'Heilserwartung und Revolution der Täboriten', 82.

[30] Above, Ch. 2 at nn. 15–16. See also H. Kaminsky, 'Chiliasm and the Hussite Revolution', *Church History*, 26 (1957), 43–71.

[31] Kaminsky, *History*, 320, 323.   [32] Ibid. 321–2, 341.

'the day of the Lord will come like a thief in the night'. In this situation, it would be an act of disobedience to God not to carry out his command to destroy his enemies and expand the Taborite *seigneurie* through compulsory migration and the seizure of the belongings of the wicked, which were forfeited to God's chosen agents. As Lawrence of Březová put it in his list of Taborite doctrines:

Further: that the Taborite brethren at this time of vengeance are angels sent to lead the faithful out of their cities, towns, and castles into the mountains, like Lot out of Sodom, and that the brethren and their supporters form that carcass to which, wherever it should be, the eagles will gather, and of which it is also written: 'Every place on which you set foot shall be yours' [Deuteronomy 11: 24]. For they are the army despatched by God throughout the entire world, to remove all scandals from Christ's kingdom, which is the church militant, and to expel the wicked from the bosom of the just, and to exercise painful vengeance on those nations which oppose Christ's law, overturning their cities, towns, and fortified places. And that in this time of vengeance there shall remain in the whole of Christendom just five cities, where the Lord's faithful must flee and seek refuge, all the rest perishing exactly like Sodom.[33]

What these examples teach us is the importance of holding a balance between a dehistoricized view of the use of Scripture, and one which emphasizes circumstance to the exclusion of all else. Certainly we need to bear in mind contexts. For example, without economic dislocation on a massive scale to stimulate migration from the west, the Anabaptists would not have been able to seize power at Münster; and without the existence of an impoverished lesser nobility to provide leadership, Tabor would not have established its *seigneurie*.[34] But within those contexts there took place a dialogue between Scripture and the needs of those who were anxiously reading it. On this point a comparison between the views of Hans Hut and Berndt Rothmann is instructive. Hut was as ready as Rothmann to embrace the use of the sword in carrying out God's will for his creation: when subjected to interrogation in 1527 he produced a flow of scriptural passages mandating violence. But all was contingent on timing: 'a Christian may well have a sword but . . . it must remain in the scabbard until God tells him to take it out.'[35] Hut's position was well characterized as 'interim nonresistance'.[36] For Rothmann, some seven years later, the 'day of wrath' after which he named his most bloodthirsty polemic had arrived: like the Taborites, he viewed his fellow-Anabaptists as themselves forming the body of angels who must carry out vengeance in God's name.[37] They were the stone in Daniel 2: 45. It is quite wrong to say that Rothmann was reaching for scriptural texts to justify his response to the situation of crisis which the Anabaptists faced at Münster: that situation had come about in large part because of the way these texts constantly weighed on the minds of such men. Though they were sometimes selective and tendentious,

[33] LoB, 'De gestis', 399–400.   [34] Cohn, *Pursuit*, 259–60; Šmahel, *La Révolution hussite*, 42–5.
[35] Klaasen (ed.), *Anabaptism in Outline*, 273.   [36] Ibid. 266.   [37] Ibid. 335.

they did not deliberately distort: for example, they displayed a serious concern that the needs of the hour should be justified in terms of both the Old and the New Testament.[38]

In the case of chiliasm Scripture played a crucial role in providing authority, and for this reason religious warfare conducted 'in pursuit of the millennium' can be described as 'holy war': in the eyes of the perpetrators the violence was not only mandated by God, it was purgative and cleansing, which meant that it was released from any of the normal constraints on war. The celebration of violence which took place in these contexts was a chilling experience, as the horrified re-action of the Hussite centre towards Taborite chiliasm shows well. The tracts of one leading chiliast, Jan Čapek, were described as being 'more full of blood than a fish-pond is of water'. Howard Kaminsky argued that 'the new violence was in-deed religious violence, orgiastic and ritualistic as well as practical in character, for its purpose was to purge the world in preparation for the "consummation of the age", and its sanction lay in the new situation created by Christ's secret com-ing, which had annihilated all traditional guides to behavior'.[39] But this removal of constraints was also short-lived, as Tabor again clearly demonstrates: in Chapter 6 we shall see how far the religious establishment at Tabor, deeply eschatological though it remained, moved from the chiliast position regarding the day-to-day conduct of war.

The situation was very different in the case of two other types of religious war in which Scripture played a part. One was the broad range of conflicts in which a *gens* or *natio* was depicted as the *populus electus*, its leaders as God's captains, and its territory as sacred soil. The emphasis in this case was heavily on the books in the Old Testament which described the Israelites' flight from Egyptian captivity and their conquest of Palestine. The Psalms were a treasure house of exhorta-tions to rely on God's help in defending the sacred, as well as of eulogies of Jerusalem. Typically, during the victory celebrations for Agincourt in October 1415 the mock castle constructed at Cheapside was adorned with a quotation from Psalm 87: 3 which equated Henry V's capital with Jerusalem: 'Glorious things are spoken of you, o city of God.'[40] But the Books of Maccabees were also cited because of the pleasing clarity with which defence of both *patria* and *fides* were associated in them. It was not at all surprising that during the debates which occurred in Bohemia in the winter of 1419–20 about the validity of defending the *lex Dei* with arms, the radicals favoured the public exposition of the Books of Maccabees.[41] In these instances, however, Scripture's role was embedded within conceptions of authority, historical traditions, and iconographic representa-tions, which together provided a rich stew of collective myth.[42] It became sup-portive rather than, as in the case of chiliasm, fundamental; a buttress rather than a foundation.

---

[38] Deppermann, *Melchior Hoffman*, 241–3.   [39] Kaminsky, *History*, 347.
[40] *Gesta*, 108.   [41] Kaminsky (ed.), 'Treatises', 528.
[42] See above all Beaune's magisterial study, *The Birth of an Ideology*.

Conversely, for those espousing a radical reform of belief, and facing military opposition, it was the group of classic passages in the Gospels, Acts, and Epistles relating to the legitimate use of violence by Christian leaders and communities which came to the forefront of attention. This applied above all to the Hussite and Protestant centre, as opposed to their chiliastic left wings. By 1400 these passages had already been subjected to almost a millennium of exegetical commentary, not least in the context of crusading apologetics. And as in the case of crusading, the just war framework provided an invaluable template for the discussion. What is most striking in the stance of Prague University Masters like John of Příbram and Jakoubek of Stříbro during the polemical debates of 1419–20 is the way they adhered to the classic criteria of the Christian just war, proper authority, just cause, and right intention. This was, very largely, a scholastic debate, and it is not hard to see why. In an atmosphere of dangerous instability, it enabled the Hussite Masters to forge a justification for the defence of the *causa Dei* by reference to such eminently respectable reference points as Gratian's Causa 23, Augustine's *Contra Faustum*, and above all, Romans 13.[43]

A century after the Prague debates, this mode of scholastic argument was looking decidedly old-fashioned. Erasmus' famous demolition of the scholastic treatment of Luke 22: 35–8, the curious passage in which two swords make an appearance at the Last Supper, was typical of the way the northern European humanists assailed the traditional exegetical treatment of texts which appeared to offer avenues into religious war, avenues which they condemned on the grounds that they traduced Christ's essential message of peace.[44] As Erasmus put it in *Dulce bellum inexpertis* (1515), one of his most savage attacks on war, 'Why should I be more impressed by the writings of Bernard or the arguments of Thomas than by the teaching of Christ?'[45] But the essential foundations of just war theory were another matter: the justice of a cause, the right of certain authorities to bear the sword in God's name, and the frame of mind of the combatants, were so deeply rooted in Christian thinking that they became central within Protestant ideology. Just war thinking was therefore able, to a remarkable degree, to transcend the confessional divide. And when the cause was perceived as holy too, it became relatively easy to move into the sphere of religious war. James Turner Johnson has argued that the hegemony enjoyed by just war thinking ousted the rationale for holy war;[46] I would rather propose that within a providential thought world it facilitated the depiction of a conflict as religious by making the conceptual leap less daunting. In terms of debates on the legitimacy of warfare, and its scriptural underpinning, the Reformation made much less of an impact than one might imagine: where the impact came, as we shall see in the

[43] Kaminsky, *History*, 513–14; Kaminsky (ed.), 'Treatises', 521–2, 527–8, 545; Seibt, *Hussitica*, 16–57.

[44] 'Moriae encomium', trans. B. Radice, ed. A. H. T. Levi, in *CWE* xxvii. 77–153, at 145–6.

[45] *Erasmus on his Times: A Shortened Version of the 'Adages' of Erasmus*, ed. and trans. M. Mann Phillips (Cambridge: Cambridge University Press, 1967), 107–40, at 130.

[46] Johnson, *Holy War Idea*, 11.

Conclusion, was in the establishment of new religious collectivities which pursued their military goals with heightened urgency and excitement.

4.2 FIGURES

Warfare and rebellion called for leadership, and when the violence was perceived in religious terms there was a natural tendency to 'messianize' these leaders. In this respect, above all, a divergence between the mainstream and the subversive or radical becomes apparent. For some leaders were in office, typically as emperors, kings, or popes, while others were either thrown up by the occasion or had seized power and were seeking to define and legitimize their role. Those in the first category found it much easier to conceptualize their position. Not only were they operating within a much more stable environment, but they enjoyed access to well-established traditions and structures of communication to disseminate their role. A telling example is Rodrigo Ponce de León's circulation amongst the Castilian high nobility of commentaries affirming the messianic status of Fernando of Aragon in 1486.[47] Problems arose when a divergence existed between messianic expectation and the policies which they prioritized, or when a widespread acceptance of their messianic role was not matched by a readiness to provide the financial and other support needed to fulfil it.[48]

We have seen that this tendency to bestow messianic status on those in power occurred most distinctively within the Joachimist pattern of thought, and particularly in relation to the roles of 'Last Emperor' and 'Angelic Pope'. What was expected may be approached through two of the more familiar sources. The first of these is the famous prophecy of Guilloche de Bordeaux for Charles VIII of France. Guilloche wrote of the king's early campaigns against rebellious French princes, culminating in a general pardon. At the age of 24 he would invade Italy and subjugate all his enemies. Rome would be conquered and Florence, 'the city of sin', would be destroyed. The evil clergy would be killed and all would be brought into obedience to the pope. Charles, now crowned as king of the Romans despite German opposition, would campaign overseas and receive a third crown, that of king of the Greeks. Victories over the Muslims would follow and a programme of forcible conversion to Christ would be carried through. Charles would bring justice to all and attain lordship over the entire earth. The culmination of this glorious reign would be his entry to Jerusalem. 'En Jhérusalem entrera et mont Olivet montrera.' There he would deposit his three crowns before dying at the age of 53.[49]

---

[47] Milhou, *Colón*, 236–8.

[48] e.g. the interesting exchange across the dinner table between Pope Nicholas V and Frederick III in 1452: Reeves, *Influence of Prophecy*, 335.

[49] C. de Cherrier, *Histoire de Charles VIII roi de France*, 2 vols. (Paris: Didier, 1868), i. 487–90. See also Labande-Mailfert, *Charles VIII*, 189, 218.

The second source is the Spanish romance *Incitamiento y conducta contra el Gran Turco a toda la Cristiandad*, which was written in celebration of Charles V's messianic role. As Juan Sánchez Montes observed, this is a highly inclusive text, which draws on Charles's universalist pretensions to make the Joachimist agenda a pan-Christian one. Charles's army would include *de buenos jinetes* from Jerez, archers from England, and soldiers from France; 'even in Ireland they will arm themselves'. It would also be socially inclusive: nobles, farm workers, and merchants alike would flock to the standards. So too would eastern Christians, for 'all the nations from the land of Prester John will appear'. With this vast if motley force Charles would conquer a wide array of lands, including the three Armenias, Arabia, Egypt, Syria, and the Indies. But his goal, as in the case of Charles VIII, would be Jerusalem, the 'Casa santa' of the Iberian Joachimist tradition. 'Once this has been achieved, Don Carlos will be embraced by the Cross which God sent us to embrace, on the same hill where Christ at the ninth hour was [nailed] to die.'[50]

The value of Joachimism, and of prophecy in a more general sense, in providing interpretative frameworks is illustrated well by Christine de Pisan's exuberant celebration of Joan of Arc's early successes, the *Ditié de Jehanne d'Arc*. As we saw in Chapter 2, it was possible to assimilate the overall 'freight' of Joan's mission into familiar thinking about the Covenant which the kingdom of France and its ruling dynasty enjoyed with God.[51] Joan's personal role, however, was more problematic: she could be compared with Moses, Joshua, and Gideon, or with Hector and Achilles, but the main point of such comparisons was to emphasize that Joan equalled or surpassed them all. Biblical heroines such as Esther, Judith, and Deborah did not lead armies as Joan was doing. Later commentators found it disconcertingly hard to place Joan: one scholar has recently drawn attention to the palpable sense of relief with which Robert Ciboule discovered in Alexander of Hales a comment to the effect that Deborah had worn masculine clothes and carried arms: 'Quod Deborah utebatur veste virili et armis militaribus ad expugnandos inimicos . . .'[52] For contemporaries like Christine this mattered less, for the wonder of victory was sufficient, 'a l'effect la chose est prouvée'.[53] But even Christine was eager to point out that Joan's mode of conduct had been prophesied by Merlin, the Sibyl, and Bede; and more importantly, to emphasize that her function was to facilitate Charles VII's accomplishment of his divinely attributed agenda. Thus she would lead him as far as Jerusalem: 'She will put paid to the Saracens by conquering the Holy Land. There she will lead Charles, whom God preserve! He will make that journey before he dies. He is the one who must

---

[50] Sánchez Montes, *Franceses, Protestantes, Turcos*, 106–8.   [51] Above, Ch. 2, at nn. 128–31.

[52] F. Michaud-Fréjaville, 'Jeanne d'Arc, *dux*, chef de guerre: Les Points de vue des traités en faveur de la Pucelle', in J. Paviot and J. Verger (eds.), *Guerre, pouvoir et noblesse au moyen âge. Mélanges en l'honneur de Philippe Contamine* (Paris: Presses de l'Université de Paris-Sorbonne, 2000), 523–31, esp. 531.

[53] *Ditié*, 33, *huitain*, 29.

conquer it. There she is destined to end her days, and both of them will acquire glory. That is where it will all end.'[54] In other words, Joan was the divinely ordained assistant of an ex officio messianic ruler: a role which closely paralleled that which Milhou concluded Columbus saw himself as holding.[55]

A vocabulary and world-view rooted in Joachimism undoubtedly helped a good deal in investing monarchs with a religious role which elevated their wars to a sacred plane. But they were far from forming a *sine qua non* for the process. Operating within the context of the 'elect nation', contemporaries of Henry V, above all the anonymous author of the *Gesta Henrici Quinti*, depicted him as God's champion, leading a Chosen People to victory over those who had offended divine justice. Indeed, under Henry, and probably with his active encouragement, the English tradition of sanctified national feeling, which had overtaken the French one as the most bullish and assertive in Europe, attained its medieval high-water mark. It is not surprising that Henry VIII, wishing to revive English patriotic feeling and bolster loyalty to himself, viewed the reign of his predecessor with approval and sponsored an updated life in English.[56]

Some radical leaders, riding a wave of popular unrest and vulnerable to the loss of support, naturally sought to bolster their position by reference to role models. Within the Joachimist pattern of apocalyptic thinking, this was easiest in Spain, with its remarkable inversion of the 'Last Emperor' in *El Encubierto*, a revolutionary leader who would bring about social justice as well as leading a crusade to regain Jerusalem. One anonymous individual made good use of this tradition when he seized power at Játiva during the *Germanías* uprising in 1522. The case was an extraordinary one. *El Encubierto* proclaimed himself to be the champion of the poor and the enemy of the unjust rich and corrupt clergy. The viceroy of Valencia, who was directing the suppression of the *Germanías*, was, he declared, one of two antichrists, the other being Charles V himself. But both would be defeated and a millennial reign of peace and justice would ensue. So powerful was the role that even after this individual had been assassinated, two other men claimed to be the *Encubierto*. Judging by the ferocious response of the authorities, the figure had enormous latent power.[57]

Why did this millenarian role model prove so attractive in Valencia, whereas in neighbouring Castile, also in rebellion at this point, and no less open than Valencia to apocalyptic anxieties and hopes, it was left unused? Sara Nalle has suggested two answers. One was that the Castilian *Comuneros* was generally a more conservative revolt than the *Germanías*. The *Comuneros* did not espouse the redistribution of goods, nor did they experience the excitement which occurred in Valencia when Alamany's *la venguda de Antichrist*, with its redistributive-cum-apocalyptic message, was republished in late 1520. Nalle's other suggestion was that 'Castilian eschatological speculation tended to be more religious in

---

[54] Ibid. 36, *huitain*, 43.   [55] Milhou, *Colón*, 286, 447–8.
[56] Allmand, *Henry V*, 432–3.   [57] Nalle, 'The Millennial Moment', *passim*.

nature and was not explicitly political'. Indeed, the 'conjuncture of conditions' which produced the Játiva *Encubierto* of 1522, in the shape of the radical currents in Valencia and the Catalan-Aragonese federation's receptivity towards subversive Joachimism, proved short-lived.[58]

Outside Iberia Joachimism did not generate a subversive tradition of any strength and radical leaders experienced more difficulty in conceptualizing their position convincingly within a religious framework. Some did not try. György Dózsa described himself as 'leader (*princeps*) of the blessed tribe of the *cruciferi*, supreme captain and subject of the king of Hungary, though no subject of the lords', a title which nicely encapsulates the fudged position adopted by his army in relation to secular authority in Hungary.[59] We shall see later that the really radical interpretation of Dózsa's leadership came not from him but from his triumphant opponents. Jan Žižka, who had much longer to contemplate his role than György Dózsa, was similar. He never tried to move beyond titles which simply expressed his position of supreme command within the Taborite and later the Orebite community. Both men, of course, were primarily field commanders: released from dependence on charisma or prophetic credentials, they had no real need to tap into a tradition like *El Encubierto*, even had one existed.[60]

Jan Bockelson's position at Münster was a particularly interesting case, since he skilfully moved from a position of power which was charismatic and prophetic, lasting from his arrival late in 1533 to September 1534, to one of institutionalized kingship as a New David. We have enough detail on Bockelson's view of his monarchic role, embedded within the admittedly hostile narrative of Herman Kerssenbrück, to allow us a clear picture of this most dramatic of millennial rulers. The seizure of power was engineered by Bockelson through an ally, the Warendorf goldsmith Johann Dusentschur, who announced at the start of September 1534 that he had experienced a vision in which God had 'revealed to me and told me to announce to you that Jan Bockelson of Leiden, man of God and holy prophet, is to be king throughout the world. He will hold power over emperors, kings, princes, and all earthly powers; he will exercise the supreme magistracy, with no superior. He will occupy the sceptre and throne of David, his father, until God the Father demands the kingdom back from him.'[61]

The sword was then taken from the Elders of Zion, who had ruled the city throughout the summer, and assigned to Bockelson, 'to subdue the peoples of the earth, and to enable you to render an account to Christ when he returns in Judgement'. Dusentschur then anointed the new king with the words 'At God's

[58] Nalle, 'The Millennial Moment', 165, 171.
[59] Fekete Nagy et al. (eds.), *Monumenta rusticorum*, no. 79.
[60] Heymann, *John Žižka*, 15, 486–9; Fudge, *Magnificent Ride*, 124–5, 152–3.
[61] *Hermanni A. Kerssenbroch . . . historica narratio*, 634–5.

command I anoint you king of the New Temple and the people of God, and pro-nounce you king of New Zion before the entire people.' It was, Bockelson re-minded his subjects, all in accordance with 1 Samuel 16: 'In the same way God commanded through his prophet that David, a humble shepherd, should be se-lected and anointed as king in Israel. Our heavenly father often works in this way, and anybody who stands in the way of his will, calls down on himself his divine wrath. Power has been vested in me over all the nations of the globe, and the use of the sword, to terrorize the wicked and defend the good.'[62]

Grafting Bockelson's Davidic commission onto a theology of millennial vio-lence was not particularly hard: it was achieved by Rothmann in the tracts which he wrote during the last months of 1534 to attempt to mobilize support for the Münster Anabaptists in the neighbouring Low Countries. Rothmann's theology did not depend on Bockelson's new status, but the idea of a New David was per-fectly compatible with the apocalyptic excitement engendered, as we saw earlier, by an eschatological reading of contemporary events. All that was needed was to cast Christ in a pacific, quasi-Solomonic guise rather than a bellicose Davidic one. The latter role could then be assigned to Bockelson: he was Christ's precur-sor, charged with carrying out his vengeance in preparation for his Second Coming. 'See! The throne of David must be re-established, the Kingdom pre-pared and armed, and all the enemies of Christ humbled by David. Then the peaceful Solomon, the eternal king and anointed God, Christ, will enter and pos-sess the throne of his father, David, and his Kingdom shall have no end.'[63] Bock-elson fitted the role well, and not just because he had once been a play-actor; he had slain his Goliath through his brilliant defence of the city in August 1534. His status was acceptable, even if the actual transfer of power in early September was blatantly stage-managed. So during the final months of Anabaptist power in Münster Bockelson ruled his New Jerusalem as a monarch, with a full set of regalia which was to fascinate contemporaries for years to come, and Münster was prepared for the Second Coming with a control so rigorous that it belied the idea that chiliastic enthusiasm naturally tended towards anarchy.[64]

For different reasons, the case of Thomas Müntzer is as revealing as that of Jan Bockelson. Müntzer's main problem was that he fitted Machiavelli's famed category of the 'unarmed prophet', a man with an urgent mission who lacked an army. As Müntzer moved between a series of formats for mobilizing force, he cast himself in a number of guises to emphasize his own role. Sometimes it was purely a matter of imagery, 'a willing courier of God', 'a disturber of the unbe-lievers', 'a servant of God', and 'a servant of God against the godless'.[65] At other

[62] Ibid. 637.

[63] Stayer, 'The Münsterite Rationalization of Bernhard Rothmann', 191, and see too n. 68.

[64] G. Vogler, 'The Anabaptist Kingdom of Münster in the Tension between Anabaptist and Imperial Policy', in Hillerbrand (ed.), *Radical Tendencies in the Reformation*, 99–116, at 108–10.

[65] *The Collected Works of Thomas Müntzer*, 54, 67, 70, 142.

times his conviction of the strength of his personal credentials and his close identification with the Old Testament prophets led him to adopt a more dramatic guise: he was Elijah, Jeremiah, Daniel, and John the Baptist.[66] But it was the signature on his last letters to his opponents, written in May 1525, which tells us most about Müntzer's self-perception: 'Thomas Müntzer with the sword of Gideon'.[67] Müntzer's personal identification with the widespread purging of society which his aggressive theology demanded was total. But he lacked a biblical model which would give adequate and credible expression to that identification. His reversion after capture to the simple signature 'Thomas Müntzer' therefore evinced, as Matheson put it, 'the collapse of his mission'.[68]

4.3 SYMBOLS AND COMMUNITIES

The importance of Scripture in proving the consonance of warfare with God's will and purpose has always been apparent. However, it is only recently that historians have grasped the significance of symbols in reflecting and consolidating belief that such consonance existed.[69] The visual representation of these signs of authority did far more than simply remind combatants of what they were doing as individuals. Together with songs, they sustained group morale and instilled a sense of common purpose. To deploy a common phrase, the whole became more than the sum of its parts. As it was put by the narrative source for the miraculous incident with which we began this chapter, '[the Hungarian *crucesignati*] all resolved to stand or fall together'.[70] But this went beyond mere group cohesion. From it authority could flow, conviction itself being enhanced by experiencing the commitment of others. In this respect the analysis of religious belief cannot help but learn from the psychology of group behaviour and the dynamics of popular movements.[71]

The Dózsa uprising again provides much food for thought, but before looking at it we should refer to its remarkable predecessor, the crusade of 1456 recruited and led by Giovanni da Capistrano. His crusaders used the *nomen Jesu* both as a battle cry and as a slogan. The latter emerges constantly from Giovanni da Tagliacozzo's acount of the campaign, above all in the long passage in which he depicted the revivalist atmosphere which prevailed in the crusaders' camp. Amidst the heightened piety, the charity and penitential zeal, the sense

---

[66] *The Collected Works of Thomas Müntzer*, 246, 300, 371; R. L. Petersen, *Preaching in the Last Days: The Theme of 'Two Witnesses' in the Sixteenth and Seventeenth Centuries* (New York: Oxford University Press, 1993), 60–1; Stayer, *Anabaptists and the Sword*, 76–89.

[67] *The Collected Works of Thomas Müntzer*, 151, 156–7.

[68] Ibid. 5. See also R. Bailey, 'The Sixteenth Century's Apocalyptic Heritage and Thomas Müntzer', *Mennonite Quarterly Review*, 57 (1983), 27–44.

[69] Housley, 'Insurrection as Religious War', 152–3.

[70] Fekete Nagy et al. (eds.), *Monumenta rusticorum*, no. 227, p. 316.

[71] In particular, the distinction between internalization and behavioural compliance is a useful one: Millward, 'Social Psychology 2', 369–70.

of order and discipline, he noted 'the frequent proclamation of the name of Jesus'.[72] In battle the Turks shouted the name of Muhammad, the crusaders that of Jesus. Victory showed above all the virtue of 'the most holy name of Jesus and his most sacred cross'. The Turks were not just filled with terror by the chanting of the name, they were literally felled and killed by its power, 'as if by javelins hurled from heaven'.[73] The battles of the ancient Israelites were thus re-enacted in southern Hungary, Capistrano himself, in a letter to the pope on 23 July, attributing his strategy to Joshua: 'more than anything else, I had repeatedly encouraged and exhorted our army, acting like Joshua in the ruins of Jericho, that when I acclaimed and invoked the most holy name, they were all to shout "Jesus" as loudly as they could. And so they did.'[74] Even if a good deal of what Giovanni da Tagliacozzo says is exaggerated, the fact remains that Capistrano hit upon a brilliant way of compensating for his troops' anxiety, inexperience, and makeshift weaponry by bolstering their morale and, at the same time, undermining that of the enemy.

The reason why the ambience of 1456 is relevant to that of 1514 is that on both occasions it was the Franciscan Observants who preached the crusade and imbued it with their distinctive spirituality. As we saw at the start of the chapter, Dózsa's beleaguered and disorientated *crucesignati* responded to the withdrawal of official church support for their crusade by stressing their direct contact with Christ. It is likely that this only emphasized a Christocentric response which had been present since the crusade was first preached by the Observants, some of whom remained with the *crucesignati* throughout the campaign. Repudiation and condemnation by both church and state, in a manner which came close to philoturkism, paradoxically reinforced a remarkable sense of community focused on a shared devotion to Christ. So far as we can see, little changed from 1456; the *crucesignati* even repeated the use of the *nomen Jesu* as a battle cry. For this devotion the cross prominently worn by all naturally served as a constant reminder. It seems likely that its importance as a uniform was greater than in 1456 because Dózsa's crusaders were confronted not by an enemy instantly recognizable as such through their clothes and weapons, but by their fellow-countrymen. In August 1514 George of Brandenburg's chaplain Matthias Künisch wrote a graphic description of how he had assumed the cross to escape detection and death when surrounded by *crucesignati* in the Maros valley at the height of the revolt.[75] Rarely in crusading history had the cross itself played such a conspicuous role as in 1514. But the cross provided much more than identification: it fashioned a powerful and defiant sense of community, one formed of elect individuals who believed themselves to be blessed. In the so-called Cegléd proclamation, a short document which forms the nearest thing we have to a rebel manifesto, this claim is insistently repeated. The *cruciferi* formed a 'blessed people', a 'holy gathering', and a 'sacred band and blessed assembly'.[76] In the

---

[72] Giovanni da Tagliacozzo, 'Relatio', 765.   [73] Ibid. 786.   [74] Ibid. 797.
[75] Fekete Nagy et al. (eds.), *Monumenta rusticorum*, no. 179.   [76] Ibid., no. 79.

near-contemporary account of the uprising by György Szerémi, the phrase *sancta crux* recurs constantly.[77]

This proved deeply unsettling for the Hungarian authorities, not least because of the sympathy which the *cruciferi* enjoyed amidst the population at large. When Bakócz tried to turn the crusade upside down by granting indulgences to anybody who would take up arms against the rebels, friars who attempted to preach this message in Buda's mendicant churches of St John and St Nicholas were threatened with violence by their enraged congregations: 'for the past twenty years the lords and nobles have [supposedly] been arming themselves; it is all villainy. Nobody should take up arms against people wearing the cross.' [78] An ideological as well as a military response was called for. From mid-May onwards, when Cardinal Tamás Bakócz called off the crusade in response to news of disturbances, the authorities were able to deny the status of the rebels as crusaders and on occasion (though not invariably) they did this. Sometimes this status was rhetorically turned against the insurgents, as when the nobles of a group of ravaged counties referred to them as 'the accursed and most wicked crucifiers who called themselves *cruciferi*, but who were really persecutors of Christ's name'.[79]

Events moved quickly, and once the revolt had been suppressed it was more important to take legislative measures to stop another one occurring than to rake over the ashes of what had happened. In fact it is in the method chosen to execute Dózsa near Temesvár in July 1514 that the shock inflicted on the authorities can be seen at its most powerful. Dózsa was compelled to sit on a red-hot 'throne' and a burning 'crown' was placed on his head. His closest followers, who had been starved for twelve days, were then forced under penalty of death to bite into his burning body and to drink his flowing blood. This execution may be construed as the predictable finale in a revolt characterized by extreme cruelty on both sides, and there were precedents, both Hungarian and otherwise, for each of its grisly elements. But as described and portrayed by contemporaries, on whom it made a deep impression, the ensemble is inescapably reminiscent of the torment and crucifixion of Christ. It is hard to escape the conclusion that Dózsa's enemies, who planned it all with great care, were passing a comment on the nature of the rebellion. Given the fact that the man they were killing had led an army of *cruciferi* permeated by strong Christocentric devotion, his death in this manner cannot have been coincidental. Marianna Birnbaum has pointed out no fewer than ten 'convergencies' between the Dózsa Passion and that of Christ.[80] She

[77] György Szerémi, 'Epistola de perdicione regni Hungarorum', in G. Wenzel (ed.), *Monumenta Hungariae historica*, vol. i (Pest: Magyar Tudományos Akadémia, 1857), at 58–70.

[78] Fekete Nagy et al. (eds.), *Monumenta rusticorum*, no. 227. See too my 'Crusading as Social Revolt', 23–4.

[79] Fekete Nagy et al. (eds.), *Monumenta rusticorum*, no. 73, and my 'Crusading as Social Revolt', 13–15.

[80] Birnbaum, 'A Mock Calvary in 1514?', 102–4.

concluded that there was no clear way to 'read' the execution. Obviously it was far from the intention of the executioners to establish a straightforward parallel between Dózsa and Christ. There were elements of carnival (the whole procedure was accompanied by music, singing, and dancing), of sardonic juridical comment, and perhaps too of ritual purging. 'Purpose and structure remain unreconciled: the social ambivalence inherent in Dózsa's persona and in the crusade's final outcome could not be fitted into the unidirectional framework of Christ's Passion.'[81]

Both dreadful and bizarre, Dózsa's death was a fitting end to a sequence of events which had throughout reflected the inverted and unstable condition of social and political relations in Hungary at this point. According to one modern historian, the very word 'crusade' was banned in Hungary after 1514.[82] As it approached its decisive encounter with the Turks, a kingdom whose rulers loudly proclaimed its status as Christendom's leading *antemurale* was thus denied access to a principal source of help. This was ironic and profoundly contradictory. For some contemporaries Mohács was not only Dózsa's revenge in a military sense, but in a providential one too: the whole of Hungary was paying the price for the treachery committed by its ruling elite. György Szerémi clearly saw the betrayal of the broad mass of the *cruciferi* by their lords as mirrored in the experience of Dózsa, who was promised his life by the vaivoda János Zápolyai but was then callously tortured to death. 'Behold, reader, the destruction of the faith (*fides*) of the Hungarians.'[83]

Within any context related directly or indirectly to crusading, the power of the cross and associated sacred symbols is undeniable. This was what fuelled the fear of Thomas Cromwell that the Pilgrimage of Grace might be transformed into a much more dangerous phenomenon by the distribution of badges of the Five Wounds at Pontefract Castle.[84] Just a few years before the Dózsa revolt, the author of a classic text of subversive Joachimism, the 'Book of One Hundred Chapters', described a sequence of apocalyptic violence in which the Archangel Michael would decree the formation of an association of bearers of a yellow cross, 'so that the words of our Savior may be fulfilled: "There shall be one flock, one shepherd"'. These *crucesignati* would have a purgative role: 'Whoever wants to join in punishing the wicked, let him take the yellow cross and raise his voice in songs of praise.' But, like the followers of El Encubierto in Alamany's *La venguda de Antichrist*, they would also have a more traditional task to fulfil; following a King Frederick, they would march to liberate the Holy Land. 'He will bear the

---

[81] Ibid. 107–8.
[82] Göllner, *Turcica*, iii. 71; C. Göllner, 'Zur Problematik der Kreuzzüge und der Türkenkriege im 16. Jahrhundert', *Revue des études sud-est européennes*, 12 (1975), 97–115, at 108. No supporting evidence is given.
[83] Szerémi, 'Epistola de perdicione regni Hungarorum', 69.   [84] Above, Ch. 3 at nn. 44–5.

yellow cross on his breast and lead a vast throng of men to reconquer the Holy Land.'[85]

The crusading context to these predictions, which were woven into a remarkably complex and idiosyncratic pattern, was a twofold one. On the one hand, the author noted at the start that 'three unclean men, the pope, the emperor, and the king of France, will wake the dragon—that is to say the Turk—from his sleep. Gruesome wars will be waged, and thousands will die. And God will cause stones to fall from the sky, and these will destroy us with fire and blood.'[86] This reference to the league of Cambrai (1508) and its apocalyptic meaning points to an interpretation of the anti-Turkish conflict which we shall explore in the next chapter. More interesting is a brief autobiographical reference in chapter 25, when the author reveals that when he was 18 he received the cross from Giovanni da Capistrano. During the fighting at Belgrade he witnessed a miracle, 'a sign from God in the heavens, a golden cross hovering above us'. The crusaders, who had been in flight at that point, rallied and with just 10,000 men killed 600,000 Turks. Nearly half a century after the events of July 1456, key elements of the campaign, its Christocentric devotion, religious excitement, and social radicalism, thus fed into the views expressed in this sprawling 'eve of Reformation' tract.[87]

But once one moves away from a context in which crusade figured, actually or (as in 1536) potentially, the power of the cross as a symbol becomes much more problematic. Several examples will illustrate this. Johann Herolt commented that the rebels in the German Peasants' War of 1524–5 wore white crosses 'as their sign, symbol, and password', while their opponents in the Swabian League displayed red ones.[88] Much the same situation arose just a few years later when the defenders of the last Florentine republic wore white crosses in opposition to the red ones worn by the imperialist besiegers.[89] In the Pilgrimage of Grace the members of the Bowes Host originally adopted a black cross as their symbol. Men fighting in the royal army customarily wore red crosses, and during a skirmish with the duke of Norfolk's men one member of the Bowes Host was mistaken for an opponent and accidentally run through with a spear. As a result the badge of Five Wounds and the Name of Jesus became alternatives as new identifying signs.[90] All three instances point towards a scenario in which crosses, even when coloured red like those of crusaders, could simply act as uniforms, as in-

---

[85] Strauss (ed.), *Manifestations of Discontent*, 234–47, esp. 234–6, 246. For the complete text see *Das Buch der Hundert Kapitel und der vierzig Statuten des sogenannten Oberrheinischen Revolutionärs*, ed. A. Franke and G. Zschäbitz (Berlin: Deutscher Verlag der Wissenschaften, 1967), with these passages at 181, 375.

[86] Strauss (ed.), *Manifestations of Discontent*, 235.

[87] *Das Buch der Hundert Kapitel*, 257. See also Cohn, *Pursuit*, 119–26.

[88] G. Franz (ed.), *Quellen zur Geschichte des Bauernkrieges* (Darmstadt: Wissenschaftliche Buchgesellschaft, 1963), no. 135, p. 417.

[89] Roth, *The Last Florentine Republic*, 193 and cf. text at 217 n. 43. See too J. N. Stephens, *The Fall of the Florentine Republic 1512–1530* (Oxford: Oxford University Press, 1983), 219.

[90] Bateson (ed.), 'Aske's Examination', 571–2; Bush, *Pilgrimage of Grace*, 182.

deed they had throughout the Hundred Years War. In the same year as Dózsa's uprising, English lords tourneying at Paris sported red crosses 'to be known for love of their country'.[91] Crosses, Five Wounds badges, the Name of Jesus: all contained latent power, but it had to be released, through the pressure of circumstances, charismatic preaching, or, as Cromwell feared in 1536, by deliberate attempts to bring to the foreground traditional associations which might otherwise be overlooked. It is striking that this was the case even in 1529, when there was an atmosphere of heightened religiosity amongst the die-hard defenders of Florence, and a Christocentric devotion of some power.[92]

One incident during the Swiss wars against the Habsburgs illustrates this point particularly well. In 1443 the *Eidgenossen* were at war with Zurich, which had thrown in its lot with the Habsburgs in the hope of making territorial gains. Customarily *Eidgenossen* wore a white cross as their uniform and the soldiers fighting for Zurich a red one.[93] But the *Eidgenossen* won a notable victory by the ruse of sporting their opponents' red cross on their chests while wearing their own white cross on their backs. After the war an anonymous Austrian poet bitterly bewailed the defeat. God, his angels, and all the saints were called on to avenge this affront to Christendom; the pope and all the prelates should give out indulgences for fighting against the *Eidgenossen* ('der babst und all prelaten sond aplass darumb geben'). Otherwise all Christian belief and obedience could soon come to an end. There should in fact be a crusade against the *Eidgenossen*, and one scholar has analysed the song as a *Kreuzlied* comparable to others against the Hussites and Turks.[94] In these circumstances the trickery with the crosses should surely be centre stage if the symbolism had any inherent resonance: instead it was passed over briefly and with no clear religious reference. 'It is of the despicable men of Schwyz that I wish to sing to you, | They sported two crosses at Zurich on the Sihl, | White behind and red in front, | That landed the pious men of Zurich in a really desperate plight.' What offended the poet much more were other alleged crimes of the *Eidgenossen*: first their use of the disembowelled entrails of Zurich's commander, the Bürgermeister Rudolf Stüssi, to make shoes, and secondly, their destruction of churches, including the stored sacrament. The first was labelled heretical ('das ist ein ketzerliche tat'), the second a disgrace ('ist der christenheit ein schand'). No such rhetoric was used in respect of the crosses.[95]

[91] S. Gunn, 'The French Wars of Henry VIII', in J. Black (ed.), *The Origins of War in Early Modern Europe* (Edinburgh: John Donald Publishers Ltd., 1987), 28–51, at 34.

[92] Above, Ch. 3, at nn. 101–5.

[93] G. P. Marchal, 'De la "Passion du Christ" à la "Croix Suisse": Quelques réflexions sur une enseigne suisse', in M. Comina (ed.), *Histoire et belles histoires de la Suisse: Guillaume Tell, Nicolas de Flüe et les autres, des chroniques au cinéma* (Basle: Schwabe, 1989), 107–31.

[94] U. Müller, 'Ein Zürich-Habsburgisches Kreuzlied gegen die Eidgenossen. Beobachtungen zur Kreuzzugslyrik des späten Mittelalters', in H. Wenzel (ed.), *Adelsherrschaft und Literatur* (Bern: Peter Lang, 1980), 259–86.

[95] Liliencron (ed.), *Die historischen Volkslieder der Deutschen*, ii. 392–4, no. 81.

There are reasons for emphasizing this point. In an article on the relationship between the crusade against the Turks and the conflict between the *Eidgenossen* and Burgundy, Claudius Sieber-Lehmann argued that 'Obviously in the area controlled by the *Eidgenossen* and on the Upper Rhine we are dealing with a secularized crusade (*säkularisierten Kreuzzug*) which is undertaken from 1474 onwards against Charles the Bold, "the Turk of Burgundy". It is no coincidence that the anti-Burgundian "crusaders" on the Upper Rhine and in the *Eidgenossenschaft* wear white crosses in 1474–1477.' Sieber-Lehmann demonstrated that there were indeed rumours of a genuine crusade against Charles in the spring of 1475; but there is no evidence that the white crosses worn by the anti-Burgundian forces were anything but coincidental.[96] For the *Eidgenossen* the colours of the crosses displayed did acquire significance: they came to associate the red cross so closely with their enemies that their priests refused to celebrate mass before it; and the cult of St George, which was closely linked with the red cross, became unpopular in Switzerland.[97] But for this very reason it is important to be as precise as possible in establishing the associations of such symbols.

And yet, when approached from a rather different direction, the formation of national consciousness among the *Eidgenossen* throws much light on the role of semiotics. A striking feature of Swiss piety at the end of the fifteenth century was the common practice of praying with arms outstretched, often described as 'publica brachiorum expansio per modum crucis', or 'beten mit "zertanen Armen"'. There was nothing inherently unorthodox in the practice: it had a long history in private devotion as a way of associating oneself with Christ's suffering and its public use had been permitted to the people of Lucerne by papal decree in 1479 and extended to Basle in 1502.[98] But for the enemies of the *Eidgenossen* it was an arrogant assertion of exceptionalism, the exact equivalent in devotional terms of their wilful and damaging political claims. Quite rightly they saw it as a means of consolidating commonality in a group which was slowly expressing a national identity. In 1504 the Dominican Johannes Winckel took issue with it and in the following year the Alsatian humanist and reformer Jakob Wimpfeling treated the subject in a tract entitled the *Soliloquium pro pace christianorum et pro Helvetiis ut resipiscant*. As Guy Marchal showed, the gist of Wimpfeling's case was that the Swiss position rested on the erroneous belief that since God had so constantly supported their cause (*judicium belli*), they were exempt from obeying the universally accepted criteria of a just war (*bellum iustum*). This belief that, as Winckel had put it, 'We are that Chosen People whom the people of Israel pre-

[96]   Sieber-Lehmann, '"Teutsche Nation" und Eidgenossenschaft', 600.

[97]   G. P. Marchal, 'Stigmatisierungskonzept und Semiotik: Annäherungen an die eidgenössische Selbstpräsentation um 1500', in *Schwaben- oder Schweizerkrieg. Ereignis und kollektive Identität*, forthcoming. I am grateful to Prof. Marchal for sending me a copy of this paper.

[98]   P. Ochsenbein, 'Beten "mit zertanen armen": Ein alteidgenössischer Brauch', *Schweizerisches Archiv für Volkskunde*, 75 (1979), 129–72; Marchal, 'De la "Passion du Christ" à la "Croix Suisse"', 121 (ill. no. 8).

figured, and whom Almighty God defended against kings and princes as the observers of his law and justice',[99] was embedded in such singular practices as praying with outstretched arms. The Swiss would 'return to their senses' if they rejoined both the political community, by ending their resistance to Habsburg authority, and the religious community, by conforming with mainstream Catholic devotional practices.[100]

In more recent studies Marchal has pursued this subject further. When they rebelled against the Habsburgs the *Eidgenossen* were guilty of a twofold scandal: they rejected lordship, and with it the functional three-order scheme so beloved of medieval social thinking, and they rejected the overarching authority of the Holy Roman Empire. Isolated and vulnerable, they located in their extraordinary run of military successes a means of establishing their legitimization; their appropriation of a special place in God's favour, while fitting the general pattern outlined in Chapter 1, was therefore particularly strident. It included a range of unusual devotional practices, not just praying with outstretched arms, but also a focus on Christocentric piety (especially the Five Wounds of the Passion) which was extreme even for the late Middle Ages. Wimpfeling was correct to identify the links between these practices and the identity of the *Eidgenossen*, for when cities like Basle joined the confederation they pointedly embraced the former. The *Eidgenossen* even distinguished between 'their' God, *der alte Gott*, and 'the God of Austria'. The religious distancing of their enemies could go no further short of assertions of 'turkification'.[101]

Symbols like crosses, or for that matter devotional practices like praying with outstretched arms, might or might not matter; it depended on whether an interaction took place with the dynamics and psychology of the community which embraced them. That interaction can clearly be viewed occurring in the embryonic Switzerland. It does not appear to have taken place in Florence in 1529, and even in the case of Hungary in 1514 the evidence is hardly overwhelming since the revolt was swiftly suppressed. Richest and most convincing is the evidence relating to the Hussite conflict. Like the *Eidgenossen*, the Hussite community was formed around religious values: indeed the assertion of exceptionalism quoted above, which Johannes Winckel put into the mouths of the *Eidgenossen*, could have been voiced word for word by the Hussites. But the Hussite example is inherently more interesting than the Swiss one because, for all their opponents'

---

[99] P. Ochsenbein, 'Jakob Wimpfelings literarische Fehde mit den Baslern und Eidgenossen', *Basler Zeitschrift für Geschichte und Altertumskunde*, 79 (1979), 37–65, at 54 n. 57.

[100] G. P. Marchal, 'Bellum justum contra judicium belli. Zur Interpretation von Jakob Wimpfelings antieidgenössischer Streitschrift "Soliloquium pro Pace Christianorum et pro Helvetiis ut resipiscant . . ." (1505)', in N. Bernard and Q. Reichen (eds.), *Gesellschaft und Gesellschaften. Festschrift Ulrich Im Hof* (Bern: Wyss Verlag, 1982), 114–37.

[101] G. P. Marchal, 'Die Antwort der Bauern: Elemente und Schichtungen des eidgenössischen Geschichtsbewusstseins am Ausgang des Mittelalters', in H. Patze (ed.), *Geschichtsschreibung und Geschichtsbewusstsein im späten Mittelalter* (Sigmaringen: Jan Thorbecke, 1987), 757–90; Marchal, 'Stigmatisierungskonzept und Semiotik', *passim*.

attempts to tar them with the heretical brush, the *Eidgenossen* remained thoroughly orthodox, while the Hussites departed from the Catholic church and faced its soldiers again and again on the battlefield.

As Thomas Fudge showed in a fine analysis of the Hussites' iconography, the Czechs had a whole range of sacred symbols and figures to place in opposition to their cross-bearing opponents.[102] First and foremost was the chalice. Lawrence of Březová referred to the Hussites as 'enthusiasts for communing with the chalice', and he narrated how the people of Prague resolved 'to oppose king [Sigismund]'s might in the name of God for the truth of communing with the chalice until their goods and bodies were exhausted'. Following the arrival of the Taborites in Prague in May 1420 to defend the city against the crusaders, he described how 'their priests preached the word of God to them every day, encouraging the people to fight for God's Law, and in particular for communion with the chalice. Devoutly they ministered to them the body and blood of the lord Jesus, in order that they would be constantly prepared and eager for God's war (*Dei bellum*).'[103] Lawrence reported that after the Hussite victory on the Vítkov many people renamed it Chalice Hill, 'because there the enemies of the chalice were laid low by those who fought with God's help on its behalf, and who displayed the sign of the chalice in red or in white on their clothing, arms, and standards'.[104]

The constant depiction of the chalice on surviving evidence makes it clear that it was central to the thinking of the Hussites. It was even painted on tiles baked during the period of the Hussite wars.[105] Above all it featured a good deal in the Jena Codex, a remarkable repository of Hussite visual ideas, albeit dating from the later fifteenth century.[106] In one battle scene in the codex a gold chalice appears on a large red banner.[107] For such roles the chalice was ideally suited. It was a straightforward symbol, easily reproduced, and it unfailingly communicated the single most important demand of the Hussites. For the 'warriors of God' in particular, the taking of communion in both kinds before joining battle served a multitude of purposes: it expressed community of belief, prepared them spiritually for death, and strengthened their sword arm. On the other hand, for those with time to ponder on it, the symbol acted as a key, unlocking a whole programme of ecclesiological reforms centring on a radical new conception of the Christian community. Veneration for the chalice was particularly strong in the case of Jan Žižka. A castle near Litoměřice which he seized from the Teutonic Knights in 1421 was defiantly renamed Chalice Castle (*Kalich*), and Žižka started calling himself 'Jan Žižka of the Chalice'. He also adopted the symbol for his coat of arms and seal.[108]

---

[102] Fudge, *Magnificent Ride*, chs. 3–4 *passim*.   [103] LoB, 'De gestis', 362–4.   [104] Ibid. 379.
[105] J. Kejř, *The Hussite Revolution*, trans. T. Gottheinerová (Prague: Orbis Press Agency, 1988), 18, 28, 78, 98.
[106] Drobná, *The Jena Codex, passim*.   [107] Fudge, *Magnificent Ride*, 246.
[108] Ibid. 163–4; Heymann, *John Žižka*, 218–19, 488–9, 491, 493.

Two other Hussite symbols are striking. One is the goose, standing for Jan Hus (*hus* means goose in Czech), and regularly depicted in visual evidence. A manuscript drawing preserved at Tabor shows a Taborite warrior carrying his battle flail over a shoulder on which the chalice is prominently drawn, with a goose tucked into his belt. The goose may be booty, depicting the legitimate seizure of food to sustain a warrior fighting for God's Law; but it also represents the sustaining teaching and example of Hus. On another picture a goose drinks from a chalice, thus bringing together in homely fashion the movement's initiator and its chief demand.[109] The other symbol is the representation of the blind Žižka. Following his death in 1424 Žižka shared prime place with Hus in the Hussite pantheon. The 'Very Pretty Chronicle' claimed that 'the people of Hradec Králové ordered Žižka to be painted on their banner, mounted on a white horse, in knightly armor, holding his battle club, as he looked when he was alive. And whenever the people of Hradec Králové went into battle under this banner, they were invincible.'[110] In what Thomas Fudge termed 'an exceptional propagandist statement', the Jena Codex even depicted Žižka as the heavenly key-holder in place of St Peter.[111]

This pseudo-cultic veneration of Hus and (to a lesser extent) Žižka invites comparison with the contemporary cults of 'national' saints like St George in England, St Denys or St Michael in France, and the Virgin Mary at Siena.[112] Effectively the Hussites' response to their condemnation by the papacy and the assault on their homeland by the crusaders was to establish an alternative community of belief. Interesting recognition of the radical nature of this response came from Sigismund. In his extraordinary tirade against the people of Prague in 1420, the king sarcastically remarked that the Hussites were abandoning long-established cultic practices at the same time that they were taking it upon themselves to inscribe Hus and his fellow-martyr Jerome of Prague in the catalogue of saints, 'whose feasts you solemnly celebrate, forgetting about the feasts of other saints'.[113] Judging from a letter of complaint which the canons of Catholic Olomouc sent to the council of Constance, the feast days of the two men were being celebrated as early as 1416.[114] In his *Historia bohemica* Aeneas Sylvius Piccolomini later wrote that the Hussites had listened to Wenceslas Koranda and Jakoubek of Stříbro 'as if they were Apostles of Christ, or angels sent from the sky'.[115] In the same way that the appropriation of saints for particular ethnic or political groups delineated, and emphasized, those groups without

---

[109] Fudge, *Magnificent Ride*, 127, 147–8.   [110] 'Very Pretty Chronicle', 10.
[111] Fudge, *Magnificent Ride*, 247, ill. on 248.
[112] S. Riches, *St George: Hero, Martyr and Myth* (Stroud: Sutton, 2000), 101–39; Beaune, *The Birth of an Ideology*, 20–69, 152–71; B. Kempers, 'Icons, Altarpieces, and Civic Ritual in Siena Cathedral, 1100–1530', in B. A. Hanawalt and K. L. Reyerson (eds.), *City and Spectacle in Medieval Europe* (Minneapolis: University of Minnesota Press, 1994), 89–136.
[113] *UB* ii. 523–5.   [114] Fudge, *Magnificent Ride*, 129.
[115] Piccolomini, *Historia bohemica*, ch. 1.

transgressing orthodox Catholic belief, so the more extreme step of venerating Hus and Žižka displayed defiance but, more importantly, expressed resolve and commonality of purpose. So too of course did the chalice, but without the humanity and the resonances of martyrdom (Hus) and victory (Žižka) which reference to the two men could create. Interestingly, the Catholic response to Žižka's renaming of his fortress in northern Bohemia as 'Chalice' was to name its Catholic neighbour 'Virgin', thereby bringing to bear the power of Catholicism's most distinctive cult.[116]

Also important was the projection of the Hussite cause in songs. Thomas Fudge summed up their role well: 'The function of popular songs assumed at least four roles: a form of witness, sign of solidarity, polemical device and expression of militarism.'[117] The great Hussite battle song 'Ye warriors of God' has long been praised for its combination of morale-boosting encouragement and exhortation to sound discipline. Ironically, its religious message was more in tune with traditional crusading theology than with the core tenets of Hussitism: no mention is made of the chalice, yet John 15 : 13 ('No one has greater love than this, to lay down one's life for one's friends'), a text beloved by crusaders and their apologists, is referred to in the third verse.[118] 'Children, let us praise the Lord', Jan Čapek's song of 1420 celebrating the battle of the Vítkov, admirably expressed Čapek's belief that song possessed, in Molnár's words, 'a cultic function in terms of holy war'.[119] Other songs were more dogmatic in content: one set out the historical basis for infant communion.[120] Probably nothing expresses and reinforces group feeling more clearly than songs, but they were just one of a whole range of comparatively new genres which worked towards that end, others being polemical satires, newsletters, and manifestos, all of course written in Czech.[121]

The sense of community achieved over almost two decades in Hussite Bohemia was not replicated elsewhere, and it is hard to see how it could have been, given its deep territorial and ethnic roots. But it is visible at times, and two contrasting examples may be offered. The first is the defence of Anabaptist Münster, especially during the six months between February 1534, when non-Anabaptists were expelled from the city, and Bockelson's assumption of monarchical power in September 1534, when the new regime of terror and favouritism proved destructive of feelings of collective identity. In April 1534, following the

---

[116] Heymann, *John Žižka*, 372.   [117] Fudge, *Magnificent Ride*, 210.
[118] Heymann, *John Žižka*, 497–8.
[119] Molnár, 'L'Évolution de la théologie hussite', 149. Song itself in Heymann, *John Žižka*, 140 n. 10; Fudge, *Magnificent Ride*, 203.
[120] Fudge, *Magnificent Ride*, 205–6.
[121] Bylina, 'Le Mouvement hussite', 60; Hruza, 'Die hussitischen Manifeste', *passim*; F. Šmahel, 'Reformatio und Receptio: Publikum, Massenmedien und Kommunikationshindernisse zu Beginn der hussitischen Reformbewegung', in J. Miethke (ed.), *Das Publikum politischer Theorie im 14. Jahrhundert* (Munich: Oldenbourg, 1992), 255–68.

bizarre death of Jan Matthys in a suicidal charge at the enemy, Bockelson persuaded the Anabaptists to abandon the city's constitution in favour of one modelled on the custom of Ancient Israel. Twelve Elders would rule the New Zion, guided by Bockelson himself in his capacity as prophet. The new constitution resonates with a conviction of divine election in which Old Testament continuity is fused with exclusive claims to true Christian status. The Anabaptists were consistently described as Israelites, Münster was 'a holy city', and they formed a *communitas Christi*. Thus clause seven of the constitution prescribed that 'whatever the Elders by common counsel decree as useful in this new state of Israel (*in hac nova Israhelis republica*) will be announced and expounded to the community of Christ and the whole company of Israel by Jan van Leyden, the prophet, acting as a faithful minister of God and of the holy magistracy'.[122]

The fifty-three ordinances established in April 1534 together form a remarkable document. Detailed and restrained, they 'reveal a secure sense of community and of organization, independent of theology', as Anthony Arthur put it.[123] Yet theology exerted its impact indirectly, for what sustained the sense of community was the constantly reiterated claim that this was 'the company of Christ' (*Gemeinde Christi*). Writing to their besiegers at this point, the Elders were perfectly capable of adopting a tone of pained indignation that this peaceful city had been subjected to a siege: 'Our wish is to enjoy not just peace but also brotherly love with all men. So what reasons can you set before God-fearing men (not to speak of God himself) for the fact that you are subjecting us to this violent and murderous siege, contrary to all written and accepted laws and without a declaration of war?'[124] This was conveniently to ignore the apocalyptic excitement of the previous winter, and the expulsion of non-Anabaptists which had taken place just a few weeks previously.[125] The cast of mind behind the latter was well expressed in the words attributed to Jan Matthys, which are soaked in the language of contamination and purging: 'The will, decree, and command of the Father is this: that unless they consent to being baptized again, the impious, who incessantly impede our pious endeavours, must be expelled from the city. Let this holy city be purged, for God's people is contaminated by contact with the impious. Drive out therefore the sons of Esau! For this place, this holy city, this mansion, this inheritance, is reserved for the sons of Jacob and the true Israelites!'[126] No less telling was the response of the Anabaptists to Matthys's call to arms: ' "Be gone from here, you impious people, and do not come back. Be off, enemies of the Father! Go away, disturber of all that is good, leave us alone! The Father's altar must be purged, the wicked seed expunged lest the sound corn be ruined.

---

[122] *Hermanni A. Kerssenbroch . . . historica narratio*, 582–6, with quote at 582.

[123] Arthur, *The Tailor-King*, 78.

[124] *Hermanni A. Kerssenbroch . . . historica narratio*, 586–8, with quote at 586.

[125] For a different view see Stayer, *Anabaptists and the Sword*, 235 (esp. n. 25), 238–9.

[126] *Hermanni A. Kerssenbroch . . . historica narratio*, 536, and cf. Matthys's earlier demand for the slaughter of non-Anabaptists, 532–3.

This is our inheritance, given to us by the Father!"'[127] Earlier, in language reminiscent of the First Crusade, Berndt Rothmann had described Münster as 'the New Jerusalem, the New Zion, the true Temple of Solomon', a prosperous city where Anabaptist immigrants, in joining their fellow-elect, would find earthly wealth as well as a heavenly treasure.[128] For a brief period some did, before they were overtaken by what James Stayer has described as the 'dreary "war communism"' of Bockelson's bedraggled Davidic kingdom.[129]

The inherent tension between the disorder generated by apocalyptic excitement and the desire to establish cohesion within a collectivity which perceived itself as sacred is well illustrated in Münsterite polygamy, introduced in July 1534 and destined to shock contemporaries even more than common ownership of goods. At first sight it looks like an example of a community shaking off the shackles of social order, continuity, and normality in the heady expectation of a decisive millennial turning point. But Ronnie Po-chia Hsia has suggested that the practice was at heart an attempt to instil order by giving the many unattached women, in a city where they far outnumbered men, a social position, albeit one which cut across accepted norms of behaviour. In his words, it was intended to create 'a fictive tribe, a chosen people, the "New Israel", a holy nation for a sacred city'.[130] Polygamy, in other words, arose from the particular circumstances in which the *Gemeinde Christi* found itself: certainly the imminent end released the 'New Israel' from former social constraints, just as it mandated setting aside their former quietism, but much more important was the need to give the elect a way to function effectively as a collectivity in the mean time. In his study of covenanting ideas, Donald Akenson defined six features of the 'covenanting mindset'. These were an emphasis on social law, enforced through religious congregations; a sharp and uncompromising view of the enemy; a militant presiding deity; the sacralization of territory; the motif of Exodus to a promised land; and the setting of great store by group purity.[131] All were present at Münster, and they had the effect, for a few months, of creating a cohesive and galvanized community.

The Anabaptists of Münster were nothing if not apocalyptic; the uskoks of Senj, on the other hand, left no traces of chiliastic belief, and the clarity of their self-image shows that a community believing itself empowered to pursue religious warfare did not have to be defined in eschatological terms. As we saw in Chapter 1, the dominant ideological theme amongst the uskoks was that they manned an *antemurale Christianitatis*.[132] Their raids against the Turks and their Christian subjects were, in their eyes, part of an unending war in defence of the faith. Venice and even Ragusa, which was tributary to the Turks, were expected

---

[127] *Hermanni A. Kerssenbroch . . . historica narratio*, 536.   [128] Ibid. 508–9.
[129] Stayer, 'Christianity in One City', 134.
[130] R. Po-chia Hsia, 'Münster and the Anabaptists', in R. Po-chia Hsia (ed.), *The German People and the Reformation* (Ithaca, NY: Cornell University Press, 1988), 51–69, at 60.
[131] Akenson, *God's Peoples*, 42.   [132] Above, Ch. 1, at nn. 57–9.

to adhere to this creed. Nothing took precedence over it, including Senj's allegiance to the Austrian Habsburgs. So the Captain at Senj commented, undoubtedly with some exaggeration, in 1542, that 'My king can command me to do whatever His Majesty pleases, but if he orders me not to harm the infidels, and to give back that which I have taken and intend to take whenever and wherever I can, I would rather lose my head than obey him.'[133]

The religious war conducted by the uskoks did not hinge on the interpretation of particular passages in Scripture, or on the leadership of messianic figures. It was rooted in popular features of the crusading tradition with which they were doubtless made familiar from the pulpit: in veneration for St George, key figure in Senjian iconography, and in the use of the battle cry 'Jesus! Jesus!', which they shared with the Hungarian crusaders of 1456 and 1514.[134] The most important way in which *antemurale* ideology affected their behaviour was through the inevitable debates about what constituted licit plunder: in a sense, who stood before and who behind the defensive ramparts they were defending. The 'foundation stone' of their *antemurale* thinking was the papal ban on trade with Muslims in war supplies and associated goods, encapsulated in the bull *In coena domini*, which was publicly recited every year by the bishop of Senj.[135] A rough and ready code concerning its application to Christians was devised and uskoks who transgressed it were ostracized or punished. But as Wendy Bracewell has emphasized, conflicts of interpretation were bound to arise and 'necessity and ideology were constantly balanced against each other'.[136]

4.4 CONCLUSION

Dependence on an *antemurale* ideology had the effect of tying the uskoks' religious warfare to the validation of the papacy, for it was above all the popes who formulated and refined that ideology, for example through the juridical act of reissuing *In coena domini* every Holy Thursday.[137] Clearly this placed the uskoks in a vulnerable position. It did not usually matter, since their relations with the papal *curia* were infrequent and mediated through several levels of authority.[138] But it is not hard to conceive of a situation in which the volatile world of European power politics could have led a pope not just to withdraw his broad-based sanction for the activities of the uskoks, but to go further and outlaw them. They would then have been placed in the same decidedly awkward situation

---

[133] Bracewell, *Uskoks*, 211.
[134] Ibid. 160. It would be interesting to know if this derived from Franciscan influence, as in Hungary.
[135] Ibid. 213–14.   [136] Ibid. 173–4.
[137] The ban had enjoyed the status of canon law since its incorporation into Pope Gregory IX's *Decretales* in 1234: J. Muldoon, *Popes, Lawyers, and Infidels: The Church and the Non-Christian World 1250–1550* (Liverpool: Liverpool University Press, 1979), 4–5.
[138] Bracewell, *Uskoks*, 156–8.

which Dózsa's crusaders faced in 1514. As we saw at the start of the chapter, the latter responded with the 'miracle of the crucifix'. It seems likely that had the uskoks faced this problem, their response would have been no less imaginative. Popes, like emperors, could be defied in favour of a higher authority. For centuries groups whose identity hinged on the pursuit of religious warfare had shown ingenuity in the way they had handled this problem.[139]

This point takes us to the heart of the issue. All the individuals and groups whom we have been looking at in this chapter shared the conviction that God had a purpose for his human creation; this purpose could be read, above all via Scripture and prophecy, in some detail. Its pursuit not only validated but could also mandate military action. The armies which carried out the action sometimes marched under the leadership of messianic figures, whether hierarchical or charismatic; at other times they wore or followed symbols which expressed their community of purpose and designated it as holy. These were bound to be contentious claims, open to a challenge which, as we shall see, some contemporaries were eager to make. But the assembling of authority which was involved was a constant feature of religious war. Without it Europeans in this period would have found it impossible to sustain the conviction that their wars were indeed holy.[140] The search for authorization may have led contemporaries into some curious intellectual alleys, and it led to some remarkable scriptural strangling and fictive constructs. The hard fact remains that it was conducted. The study of religious war in this period therefore supports two generalizations: Christians have rarely found it a straightforward process to sanctify their warfare; but they have usually managed to do so.

---

[139] Housley, *Later Crusades*, 332, 351–62.   [140] Cf. Johnson, *Holy War Idea*, ch. 4 *passim.*

CHAPTER FIVE

The Three Turks

So far we have looked at a number of the factors which shaped violence systematically executed in the name of God, in particular the existence of sacred lands and communities, and the appropriation by individuals or groups of divinely mandated missions. In the last chapter we examined how the force which was assembled was validated, depicted, and directed. We will now look at the nature of the enemy. In the fifteenth and early sixteenth centuries this meant to a large degree the Turk, who became the normative foe of Christendom, the embodiment of Islam. The Turk was far from being a flat or static image of hostility. On the contrary, 'turkishness' was a multifaceted and changing identity. It was a prism, which depending on time and context reflected every aspect of Christian thinking about religious warfare: its vigour and triumphalism, its anxiety and tensions, its traditionalism, and its openness to new ideas and information. Consensus was impossible, the image of the Turk (*imago Turci*) revealing above all the tumultuous and contradictory variety of ideas which existed about the practice of religious war.

5.1 EXTERNAL TURKS: THE OTTOMANS

The Ottoman Turks were an Islamic military power whose victories and conquests were too substantial and close at hand to be ignored. This meant that throughout our period, and especially from the mid-fifteenth century onwards, the dominant image of the Turk focused on the Ottomans as a power and, in personal terms, on the ambitions of their sultans.[1] That image was developed in particular in response to the landmark events of the Ottoman advance, the fall of Constantinople in 1453, the siege of Rhodes and capture of Otranto in 1480, the destruction of the Mamluk sultanate in 1516–17, and the defeat of the Hungarians at Mohács in 1526. It encapsulated features which in their basic form were fairly straightforward, almost truisms. Thus it was commonly believed that the Turks benefited from an extraordinary concentration of power and exercised military virtues which, as the Venetian historian Marcantonio Sabellico noted, the Christians simply could not match.[2] The janissaries in

---

[1] Göllner, *Turcica*, iii *passim*.
[2] F. Tateo, 'Letterati e guerrieri di fronte al pericolo turco', in his *Chierici e feudatari del Mezzogiorno* (Bari: Laterza, 1984), 21–68, at 27.

particular were a match for the Spartans, trained to endure incredible hardships, disciplined, and obedient. The Turks were fanatical Muslims: indeed, to all intents and purposes they *were* Islam.[3] They combined an unquenchable will to conquer with an unflagging animosity towards the Christian faith. Such features could only be countered by a similar pooling of resources and endeavour on the part of the entire Christian community.

Rather more interesting was the way in which contemporaries forged relationships between the dynamics of Ottoman power and the ideological world in which they lived. It is possible that the first person to establish the inherent aggressiveness of the Ottoman sultanate, through an accurate reading of its military structure, was Cardinal John Bessarion, the Greek exile who devoted his later life to opposing the Turkish danger.[4] By Luther's day it had become axiomatic that the Turks were by nature conquerors.[5] Bessarion and his contemporaries, such as George of Trebizond and Isidore of Kiev, also developed what has been described as a 'domino theory' emphasizing the interdependence of the Christian states threatened by the Ottomans.[6] Connected with this was the idea that certain states and cities had the role of 'bulwark of Christendom' (*antemurale Christianitatis*). We have seen that it was actively promoted in relation to Hungary, but it was also applied with vigour to Venice and Rhodes. The fall of Belgrade in August 1521 was seen by many as opening up Hungary to attack, and the surrender of Rhodes just a few months later made Crete and Cyprus similarly vulnerable.[7] As we saw in Chapter 1, the *antemurale* image was rooted in a particular view of Catholic Europe forming a *respublica christiana* under the tutelage of the papacy.[8] But one reason for the enduring popularity of the *antemurale* metaphor was a corresponding image of the Ottoman sultanate as a powerful tide crashing against a sea wall. It was used in a telling way by Constantine Ostrovica, a Serb taken prisoner at Novo Brdo in 1455, who was drafted into the janissary corps, served in several campaigns, was captured by the Hungarians in 1463, and subsequently wrote his memoirs.[9]

The nature of the Turkish threat was highlighted above all in calls for a crusading response to the Ottomans, and in a somewhat more dispassionate way in the massive corpus of descriptive and historical literature about the Turks which proliferated from the mid-fifteenth century onwards.[10] Both the calls to crusade and the literature were systematically analysed by R. C. Schwoebel a generation

---

[3] Göllner, *Turcica*, iii. 5.

[4] R. Schwoebel, *The Shadow of the Crescent: The Renaissance Image of the Turk (1453–1517)* (Nieuwkoop: B. de Graaf, 1967), 158.

[5] Luther, 'On War against the Turk', 178.   [6] Hankins, 'Renaissance Crusaders', 120.

[7] Thomas More, 'A Dialogue of Comfort against Tribulation', ed. L. L. Martz and F. Manley, *CWSTM* xii, p. cxxiv.

[8] Above, Ch. 1, at nn. 84–5.   [9] Göllner, *Turcica*, iii. 5 n. 2, 12 n. 8.

[10] On the historiography see D. Mertens, ' "Europa, id est patria, domus propria, sedes nostra . . .". Zu Funktionen und Uberlieferung lateinischer Türkenreden im 15. Jahrhundert', in Erkens (ed.), *Europa und die osmanische Expansion*, 39–57.

ago, and they have recently received fresh attention from such scholars as James Hankins, Michael Heath, Kenneth Setton, and Francesco Tateo.[11] Several aspects of this image call for special comment in the light of what follows. The first is the theme that the consequences of the Ottoman conquests included not just the extinction of the Christian faith, but also the end of civilized values. The Turks were barbarians, enemies of the New Learning based on classical texts and values, which by 1453 was already well entrenched in Italy and had stalwart supporters in Popes Nicholas V and Pius II. The conquest of Constantinople, a city revered by the humanists as a treasury of ancient texts, was lamented as a devastating blow to classical Greek culture. 'How many names of great authors have now perished?', Aeneas Sylvius Piccolomini rhetorically asked. 'It is a second death for Homer and Plato.'[12] Michael Heath was not going too far in describing the conquered Byzantine lands as 'the holy places of humanism'.[13]

It is in this light that the important debate on the ethnic origins of the Turks has to be assessed. During Coluccio Salutati's generation it became fashionable to view the Turks (*Turci*) as the descendants of the Trojans (*Teucri*). After 1453 this was increasingly regarded as unacceptable, for several reasons. In the first place, it placed the ethnic origins of the Turks within the very classical world whose legacy of learning and insight they were intent on destroying. It also gave their conquests over the Greeks a spurious air of legitimacy, in so far as they were avenging the expropriation of their ancestors. And it established a dangerous affinity between the Turks and the many European states which had nurtured origin myths based on a supposed flight to the west by Trojans who survived the fall of their city. This could erode the 'otherness' of the Turks and facilitate their assimilation into the diplomatic world of the European states, to the detriment of a crusading response. Not surprisingly, therefore, Pius II was one of the most determined opponents of the 'Trojan origins' theory. 'In order to confute the error of those who affirm that the Turks are of Trojan race and call them Teucrians', the pope argued that they were descendants of the barbarian Scythians, and he was instrumental in driving *Teucri* out of use and establishing *Turcae* as an alternative plural noun to *Turci*.[14] In 1528 Andrea Cambini summarized the orthodox position well in his very popular *Libro della origine de Turchi et Imperio delli Ottomani*: 'Some writers, especially contemporary ones, have maintained that the nation of the Turks is descended from the Trojans and have their origins at Troy, on the basis that they have overrun the lands where ancient Troy was situated. But that is wholly false, because the people who presently inhabit Asia Minor, where the Ottomans exercise lordship, are by nature barbarous and cruel, showing their origins in the Scythian nation.'[15] For the Turks there was no

---

[11] Hankins, 'Renaissance Crusaders'; M. J. Heath, *Crusading Commonplaces: La Noue, Lucinge and Rhetoric against the Turks* (Geneva: Droz, 1986); Setton, *PL*; Tateo, 'Letterati e guerrieri'.
[12] Schwoebel, *The Shadow of the Crescent*, 9.   [13] Heath, *Crusading Commonplaces*, 29.
[14] Hankins, 'Renaissance Crusaders', 135–42.   [15] Göllner, *Turcica*, iii. 237 n. 60.

escape: 'They were born barbarians and would never be otherwise.'[16] As Göllner noted, the point of the exercise was to establish a blanket legitimization of war against the Turks as the arch-enemies of Christians.[17] We shall see that an added advantage of this reading was that it made possible the identification of the Ottomans with Gog and Magog.

A related aspect of the image which formed during the fifteenth century was that of Turkish inhumanity. Increasingly, the Turks were condemned not just as *infideles* but as *immane genus*. Here again the imprint of humanist culture was being felt, since *immanitas* was the lexical opposite of *humanitas*.[18] But what was emphasized was the brutality of the Turks. As Erich Meuthen put it, 'the image of the Turks in the West was painted as a lurid mixture of bloodlust, bestial cruelty, and perversion'.[19] Nowhere was this *imago Turci* more apparent than in the curious genre of *Absagbriefen*, spurious Ottoman declarations of war, in which threats of the most extreme violence abounded.[20] Although it relied on scriptural antecedents, to a large degree this stereotype was enlivened by lurid accounts of what happened at Constantinople in 1453, in descriptions of rape and excess which became a *topos* of overwhelming familiarity as it was channelled through papal appeals and crusading sermons.[21] The ruthlessness of Ottoman military procedures became legendary. In particular, their habit of impaling prisoners was singled out for comment after the fall of Negroponte and Otranto.[22] There is some evidence that impaling was regarded as a peculiarly Turkish manner of execution. Those Christian countries where it was practised, notably Hungary and Transylvania, had good reason to be familiar with Ottoman ways.[23] It was asserted in one late source that the Senj uskoks, who were notoriously brutal, reserved impaling for their Ottoman opposite numbers, the *martoloses*.[24] The anonymous author of *An die Versammlung gemeiner Bauernschaft* (1525) speculated that impaling could become the fate of the rebel peasants in Germany if they were defeated, together with slavery 'in the Turkish manner, like cattle, horses, and oxen'.[25] The most notorious feature of this slavery was un-

---

[16] Meserve, 'Medieval Sources', 411.

[17] Göllner, *Turcica*, iii. 229: 'Es ging den Historikern nur darum, durch ihre Schriften eine Dokumentation für den Krieg gegen die Türken zu liefern.'

[18] Hankins, 'Renaissance Crusaders', 122, noting his own debt to the work of Tateo.

[19] E. Meuthen, 'Der Fall von Konstantinopel und der lateinische Westen', *HZ* 237 (1983), 1–35, at 4.

[20] Göllner, *Turcica*, iii. 23–4.

[21] e.g. Meuthen, 'Der Fall von Konstantinopel', 6 n. 15 (Giovanni da Capistrano); 'Bessarions Instruktion für die Kreuzzugspredigt in Venedig (1463)', ed. L. Mohler, *Römische Quartalschrift*, 35 (1927), 337–49, at 339–40 (Cardinal Bessarion).

[22] Cf. Cunningham and Grell, *The Four Horsemen of the Apocalypse*, 142–4.

[23] Schwoebel, *The Shadow of the Crescent*, 126, 132, 178, noting the case of John Tiptoft, Edward IV's constable, a Turcophile who practised impaling in England. See too Meuthen, 'Der Fall von Konstantinopel', 8–9 n. 23.

[24] Bracewell, *Uskoks*, 188.

[25] M. G. Baylor (ed. and trans.), *The Radical Reformation* (Cambridge: Cambridge University Press, 1991), 101–29 at 125.

doubtedly the *devsirme* system of child abduction from Christian areas which had been conquered, with a view to their later employment in the sultan's army and civil administration. This was fiercely criticized on humanitarian as well as religious grounds: it led to apostasy but it also broke the natural bonds of family life.[26]

The Otranto expedition of 1480 provides a particularly useful case study of European views about Turkish brutality. Francesco Tateo has noted that the cruelty practised by the Turks was elaborated on as the campaign's historiography developed.[27] It found rich early expression in Giovanni Albino's *De bello Hydruntino*, which was written around 1495. The Turks were characterized as an inherently brutal people: 'that people is driven by filthy lust, suckled in wild disorder, and knows nothing of piety or the sacred. From an early age, they become accustomed not to ease beneath roofs, but to fierce combat and the snows of winter, delighting in the shedding of human blood.'[28] Their way of waging war was different from that of the Italians. 'The barbarians do not follow the Italian practice, that those who dismount and cast aside their weapons once defeated are spared their lives. Rather, they cherish blood as warfare's finest prize.'[29] Their soldiers were even rewarded for decapitating their enemies.[30]

This barbarization of the Turks was accompanied by attempts to locate them within an eschatological reading of events. As a process this was sanctioned at the highest level, for in the crusade bull which he issued in response to the fall of Constantinople, Pope Nicholas V made a direct reference to Revelation 12: 3 and the widespread identification of the Turks with its 'great red dragon, with seven heads and ten horns, and seven diadems on its heads'.[31] It has been amply demonstrated that the sense of anxiety created by the Ottoman advances is apparent in the numerous prophecies which circulated during the aftermath of each major success.[32] Some exegetes identified the Turks as the *flagellum Dei*, the chosen agent of God's wrath, and sultans like Mehmed the Conqueror as 'Antichrist's forerunner'.[33] Others eagerly scanned the key scriptural texts for predictions of the sultanate's impending fall. On the basis of Ezekiel chapters 38–9 and Revelation 20: 8, some commentators identified the Turks with Gog and Magog and wrote of a great Last Battle in which they would be wiped out after a career of destructiveness. The Joachite Johannes Lichtenberger specified in 1488 that they would lay waste Poland, Meissen, Thuringia, Hesse, and Prussia before encountering defeat near Cologne. His reading was influential,

---

[26] Heath, *Crusading Commonplaces*, 34–6.   [27] Tateo, 'Letterati e guerrieri', 46–7.
[28] L. G. Rosa et al. (eds.), *Gli umanisti e la guerra otrantina: testi dei secoli XV e XVI* (Bari: Dedalo, 1982), 58.
[29] Ibid. 76.   [30] Ibid. 62.   [31] Andermann, 'Geschichtsdeutung und Prophetie', 36.
[32] Niccoli, *Prophecy and People, passim*.
[33] R. M. Dessi, 'Entre prédication et réception: Les Thèmes eschatologiques dans les "reportationes" des sermons de Michele Carcano de Milan (Florence, 1461–1466)', in A. Vauchez (ed.), *Les Textes prophétiques et la prophétie en Occident (XIIe–XVIe siècle)* (Rome: École Française de Rome, 1990), 457–79, at 464, 474; O'Malley, *Praise and Blame*, 190–1.

causing Luther and Melanchthon among others to write of the Turks as Gog and Magog and to expect that a Last Battle would occur within their lifetime.[34] The Wittenberg Bible of 1534 even used a depiction of the Ottoman siege of Vienna five years previously to illustrate Revelation 20: 9, the siege of 'the beloved city' by the forces of Gog and Magog.[35] A combination of natural reason, mathematics, and recent prognostications led Cardinal Carvajal to predict the imminent end of Islam in 1508, tying it to a call for a crusade led by the Emperor Maximilian.[36] Some eschatologists who were fascinated by Turkish might predicted the establishment of an Ottoman world-empire, accompanied or followed by their conversion. It has been suggested that this inverted image of the Turk as, potentially, a 'Good Emperor' was an innovation of the early sixteenth century. Certainly it was an ingenious way of synthesizing admiration for Turkish might and despair at the condition of Christian government, all within the context of the 'mirror for princes' literature of the times.[37] Common to all such approaches was the goal of making sense of the Turks within a providential framework which paralleled that of fixing their ethnic origins.

These approaches were inherently group-based and were related to the military agenda and successes of the sultanate. Above all, the Turks were noted for their military ability, and those crusading apologists who played down this ability in order not to discourage their audience were unconvincing.[38] But there was another side to European interest in the Turks. There was an increasing curiosity about the Turks as individuals coupled with an appreciation of the virtues and strengths of Ottoman civil society, which was held up as a mirror to demonstrate the failings of Christian communities. Some Europeans who travelled or lived in Ottoman lands proved capable of 'compartmentalizing' their religious antipathy and viewing other features of Turkish society objectively; they lauded the sobriety, discipline, and piety of the Turks at home. These features were strongly present in Bertrandon de la Broquière's *Le Voyage d'outremer*, a report written for Philip the Good on his extensive tour of the Mamluk and Ottoman lands in 1432.[39] The *Tractatus de moribus condicionibus et nequicia Turcorum* (1479/80) by George of Hungary, a Transylvanian who spent two decades in Turkish captivity, set new standards of accuracy and detail (though not of admiration).[40] There existed too a 'Turkish chic' which paralleled that recently described by Stephen Rowell in the case of fourteenth-century

---

[34] Andermann, 'Geschichtsdeutung und Prophetie', 46–8; Brecht, 'Luther und die Türken', 18–19; Göllner, *Turcica*, iii. 337–8.

[35] Cunningham and Grell, *The Four Horsemen of the Apocalypse*, 30.

[36] Minnich, 'The Role of Prophecy', 113–17.

[37] O. Niccoli, 'High and Low Prophetic Culture in Rome at the Beginning of the Sixteenth Century', in Reeves (ed.), *Prophetic Rome*, 203–22, at 207–8, 210, and cf. her *Prophecy and People*, 113; Göllner, *Turcica*, iii. 95.

[38] This point is well explored by Heath, *Crusading Commonplaces*, ch. 2 *passim*.

[39] Schwoebel, *The Shadow of the Crescent*, 101–6.   [40] Ibid. 208–9.

Lithuania.[41] It was manifested in the wearing of Turkish costume at tableaux and plays, and in the occasional appearance at courts of dwarfs and giants of Turkish origin. Sir John Paston noted the arrival of a Turkish dwarf at Edward IV's court in 1470, 'a wele vysaged felawe, off the age of xl. yere'.[42] It is plausible that interest in the 'exotic' element increased with distance from the threat of actual Turkish attack, in the same way that these lands were less susceptible to apocalyptic readings and to 'anxiety literature' arising from the *Türkenfurcht*.[43] The fact that German apocalypticism was characterized by anxiety and French by triumphalism probably has a similar explanation.[44]

The presumption that greater knowledge of the Ottoman sultanate in itself eroded hostility towards the Turks has largely faded.[45] This is undeniably a historiographical step forward. It entails according European commentators in the fifteenth and early sixteenth centuries a certain degree of credit for grasping the situation which they faced. Göllner remarked on the fact that one of the most popular pieces of *Turcica* in the later sixteenth century was the account of Bartholomej Georgijević, who was captured at Mohács and escaped from captivity in 1539: his bitterly antagonistic work, *De afflictione tam captivorum quam etiam sub Turcae tributo viventium Christianorum* ('On the Afflictions Both of Captives and of Christians Living as Tributaries of the Turks'), first published in 1544, went through forty-three editions by 1600 in a number of languages.[46] But in the circumstances of the time this was hardly surprising. Nothing that was recorded by de la Broquière, George of Hungary, or the many western commentators on the sultanate who followed in their footsteps gave cause for hope that the fundamental aggression of the Ottomans would simply fade away. Their conversion might be hoped for and was certainly predicted often enough, but failing that, the tendency towards conquest, and the barbarism and brutality which in western eyes were associated with it, were dominant features of the 'Grand Turk' and his armies.

5.2 INTERNAL TURKS: 'WORSE THAN THE TURKS'

That the hostile image of the Turks constructed in response to their successes was widely publicized is beyond question. It was the official ideology of the papal *curia*, was actively proclaimed whenever crusade preaching was set in motion,

---

[41] S. C. Rowell, 'Unexpected Contacts: Lithuanians at Western Courts, *c.*1316–*c.*1400', *EHR* 101 (1996), 557–77.
[42] Schwoebel, *The Shadow of the Crescent*, 92.
[43] Andermann, 'Geschichtsdeutung und Prophetie', 39.   [44] Göllner, *Turcica*, iii. 340.
[45] See esp. Schwoebel, *The Shadow of the Crescent*, ch. 8 *passim*. On George of Hungary see M. Thumser, 'Türkenfrage und öffentliche Meinung. Zeitgenössische Zeugnisse nach dem Fall von Konstantinopel (1453)', in Erkens (ed.), *Europa und die osmanische Expansion*, 59–78, at 68–74.
[46] Göllner, *Turcica*, iii. 27 and see too 12 n. 10.

and enjoyed the public backing of European rulers and their official circles.[47] Its
failure notwithstanding to bring about collective action against the Ottomans is
of course one of the dominant themes of fifteenth-century crusading. There
existed a whole genre of 'if only' commentaries, which essentially lamented the
diversion into internecine disputes of blood, money, and effort which might have
been employed against the common foe.[48] But it would be wrong to focus on that
failure at the expense of exploring other effects of the prevalence of this image.
James Hankins has suggested that one consequence was the forging by Italian
humanists of an association between European society and civilization which
was of massive significance for the overseas discoveries and conquests which
were about to take place.[49] Another was the introduction of the image, in an
internalized form, into Christian Europe. In a Christian community riven by
political, social, and religious conflicts, the image of 'turkishness' was repeatedly
applied to the Christian enemy. It signalled the opposite of the burgeoning
triumphalism detected by Hankins in the labelling of the Ottomans as barbarians—the recognition of deep differences within the Christian world, which
paradoxically were best expressed in terms of the rift between that world and its
bitterest foe. Claudius Sieber-Lehmann put it well: 'The external, heathen
opponent possessed an equally dangerous *doppelgänger* in the shape of the
unbelieving foe within Christendom itself.'[50] Sieber-Lehmann saw in this an
appropriation by the lay world of the church's vocabulary of condemnation;
thereby echoing an argument advanced by others in relation to a much earlier
period.[51] But it could equally well be viewed as a consequence of the fact that,
as we noted in Chapter 3, the language of crusade retained the ability to impact
in a wide variety of ways on regional and national societies in which it was
preached.[52]

Some of the most cutting accusations to the effect that Christians were acting
in a 'Turkish' manner related to crusade planning.[53] They fitted into a framework
of thinking about the need to prioritize the crusade which by 1400 already went
back two centuries simply in terms of papal policy on the crusade; in the more
general sense of Catholic thinking about sacred violence it had an even longer
pedigree. The threat from within must be dealt with before the threat from external foes like the Ottomans could be countered, because the internal threat hindered the successful operation of the external crusade. Such hindrance could be

---

[47] Though different views might be expressed in private: Hankins, 'Renaissance Crusaders', 131–2.
[48] e.g. the bishop of Exeter commenting on the second battle of St Albans in 1461: Schwoebel, *The
Shadow of the Crescent*, 11.
[49] Hankins, 'Renaissance Crusaders', 145–6.
[50] C. Sieber-Lehmann, 'Der türkische Sultan Mehmed II. und Karl der Kühne, der "Türk im
Occident" ', in Erkens (ed.), *Europa und die osmanische Expansion*, 13–38, at 38.
[51] Ibid., and cf. his ' "Teutsche Nation" und Eidgenossenschaft', 601. For the earlier period, see
S. Schein, 'Philip IV and the Crusade: A Reconsideration', in P. W. Edbury (ed.), *Crusade and Settlement*
(Cardiff: University College Cardiff Press, 1985), 121–6, at 122.
[52] Above, Ch. 3, at nn. 4–10.   [53] Setton, *PL* ii–iv, contains a wealth of information on this.

deliberate: Göllner remarked that 'no accusation in contemporary polemics found greater resonance than the assertion that an enemy regime had secretly allied with the sultan and by so doing was increasing the Turkish threat'.[54] But the ties between the 'external' and 'internal' Turk need not be so tangible. When Pope Pius II was criticized by his cardinals on the grounds that his warfare in Italy stood in the way of the planned crusade he replied with some spirit: 'We fought for Christ when we defended Ferrante [of Naples]. We were attacking the Turks when we battered the lands of Sigismondo [of Malatesta, the lord of Rimini].'[55] Shortly before this, George Scanderbeg, champion of the Albanian resistance against the Turks, responded in a similar way to criticism by John of Taranto of his services to the Aragonese dynasty of Naples by asserting that 'my cause is as righteous now as when I attack the Turks and you are no better than a Turk'.[56] Much the same thinking lay behind Cardinal Wolsey's justification of England's war in France in 1522, when he received news of the siege of Belgrade and was asked for English support: 'The real Turk is he with whom we are occupied, and I know no other Turk.'[57]

The crusade itself was a double-edged sword. In 1464 Philip the Good of Burgundy threatened to deploy the crusade against the people of Liège, whose insurrection stood in the way of his crusade plans.[58] Eleven years later the situation was reversed: the federated enemies of Charles the Bold believed that the papal legate had instructions from the pope that he was to preach a crusade against Charles should he prove recalcitrant: 'that he should preach and proclaim the cross against him as an unbelieving Hussite (*als ein ungloibigen hussen*)'.[59] This was far from being a unique scenario. The Swiss *Eidgenossen*, who a year after this letter celebrated their great victory over 'the western sultan' at Murten as proof that they were the new Israelites, had themselves been condemned as enemies of Christendom, against whom a crusade should be declared, in 1443.[60] For sheer convolution, however, such cases could not match the situation which developed during the league of Cambrai. The league was formed in December 1508 and one of its professed goals was the promotion of a

---

[54] Göllner, *Turcica*, iii. 25.

[55] Pius II, *Commentaries*, trans. F. A. Gragg, in *Smith College Studies in History*, 22 (1936–7), 25 (1939–40), 30 (1947), 35 (1951), 43 (1957), 5 vols. (Northampton, Mass., 1936–57), at 43 (1957), 818–19.

[56] Ibid. 35 (1951), 458–9.

[57] G. A. Bergenroth (ed.), *Calendar of Letters, Despatches, and State Papers, Relating to the Negotiations between England and Spain*, ii: *Henry VIII, 1509–1525* (London: Longmans, 1866), 444. See also R. P. Adams, *The Better Part of Valor: More, Erasmus, Colet and Vives on Humanism, War, and Peace, 1496–1535* (Seattle: University of Washington Press, 1962), 210; R. J. Schoeck, 'Thomas More's "Dialogue of Comfort" and the Problem of the Real Grand Turk', *English Miscellany*, 20 (1969), 23–37, at 28.

[58] *Œuvres de Georges Chastellain*, ed. J. Kervyn de Lettenhove, 8 vols. (Brussels: F. Heussner, 1863–6), iv. 455–60, 468–70.

[59] Sieber-Lehmann, 'Der türkische Sultan Mehmed II. und Karl der Kühne', 14 n. 3. The equation with the Hussites is unusual.

[60] Liliencron (ed.), *Die historischen Volkslieder der Deutschen*, i, nos. 79, 81, ii, no. 144; Müller, 'Ein Zürich-Habsburgisches Kreuzlied', *passim*.

crusade against the Turks.[61] The Venetians thus found themselves charged with Turcophilia by the allies. It was an embarrassing position for a city which cherished its role as a leading *antemurale Christianitatis* on the basis of its costly and damaging wars against the Turks in 1463–79 and 1499–1502.[62] But it did not stop the Venetians making use of the league's crusading agenda in their own dealings with the Ottomans, arguing for Turkish assistance to enable them better to resist the allies in their capacity as a form of *antemurale Turcorum*. Even if Turkish troops were not deployed, the threat alone could be useful in negotiations with the pope: in January 1510 the Venetians reminded Julius II how hard it had proved to expel the Turks from Otranto in 1481.[63] The response of the Emperor Maximilian was to attempt to bring the Ottomans into the war against the Venetians on the basis that Venice was in a position to assist the crusade.[64]

At first glance both the Venetian and the imperial positions on these occasions seem astonishingly duplicitous. But the first was based on a sound legal rationale and the second possessed a logic of sorts. In the fifteenth century Rodrigo Sánchez de Arévalo had argued that bulwark states, including his native Castile, were entitled to form alliances with the infidel if the circumstances called for it.[65] A verse lament circulated after the battle of Agnadello (1509) made it apparent that this was precisely the situation which the Venetians saw themselves facing:

> If neither peace nor truce befall
> Then on the Grand Turk's might I'll call
> By sea and land with me to fight
> As is a desperate person's right.[66]

Another piece of doggerel portrayed the Venetians abandoning St Mark, 'iniusto, ingrato, vano', in favour of Muhammad.[67] By contrast, the allies' deployment of the Turks *against* Venice could be justified on the grounds that Venetian aggression in Italy hindered the operation of their league's crusade. The road to the Holy Sepulchre lay over the ruins of the Venetian empire: 'Crusaders! You want to see the Holy Sepulchre! Well, now the way to Jerusalem has been opened.'[68] The overall problem was that so many arguments had been developed centring around prioritization, indirect assistance, and the acceptance of the

---

[61] Setton, *PL* iii. 54–5; M. Brunetti, 'Alla vigilia di Cambrai: La legazione di Vincenzo Querini all'imperatore Massimiliano (1507)', *Archivio veneto*, 10 (1926), 1–108.

[62] e.g. Setton, *PL* iii. 67 nn. 80–1. Cf. Giles of Viterbo's lavish praise of Venice in December 1507: 'Fulfillment', 327.

[63] Setton, *PL* iii. 75–7. Cf. ibid., iii. 148 n. 31, for a similar scenario after the battle of Novara in 1513. Generally on Venice and the Turks see Preto, *Venezia e i Turchi*.

[64] Setton, *PL* iii. 89.

[65] R. H. Trame, *Rodrigo Sánchez de Arévalo 1404–1470: Spanish Diplomat and Champion of the Papacy* (Washington: Catholic University of America Press, 1958), 165–6; Schwoebel, *The Shadow of the Crescent*, 204.

[66] Niccoli, *Prophecy and People*, 57 n. 74.   [67] Göllner, *Turcica*, iii. 69, and cf. 129.

[68] Ibid. 70. Cf. Niccoli, *Prophecy and People*, 25–8.

undesirable provided that it served a greater good, that virtually any alignment of forces could be justified by the early sixteenth century. Just war theory had reached a similar impasse owing to the constant broadening of its field of reference. In the same way that virtually any war could be justified, so the Turks could be fought virtually anywhere.[69]

Acting in a Turkish way, however, went far beyond these specific accusations of favouring the cause of the Ottoman sultan, whether overtly or indirectly. The sultanate itself was not necessarily part of the equation. Erasmus noted that the accusation 'acting like a Turk' had become common in his day.[70] To some extent this simply provided a definition of the worst possible behaviour, as in Erasmus' own charge against English sailors that they treated foreign visitors to their country so brutally that it was preferable to fall into the hands of the Turks, or in the humanist's declaration in 1535 that he would be better off amongst the Turks than living again at Freiburg.[71] For the Christians of Croatia living on the frontier 'worse even than a Turk' was a measure of extreme wickedness.[72] But it could carry a much more severe message. The tendency to associate the Turks with uncivilized behaviour, both in the practice of warfare and in such procedures as the *devsirme*, established the possibility of attaching the label to enemies or rulers whose own activities were equally reprehensible. It is noticeable how easily Philip the Good slipped from the idea of directing a crusade against the rebels of Liège on the basis of their impeding his crusade against the Turks, into a crusade on the grounds of their inherent wickedness: 'You watch out that I don't march on you, and that you become the Turks and the Turkey against whom I direct my crusade (*voyage*); for you too are a false and wicked generation, in rebellion against God and his holy church, and my crusade will be as well employed against you as against the infidels.'[73] In the course of the reversal of roles noted above, the enemies of Charles the Bold established parallels between the duke and Sultan Mehmed II, in particular their tyranny and cruelty.[74] Around 1500 the Swiss were frequently labelled as Turkish by their enemies.[75] In a particularly virulent attack in 1505 Jakob Wimpfeling described them as all but Alpine janissaries: 'The Turks and Hussites show greater piety than these forest-dwellers, hardy, menacing, ferocious, hot-tempered, constantly in arms, always ready to fight, feasting on Christian blood and gorging themselves on the

---

[69] Göllner, *Turcica*, iii. 62, 76. On the just war see W. F. Bense, 'Paris Theologians on War and Peace, 1521–1529', *Church History*, 41 (1972), 168–85; H. A. Lloyd, 'Josse Clichtove and the Just War', in A. Ayton and J. L. Price (eds.), *The Medieval Military Revolution: State, Society and Military Change in Medieval and Early Modern Europe* (London: I. B. Tauris, 1995), 145–62.

[70] Partner, *God of Battles*, 180.

[71] *Opus epistolarum Des. Erasmi*, i. 563, no. 295, xi. 228, no. 3054. Cf. earlier comments about Basle, ibid., v. 419, 423, 434, nos. 1431, 1433, 1437.

[72] Bracewell, *Uskoks*, 33.   [73] *Œuvres de Georges Chastellain*, iv. 470.

[74] Sieber-Lehmann, 'Der türkische Sultan Mehmed II. und Karl der Kühne', *passim*.

[75] Sieber-Lehmann, '"Teutsche Nation" und Eidgenossenschaft', 599; Ochsenbein, 'Jakob Wimpfelings literarische Fehde', 58–9.

conflicts of kings.'[76] In 1507 the prince-bishop of Bamberg told the Venetian envoy Vincenzo Querini that Louis XII's treacherous behaviour towards the Holy Roman Empire had shown that he was as bad as any infidel.[77] Louis was again the target of attack in 1512, when Henry VIII insisted to the Emperor Maximilian that the launching of a crusade against the Turks must take second place to the destruction of French power in Italy. The emphasis was on a 'worse than Turkish cruelty', which had shown that the French were the 'worse-than-infidels who are in the middle of Christendom'. Within the lands of the church they were guilty of massacring old men, women, and children, raping nuns, and desecrating church altars, the classic symptoms of barbaric behaviour.[78]

The poet Guizzalotti wrote of the sack of Prato in 1512 that 'Never were Christians worse treated | Even by the unbelieving Turks | than the people of Prato at the hands of the vicious Spaniards.'[79] It has been noted that such an accusation was used with particular frequency by all sides during the Italian wars.[80] It was directed against the French from the start of the conflict, while it was remarked of the imperialists during the siege of Florence in 1530 that 'there were never Turks or other nation who did worse to their enemies than did they . . . burning houses, seizing captives, sacking and ruining the neighbourhood'.[81] This might be dismissed as a figure of speech, or the desperate search for a yardstick with which to describe warfare of an alarming and unfamiliar brutality, were it not for two considerations. One was the relative ease with which domestic wars could be lifted to a sacred plane precisely by the introduction of such language. In this regard the situation in England in 1512 is instructive. Henry VIII's bitter attack on French *crudelitas*, quoted above, was written at a time when the English were angling for the grant of full indulgences to the troops who embarked to fight in France.[82] But the wording used in the king's reply to Maximilian was astute: the atrocities committed by the French were so great that the English cause was effectively a crusade whatever its precise status. 'Our opinion was that this would be just as acceptable and welcome to the Almighty as

[76] C. Sieber-Lehmann and T. Wilhelmi (eds.), *In Helvetios—Wider die Kuhschweizer. Fremd-und Feindbilder von den Schweizern in antieidgenössischen Texten aus der Zeit von 1386 bis 1532* (Bern: Verlag Paul Haupt, 1998), 186, a passage notable for Wimpfeling's extraordinarily inaccurate history.

[77] Setton, *PL* iii. 44.

[78] *I diarii di Marino Sanuto*, ed. R. Fulin et al., 58 vols. (Venice: Commercio di Marco Visentini, 1879–1903), xiv, cols. 425–7. Summaries in J. S. Brewer et al. (eds.), *Letters and Papers, Foreign and Domestic, of the Reign of Henry VIII*, 21 vols. and addenda (Vaduz: Kraus Reprint, 1965), i. 561–2, no. 1215; R. Brown (ed.), *Calendar of State Papers and Manuscripts, Relating to English Affairs, Existing in the Archives and Collections of Venice, and in Other Libraries of Northern Italy*, ii: *1509–1519* (Nendeln: Kraus Reprint, 1970), 69–70, no. 178. See also Setton, *PL* iii. 130.

[79] Setton, *PL* iii. 133 n. 146.

[80] Schwoebel, *The Shadow of the Crescent*, 213, cites three instances from Florentine, Venetian, and imperialist sources, noting that there are 'hundreds of examples'. *Cassell's Italian–English Dictionary* (7th edn., 5th imp., 1972) translates *turchescamente* as 'like a Turk; roughly, cruelly'.

[81] Roth, *The Last Florentine Republic*, 169; A. Denis, *Charles VIII et les Italiens: histoire et mythe* (Geneva: Droz, 1979), 91.

[82] *Letters and Papers*, 63–4, no. 169: Henry VIII to Cardinal Bainbridge, 31 May 1512.

if we were to take the field against the Turks and Saracens; and we do not doubt that those who fall in this most pious and sacred cause will win the prize of eternal life.'[83]

The other consideration which should make us think twice about dismissing the Turkish analogy as a figure of speech is the constant interplay, both at diplomatic and at prophetic level, of the Italian wars and the advance of the Turks. We have already witnessed this in relation to the league of Cambrai in 1508–10,[84] and it is useful to bear in mind that what appears to be a cynical manipulation of crusading ideas during those years occurred at the same time as a wave of busy negotiations for a crusade against the Turks involving powers which had no stake in the Italian conflict.[85] A prophecy by a supporter of papal policy, which was probably printed during the early months of 1510, predicted the defeat of Venice, followed by the defeat and conversion of the Turks.[86] The use of the theme of 'turkishness' in warfare between Christian powers hinged on the readiness with which such warfare could be placed within a religious frame of reference, and the high level of anxiety generated by the Ottoman threat combined with a perception of Christendom's pervasive disunity in confronting it. Of course it was convenient to reach for the label of 'Turk', but it would be wrong to deduce from this that the label had lost its power to shock.

Some of these patterns recurred in relation to the use of the theme of 'worse than the Turks' during insurrections within individual states. Given the tendency to use the admirable qualities of Ottoman society and government as a mirror for a radical critique of Christian failings, this was almost inevitable. In the Holy Roman Empire in particular, where the issue of reform was inextricably bound up with the provision of defence against the Turkish threat, it was hard to avoid pointing out the contrast between domestic disorder and the harmony perceived in the Ottoman system.[87] Around 1438 the author of the 'Reformation of Sigismund' portrayed a Turk advising a Christian to deal with the 'Turk at home' first: 'You take away your neighbor's goods and wealth; you destroy your fellow man's dignity; you even claim his person for your own. Is this done according to your savior's word and command? Now you plan to come across the sea and wage war upon us, and gain eternal life by vanquishing us. But you deceive yourselves. It would be a far better deed were you to remain at home and do battle with the false Christians in your midst, showing them the way to righteousness.'[88] In 1454 Hans Rosenplüt's *Des Türken vastnachspiel* put forward a similar case; as Göllner put it, 'adopting the perspective of the Common Man,

---

[83] *I diarii di Marino Sanuto*, xiv, cols. 425–7.   [84] Above, Ch. 4, at n. 86.
[85] Housley, 'Holy Land or Holy Lands?', 232–3.   [86] Niccoli, *Prophecy and People*, 25–8.
[87] Cf. T. Vogtherr's comments in '"Wenn hinten, weit, in der Türkei . . .". Die Türken in der spätmittelalterlichen Stadtchronistik Norddeutschlands', in Erkens (ed.), *Europa und die osmanische Expansion*, 103–25, at 116, 125. See also Bohnstedt, 'The Infidel Scourge of God', 17–18; Freedman, *Images of the Medieval Peasant*, 52–3.
[88] Strauss (ed.), *Manifestations of Discontent*, 7–8.

Rosenplüt completely demolished the schematically hostile view of "the heathen" '.[89] Such comments accelerated in the early sixteenth century. In 1518 Erasmus wrote to John Fisher that 'it looks as though the state of the common people will soon be such that the tyranny of the Grand Turk would be more bearable'.[90] The author of the *Turcken puechlein* (1522) had his imaginary Turk encourage Christians to flee eastwards, where they would discover a just administration and religious tolerance under Ottoman rule, and a year later the paradox of Christian lordship being worse than subjection to the Ottomans was highlighted by a worried Pope Adrian V.[91] During the German Peasants' War the theme was picked up by the author of *An die Versammlung gemeiner Bauernschaft*, who wrote that lordship had become so oppressive that the peasants would be better off under the Turks; at least they would allow the free preaching of the gospel.[92] The rebellious peasants of Hegau agreed, as evidently did those from the Black Forest who fled to Turkish lands after the revolt.[93] Such unfavourable comparisons were especially common in the Empire but they were made elsewhere, especially when the stresses of social and economic change were exacerbated by religious upheaval. For example, the description of Thomas Cromwell and his advisers during the Pilgrimage of Grace as 'those southern Turks perverting our laws and spoiling Christ's church' may seem like a mere turn of phrase, but it acquires much more serious connotations when one recalls the contemporary horror for the *devsirme* system and other abuses of Ottoman government.[94]

The situation in regions which shared a frontier with the Turks was particularly delicate. To start with, first-hand knowledge of the Turks and their ways gave point and depth to comparisons between the brutal behaviour and oppressive lordship of Christian rulers, and those of the Ottomans. Secondly, the need to maintain strong frontier defences against the Turks brought to the foreground a functional definition of lordship in terms of the provision of protection and military leadership. When these were not in evidence the social order could be seen as losing its legitimacy. This was of course a precise mirror-image within a community of the situation which developed with regard to Venice during the Italian wars in the early sixteenth century as the *antemurale* showed signs of turning quisling. As we saw in Chapter 3, there is evidence that the peasant crusaders who relieved Belgrade in 1456, to a large extent without assistance from the Hungarian nobility, nourished insurrectionary ideas in the aftermath of their great victory, and that Giovanni da Capistrano and János Hunyadi dealt with it by dispersing the entire army.[95] A clearer example occurred in Upper Styria in

---

[89] Göllner, *Turcica*, iii. 357. See also Thumser, 'Türkenfrage und öffentliche Meinung', 74–7.
[90] *Opus epistolarum Des. Erasmi*, iii. 238, no. 784.
[91] Göllner, *Turcica*, iii. 316–17.   [92] Baylor (ed. and trans.), *The Radical Reformation*, 119–20.
[93] Blickle, *The Revolution of 1525*, 128; Franz (ed.), *Quellen zur Geschichte des Bauernkrieges*, 582, no. 202.
[94] Bush, *Pilgrimage of Grace*, 208.   [95] Above, Ch. 3, at nn. 19–21.

1478 when a peasant league was organized to defend the region against the Turks, and denounced noblemen who were allegedly acting as guides for the latter. The conservative chronicler Jakob Unrest viewed the league's proclaimed goal of self-defence as a sham: 'The common opinion was that they wanted to go the way of the faithless Swiss. This false undertaking they camouflaged with the claim that they intended their *Bund* to be directed only against the Turks. But when this was compared with their own words and deeds, it was clearly not the case.'[96] Appropriately, God punished such deceptive behaviour by sending the Turks to lay waste the farms of the peasants who had wickedly formed the league.[97]

Jakob Unrest's hostility makes him a problematic source for the events of 1478, and the Dózsa rebellion of 1514 offers somewhat better evidence of the views of peasants who were placed in this truly no-win situation. No surviving text portrays the Hungarian *cruciferi* going so far as to accuse their nobles of openly allying with the Turks. But when the crusaders turned their arms against their nobles, they made it clear that they regarded their noble elite as effectively 'turkified' because of their refusal to provide leadership for the campaign. In Hungary there was an additional twist to the breakdown of functional lordship, because since the thirteenth century social divisions had been accounted for in terms of the failure of the serfs' ancestors to answer a call to arms in 700: thus 'a hereditarily transmissible curse was created'.[98] There is evidence that the peasant *cruciferi* were aware of this myth in the way Dózsa chose to summon his followers.[99] In these circumstances it was naturally galling that peasants had to provide for their own defence, and it is easy to understand the anger experienced when the Hungarian nobility took steps to hinder peasant mobilization. Nonetheless, the pseudo-historical division into free and unfree was deployed as an argument to justify the legal reinforcement of serfdom in the aftermath of the revolt. It was ironic in the extreme that this myth of ancestral cowardice was used alongside the charge of violent rebellion.[100]

It was in the interests of the Hungarian monarchy to suppress the insurrection of 1514, but in general the court shared the anxiety of the rebel crusaders about the chronic particularism and factionalism of Hungary's nobility. In 1526, on the very eve of catastrophe at Mohács, King Louis II of Hungary was reported as passing the revealing comment that 'he was more afraid of the Turks of Hungary than of the Turks of Turkey'.[101] A report written after Mohács stated

---

[96] Unrest, *Österreichische Chronik*, 93.

[97] Ibid. 95, 99: 'Nun hort und merckt, ob die untrewen pawrn, die den pundt gemacht haben, nicht gestrafft syn worden, wo die Turckhn am maysten geczogen, gelegen und gepranndt haben im lanndt Kernndten, da ist die pundnus am maysten gewessen. Das soldt nyemannt anders messen, dan es sey ain besundre straff von Got, der die ubermuettigen, die sich selbs nicht erkennen wellen, nyedert.'

[98] Freedman, *Images of the Medieval Peasant*, 118–26, with quote at 126.   [99] Ibid. 277–8.

[100] Ibid. 124, referring to the decrees of 19 Nov. 1514, in Fekete Nagy et al. (eds.), *Monumenta rusticorum*, 270–1, no. 202.

[101] Brewer et al. (eds.), *Letters and Papers*, iv. 925, no. 2056.

that 'those lords of Hungary who have escaped are not making any attempt to recruit the army, but are committing worse cruelties than the Turks, spoiling and burning their own domains'.[102] With Ferdinand of Habsburg now on the throne, these social fissures were complemented by national antagonisms: Ferdinand's Landsknechts distrusted the Hungarians, regarding them as worse enemies than the Turks.[103]

The scenario which had briefly manifested itself in Upper Styria in 1478 in response to Turkish raids threatened to reappear once Mohács had all but removed the Hungarian bulwark. The central European German lands were exposed to attack, and the failure of the authorities to defend them could be construed as 'turkishness'. The theme was vigorously advanced in a number of pamphlets which lambasted nobles and Landsknechts alike.[104] Interestingly it was Luther, whose own supporters benefited so markedly from the Ottoman pressure on the Habsburgs,[105] who presented one of the strongest attacks on the indolence of the imperial estates. In his 'On War against the Turk' (1529) Luther put into the mouth of an imaginary papal legate a speech in which he castigated the failure of authorities appointed by God to defend their subjects. The suggestion was made that they had forged 'a secret covenant with the Turk'. 'In this', the legate remarked, 'you are steadily becoming Turks to your own subjects.' It was time to stop discussing religious matters, as the Reichstags had done since 1526, and focus on the first duty of Christian lords, which was to stop their people 'being taken captive, put to shame, plundered, slain, and sold by the Turk'.[106] One Lutheran pamphleteer asserted that all who refused to take part in such a war were to be branded as Turks.[107]

The image of the Turk could thus be directed inwards both in relations between Christian powers which found themselves in a state of war, and in the process of legitimizing insurrection. It functioned as a yardstick by which the propriety of international behaviour could be assessed in a world of rapidly changing diplomatic relations, and the adequate functioning of lordship might be gauged. Probably its most imaginative use, however, took place in yet another context: that of revolt against the structures and practices of the Catholic church. In the late fourteenth century Wyclif had argued that the rise of Islam was a consequence of the growth of worldliness in the church: from this perspective the threat posed by the Turks and the corruption of the church were connected, and any attempt to deal with the Turks simply through the applica-

[102] Brewer et al. (eds.), *Letter and Papers*, 1114, no. 2496.
[103] Göllner, *Turcica*, iii. 91, and see also 51 for earlier criticism that the Hungarians failed to welcome crusaders from abroad.
[104] Ibid. iii. 185.
[105] S. A. Fischer-Galati, *Ottoman Imperialism and German Protestantism 1521–1555* (Cambridge, Mass.: Harvard University Press, 1959).
[106] Luther, 'On War against the Turk', 188–9. Cf. Göllner, *Turcica*, iii. 188–9.
[107] Göllner, *Turcica*, iii. 190.

tion of force would fail.[108] Melanchthon developed this historicism by pointing to the promulgation of the doctrine of transubstantiation at the Fourth Lateran Council as the exact moment when the corruption of the papacy gave rise to the origins of Turkish power.[109] A generation later Heinrich Müller claimed that the papacy's corruption began in the same period as Islam's rise to power, when Boniface III received Byzantine backing for overarching supremacy in the church.[110] There was much in common between this pessimistic view of Christianity's historical development and the depiction of the Turks as the *flagellum Dei*. It was no coincidence therefore that Luther, who espoused Wyclif's viewpoint on the historical decline of the church, also subscribed to the *flagellum Dei* approach. For a time he controversially adopted full-scale quietism in the face of the Ottoman advance,[111] and even when counselling war against the Turks in 1529 he emphasized their providential role: 'If we will not learn from the Scriptures, we must learn from the Turk's scabbard . . . Fools should be beaten with rods.'[112]

The main feature of Luther's position, however, was the links which he drew between the papal office and the Turks.[113] On occasion Luther was content to adopt a straightforward 'worse than the Turks' stance in regard to 'hos Romanos Turcissimos Turcas'. 'No Turk', he wrote in his tract 'To the Christian Nobility of the German Nation' (1520), 'could have devastated Italy and suppressed the worship of God so effectively.'[114] Appropriately enough, one of the features of papal activity which most clearly established the Roman church's claim to being 'Turk-like' was its fraudulent behaviour in pocketing the contributions made by the faithful 'under cover of the Turkish war'.[115] 'Everybody knows that not a cent of the annates, or of the indulgence money, or of all the rest, is spent to fight the Turk. It all goes into their bottomless bag.'[116] In 1520, with Belgrade still in Christian hands and the Hungarian *antemurale* standing firm, Luther took the stance that this 'Turk at home' should be dealt with first: 'If we want to fight against the Turks, let us begin here where they are worst of all.'[117] The same approach featured in his 'Treatise on Good Works', also written in 1520: 'Now these are the real Turks whom the kings, princes, and nobles ought to attack first,

---

[108] R. W. Southern, *Western Views of Islam in the Middle Ages* (Cambridge, Mass.: Harvard University Press, 1962), 77–83.

[109] G. H. Williams, 'Erasmus and the Reformers on Non-Christian Religions and *Salus extra Ecclesiam*', in Rabb and Seigel (eds.), *Action and Conviction in Early Modern Europe*, 319–70, at 352.

[110] Göllner, *Turcica*, iii. 179.

[111] Twenty years after Luther advanced his quietist argument, Francisco de Vitoria still believed the reformer was a pacifist: 'On the Law of War', 296.

[112] 'On War against the Turk', 167, and see 162–3 for Luther's comments on his earlier stance.

[113] The topic has been much studied. See, most recently, Mau, 'Luthers Stellung zu den Türken'; Brecht, 'Luther und die Türken'.

[114] 'To the Christian Nobility of the German Nation', trans. C. M. Jacobs, in *LW* xliv. 115–217, at 141.

[115] Schoeck, 'Thomas More's "Dialogue of Comfort"', 29 n. 15.

[116] 'To the Christian Nobility of the German Nation', 144.   [117] Ibid. 156.

not in their own interest, but for the benefit of Christendom and the disgrace of the divine name.'[118] In this, again, he was following in the footsteps of Wyclif, who had suggested during the Great Schism that the forces of the crusade assembled by each obedience against the other should be directed to bring them both down.[119] But Luther explored the Turk/pope analogy with much greater subtlety than Wyclif: his commentary conveyed the impact of a century of destructive conquest on the one hand, and disappointed hopes for the reform of the church on the other. Extended quotation is necessary.

If the Turk destroys cities, country, and people, and lays waste the churches, we think a great injury has been done Christendom. Then we start complaining, and urge kings and princes to wage war. But when faith collapses, love grows cold, God's word is neglected, and all manner of sin takes control, nobody thinks of fighting. In fact, pope, bishop, priests, and clergy, who ought to be the generals, captains, and standard-bearers in this spiritual warfare against Turks of a far deadlier spiritual kind, are themselves the very princes and leaders of such Turks, of a devilish army, just as Judas led the Jews when they took Christ prisoner. It had to be an apostle, a bishop, a priest, one of the best, who began the work of slaying Christ. And in the same way, too, Christendom is being destroyed not by the Turks, but by those who are supposed to defend it. And yet they go on being so senseless that they want to eat the Turk alive, and at the same time they set fire to their own house and sheep stall and let them burn away, sheep and all, and worry more about the wolf in the woods.[120]

In Luther's overall view of the world the mutual antagonism of pope and sultan was irrelevant: they were both agents of the devil. As he put it in 'On War against the Turk', his most considered reflection on the Ottoman threat, which was published in February 1529, 'Just as Herod and the Jews hated each other, though both stood together against Christ, so Turk and papacy hate each other, but stand together against Christ and his kingdom.'[121] Days after 'On War against the Turk' was first printed, Luther wrote in heavily apocalyptic mode to Wenceslas Link, 'Rome falls, kings fall, popes fall, and obviously the world will tumble, just as a big house which is about to collapse begins its decay with little cracks. Only the Turk, the final Gog and Magog, is to glory in his supreme victory and is [then] to perish, together with his companion, the pope.'[122] Both pope and Turk bore a relationship to Antichrist. In 1529, with the Ottoman threat to the Germanic lands at the forefront of his mind, Luther wrote, 'Just as the pope is the Antichrist, so the Turk is the very devil incarnate.'[123] His response to the question, against whom should the Christian first take up arms?, had by now

[118] 'Treatise on Good Works', trans. W. A. Lambert, in *LW* 44, 15–114, at 90.
[119] John Wyclif, 'Cruciata', in *John Wyclif's Polemical Works in Latin*, ed. R. Buddensieg, 2 vols. (London: Trübner & Co., 1883), ii. 577–632, at 596.
[120] 'Treatise on Good Works', 70.   [121] 'On War against the Turk', 200.
[122] *Letters*, ii. 216–17, no. 190.
[123] 'On War against the Turk', 181; cf. Göllner, *Turcica*, iii. 178–9.

shifted from pope to Turks, but he did not doubt that the pope would also have to be dealt with.[124] So too would radical sectarians like the late Müntzer, whom Luther rather clumsily brought into the equation by comparing him with the Ottoman sultan in his determination to wipe out all authority but his own.[125]

The last member of Luther's unholy trinity had also accepted the need to prioritize in dealing with Christ's enemies. Although he shared Luther's belief in the eschatological significance of the Ottoman Turks,[126] Müntzer advocated dealing with the Turk at home first. Writing to the people of Sangerhausen in July 1524, Müntzer declared that 'anyone who wants to fight the Turks does not need to go far afield; the Turk is in our midst'.[127] It is possible that Müntzer, like Luther, would have changed his priorities if he had lived long enough to hear of the siege of Vienna, but to the end he maintained his view that the 'the Turk is in our midst'. In May 1525, shortly before his capture and death, he threatened Ernst of Mansfeld ('You miserable, wretched sack of worms') with a kind of inverted crusade: 'all the brethren will be ready to risk their life-blood, as they have been hitherto against the Turk. Then you will be hunted down and wiped out, for everyone will be far keener to gain an indulgence at your expense than those which the pope used to give out.'[128] Equally striking is the position taken up by the Anabaptist Michael Sattler in 1527. In contrast to Müntzer, Sattler was a doctrinal pacifist who rejected the idea of fighting either the Turks or his Christian opponents, but he could not resist making the by-now familiar comparison between the two, to the detriment of the latter: 'I said that, if warring were right, I would rather take the field against so-called Christians who persecute, capture, and kill pious Christians than against the Turks . . . [For] the Turk is a true Turk, knows nothing of the Christian faith, and is a Turk after the flesh. But you who would be Christians and who make your boast of Christ persecute the pious witnesses of Christ and are Turks after the spirit.'[129]

5.3 THE INTERIOR TURK

'Let the Christian . . . not hate any man at all in so far as he is a man . . . Let him be the enemy only of vice . . . [Let us assume that he has to deal with] an adulterer, a sacrilegious person, a Turk; one should abhor the adultery, not the man;

---

[124] 'On War against the Turk', 180–1, 183, 196, 198–200, and see Williams, 'Erasmus and the Reformers', 348.

[125] 'On War against the Turk', 180, 183.

[126] *The Collected Works of Thomas Müntzer*, 371. Cf. Scott, *Thomas Müntzer*, 32–9; D. Fauth, 'Das Türkenbild bei Thomas Müntzer', *Berliner theologische Zeitschrift*, 11 (1994), 2–12.

[127] *The Collected Works of Thomas Müntzer*, 90. Cf. Stayer, *Anabaptists and the Sword*, 76.

[128] *The Collected Works of Thomas Müntzer*, 154–6. Note the use of the past tense with reference to the crusade.

[129] Klaasen (ed.), *Anabaptism in Outline*, 270. Cf. Stayer, *Anabaptists and the Sword*, 124.

show one's aversion for the sacrilege, not the man; kill the Turk, not the man. He should make every effort that the impious man that the other has made of himself should perish, but that the man that God made should be saved.'[130] This striking passage from Erasmus' *Enchiridion militis christiani* serves as an excellent summary of the third image of the Turk. It is somewhat similar to Sattler's approach, and there were precedents. Some fifteenth-century preachers had 'interiorized' the Antichrist,[131] and Pius II had emphasized that he was not hostile to Mehmed II as a man, only to the sultan's deeds.[132] But above all the image is associated with Erasmus' religious programme. As its title suggests, 'The Handbook of the Christian Soldier' was intended to be a guide to everyday religious life; in that respect the absence of an eschatological perspective, of the type which gave a particular urgency to the views of a Luther or a Müntzer, is not surprising. Nonetheless, the passage is typical of Erasmus' overall approach.

In some ways Erasmus accepted the first image of the Turk, in so far as the word for him summed up impiety, violence, and barbarism.[133] It was above all a frame of mind, but for somebody as essentially societal in his thinking as Erasmus, this was far from denying that it took shape in objective reality. It drove the wheels of Ottoman aggression in the form of the sultan's armies and government. However, it could thrive equally well in Christian countries. It was the way of thinking and behaving which was antithetical to the philosophy of Christ (*philosophia Christi*), and its uprooting, both in so-called Christian countries and amongst the Turks themselves, would pave the way for the kingdom of Christ. Indeed, Erasmus wrote in 1527 that if 'the Turk within' could be overcome, the actual Turks and Jews would be so overcome with admiration that missionary work would hardly be necessary: 'Witnessing our good deeds, both Turks and Jews would glorify our heavenly father and desire to enter such company.'[134] On the other hand, if the Turk within individuals, together with its many political and social expressions, continued to prosper, it would scarcely matter whether an actual Ottoman conquest occurred or not; 'turkishness' would be triumphant amongst peoples who remained notionally Christian. Victory or defeat in the military struggle between 'Christians' and 'Turks' would then be irrelevant, for as Jacobus de Voragine had put it in the *Legenda aurea*, 'What would we gain from overcoming the barbarians, if we are conquered by cruelty?'[135]

These were views which changed little throughout Erasmus' maturity, irrespective of whether the backcloth was the crusade planning of Leo X, the anti-Turkish campaigns of Charles V, or the crusade preaching which followed the

---

[130] Desiderius Erasmus, 'Enchiridion militis christiani', trans. C. Fantazzi, ed. J. W. O'Malley, in *CWE* lxvi. 1–127, at 93–4.

[131] Dessi, 'Entre prédication et réception', 466.

[132] Pius II, *Epistola ad Mahomatem II*, ed. and trans. A. R. Baca (New York: Peter Lang, 1990), 117.

[133] *Opus epistolarum Des. Erasmi*, x. 3, no. 2636.

[134] Ibid., vi. 490, no. 1800.

[135] Jacobus de Voragine, *Legenda aurea*, ed. T. Graesse (repr. Osnabrück: Otto Zeller, 1965), 70.

siege of Vienna in 1529.[136] In the *Institutio principis christiani* (first edition 1516), he commented, 'judging by the people who fight this kind of war [the crusade] nowadays, it is more likely that we shall turn into Turks than that our efforts will make them into Christians. Let us first make sure that we are truly Christian our-selves and then, if it seems appropriate, let us attack the Turks.'[137] In a letter in October 1518 he wrote that civilized values could perish perfectly easily without the help of the Turks,[138] and in the prefatory letter to the 1519 edition of the *Enchiridion militis christiani* he wrote that unless Christians mended their ways, 'we shall degenerate into Turks long before we convert the Turks to our way of thinking'.[139] In 1525 he expressed his gloom that 'the whole of Christendom [is] sinking into a state of Turkish barbarism',[140] and in 1528 he was prepared to com-ment to Mary of Hungary, whose husband had fallen fighting the Turks at Mohács, that '[it does not] show Christian clemency to kill a Turk for no other reason but that he is a Turk'.[141]

Given Erasmus' loathing for warfare, this definition of 'turkishness' as the antithesis of true Christian values was bound to encompass a condemnation of contemporary fighting men on precisely the same grounds of barbaric behaviour that the Turks were attacked by so many exponents of a crusading response. Crusading enthusiasts were of course well aware of this paradox. Matthias Kretz, for example, 'a representative of traditional crusading ideology' who preached 'A Sermon on the Campaign against the Turk' in 1532, hoped that the participants would 'fight not in order to gain great honor and glory, nor to ac-quire lands and possessions, nor out of anger and a desire for vengeance. Such motives are Turkish, not Christian, and one cannot vanquish Turks with Turks.' Kretz was not overly optimistic, given that many of the Emperor's troops would be 'loot-mongers, blasphemers, drunkards, gamblers, lechers, etc'; he sought refuge in hopes for their moral conversion as they contemplated the cause for which they were fighting.[142] Erasmus was beyond such hopes by this point. For him European mercenaries were 'a barbarian rabble, made up of all the worst scoundrels', as he put it in his *Institutio principis christiani*,[143] while the merce-naries who sacked the Dutch town of Asperen in 1517 showed 'more than

---

[136] N. Housley, 'A Necessary Evil? Erasmus, the Crusade, and War against the Turks', in J. France and W. G. Zajac (eds.), *The Crusades and their Sources: Essays Presented to Bernard Hamilton* (Aldershot: Ashgate, 1998), 259–79, repr. in *CWMRE*, study XVIII, and bibliography cited in nn. 1–2. See also R. G. Musto, 'Just Wars and Evil Empires: Erasmus and the Turks', in J. Monfasani and R. G. Musto (eds.), *Renaissance Society and Culture: Essays in Honor of Eugene F. Rice, Jr.* (New York: Italica Press, 1991), 197–216.

[137] 'Institutio principis christiani', trans. N. M. Cheshire and M. J. Heath, ed. A. H. T. Levi, in *CWE* xxvii. 199–288, at 287.

[138] *Opus epistolarum Des. Erasmi*, iii. 403, no. 868. [139] 'Enchiridion militis christiani', 11.

[140] *Opus epistolarum Des. Erasmi*, vi. 95, no. 1581 and cf. vi. 111, 149, nos. 1584, 1597.

[141] 'De vidua christiana', trans. J. T. Roberts, ed. J. W. O'Malley, in *CWE* lxvi. 177–257, at 234.

[142] Bohnstedt, 'The Infidel Scourge of God', 41, 43–4 and cf. 34–5. For the description of Kretz see Göllner, *Turcica*, iii. 197.

[143] 'Institutio principis christiani', 282.

Turkish ferocity'.[144] The logical conclusion of this train of thought was that armed resistance to the Turks was futile because it involved the triumph of 'turkishness'. Ends and means could not be uncoupled. If, in 1530, he was prepared to sanction a defensive war against the Turks, it was on the strict understanding that 'interior turkishness' must be dealt with first.[145]

5.4 THE IMAGES COMBINED: THOMAS MORE AND THE TURKS

It is clear that the Erasmian image of the Turk was ideologically opposed to a violent response towards the Ottomans, and a fortiori to any attempt to clothe that response in religious garb. As Erasmus expressed it in a letter written in April 1531, 'some are Lutherans, others Zwinglians, and others Anabaptists; but my fear is that by fighting with the Turks we shall ourselves become Turks'.[146] In practice the second image too was difficult to reconcile with an active engagement with the Ottoman advance, since it sprang from fractures within the Christian commonwealth which impeded a unanimity of response to the external threat. The three views would seem therefore to have been irreconcilable. To that extent they mirrored the polemical exchange which took place early in 1420 between Jakoubek of Stříbro and John of Jičín on the meaning of 'Babylon'. The Taborite reading of Babylon as the corrupted church was the equivalent of the Turks qua Turks, and it underpinned their doctrine of flight from such evil on the basis that it would soon be subjected to God's wrath. In opposition to this Jakoubek argued that Babylon was the *corpus antichristi*, the group of individuals, both clerical and lay, who were corrupt: it could not be geographically pinned down as the Taborites believed. The third meaning of Babylon, that of spiritual confusion and distress working within the individual believer's soul, was akin to Erasmus' 'Turk within'. As a dedicated reformer, Jakoubek objected just as fiercely to John of Jičín's attempt to identify him with the pseudo-Erasmian approach as he disagreed with the Taborite doctrine of flight and its aberrant offspring, apocalyptic holy war.[147]

A form of synthesis of the three images of 'turkishness' could nonetheless be achieved. When Jakob Wimpfeling strenuously attacked the Swiss in 1505 for their disobedience to Maximilian, labelling them as 'worse than the Turks', it was against a background of hope that their undoubted military virtues could be turned against the Ottomans. The latter war, he wrote, together with the conflict against 'the Turk within', formed the Christian's two proper fields of combat: 'our wars should be with the enemies of our souls, the apostate angels . . . [and]

[144] *Opus epistolarum Des. Erasmi*, iii. 65, no. 643.
[145] 'Utilissima consultatio de bello Turcis inferendo', ed. A. G. Weiler, in *Opera omnia Desiderii Erasmi Roterodami* (Amsterdam: North-Holland, 1969–), v/iii. 1–82.
[146] *Opus epistolarum Des. Erasmi*, ix. 259, no. 2485.   [147] Kaminsky (ed.), 'Treatises', 534–44.

with the wicked enemies of your name, o Christ, the most inhuman Turks.'[148]
Much more impressive than Wimpfeling's synthesis, however, was that advanced by Thomas More. In the course of his writings More managed to give
very clear expression to all three images. In the first place, he repeatedly subscribed to the view that the Turks represented a danger to the faith and civilization of Christian Europe, and that they must be resisted by common action. In
the course of a harsh critique of Christopher St German's *Salem and Bizance*,
published in 1533, he conceded that 'I well allow therfore and lyke not a lytell the
great good mynde of Salem toward the vanquysshyng of the great turke and con-
querynge of the holy lande'.[149] He adopted his most elevated tone when writing
about the common defence of Christendom:

And by this reason is not only excusable but also commendable the comen warre which
euery peple taketh in ye defence of theyr countre agaynst enemyes yt wold inuade it syth
yt euery man fyghteth not for ye defence of him selfe of a pryuate affeccyon to hym self
but of a crysten charyte for ye sauegard & preseruacyon of all other. Whych reson as it
hath place in all batayle of defence so hath it most especyally in the batayle by whyche we
defende the crysten countrees agaynste the Turkys in that we defende eche other fro farre
the more parell and losse both of worldly substance bodyly hurt and perdycyon of
mennys soules.[150]

Whether or not More envisaged this common action taking the precise form
of a crusade is hard to tell. He certainly regarded its conduct as the responsibility of the princes, who held the sword for that end.[151] Towards the end of his public career he expressed his concern that Charles V's efforts against the sultan
should not be impeded by English foreign policy, because the Emperor was fighting for the good of the entire faith.[152] He scornfully rejected the claim that past
failure proved that God had not supported the Christian cause, taking a much
more historically conditioned and, at first sight, modern view of the reason for
failure: 'For whan crysten prynces dydde theyr deuoyre agaynst myscreauntes
and infydels there be storyes and monumentes ynoughe that wytnesse the
manifest ayde and helpe of god in grete vyctoryes gyuen to good crysten prynces
by his almyghty hande.'[153] It was division and apathy, and the short-sighted pursuit of selfish or vainglorious objectives, that brought defeat.[154]

More also eagerly seized on the idea of Christian groups adopting Turkish
ways in his spirited response to the Protestants. Particularly important in this

---

[148] Sieber-Lehmann and Wilhelmi (eds.), *In Helvetios*, 166, 170, 174–6.
[149] Thomas More, 'The Debellation of Salem and Bizance', ed. J. Guy et al., *CWSTM* x. 222.
[150] Thomas More, 'A Dialogue Concerning Heresies', ed. T. M. C. Lawler et al., *CWSTM* vi. 415.
[151] Ibid.
[152] P. de Gayangos (ed.), *Calendar of Letters, Despatches, and State Papers, Relating to the Negotiations between England and Spain*, iv. 2: *Henry VIII, 1531–1533* (London: Longmans, 1882), 114.
[153] More, 'A Dialogue Concerning Heresies', 413.
[154] Ibid. 413–14; More, 'A Dialogue of Comfort', 7–8, 224.

regard was his *A Dialogue Concerning Heresies*, written in 1529 at the request of Bishop Cuthbert Tunstall. Given More's deep knowledge of St Augustine,[155] it is not surprising that he embraced the traditional argument that heresy presented a graver danger to the church than did external assault.[156] But he was also attracted by the more pragmatic approach which compared the actual behaviour of Turks and unfaithful Christians to the disadvantage of the latter. The impiety of the Lutherans, especially their iconoclasm, was worse than that of the Turks: at least the latter showed reverence for the Virgin Mary, 'whose name the Lutherans hardly endure'.[157] Most importantly, More accused the Lutheran troops of Charles V who sacked Rome in 1527 of behaving worse than the Turks ever had on such occasions. He described their atrocities in graphic terms which even today retain the power to shock.[158] He argued that if the Turks were to take advantage of Lutheran quietism to invade and conquer more Christian lands, they would find the heretics willing collaborators: 'it is lytell doute whose parte they wyll take and that crysten people be lyke to fynd none so cruell Turkes as them.'[159] Such arguments were being advanced by other Catholic polemicists at this point: Johannes Eck, for example, claimed in 1532 that 'it would be preferable to live among the Turks than among these apostates and wicked Christians', while Johannes Cochlaeus wrote in 1529 that Luther was inflicting more damage on the church than were the Turks.[160]

Much of More's anti-Protestant polemic was hastily written and tendentious in character. But four years after he wrote *A Dialogue Concerning Heresies* he did manage to take a more Erasmian view of the reformers. With public office and its duties behind him, he wrote 'as touchynge heretykes, I hate that vyce of theyrs & not theyr persones and very fayne wolde I that the tone were destroyed, and the tother saued'.[161] With such comments we are close to heresy as 'interior turkishness'. A similar moderation is on display in More's handling of the external/ internal threat in his *Debellation of Salem and Byzance*, written just a few months after the *Apology*. The *Debellation* was the most extended work in More's polemical exchange with the legal reformer Christopher St German. This began when St German published his *A Treatise Concerning the Division between the Spiritualty and the Temporalty* at the end of 1532 or the beginning of 1533. St German called for the end of the clergy's immunity from royal justice, a reform of the procedures followed in church courts, especially when investigating charges of heresy, and the stripping of legislative powers from the convocations

[155] In his early twenties he lectured on 'The City of God' at St Lawrence Jewry: P. Ackroyd, *The Life of Thomas More* (London: Chatto & Windus, 1998), 100–2.

[156] More, 'A Dialogue Concerning Heresies', 405–10. Cf. Cuthbert Tunstall, writing to Erasmus in 1523: *Opus epistolarum Des. Erasmi*, v. 290–3, no. 1367.

[157] Thomas More, 'Responsio ad Lutherum', ed. J. M. Headley, *CWSTM* v. 688–91.

[158] More, 'A Dialogue Concerning Heresies', 370–2.   [159] Ibid. 412.

[160] Göllner, *Turcica*, iii. 196–8, arguing that the Lutheran polemicists made a greater impact.

[161] Thomas More, 'The Apology', ed. J. B. Trapp, *CWSTM* ix. 167.

of Canterbury and York. More fought back on the church's behalf in his *Apology* and St German replied with *Salem and Byzance* (September 1533).[162]

St German's work consists of a dialogue between two Englishmen whose names happen to be Salem and Byzance. 'Just why St German invented such characters is far from plain', John Guy, one of the editors of More's *Debellation*, has commented;[163] in fact the reason, as Guy suggests, is made clear enough in chapter 22, when Salem points out the coincidence that their names resemble the two great patriarchal cities which had been conquered by the Turks. If only relations between the laity and the spirituality were placed on a sound footing, they could proceed to a great crusade, 'the one with prayour, the other with power, ayenst the most cruell ennemies of all Christen religion, that are the Turkes, and all the cursed secte of Mahumete'. The two cities could then be reconquered, and their inhabitants brought back to the faith, for 'howe greatte pitie it is, to se so many people as be in the sayde cities and in the countreys theraboute, lye in the danger of the divel, and daily perishe by their infidelitie, to their eternalle damnacion, as there dothe, and that yet christen men loke no more upon it then they do'.[164] One powerful motive lying behind legal reform was therefore a crusade, and St German reminisced about the time when Henry VII's letters advocating such a crusade had been read out aloud in Star Chamber, when Warham, the archbishop of Canterbury and More's own patron, had been chancellor and St German himself present, 'where it was my chaunce then to be, and with other to here them redde'.[165]

These concluding chapters of *Salem and Byzance* presented More with a delicate situation. The author of *Salem and Byzance*, whom he could not identify for reasons of personal safety, was no Protestant, attacking the faith from within and denying the very substance of the church's traditional teachings. We have seen that More applauded St German's personal hope for a crusade; he also commended the fact that he had no quarrel with 'suche poyntes of the catholyke fayth as heretykes nowe labour to destroye, as prayenge to sayntes, pylgrymage, and purgatory, & the sacraments, and specially the blessed sacrament of the awter'. But an assault on the church's legal immunities and privileges could be just as perilous as such a doctrinal challenge: 'I mysse lyke mych agayn, that as he wold dylate the fayth, by force of sworde in farre cuntres hense: so he laboreth to chaunge and take away the good & holsome lawes, wherby the fayth is preserued here at home.'[166] St German's own reply, which came only after More's execution, was predictable: it was better to push on with the reform of the church than with a crusade. In his unpublished 'Dyalogue Shewinge What we be Bounde to

---

[162] More, 'The Debellation of Salem and Bizance', pp. xvii–xx.   [163] Ibid., p. xx.
[164] St German, 'Salem and Bizance', 383–4.
[165] Ibid. 390–1. This was almost certainly in 1507: see Housley, 'Holy Land or Holy Lands?', 232–3.
[166] More, 'The Debellation of Salem and Bizance', 222.

Byleve as Thinges Necessary to Salvacion, and What Not' (1537), he wrote that the former was 'more plesaunte to god . . . then it were to endevour theym self to dryve all turkes, sarysyns, and other infidels owte of all countryes that they have wrongfully taken from Cristen men'.[167]

This exchange between More and St German demonstrates that the debate about the 'external' and the 'internal' Turk could be steered in both directions, towards reform and its rejection, without infringing the context of Christian unity and its function as an essential precondition for the defeat of Islam. John Guy pointed out that both protagonists in this highly technical debate shared such concerns however much they disagreed on other matters.[168] The full complexity of More's position, however, emerges not in *The Debellation of Salem and Byzance*, but in his *Dialogue of Comfort against Tribulation*, which he wrote in 1534 when incarcerated in the Tower of London. The advance in this contemplative work is that More incorporated his own version of the third image, the 'interior' Turk. And the strength of his treatment lies in his ability to give this image real shape and substance by associating it with apostasy. For instead of the somewhat abstract conceptualization of 'Turkish' behaviour which his friend Erasmus had earlier diagnosed, More addressed the pressure to undertake formal conversion to Islam which confronted Christian communities which had been overrun by the Turks and made subject to the sultan's rule.

The precise scenario depicted by More was both imaginative and relevant: Hungary in 1527–9, when the *antemurale* had been breached at Belgrade and Louis II's army smashed at Mohács. Another great assault was imminent and János Zápolyai, vaivoda of Transylvania and one of the rival claimants to the Hungarian throne, was actively negotiating with the Turks. Ordinary Hungarians, represented in the dialogue by Uncle Antony and Nephew Vincent, had to anticipate conquest and heavy pressure to convert. It was a testing time for the conscience of every Christian: given what was likely to occur it was essential that 'euery man & euery woman both, appoynt with goddes helpe in their own mynd beforehand what thyng they intend to do yf the very worst fall'.[169]

Much of the dialogue took the form of an exegesis on Psalm 91, especially verses 5–6, one of the most revered scriptural statements of the various types of trial which could test the believer. More viewed the pressure to convert as an example of the fourth sort of trial, 'the destruction that wastes at noonday' or 'midday devil', and he was under no illusions about the double impact which would be exerted by the attractions of Ottoman favour to converts and the fear of their atrocities against recalcitrants. The dialogue was a reasoned plea for steadfastness on the basis that nothing the Turks could do, in terms of either reward or punishment, could possibly compare with the joys of Heaven or the terrors

---

[167] J. Guy, 'The Later Career of Christopher St German (1534–1541)', app. C in *CWSTM* x. 393–417, at 413.

[168] Ibid. 417.　　　[169] More, 'A Dialogue of Comfort', 195.

of Hell. The peroration, in which Uncle Antony exhorted his nephew, and all Hungarians, to fix their eyes on the sufferings of Christ and the martyrs, was one of the finest passages More ever wrote. In one piece of remarkable word-painting More imagined that the entire Turkish army stood before Antony and Vincent, sounding all their musical instruments and firing all their guns at once. The sight and sound would be terrifying, but if at the same time the demons were to rise out of Hell and the sufferings of the damned be made visible, 'we wold wax so ferd of that sight, that as for the Turkes hoste, we shuld scantly remembre we saw them'. And if the wonders awaiting the believer in Heaven were also revealed, 'there wold I wene be no man that ones wold shrinke therat but euery man wold run on toward them in all that euer he might, though there lay for malice to kyll vs by the way, both all the Turkes tourmentours, & all the devilles to'.[170] In other words, apostasy lost its attractions when viewed from a properly Christian perspective, in which life on earth was but preparation for eternity.

In the preface to his 1573 edition of *The Dialogue of Comfort against Tribulation*, the Catholic exile John Fowler emphasized the text's universality: even Turks who had been taken prisoner by Christians would find in it reason to make their captivity less painful to endure.[171] Nonetheless, the actual Turks were far from functioning simply as a backcloth for the work. More depicted Ottoman conquest, and the effects of occupation, in graphic and sombre language which was fully in accordance with the first image of the Turks. Both his learning and his experience of public service in the 1520s stood him in good stead to provide an accurate but thoroughly engaged account of what the Ottoman military advance meant for the Hungarians whom he chose to act as his spokesmen. At the very start Vincent provided a description of the Ottoman threat which encapsulated much of that image: 'There falleth so contynually before the eyen of our hart, a fearefull imaginacion of this terryble thyng his myghty strength and power, his high malice and hatryd, & his incomparable crueltie, with robbyng, spoylyng, burnyng, and layng wast all the way that his armye commeth than kyllyng or carying away, the people far hens fro home and there seuer the couples & kyndred asonder, euery one far from the other some kept in thrauldome, & some kept in prison & some for a tryumph tormentyd and kyllid in his presens.'[172] At other points in the work More showed a detailed grasp of the varied approach taken by the Ottomans towards conversion in the lands which they overran, and an acceptance of the role which the Turks were believed to play within Christian eschatology.[173]

Given the circumstances in which More was writing, however, the work can hardly be read without reference also to the second image which we have examined. More was severe in his castigation of János Zápolyai's party—'for of Turkes naturall this countrey lakketh none now'—and regarded the prospects

---

[170] Ibid. 315.   [171] Ibid. 486.   [172] Ibid. 6.   [173] Ibid. 190–5.

of Hungarian Christians under their yoke as worse than Ottoman conquest pure and simple: 'for there ys no born Turke so cruell to christen folke, as is the false christen that falleth fro the faith.'[174] Such remarks inevitably bring to mind the self-serving supporters of Henry VIII's Act of Supremacy, even if the association of the king himself with the sultan is more problematic. Frank Manley, writing in the introduction to the Yale edition of the dialogue, was probably right to warn against a reading which is rigidly allegorical: 'Rather than an allegory More creates a loose, metaphoric analogy.'[175] It is striking that the confessional divide in the Empire is somewhat played down in the dialogue. Indeed, in response to a gloomy comment by Vincent, Antony advanced three reasons for hope, possibly culled from the religious peace of Nürnberg (1532) or Cadan (1534). The first was that there had been recent intimations of a settlement between reformers and Catholics, the second that the parties had agreed to call a truce in their polemical strife while this was being negotiated, and the third that they had recognized the need to mobilize 'a comen power in defence of cristendome ageinst our comen ennymy the Turke'.[176] More broadly, Alistair Fox has suggested that More's use of the word 'christendom' where formerly he would have used 'church' was a tactful attempt to avoid sectarianism by reference to a collectivity to which Lutherans could feel they still belonged; they too 'professed Christ's name'. Even the clash between faith and works was to some extent played down.[177]

The danger of an actual alliance between infidel and heretic was replaced by a much subtler approach to their relationship. More made it clear that it was not simply a question of apostasy, or even of apostates behaving worse than their Turkish masters; there was also the danger of a corrosion of the Christian position when those who leaned towards apostasy were increasingly vociferous in their praise of the religious practices of the Turks, and increasingly critical of the Christian church. More described an insidious 'drift' towards apostasy in a Hungary poised on the edge of disaster:

For like as before a greate storm, the see begynneth sometyme to worke & rore in hym selfe ere euer the wynd waxeth boystuouse so my thinke I here at myn eare some of our owne here among vs, which with [in] these few yeres could no more haue born the name of a Turke than the name of the devill, begyn now to fynd little faute therin ye and some to prayse them to, litle & litle as they may more glad to find fawtes at euery state of christendome, prestes, princes rites ceremonies sacramentes laues and custumes spirituall temporall & all.[178]

By focusing on the theme of apostasy, More was therefore able not only to forge an unusually subtle link between the real Turks and the 'Turks at home',

[174] More, 'A Dialogue of Comfort', 6–7, 195.   [175] Ibid., introd., p. cxxxiv.
[176] Ibid. 38, 349.   [177] A. Fox, *Thomas More: History and Providence* (Oxford: Blackwell, 1982), 236–7.
[178] More, 'A Dialogue of Comfort', 192.

but also to tie in with both images the danger emanating from 'the Turk within'. The resulting argument was an astonishing *tour de force* on an intellectual level, and it naturally drew much emotional power from More's own circumstances. The similarity between the Hungarians' plight and More's own situation in the Tower was inescapable, and the passage on torture in particular remains deeply moving.[179] More was unwilling to draw out the comparison between the plight of the Hungarians and that of Catholics in England, but in 1573 the Catholic exile John Fowler did not shy away from doing so. In spite of recent disasters like the conquest of Cyprus, the actual Turks, 'blessed be God', were still far off. But 'would God al their Turkish fasshions and persecutions were as farre of from vs to, & that Christian Charitie did raigne more truly and plentifully in the hartes of al that beare the name of Christians in Christendome'.[180]

At the end of our period, one Catholic thinker thus succeeded in creating strong links between the very different images of the Turk. They possessed an essential unity in so far as they were all expressions of the devil's work in the world. The Turk was the instrument of the devil: 'The Turkes are but his tourmentours, for hymselfe doth the dede.'[181] This was so whether he operated overtly through his creations, Islam and the Ottoman state, covertly by undermining the unity of Christendom and spreading schism and heresy, or most insidiously, within the minds of individual Christians whom he lured into apostasy. The dialogue offered a remedy for the third approach: 'Stand up to the Devil and he will flee from you.' 'And let vs fence vs with fayth, & comfort vs with hope, & smyte the devill in the face with a firebrond of charitie.'[182] The remedies for the first and second approaches were of course not individual but collective: the mounting of a common defence against the Ottomans, and the maintenance of Christendom's religious unity by defending the church through word and deed. More argued strongly for the first and actively pursued the second.[183] If both were in a state of extreme disarray at the time he wrote, this was far from causing him to despair. The overall coherence of More's perspective on 'turkishness' was a rare achievement. It sprang from an unrelenting optimism about God's providential purpose, and it involved ignoring or at least pushing into the background those crippling deficiencies in the contemporary church which concerned Erasmus and drove Luther into revolt. It also owed much to More's own many-sided character and career, encapsulating as he did the roles of convinced defender of Christendom, resolute opponent of heresy, and advocate of martyrdom.

---

[179] Ibid. 244–9.   [180] Ibid. 486.   [181] Ibid. 317.   [182] Ibid. 317–18.
[183] Cf. More's assertion at his trial that in matters of faith he stood by the authority of Christendom rather than that of the political or ecclesiastical institutions of England. Ibid., introduction, p. cxxix.

CHAPTER SIX

The Critique of Religious War

In the summer of 1524 the evangelical community of Orlamünde replied to a request from Allstedt that they join the league which Thomas Müntzer had established in order to further the radical Reformation through violent means. Their letter was headed 'On the Christian Way to Fight' and its gist was straightforward: 'we can have no resort to worldly weapons in this matter. This is not what we are commanded to do.' The use of force they rejected on the basis of Matthew 26: 52, Christ's command to Peter to put his sword away in Gethsemane, and Ephesians 6: 13 ff., Paul's description of the spiritual armour which the believer should wear. This was followed by a close critique of the practice of covenanting, the argument being that the Allstedters had misinterpreted 2 Kings 23: 3. Josiah covenanted with God rather than with his own people. To covenant with others was to infringe Matthew 6: 24, 'no one can serve two masters'. Such associations both infringed the freedom of the true Christian to serve God and betrayed a lack of confidence in his almighty power.[1]

Müntzer had no patience with such arguments. It was only possible to adhere to the covenant with God if one *did* covenant with others, and in a letter which he wrote to the intendant John Zeiss at this time he claimed that the individual's experience of God's testimony provoked action, not passivity: 'if the elect simply ought to let themselves be martyred on the basis of this counterfeit goodness and faith then the depths of the knavery of the godless would never be exposed.'[2] As Berndt Rothmann put it during the apocalyptic excitement of the Münsterite kingdom, 'we, who are covenanted with the Lord, must be his instruments to attack the godless on the day which the Lord has prepared'.[3] These were cogent arguments given the premises of activists like Müntzer and Rothmann, but they were no more inherently sound than the stance taken up by the people of Orlamünde: that the adoption of violent means for religious ends was fundamentally at odds with the Christian faith since it ran counter to the teachings of Christ and his Apostles. They picked their texts well. Matthew 26: 52 was a *locus classicus* in medieval discussion of the church and war, while Ephesians 6 was a

---

[1] *The Collected Works of Thomas Müntzer*, 93–4. Cf. Scott, *Thomas Müntzer*, 76–7.

[2] *The Collected Works of Thomas Müntzer*, 100–3, with quote at 103. See also H.-J. Goertz, 'The Mystic with the Hammer: Thomas Müntzer's Theological Basis for Revolution', in Stayer and Packull (eds.), *The Anabaptists and Thomas Müntzer*, 118–32.

[3] Klaasen (ed.), *Anabaptism in Outline*, 335.

favourite text for anybody who regarded religious warfare as confused thinking: it had been approvingly referred to in 1410 by Jakoubek of Stříbro before the militarization of the utraquist cause, it was central to the thinking of Peter Chelčický, and it would be cited a few years later by Bishop Hugh Latimer when he denounced the Pilgrimage of Grace.[4] But the Orlamünde letter addressed a second contentious issue: that the violent pursuit of religious ends involved human associations and actions which were sinful. In the language of the reformers, they shattered the covenant between the believer and God. These two viewpoints, and their repeated expression in the fifteenth and early sixteenth centuries, will form the substance of this chapter, together with a third which arose not in the context of wars between states, or revolutionary activity of the type envisaged by Müntzer, but in that of European overseas expansion: that the use of violence was counterproductive to the goal of converting the gentiles.

6.1 THE PROBLEM OF AGENCY

As we saw in Chapter 4, a providential world-view caused the problem of human agency to become linked, through military failure, with a perceived lack of divine sanction. Unless one fell back on the inscrutability of God's mind, failure when ostensibly fighting on behalf of his cause had to indicate one of two things: either that the cause was not in fact God's; or that it was human agency that was at fault. The defeated radical sectarians adopted the second approach. In his last letter, written to the evangelicals of Mühlhausen after his capture and torture in May 1525, Thomas Müntzer roundly blamed the insurgents' pursuit of their self-interest for the defeat at Frankenhausen. 'Dear brothers, it is quite crucial that the sort of disaster which befell the men at Frankenhausen should not be your lot too: there is no doubt of its root cause: that everyone was more concerned with his own self-interest than in bringing justice to the Christian people.'[5] Jan Bockelson took the same approach after the fall of Munster: the elect of the New Jerusalem had simply been unequal to the solemn task of renewal placed on their shoulders.[6] More generally, Peter Blickle has emphasized that all the major Protestant reformers perceived very clearly the danger of a materialist motivation usurping their spiritual programme.[7]

---

[4] Above, Ch. 2, at n. 10; *Sermons by Hugh Latimer Sometime Bishop of Worcester*, ed. Canon Beeching (London: J. M. Dent & Co., 1906), 22–9, esp. 26. The similar ideas expressed in 2 Cor. 10: 4 were used by Jan Kalenec in a criticism of Zwinglian warfare in the 1540s: see P. Brock, *The Political and Social Doctrines of the Unity of Czech Brethren in the Fifteenth and Early Sixteenth Centuries* (The Hague: Mouton & Co., 1957), 250.

[5] *The Collected Works of Thomas Müntzer*, 160–1: a problematic letter given the circumstances and the strong probability of the scribe's intervention.

[6] Stayer, *Anabaptists and the Sword*, 278.

[7] P. Blickle, 'Social Protest and Reformation Theology', in K. von Greyerz (ed.), *Religion, Politics and Social Protest: Three Studies on Early Modern Germany* (London: George Allen & Unwin, 1984), 1–23, at 15–16.

A similar dilemma could occur within the much less volatile context of national or dynastic messianism. When, in 1495 and 1498, Savonarola warned Charles VIII of France that he would cease to be God's chosen instrument unless he behaved more acceptably,[8] the prophet could have reminded Charles of recent history. In two texts written in 1422, when the Valois cause was at its nadir, Alain Chartier addressed the sad condition of the defeated and divided French kingdom. In his *Dialogus familiaris et sodalis* Chartier asked why the French were suffering so much more than other peoples whose behaviour was just as wicked. Divine judgements were unfathomable, and given time all would receive their just rewards. But the French, as God's Chosen Ones, had let God down particularly badly and therefore had to suffer the more: 'Compared with other Christian peoples we have received the most from the Lord's hand, so when we ungratefully set aside our fear of God, we deserve to be the more severely chastised by him.' It was not God who had forgotten the devotion of the Merovingians and Carolingians, but the French themselves. A revival of piety and patriotic spirit must accompany that of *disciplina militaris* if the French covenant with God was to be renewed.[9] Chartier advanced similar arguments in *Le Quadrilogue invectif*. Inconstancy, lack of fortitude, and the divisive pursuit of self-interest were divine visitations. Henry V, 'ce flaiel de persecution', acted as God's agent, and the only question was whether the French were being punished or had been sentenced to extinction.[10]

At the same time that Chartier wrote, the Hussites too were considering the problem of human agency in God's cause. Lawrence of Březová, as ever the best spokesperson for the Hussite centre, reported the response of the priests of Prague to the defeat of Jan Želivský's army at Most in August 1421. God punished those who fought for the wrong reason. 'When we fought with compassion and humility in defence of his most sacred truth, God helped us and everything fell into our laps. But now our brethren have embraced wicked ways, and they fight not for the truth but for spoils, mercilessly seizing the belongings of the poor, and killing their fellow-humans more cruelly than the heathens. So the Lord in his anger has permitted us to be afflicted.'[11] Given the emphasis placed by the Hussite centre on right intention, in accordance with their legal approach to the validation of the war, this may be expected. What is striking is the attention given to the same subject by the Taborites. Their warfare was immensely successful. Not only did they repel the crusaders and defeat their royalist neighbours in southern Bohemia, but they established a rich and powerful *seigneurie*. And that was precisely the problem: successful agency brought rewards which

---

[8] Fra Girolamo Savonarola, *Lettere e scritti apologetici*, ed. R. Ridolfi et al. (Rome: Angelo Belardetti Editore, n.d.), nos. 20, 21, 28, 29, 80.

[9] *Les Œuvres latines d'Alain Chartier*, ed. P. Bourgain-Hemeryck (Paris: Éditions CNRS, 1977), 245–325, esp. 300–6.

[10] Alain Chartier, *Le Quadrilogue invectif*, ed. E. Droz (Paris: Honoré Champion, 1923), 4, 6.

[11] LoB, 'De gestis', 492. For the battle see Heymann, *John Žižka*, 248–52.

could so easily distort and pollute motivation. The discussion which resulted was part of a broader debate about how Tabor should evolve once it had shed its early chiliasm and communism; but for us it is especially illuminating because Tabor's longevity and organizational finesse caused its leaders to address the issue of exactly how to conduct a religious war to a remarkable depth.

The manner in which the war was waged was a central concern of Tabor's greatest commander. When Žižka won what may have been his most resounding victory, at Německý Brod in January 1422, he was unable to prevent his troops from burning and ransacking the captured town. Although Žižka celebrated his success in grand style, he viewed the indiscipline of his soldiers as primarily responsible for the disappointments which followed in 1422–3. In two remarkable letters written on 26 March and 1 April 1423 he summoned allies to send representatives to a meeting at Německý Brod at Easter, where strategic decisions would be made, but only after the public performance of penance for the 'greed, pillage, haughty wantonness and betrayal' of January 1422. 'There, at the very place where we have sinned, we will do penance and repent our sins.'[12] It was probably no coincidence that not long after the Německý Brod meeting Žižka drew up his famous 'Statutes and Military Ordinance'. This detailed document ranged over an impressive array of disciplinary and organizational matters, setting them all within the context of a war fought explicitly and exclusively for God. 'And thus, if we observe, keep and fulfill the salutary articles written above, the Lord will be with us with His grace and His help. For thus it behooves us to act in the fight for God.'[13]

Žižka had left Tabor by the time of the meeting at Německý Brod. Another prominent Taborite, however, has also left detailed views on the community's waging of war. Nicholas of Pelhřimov (Mikuláš Biskupec) was elected bishop of the Taborites in the autumn of 1420 and was still there thirty-two years later when the city fell. He spoke for the Taborites on many occasions, notably at Prague in 1420, at Konopiště Castle in 1423, and at Basle in 1432–3. Amedeo Molnár characterized Nicholas as exercising 'a tutelary function in the Taborite struggle and in the organisation of the church', and holding 'one of the positions of highest responsibility in the Taborite revolution, in which he acted as "speaker"',[14] while Thomas Fudge included him among the 'grand old men' of the Hussite reformation.[15] He was Tabor's most impressive theologian and ideologist,[16] and his opinions were therefore not just interesting but influential.[17]

---

[12] Heymann, *John Žižka*, 491–2, and see too 300–3, 361–5.

[13] Ibid. 492–7, with quote at 496; good analysis ibid. 374–84.

[14] Nicholas of Pelhřimov, *Confessio Taboritarum*, ed. A. Molnár and R. Cegna (Rome: Istituto Storico Italiano per il Medio Evo, 1983), 'Introduzione', 41.

[15] Fudge, *Magnificent Ride*, 283.

[16] 'The ablest writer of the Taborite brotherhood': Bartoš, *Hussite Revolution*, 63.

[17] Fudge, *Magnificent Ride*, 109–10, 112, 141–2, 156, 176.

The tensions which came to beset Tabor's practice of warfare are most clearly revealed in the *Chronicon Taboritarum* composed by Nicholas with the assistance of John of Lukavecz during the decade which followed Tabor's downfall at the battle of Lipany (1434).[18] Nicholas's goal in writing this history is aptly summarized in the title often accorded it, 'the cause of the priests of Tabor', and the text is a highly selective one. In Molnár's words, 'Far from telling the history of events, Nicholas presents a balance sheet of the revolution. He does this as apologist for the intentions which presided over this mighty insurrection, as both eyewitness and active agent in a struggle whose goal was most faithfully kept in sight and defended by the Taborites.'[19] Nicholas narrated how the leaders of the entire Hussite community were driven with enormous reluctance into the armed defence of their position by the repeated refusal of the Catholic authorities to grant them a proper hearing. This war was conducted in accordance with established practice: 'This war was set in motion with great care and in accordance with the rulings of the virtuous warriors of ancient times, as confirmed and set out in detail by the said Masters of Prague and the priests of the kingdom of Bohemia, who then and from the start worked alongside the people.' Despite this care, abuses (*deordinationes*) had occurred. 'Alas, as time proceeded, this war was diverted into great abuses by many who took part in it in fraudulent fashion, with quite other intentions. They worked always against the will and intention of the faithful, who opposed them in faithful and catholic fashion in defence of the good.'[20] These *deordinationes* were against the wishes of the majority, and the priests of Tabor responded by calling a series of reform assemblies, at Písek in 1422, Tabor in 1424, and Klatovy also in 1424.[21] Restraining decrees were passed and it was agreed that they should be read out in public.[22]

The 'more notable' of these decrees were described at considerable length by Nicholas. In the first place, it was acknowledged that some priests had interpreted Scripture in such a way as to justify acts of oppression, cruelty, and greed. Rather than reading into the Bible whatever they pleased, and applying scriptural prophecies to situations as and when they chose, the priests should ensure that their interpretations were soundly based and 'accorded with the life and teaching of Christ and the holy Apostles'.[23] Secondly, the military activity of the priests themselves was regulated. They were forbidden to fight in person, to shed blood and kill, to command troops, to exhort soldiers to slaughter others, or in any way to excuse or help bring about unacceptable behaviour in the field. The priest's role was closely defined: 'he may be present in just wars fought for the cause of God, exhorting the combatants to conduct it in a just and holy manner.'[24]

---

[18] 'Chronicon Taboritarum', *passim*.
[19] A. Molnár, 'Réformation et révolution: Le Cas du senior taborite Nicolas Biskupec de Pelhřimov', *Communio viatorum*, 13 (1970), 137–70, at 138.
[20] 'Chronicon Taboritarum', 481.
[21] Ibid. 482. For the dates see *Confessio Taboritarum*, 291 nn. 2–4.
[22] 'Chronicon Taboritarum', 482.   [23] Ibid. 482.   [24] Ibid. 483.

The third set of decrees focused on the authority for waging war, and they remind one strongly of the debates which had taken place in the winter of 1419–20 when the legality and mode of conduct of a war in defence of the Hussite cause were discussed at Prague. The position set out in these Taborite decrees was highly conservative, remarkably so for a community which still faced a powerful external threat. They are however confirmed by the surviving decrees of a Taborite assembly at Písek in February 1426. These stated that 'They intend to conduct an orderly and Christian form of war, based on and established in the law of the holy Gospel. Such a war arises not from one's own will but in response to oppression, when somebody is resolved to use violence to deter his victim from the pursuit of the good, and it proves impossible to make the oppressor desist by any other means. They intend and desire to avoid disorderly and inhumane warfare, unfounded in the New Testament, nor do they wish to assist anybody engaged in such warfare.' The emphasis on the contrast between *ordinaciones christiane* and 'bellis inordinatis et inhumanis' shows clearly the important place within Taborite thinking of a war waged in a manner which did not indecently flout New Testament ideals. The contrast of course was with the war which was being waged by their Catholic opponents, as the 1426 decrees showed by the clause 'They wish to assist the land of Bohemia in an orderly way, defending and protecting it against foreigners (*alienigenae*) and other disorderly agents of violence and devastation, who are opposed to God and his faith, maintaining this good order as far as the loss of property and person.'[25]

It was firmly restated that true Christian wars (*bella christiana*) fitted certain criteria, which were essentially Augustinian in origin: they must accord with the New Testament and they must be pursued by a legitimate authority, or failing the latter, by the 'Christian people' itself or somebody acting responsibly in its name, inspired by God (*spiritu Dei agitato*) and fired by a just cause. The enemy must be guilty of serious crimes such as a violent assault on the *respublica*, or the intention to destroy the faith, and he must be clearly unresponsive to attempts to restrain his actions by peaceful means. He should be killed out of necessity rather than from cruel vengeance or to gain his goods. The conflict must be waged in accordance with the writings of 'the holy doctors in law' and its guiding spirit must be charity, 'to the extent that the combatant engages his human opponent with charity, and is always ready to spare him, as long as the enemy is sincerely prepared to choose the way of truth'.[26] As Erasmus would later express it, they should 'kill the Turk and not the man'.[27]

Other decrees recorded by Nicholas dealt with the broader subject of Tabor's relations with its neighbours. The priests condemned the practice, common to all the radical brotherhoods, of exacting the punitive tribute payment called

[25] *UB* ii. 509–11.   [26] 'Chronicon Taboritarum', 484.
[27] Above, Ch. 5 at n. 130. For other later echoes see B. Lowe, *Imagining Peace: A History of Early English Pacifist Ideas, 1340–1560* (University Park: Pennsylvania State University Press, 1997), 224–6.

holdy from people who embraced Hussite beliefs and even fought for them. In some cases utraquist peasants had even been compelled to pay *holdy* when they were already forced to pay tribute to the enemy because the Taborites had been unable to protect them. At most money could be asked for on a voluntary basis, *caritative*. Instead of being harassed for making tribute payments to the enemy, Hussite communities exposed to their attack should be offered effective protection. Many extreme Taborites had been far too ready to assume that individuals whose allegiance was doubtful were supporters of the Catholics, even when they made public statements of their adherence to the Four Articles. Much the same applied to the wives of Catholic nobles. They should be judged by their own actions rather than those of their husbands.[28] Overall, and in much the same way that proven enemies were if at all possible to be won over 'by the road of piety', every effort should be made to avoid making enemies of friends by harsh treatment.

Lastly, the mounting of expeditions solely for the purpose of collecting booty called for special attention. Such 'disorderly excursions', directed at areas both inside Bohemia and outside it, were the more strongly condemned because they sometimes involved press-ganging. It was established that the practice was neither just nor 'expedient for the winning of beatitude'.[29] Priests who knew that the chief goal of an expedition was the extortion of money from the poor were permitted to exclude its participants from communion when they were about to set out and on their return. This was viewed as an interim measure until the radical communities could devise a more appropriate means to stop the practice occurring.

These reforming decrees were in part intended to prove that Tabor in its heyday was far from being the rogue member of the Hussite coalition which its enemies claimed. Indeed, later in their chronicle Nicholas of Pelhřimov and John of Lukavecz used the decrees as proof that Tabor's stance on warfare was wholly in line with Prague's.[30] One of the charges laid at Tabor's door was that 'The Taborite priests, or certain among them, do not denounce the current wars to men, and yet they cannot and do not know how to reconcile them in detail with God's law or the writings of the saints.'[31] In reply, the priests of Tabor first recounted the origins of the war in the measured military response of the Hussite coalition to the violence with which its adherents had been threatened. Tabor assented to this response in so far as it was waged *in caritate*, out of necessity, and after repeated attempts to persuade the enemy to desist through non-violent means. And secondly, the reforming decrees passed in an attempt to suppress *deordinationes* demonstrated that the Taborites knew very well how to reconcile the conduct of the war with both God's Law and Scripture. Nicholas

---

[28] 'Chronicon Taboritarum', 484–6. For one example (the chatelaine of Moravsky Šternbeck) see Bartoš, *Hussite Revolution*, 57.

[29] 'Chronicon Taboritarum', 486.   [30] Ibid. 687–9.   [31] Ibid. 687.

took a very similar line, at times using identical language, in his *Confessio Tabori-tarum* (completed in 1435), in his repudiation of the charges directed against Tabor by John Rokycana.[32]

Were these sweeping decrees effective? In their own defence the priests of Tabor acknowledged only partial success. 'We regret everything relating to these abuses, which were contrary to the common intention of us all, as well as to the decree imposed on all of the people to whom we preach; and we believe that similar excesses are practised, contrary to the intentions of the Masters [of Prague], amongst people subject to their influence.'[33] Nicholas of Pelhřimov returned to the subject in the cycle of sermons which he wrote on the Apocalypse c.1430. In an illuminating essay on the cycle, Howard Kaminsky has recently argued that Nicholas's goal was to place Tabor's evolution in an eschatological framework, 'an eschatological image of Tabor as complement or alternative to the historical Tabor whose spokesman he was and would remain'.[34] This had the obvious effect of emphasizing the holiness of the burden carried by the Hussites as contemporary apostles, people who had been chosen to disseminate God's word, and the incongruity of the *deordinationes* perpetrated during their conflict. Nicholas's text reveals his unease about the possibility of the Czechs losing their status as the Chosen People through bad behaviour. 'But if we cut ourselves off from him, he will abandon us, and he will bestow these gifts on a people whose language we know not . . . And should we Czechs prove proud, as I have said, he will give these gifts and great glory and honour to some [other] tribe or people, at present unheard of, as it was at the beginning.'[35] In other words, the Czechs could easily confront the same divine punishment which Alain Chartier, at precisely this point, believed to be facing the French.

What this meant Nicholas elsewhere spelled out in some detail. Men were transferring their services from one army to another, fighting for Sigismund 'and his tyrants', for the forces of Prague, for Mount Horeb, or for Tabor, 'and whichever party they favour or community they belong to, they commit horrendous sins, with no true penitence to follow'.[36] Nicholas was very concerned about Tabor's moral health as a community. Its degeneracy from its original values he described in language of great immediacy, enlivening his Latin text with proverbs in the vernacular. 'When things are going well our warriors often go out in the armies, but in time of adversity they creep into the hedges with the grasshoppers.'[37] The laity were consumed by greed, obsessed with booty, given over to gluttony and drunkenness. They had taken all too literally the promise in the Hussite battle hymn that 'Christ will reward you for what you lose'. Gold and

---

[32] *Confessio Taboritarum*, 289–92.   [33] 'Chronicon Taboritarum', 689.
[34] Kaminsky, 'Nicholas of Pelhřimov's Tabor', 144. Regrettably this revealing text has not been published, but it is quoted at length in Kaminsky's article and in Bartoš, 'Táborské bratrstvo'.
[35] Kaminsky, 'Nicholas of Pelhřimov's Tabor', 147 n. 24.
[36] Ibid. 153 n. 54   [37] Ibid. 157 n. 70.

silver had been piled up 'under the cover of holy war for the Lord's Law' (*sub titulo belli sancti pro lege domini*), and Tabor's armies were full of men who 'would not fight for the truth, if they did not hope that through warfare they would acquire material goods in abundance'.[38] Nor were people as pious as they had once been. They resented the rigour of the Taborite regime, pined for the colour and music of the Roman liturgy, skipped church services, and missed communion. There were some who turned the very justification of the war on its head, saying that if God's Law were being practised there would not be this incessant warfare between Christians.[39]

Nicholas's text cannot be taken as a barometer reading of the social and religious condition of Tabor *c*.1430. As Tabor's leading priest he was likely to be disappointed by the values of his flock, and this critical stance was sharpened by the eschatological context of the whole sermon series. Much of it does ring true. F. M. Bartoš detected a growing antagonism towards the field armies at this time, as they came to be blamed for Bohemia's endemic condition of warfare and more specifically for bringing back plague from their forays abroad.[40] At the council of Basle in 1433 Prokop the Bald admitted the continuing problem of *deordinationes*: 'Your reverences may be certain of this, that we detest the abuses committed during the conduct of military operations, however they happen; we heartily regret them, and we shall not cease pursuing those guilty of them.'[41] In the following year an alderman of Tabor called Simon warned that heavy taxation had alienated the subject communities from the radical brotherhoods.[42] But more significant than the text's evidential status is the precise nature of its urgent call for reform. Kaminsky suggested that Nicholas's aim was to restore the early dynamism of his community, but without going so far as to revive the chiliasm which had been fundamental at its foundation but which he condemned as a false reading of Scripture.[43] Eschatology without chiliasm entailed stressing the spiritual urgency of the struggle against Antichrist, and the need for that struggle to be waged by those who were worthy of their cause. 'Fighting for God's Law means fighting with charity, because the goal of that Law is charity.'[44]

Nicholas's own position was nuanced and fascinating. He was no Jan Čapek or Thomas Müntzer. He acknowledged that sanctifying warfare was a dangerous step, not to be undertaken lightly: 'Let us be specific about exactly why the conflict is to be sanctified (*propter quod sanctificandum est prelium*), when, and against whom. Just as the restless David was unworthy to build the Temple, while his

---

[38] Kaminsky, 'Nicholas of Pelhřimov's Tabor', 157 nn. 68–9, and see too Bartoš, 'Táborské bratrstvo', 113–14.

[39] Kaminsky, 'Nicholas of Pelhřimov's Tabor', 157–8; Bartoš, 'Táborské bratrstvo', 119.

[40] Bartoš, *Hussite Revolution*, 114. See too Fudge, *Magnificent Ride*, 281.

[41] *Monumenta conciliorum generalium*, i. 419–20.

[42] Bartoš, *Hussite Revolution*, 125. For the disquiet caused by the way the Taborites fought their wars see also Heymann, *John Žižka*, 463, 470.

[43] Kaminsky, 'Nicholas of Pelhřimov's Tabor', 164.

[44] Bartoš, 'Táborské bratrstvo', 114. Cf. Molnár, 'Réformation et révolution', 144–5.

peaceful son Solomon was, so cruel and restless men will not be able to restore the Temple.'[45] Indeed, there are strong indications, both in this text and in the *Chronicon Taboritarum*, that he would have much preferred a non-violent response to the Catholic assaults on the Hussites. In October 1436 he asserted that his advocacy of God's Law was not conditioned by warfare: it had begun before the 'wars of our times' and it had continued after the fighting came to an end at Lipany.[46] His abhorrence for violence found expression in the Taborite reforming decrees relating to the use of the death penalty to punish condemned criminals, which perfectly reflected his views on the conduct of the war. Such individuals had often been treated too harshly. They were only to be executed under the sanction of legally constituted authority, in cases of necessity, and if there was New Testament justification for it. Old Testament prescriptions were valid only if they accorded with the teaching of Christ and the practice of the early church. The sixteen conditions of charity must be observed and the law of nature should be followed: do to others only what you would wish to be done to you.[47]

Nicholas supported Tabor's wars. Militarized by his strong eschatological leanings, and convinced of God's support by the victories of the 1420s, he was realistic enough to accept that even war plunder was licit, provided it was taken from 'men who bear not God's symbol on their chests'.[48] In 1432 the Prague Masters and priests asserted that 'however just the cause, goods belonging to others must not be seized, coveted, or damaged; and the faithful common folk must not be oppressed in material terms'. They supported this with a citation from Romans 3: 8, 'let not evil be done so that good may result'.[49] To this the Taborites agreed, 'with the exception of a reasonable reading of the scriptural passages cited below, and of similar texts', following this with a barrage of citations validating the spoliation of the unrighteous.[50] Hussites captured by the Catholic lord of Rožmberk claimed that Nicholas had incited them to commit their acts of violence against his lands.[51] But he was unusually alert to the dangers which successful warfare brought for the Taborites: it could nullify their role in divine history, and given the many deficiencies in the position taken up by the Hussite centre, this could rob the utraquist cause as a whole of its eschatological momentum. What remained, 'a program for a national or territorial reformation on the basis of the existing societal order', was not to Nicholas's taste.[52]

In point of fact, what took place was not the continuing degradation of Tabor's original ideals through success, but the disastrous defeat of the field

---

[45] Bartoš, 'Táborské bratrstvo', 114.   [46] Molnár, 'Réformation et révolution', 147, 152 n. 63.
[47] 'Chronicon Taboritarum', 484, and cf. *Confessio Taboritarum*, 343, 351. See also Bartoš, *Hussite Revolution*, 93–4, on Nicholas and capital punishment.
[48] Kaminsky, 'Nicholas of Pelhřimov's Tabor', 165 n. 102.   [49] *Confessio Taboritarum*, 343.
[50] Ibid. 351. The scriptural texts were 1 Cor. 9: 7, 1 Cor. 3: 21, Wisd. 10: 20, Prov. 13: 22, and Matt. 12: 4.
[51] Fudge, *Magnificent Ride*, 258.   [52] Kaminsky, 'Nicholas of Pelhřimov's Tabor', 163.

armies at Lipany. Faced with the withdrawal of divine backing and the threat of a compromise settlement with the deceitful Sigismund, the leaders of the Taborite federation passed a series of striking decrees at an assembly held at Tabor in December 1435. They agreed that the 'fine and ridiculous phrases' of the Emperor were not to be trusted. They restated their allegiance to the Four Articles. But they went on to acknowledge 'how in our times, above all, the lord God has worked his vengeance in so many ways on the overt enemies of truth, on hypocrites, but also on us, because of sins and abuses'. To stave off further punishment, sinning, especially 'worldly pride', was to be uprooted, and a day's fast each week was decreed throughout the period leading up to Lent. Provision was made for intervention by a neighbouring Taborite community in the event that any community was plunged into schism, and the Taborite federation as a whole was to strive to speak with one voice. In this way Tabor tried, almost certainly under Nicholas's guidance, to cope with the unfamiliar pain of defeat.[53]

6.2 CONDEMNATION

Turning from Nicholas of Pelhřimov to his contemporary Peter Chelčický, we move from an acceptance of holy war provided it was fought within precise and forbidding parameters, to a thoroughgoing condemnation of it. This was not because his religious ideals were less radical or his convictions less firm than Nicholas's: it was because he associated warfare with the very regime which he opposed, and with the spiritual evil which underpinned it. In a fine study of Chelčický's views, Kaminsky argued that 'his is the only body of Hussite theory that may qualify as genuinely original', the reason being that Chelčický was uncompromising in pursuing the societal implications of his religious views.[54] He did not take the escape route of eschatology, which legitimized secular power by allocating to it a role within a divine programme which could not be realized without it. The oxymoron of holy war could not be made acceptable in this way, let alone in the conservative, legal frame of reference used by the Prague Masters. The circle could not be squared.

The first solid evidence for Chelčický's engagement with the issue is his undated treatise 'On Spiritual Warfare'. The treatise was a commentary on Ephesians 6, and formed a classic statement of the view that for every Christian the true enemy is the devil (the 'interior Turk' of Chapter 5), against whom the only effective armour is spiritual. Actual warfare featured in the treatise in two

---

[53] *UB* ii. 451–3, no. 954.

[54] H. Kaminsky, 'Peter Chelčický: Treatises on Christianity and the Social Order', *Studies in Medieval and Renaissance History*, 1 (1964), 105–79, at 109. For other studies of Chelčický see F. Seibt, 'Peter Chelčický', in K. Bosl (ed.), *Lebensbilder zur Geschichte der böhmischen Länder*, vol. i (Munich: Oldenbourg, 1974), 49–61, repr. in Seibt, *Hussitenstudien*, 209–16; M. L. Wagner, *Petr Chelčický: A Radical Separatist in Hussite Bohemia* (Scottdale, Pa.: Herald Press, 1983).

respects. First, it provided Chelčický with analogies which served to emphasize his point about internal struggle. For example, Taborite Písek's preparation for a siege by its enemies was compared to the Christian withstanding devilish temptation by cutting himself off as far as possible from worldly concerns. Secondly, it was portrayed as one way in which the devil could break down the spiritual defences of the Christian. This meant that in defending the Law of God the Hussites laid themselves open to spiritual subversion, and in one memorable passage Chelčický confronted this dilemma head on:

When [the Taborites] march up [to a fortress] with their war-machines, seeking to smash down the walls within which the Devil dwells among the evil people who have shut themselves up there, the Devil doesn't care. When the attackers smash the walls and mercilessly destroy the evil people, the Devil goes out from those walls and into them, and he will dwell in their cruel and loveless hearts. Nor will it be easy for them to besiege their hearts with machines, for they don't even see that the Devil is there. And so no physical power or strength will destroy him, for with his cleverness he can easily bring it about that all those who wish or think to destroy his dominion by the power and strength of this world, that they fight on his side, serve him thus, and exalt him higher than ever.[55]

Kaminsky has argued plausibly that Chelčický probably wrote 'On Spiritual Warfare' in the autumn of 1420 during the debate at Písek about Tabor's participation in the defence of Bohemia. The date is significant, for a number of recent events had propelled the Taborites along the road of social and religious stability, bringing with it the embrace of military power. Chiliasm and purgative violence, which Chelčický portrayed as other means by which the devil cunningly worked to destroy true Christian belief, had been decisively rejected. The Taborites had assisted in the defence of Prague against the royalist siege. Nicholas of Pelhřimov had been elected bishop of Tabor in September with the task of organizing its new church. In the following month, when the customary day for collecting rents came around (St Gall's Day, 14 October), Tabor began acting as *seigneur* in southern Bohemia. In his treatise 'On the Triple Division of Society' (written *c.*1425), Chelčický recalled the Písek debate: 'some of your party's priests in your party's town of Písek agued against me with these and other ideas, seeking thereby to confirm power to themselves, as it were through faith.' Chelčický also recalled the basis on which they did so, paraphrasing Jakoubek of Stříbro: '[that] it is a just idea according to Christ's faith that power should defend the Law of God with the sword, [and that] you people and the masters [of the University of Prague] were truly in accord with the faith in this matter, when you began to fight for the Law of God.'[56]

These details are important because they establish Chelčický's highly

[55] Kaminsky, 'Peter Chelčický', 119–20.
[56] Peter Chelčický, 'On the Triple Division of Society', in Kaminsky, 'Peter Chelčický', 137–67, at 150–1, and see too 174–7 on the Písek debate.

respected position within the intellectual debates about the armed defence of the Hussite cause, and the future development of Tabor, which occurred in the 1420s.[57] Even when both men were being besieged in Prague in 1420 Chelčický discussed the legitimacy of the war with Jakoubek of Stříbro; his own stance of course was the one which he was soon to set out in 'On Spiritual Warfare', and Jakoubek did not find it easy to argue against him with conviction.[58] Kaminsky noted that the phraseology attributed by Chelčický to Jakoubek in the previous paragraph was very similar to that used by Nicholas of Pelhřimov in his *Chronicon Taboritarum*, and it is possible that 'On the Triple Division of Society' was actually addressed to Nicholas, who certainly adhered to the views with which Chelčický contended throughout the treatise.[59] Nicholas's own concerns about the conduct of the war made him a sympathetic audience for Chelčický's arguments, even if he ultimately rejected them.[60] Kaminsky advanced the attractive suggestion that in 1420 Chelčický was caught out by his opponents' use of the traditional scholastic ideology based on divinely attributed social roles, and that the later treatise was a belated reply, which took some years to appear because Chelčický had to read up on the subject and think through his position.[61] Indeed, he prefaced his new work with the comment that he had 'diligently collected the writings of all the priests of Tabor and of the Prague masters from the beginning of the war, and I have pondered on what they have said and are still saying about [the status of secular] power'.[62] By the mid-1420s it was of course too late to exert much influence on the way Hussitism had developed militarily, indeed it was probably too late even in 1420. But the result was a fully elaborated critique of the way the defence of 'God's Law' in Bohemia had been and continued to be justified by Nicholas of Pelhřimov and Jakoubek of Stříbro.

At the heart of Chelčický's 'On the Triple Division of Society' resides the conviction that secular power and Christian belief were not capable of institutional fusion, i.e. no matter how outstanding its merits, no system of secular power could be described as inherently Christian in nature. 'This division in two parts, the secular order through power and Christ's order through love, sets them far apart, and it must be understood that these two orders cannot stand together so that both would be included under the name of one Christian faith.'[63] The only scriptural texts which truly supported a sanctified secular order were Old Testament ones, and Chelčický simply ruled them out of court: 'For if power were supposed to be administered through Christ's faith by means of battles and punishments, and try to benefit Christ's faith with those battles and punish-

---

[57]   Cf. Brock, *Political and Social Doctrines*, 36.
[58]   Kaminsky, 'Peter Chelčický', 114; Brock, *Political and Social Doctrines*, 32.
[59]   Chelčický, 'On the Triple Division of Society', 137 n. 2, 150 n. 10.
[60]   Kaminsky, 'Peter Chelčický', 125: 'Peter continued for some years to serve as a kind of unofficial conscience for the Taborite leaders, whose highly creditable inner uncertainties would be revealed in their discussions with their neighbor.'
[61]   Ibid. 177.   [62]   Chelčický, 'On the Triple Division of Society', 137.   [63]   Ibid. 143.

ments, then why would Christ have abolished the Jewish Law and established a different, spiritual one? If he had wanted people to cut each other up, to hang, drown, and burn each other, and otherwise pour out human blood for his Law, then that Old Law could also have stood unchanged, with the same bloody deeds as before.'[64] Historically, the conflation of secular power and faith had brought about the very abuses against which the Hussites were rebelling, and it would be folly to repeat the mistake, even with the best intentions. Romans 13, the most important passage standing in the way of Chelčický's viewpoint, was set aside by reference to its context: Paul was addressing a situation in which he knew that to oppose the Roman Empire would be counterproductive to the spread of the early church.[65] 'The Apostle does not, by his words, bring the sword of power under Christ's law or make it lord over the faithful, but rather, for reasons of necessity, admonishes the faithful to be obedient to the pagan powers in whose domains they have their homes.'[66]

Having established that secular power and faith existed in totally different spheres, Chelčický turned his attention to the proposition that the social order itself in those lands which were loyal to utraquism was divinely instituted for the purpose of defending the Hussite reform programme, effectively that the Hussite community was the *corpus Christi* personified. The gist of the case was not dissimilar to what had already been stated: that key texts such as 1 Corinthians 12 (the interdependence of the body's parts) should be read as referring to spiritual gifts rather than physical or social matters; and that scriptural exegesis generally should operate strictly in terms of intention: 'It is proper for a man to cite a case in the Bible in aid of his own ideas only when it seems that the scriptural text may itself have the idea that is in his mind.'[67] Once the camouflage of such scriptural misinterpretation was removed it was apparent that the social order had nothing to do with the faith: 'The triply divided Christian people, carnal and full of dissension, neither can nor ever will have that unity and love of one another; it is the world, and it has in itself only worldly desires.'[68]

The incongruity of the proposition that the social order was divinely appointed elicited from Chelčický language fully as colourful as that used by Nicholas of Pelhřimov in his critique of Tabor just a few years later. But the accusations which Nicholas levelled against Taborite society were exceeded in range and bitterness by Chelčický's depiction of a Bohemia thrown into turmoil by the war, and a social order which he regarded as riddled with injustice. All his sympathies lay with the common people, whose goods were stripped off them by an oppressive military and clergy. His harshest words were reserved for the former. Rather than being the defenders of God's Law, they arbitrarily seized the goods of the ordinary peasants: '[They] ride out from the towns in the evening, visit the chests and cattle of the peasants, or whatever they meet up with—ardent

---

[64] Ibid. 139–40.   [65] Ibid. 147–8.   [66] Ibid. 150.   [67] Ibid. 154.   [68] Ibid. 156.

lovers of God's law, they cannot leave even so much as a cheese where they find it!'[69] Or as he put it in his *Postilla*: 'The labouring people is stripped of every-thing, downtrodden, oppressed, beaten, robbed, so that many are driven by want and hunger to leave their land. Some even must pay their dues to castle or town thrice over, even four times, now to one side, now to the other. For otherwise they would be driven from house and fields. And what is not taken from them by the castle in dues is eaten up by the armies . . . that prey upon the land.'[70] Chelčický's response to the Taborite priests' defence of their community's prac-tice of plundering its enemies was therefore multi-layered: first strip away the scriptural camouflage, especially the superseded Old Testament citations, and then reveal the sordid reality in all its injustice. Lacking Nicholas's belief that Tabor, for all its faults, had an eschatological role to fulfil, Chelčický could not disguise his contempt: 'To attempt, therefore, to use the teachings of Scripture to order the Body of Christ in this way is to order the world under the cover of Christ's faith, to disguise the course of secular affairs as the service of Christian Law.'[71]

Despite later advocacy of his views by Tolstoy, Peter Chelčický remains a comparatively obscure figure within European intellectual thought.[72] The re-verse is true of the man who a century later reiterated many of the arguments which Chelčický had employed. Erasmus' loathing for war was one of his most consistent preoccupations, but it found its most telling expression in a number of works written between 1511 and 1517, especially *Moriae encomium* (1511), *Dulce bellum inexpertis* (1515), *Institutio principis christiani* (1516), and *Querela pacis* (1517).[73] His stance was more societal than Chelčický's had been, to the extent that he identified and condemned the numerous evils brought about by war; as he put it in a letter to Wolfgang Capito in 1517, 'every vestige of true religion, of just laws, of civilized behaviour, of high moral standards and of liberal arts among the incessant clash of arms is either killed outright by a licentious soldiery, or at best is brought to the lowest ebb'.[74] Nevertheless, at the centre of Erasmus' re-jection of war lay the conviction that it was irreconcilable with Christian faith,

---

[69] Chelčický, 'On the Triple Division of Society', 163.

[70] Brock, *Political and Social Doctrines*, 58–9.

[71] Chelčický, 'On the Triple Division of Society', 167.

[72] In 1957 Peter Brock wrote that Chelčický's name 'has scarcely been heard of outside the frontiers of his native country': *Political and Social Doctrines*, 25. The situation has not changed much since then. For a recent assessment see W. Iwańczak, 'Between Pacifism and Anarchy: Peter Chelčický's Teaching about Society', *JMH* 23 (1997), 271–83.

[73] See *Guerre et paix dans la pensée d'Érasme*, ed. J.-C. Margolin (Paris: Aubier Montaigne, 1973); L.-E. Halkin, 'Érasme, la guerre et la paix', in *Krieg und Frieden im Horizont des Renaissancehumanismus* (Weinheim: Acta Humaniora, 1986), 13–44, repr. in his *Érasme: Sa pensée et son comportement* (London: Variorum, 1988), study XV; Adams, *The Better Part of Valor*; J. A. Fernández, 'Erasmus on the Just War', *Journal of the History of Ideas*, 34 (1973), 209–26; P. Brachin, '*Vox clamantis in deserto*: Réflexions sur le pacifisme d'Érasme', in J.-C. Margolin (ed.), *Colloquia erasmiana turonensia: douzième stage international d'études humanistes, Tours 1969*, 2 vols. (Toronto: University of Toronto Press, 1972), i. 247–75.

[74] *Opus epistolarum Des. Erasmi*, ii. 488, no. 541.

because 'the sum and substance of our religion is peace and concord'.[75] It followed that the very idea of a war fought in response to a divine mandate, in pursuit of religious goals, or even in a Christian manner (the *bella christiana* of the
Hussites), was nonsense. Raffaele Puddu expressed these central tenets well: 'the
hinges of Erasmus's thinking on war are an absolute denial of the possibility of a
Christian soldiery, and a harsh polemic against the church's role in justifying and
absolving it.'[76]

For Erasmus the context of condemnation was very different from that faced
by Chelčický. There were two types of religious war being advocated or waged at
the time Erasmus wrote the series of works referred to above. First, as we have
seen, many clerics were giving enthusiastic support to the dynastic wars of
Europe's rulers. In England in 1512–13 this included proclaiming the plenary indulgences which Pope Julius II had granted Henry VIII for his war with Louis
XII of France.[77] Erasmus may have been thinking specifically of this when, in
Dulce bellum inexpertis, he castigated the cleric who 'from the sacred pulpit
promises pardon for all the sins committed by those who fight under the banners
of his prince'. A few lines further on he described how 'two armies march against
each other each carrying the standard of the Cross, which in itself might teach
them how Christians should conquer. Under that heavenly banner, symbolising
the perfect and ineffable union of all Christians, there is a rush to butcher each
other, and we make Christ the witness and authority for so criminal a thing.'[78]
However, fourteen years later, in *Charon*, Erasmus referred to the practice in a
much more general way in the course of an attack on the friars: 'To the French
they preach that God is on the French side: he who has God to protect him cannot be conquered! To the English and Spanish they declare this war is not the
Emperor's but God's . . . [And] if anyone does get killed, he doesn't perish
utterly but flies straight up to heaven, armed just as he was.'[79]

If the sanctification of dynastic and national warfare was an unmitigated evil,
there was not much more to be said in favour of the second type of religious war,
the crusade which Pope Leo X was strenuously attempting to organize against
the Turks.[80] Even when he wrote to the pope in May 1515 with the request that
he be allowed to dedicate his edition of Jerome to him, Erasmus found it hard to
bring himself to praise Leo's crusade project.[81] In correspondence with friends

[75] Ibid., v. 177, no. 1334.
[76] R. Puddu, *Il soldato gentiluomo: Autoritratto d'una società guerriera: La Spagna del Cinquecento*
(Bologna: Società Editrice il Mulino, 1982), 80.
[77] Brewer et al. (eds.), *Letters and Papers*, 63–4, no. 169; Tyerman, *England and the Crusades*, 359.
[78] *Erasmus on his Times*, 116–17.
[79] *The Colloquies of Erasmus*, ed. and trans. C. R. Thompson (Chicago: University of Chicago Press,
1965), 391–2. This was an exact (though unintentional) replication of what Taborite chiliasts had claimed
on behalf of their combatants in 1420: 'et si quispiam de eorum fratribus fuerat ab aversariis interemptus,
mox cum gaudio ubicunque locorum eundem sepelierunt dicentes: "eum in causa Dei decessisse, et sine
omni post hanc vitam purgatorio . . . coelos penetrasse"': LoB, 'De gestis', 411.
[80] K. M. Setton, 'Pope Leo X and the Turkish Peril', *Proceedings of the American Philosophical Society*,
113 (1969), 367–424.
[81] *Opus epistolarum Des. Erasmi*, ii. 84–5, no. 335.

he was much more openly critical. He focused his attention on the abuses associated with crusading, notably the sale of indulgences and the financial frauds practised by pope and princes alike, but there was no doubt that underlying these attacks there lay a rejection of the very idea of a holy war. It was simply irreconcilable with what Erasmus termed the *philosophia Christi*, the entirety of the religious message encompassed in the life and teachings of Jesus. As he succinctly expressed it to Leo X in 1515, 'To fight the Turks we get no instructions from Christ and no encouragement from the apostles.'[82]

This remark of course brings us to the heart of Erasmus' intellectual affinity with Chelčický: both men demilitarized Scripture. In the first place, they regarded the Old Testament, which provided such rich material for advocates of holy war, as having been superseded by the new dispensation. Chelčický's comment on Christ's abolition of the Jewish Law was mirrored in Erasmus' remark that if the wars of the Israelites were to be viewed as a literal prefigurement of how Christians should behave, then the latter should stop eating pork.[83] Secondly, they both insisted on a reading of the New Testament which took fully into account both the intentions of the authors and the circumstances in which they wrote. Chelčický dismissed the traditional methods of scholastic exegesis: 'I do not allow this to be a true way of founding something in the Law of Christ—to milk it violently out of various passages in the Scriptures, and to put something into the foundation just because the Scriptures mention it or name it. It is a false sort of foundation, hiding under beautiful language like a robber who sneaks into a home at night and takes what is in it.'[84] Erasmus found this a wholly persuasive argument, and while he worked in a period in which biblical scholarship was much more advanced than it had been in Chelčický's lifetime, his method was essentially the same. Chelčický had undercut his opponents' reliance on Romans 13 by emphasizing context; Erasmus performed a similar exercise with Luke 22: 36–8 (the two swords in the Upper Chamber), another classic text for religious war, although his own reading of this very problematic passage was actually no less strained than that of the scholastics whom he mocked.[85]

Erasmus' concern to reveal the essence of the *philosophia Christi* led him to go one step further in his assault on scholastic exegetical practice. He refused to invest any especial authority in the writings of the Church Fathers, even such figures as St Augustine and St Bernard, in cases when their views conflicted with what he saw as the correct reading of Scripture.[86] Chelčický's learning was too slender for this to become an issue: his grasp of Latin was weak and he showed no signs of having encountered the writings of the Church Fathers.[87] Nevertheless,

---

[82] *Opus epistolarum Des. Erasmi*, ii. 84–5, no. 335. For more detail on Erasmus' treatment of Leo X's crusade project see Housley, 'A Necessary Evil?', 261–6.

[83] *Erasmus on his Times*, 127.   [84] Chelčický, 'On the Triple Division of Society', 154.

[85] Erasmus, 'Moriae encomium', 145–6.   [86] *Erasmus on his Times*, 130.

[87] Kaminsky, 'Peter Chelčický', 109–10; Brock, *Political and Social Doctrines*, 31.

the common concern of the two men to demilitarize Scripture produced some strikingly similar results. The internalization of combat in Chelčický's 'On Spiritual Warfare' had its equivalent in one of Erasmus' most famous and popular works, *Enchiridion militis christiani*, first published in 1503.[88] And in much the same way that Chelčický had argued that Tabor's warfare would have the effect of undermining the spiritual health of its soldiers, Erasmus used the preface to a new edition of *Enchiridion* published in 1518 to question the effects of Pope Leo's planned crusade: 'the result may extend the kingdom of the pope and his cardinals; it will not extend the kingdom of Christ.'[89]

A further parallel resides in the way an assault on religious war went hand in glove with a wider field of criticism. Chelčický was alarmed that a religious goal, the preservation of God's Law following its rediscovery by the Hussites, would be subverted by contact with secular power if it were defended by the sword, no matter how well intentioned that defence. Erasmus, on the other hand, suspected intention rather than simply lamenting effect. When Christendom's authorities talked about crusading, what they really had in mind was the extension of their own powers: 'The princes, together with the pope, and I dare say the Grand Turk as well, are in league against the well-being of the common people.'[90] More broadly, both men were deeply critical of their societies, particularly the roles played by the military class and the clergy. Each viewed the conflation of war with religion as a symptom of society's ills, and a hindrance to true Christian faith, God's Law in Chelčický's case, the *philosophia Christi* in Erasmus'.

Chelčický viewed the military defeat of the Hussite cause as preferable to its defence by the use of force. This was because he did not equate defeat with extinction. Defeat would actually facilitate the diffusion of God's Law through *imitatio Christi*, the example of its martyred adherents serving to win others over to their belief. Indeed, one good reason for not defending God's Law with force was that suffering priests made converts.[91] Erasmus could not exercise the same degree of hope when contemplating the advance of the Ottoman Turks. Their victory could well mean not just the extinction of the Christian faith but also the annihilation of the humanist cause. In his *Consultatio de bello Turcis inferendo*, written in 1530 for reasons which remain less than clear, Erasmus therefore advocated a defensive war against the Turks, albeit with extreme reluctance. It was certainly not to be a religious war, although to enlist God's support it must be promoted and waged in a spirit of piety.[92] Indeed, it could only succeed 'if before all else we placate the Lord's wrath, if our intention is unsullied and proper, if our whole trust lies in Christ, if we fight under His banners, if He triumphs in us,

---

[88] Erasmus, 'Enchiridion militis christiani', *passim*.

[89] *Opus epistolarum Des. Erasmi*, iii. 365, no. 858.

[90] Ibid. 429, no. 891, and see too iii. 426, no. 887, iii. 524, no. 936.

[91] Chelčický, 'On the Triple Division of Society', 151. Passages like this one are important for Seibt's argument ('Peter Chelčický', 212–13) that Chelčický was akin to Francis of Assisi.

[92] Housley, 'A Necessary Evil?', 267–8, 274–8.

if we heed the commands of our God, as if we were attacking the enemy under His eyes'.[93] This reads like an exhortation to crusade, but in fact it is the language of *Enchiridion militis christiani*. Erasmus was nevertheless contemplating a war, and he could not do so with any optimism. We have seen that he believed the price of defeating the 'Turk without' to be the triumph of the 'Turk within'.[94] On this point he was no less sensitive than Chelčický. But whereas Chelčický was inherently separatist in his approach, Erasmus was so engaged with the values of humanist reform that he could not contemplate their destruction by the Turks with equanimity.[95]

The challenge which the Turks posed to Erasmus' rejection of war took a more diverse form in the case of religious groups in this period which embraced pacifist ideals. The Unity of Czech Brethren, which was founded in the winter of 1457–8 and broke with the utraquist church in 1467, acknowledged Chelčický as its spiritual father. His influence is apparent in the writings of Brother Řehoř, the key figure in the early history of the movement. For example, Řehoř wrote in 1461 that 'not only are [the civil authorities] not entitled to use force in matters of faith, but they should also refrain from defending the faith by the sword. For Christ sent out his apostles into the world to preach the gospel without the help of the civil power, of magistrates, of hangmen or of armies.'[96] By this point the military might of Tabor, which had sheltered Chelčický and his small band of followers, had been broken. When conscription was introduced to defend Bohemia against another crusade in 1467, the Brethren underwent a three-year period of persecution for their refusal to bear arms. It was not long before the possibility of a Turkish incursion had to be faced, and the response of the Brethren remained resolute: 'And they say this, that if the Turk or any other enemy were to attack them, they would not wish to defend themselves, preferring to die in their simplicity, and they conclude from this, that fighting is not permissible, either for justice or for faith: evil must be borne in simplicity.'[97]

What rendered this absolute pacifism untenable in the long run was the success of the Brethren in recruiting members from amongst the better-off, who wanted to hold office and therefore resented the denigration of civil power, including its use of force. In the early sixteenth century the Brethren's doctrines underwent wholesale revision. Led by Br. Lukáš, prominent members of the Unity adopted and justified a stance on warfare situated between those taken up by Peter Chelčický and Nicholas of Pelhřimov: probably the closest equivalent in the Hussite period had been Jakoubek of Stříbro. As Lukáš defined their position, 'We have not cut ourselves off, nor have we the intention, as the Taborites

---

[93] Erasmus, 'Utilissima consultatio', 68.   [94] Above, Ch. 5, at nn. 136–45.
[95] On this point J.-C. Margolin, 'Érasme et la guerre contre les Turcs', *Il pensiero politico*, 13 (1980), 3–38, presents a sound balance. See also O. Schottenloher, 'Erasmus und die Respublica Christiana', *HZ* 210 (1970), 295–323.
[96] Brock, *Political and Social Doctrines*, 89.   [97] Ibid. 93 n. 44.

and others have had, of taking up the sword in defence of the faith.' It remained preferable for a Brother to send substitutes to war rather than fighting in person, but killing God's enemies *caritative*, 'justly and without hatred', was not contrary to the faith. Lukáš was even prepared to dismiss Chelčický's pacifism as an overreaction to the excesses of Tabor's religious warfare, and he criticized the erstwhile authority for hypocrisy in enjoying the protection of the very people whose activities he condemned. 'Thus the wheel had come full circle.'[98]

Although this volte-face in the Czech Brethren's position was not driven primarily by the Ottoman threat, it certainly made their response to that threat much less problematic. As early as 1502 Br. Tůma Přeloučský called on the rich to stop oppressing the poor and instead to perform their duty in defending Christendom, 'for if ever there was a time since the beginning of the Christian faith when it was necessary to fight against the Turks, it is now'.[99] Thus a Chelčický-like assault on social injustice was coupled with an acceptance of the just war and the protective duties of lordship, rather than forming part of a broader critique of the activities of the devil in the material world. By the time the leading revisionist, Br. Lukáš, died in 1528, the catastrophe at Mohács had drastically increased the likelihood of Turkish incursions into Moravia and even Bohemia. Although there remained a rump of Brethren (the 'Minor Party') who clung to the Unity's original pacifism, the majority were now willing to play their role in staving off the Turkish armies. In 1530 the Unity published an official guide for believers who fell into Ottoman captivity while on active service. That service was regarded not just as acceptable but as honourable.[100]

'If the Turks should come, we ought not to resist them. For it is written [Matt. 5: 21]: Thou shalt not kill.'[101] This comment by Michael Sattler at his trial in 1527 showed that some contemporaries of Erasmus still adhered to Chelčický's views. Indeed, in 1559 a conference of elders among the Czech Brethren specifically denounced the quietist stance of Anabaptists who followed Sattler's line.[102] The essentially linear evolution of ideas which is so clear in the case of the Czech Brethren was not replicated amongst the Anabaptists. Rather, the debate about the validity of religious violence which the Anabaptists conducted resembled from the start the full spectrum of the Hussite coalition. It was different to the extent that it lacked the compact territorial base of Hussitism, and it was profoundly shaped by a single watershed event: the Münster uprising of 1534–5. Prominent Anabaptists like Pilgram Marpeck, Menno Simons, and Jakob Hutter reacted against the embrace of violence by Hans Hut and Melchior Hoffman, and its short-lived but remarkable practice at Münster, by advocating

---

[98] Ibid. 182–205, esp. 191–8. See too the judgement of the earlier historian of the Czech Brethren, Anton Gindely, cited ibid. 273.

[99] Ibid. 230–1.   [100] Ibid. 271.

[101] Klaasen (ed.), *Anabaptism in Outline*, 270. See also Stayer, *Anabaptists and the Sword*, 124.

[102] Brock, *Political and Social Doctrines*, 271.

strict pacifism. Their approach was essentially that of Chelčický: the Old Testament had been superseded,[103] and Christian faith and the use of force were incompatible because of the dichotomy of spirit and flesh. It followed that, in Marpeck's words, 'no true Christian may exercise force in the name or under the cover of Christ and the gospel or faith in Christ'.[104] Separatism was the inevitable outcome, especially for those who joined Hutter in rejecting even the payment of war taxes: 'for how could we be innocent before our God if we did not go to war ourselves but gave the money that others could go in our place?'[105] These pacifists did not enjoy the protection of communities which were prepared to fight for their faith, as had been the case with Chelčický and Tabor. Michael Sattler, an extreme pacifist whose Schleitheim confession espoused passivity in its sixth clause, was burnt at the stake in 1527. Hutter was tortured and burnt to death nine years later.[106]

Probably the most important of the early Anabaptists to adhere to the movement's *Stäbler* (pacifist) wing rather than to its *Schwertler* (activist) one was Menno Simons. His brother was killed in Friesland in 1535 during the Münster rebellion and Simons wrote a condemnatory tract 'On the Blasphemy of Jan of Leyden'. For the remainder of his life Simons was anxious to dissociate himself and his followers from the Münsterite excesses. Again and again he insisted on a spiritual interpretation of the conflict which every true believer faced, a reiteration with a vengeance of Ephesians 6: 'Our wagon fortress is Christ, out weapon of defence is patience, our sword is the word of God and our victory is free, firm and undisguised faith in Jesus Christ.'[107] Simons was heavily influenced by Erasmus and he had no apocalyptic leanings. The triumph of the faith and the reward of the faithful would come in God's time. His followers (the Mennonites) and those of Hutter (the Hutterites) joined the Unity of the Czech Brethren's Minor Party among the religious groups carrying forward the rejection of religious war into the modern period.

6.3 WAR AND CONVERSION

'True believing Christians are sheep in the midst of wolves, sheep for slaughtering, and must be baptised into anxiety and dereliction, tribulation, persecution, suffering and dying, must be tried in the fire and find the fatherland of eternal rest not by throttling their bodily, but their spiritual (foes); then they will attain

---

[103] Brock, *Political and Social Doctrines*, 183–4, showed that the reinstatement of the Old Testament was a major step in the abandonment of Chelčický's views.
[104] Klaasen (ed.), *Anabaptism in Outline*, 263.   [105] Ibid. 252–3.
[106] For one reflection of the pacifist wing of Anabaptism see Bohnstedt, 'The Infidel Scourge of God', 49–50.
[107] Stayer, *Anabaptists and the Sword*, 310–21, with quote at 318.

to it.'[108] Conrad Grebel's denunciation of violence in a letter to Müntzer in September 1524 eloquently encapsulated the position of men like Chelčický, Erasmus, and Simons. At the time Grebel wrote, sectarian strife within Christian Europe and the assault by the Ottoman armies in the east made his metaphor all too convincing. But as a result of the overseas discoveries many contemporaries found themselves in the position not of sheep but of sheep-dogs, bringing unbelievers into the single flock prophesied in John 10: 16, the text on which Joachites placed such store. By so doing they were fulfilling an eschatological purpose, one fully as compelling as that which drove sectarian activists like Thomas Müntzer and Jan Bockelson. The connection between war and conversion was bound to be addressed, and many of the arguments deployed against religious war in Europe found a new theatre. In acting as sheep-dogs, would Christians overseas become wolves?

In the course of the fifteenth century a sophisticated debate developed on the relations between Christianity and Islam in terms of crusade and conversion. The key figures were the Castilian theologian and conciliarist Juan de Segovia and the German cardinal Nicholas of Cusa. Both men were encouraged by the apparent success of dialogue with the Greeks and utraquists to hope that similar methods might succeed with the Muslims.[109] In 1454, one year after the Turkish seizure of Constantinople, Juan questioned the efficacy of crusade as a means of defeating Islam. Historically, it was Islam which triumphed through arms, while Christianity achieved its successes through persuasion and example. He pointed to the failure of so many crusades in support of his thesis. The Christian powers should seek to make peace with Islamic rulers and then undermine their faith through public disputations, in which the Christian cause would emerge triumphant.[110] Juan's correspondent on this occasion, the prolific Nicholas of Cusa, famously argued for dialogue rather than conflict in his *De pace fidei* (1453).[111] By the early sixteenth century many intellectuals had come to adopt the same viewpoint, including Erasmus. He asserted that a large-scale programme of missionary activity was the way to deal with the Turks, although it is likely that he took this view because of his horror at a crusading response.[112] More

---

[108] *The Collected Works of Thomas Müntzer*, 121–32, at 127. See also Stayer, *Anabaptists and the Sword*, 102–3; H.-J. Goertz, 'A Common Future Conversation: A Revisionist Interpretation of the September 1524 Grebel Letters to Thomas Müntzer', in W. O. Packull and G. L. Dipple (eds.), *Radical Reformation Studies: Essays Presented to James M. Stayer* (Aldershot: Ashgate, 1999), 73–90.

[109] Southern, *Western Views of Islam*, 86–94; Hankins, 'Renaissance Crusaders', 128; T. M. Izbicki, 'The Possibility of Dialogue with Islam in the Fifteenth Century', in G. Christianson and T. M. Izbicki (eds.), *Nicholas of Cusa in Search of God and Wisdom* (Leiden: Brill, 1991), 175–83; J. E. Biechler, 'A New Face toward Islam: Nicholas of Cusa and John of Segovia', ibid. 185–202.

[110] D. Cabanelas Rodríguez, *Juan de Segovia y el problema islámico* (Madrid: Universidad de Madrid, 1952); Echevarria, *The Fortress of Faith*, 34–40.

[111] Nicolaus Cusanus, *De pace fidei*, ed. R. Klibansky and H. Bascour (London: Warburg Institute, 1956).

[112] e.g. Erasmus, 'Utilissima consultatio', 82; Housley, 'A Necessary Evil?', 273–4.

interesting is the readiness of some high-ranking Catholic reformers to place their hopes in conversion. Cardinal Cajetan, Luther's opponent, argued in a sermon in the papal chapel that 'holy words and holy lives, not armies, are the instruments of conversion'.[113]

Yet this debate was not paralleled in the case of overseas discoveries. The African and Atlantic ventures of the Portuguese lay at the origins of the sequence of events which culminated in Columbus' voyages, and political weakness compelled the Renaissance papacy to adopt an acquiescent and unchallenging position when approached with requests for privileges in favour of these ventures. This is most notably evident in Pope Martin V's bulls to John I following the Portuguese capture of Ceuta in 1415. Their preambles are revealing because John I's tendentious interpretation of Portuguese motives and goals 'in African parts and elsewhere' was adopted with little if any modification. Thus in April 1418 crusade indulgences were granted for further conquests 'to conquer those parts and bring them to Christianity',[114] while the right to trade with neighbouring Muslims was granted in the hope that cordial economic relations would foster receptivity to the gospel's message.[115] It is hard to avoid the conclusion that the pope was agreeing to whatever was asked of him by the king, or more likely his son Henry, whom John I had placed in charge of administering Ceuta.[116] The papacy's flaccid acceptance that any military engagement with non-Christians constituted praiseworthy activity was not at all far from the flexible mindset associated with chivalric crusading, of which Henry would remain the prime exponent throughout his life.

There are few echoes in these documents of the thirteenth-century canonistic debate about the natural rights of non-Christians.[117] *Rex regum*, the crusade bull of 4 April 1418, which set a pattern for later ones, described King John as engaged in the process of spreading (*propagatio*) the faith, to the exaltation of Christ's name and the extermination (*exterminium*) of his enemies.[118] The king was aiming to subjugate the Saracens, to bring the lands which they occupied to the Christian faith. Such generalizations betrayed a failure to discriminate or even to show much interest. In one bull of April 1418 sanctioning the conversion of a mosque or synagogue at Ceuta into a cathedral, the old belief was even repeated that Muslims worshipped idols and images.[119] *Super gregem dominicum* of July 1418 treated the conversion or annihilation of the Muslims of Morocco as more or less equally palatable alternatives.[120] In a metaphor which was almost as attractive to contemporaries as that of the rampart or bulwark, Ceuta was

---

[113] O'Malley, *Praise and Blame*, 236, and cf. J. W. O'Malley, 'The Discovery of America and Reform Thought at the Papal Court in the Early Cinquecento', in F. Chiappelli et al. (eds.), *First Images of America: The Impact of the New World on the Old*, 2 vols. (Berkeley and Los Angeles: University of California Press, 1976), i. 185–200, at 192–3.

[114] *MH* ii. 278, no. 142.   [115] Ibid. 280, no. 142.   [116] Russell, *Prince Henry*, 59–80.
[117] Muldoon, *Popes, Lawyers, and Infidels*, 3–48.   [118] *MH* ii. 283, no. 143.
[119] Ibid. 288, no. 144.   [120] Ibid. 300, no. 146.

depicted as the key to Africa (*clavis tocius Africe*).[121] But with no real steering in any direction being given by the papal *curia*, the 'door' which it opened could lead to conversion, conquest, or annihilation.

If there is any logic in these documents, it resides in the association of military conquest with proselytizing, as proclaimed, for instance, by Henry's publicist Zurara.[122] But there was no demand for proof of action in terms of missionary activity and, as Peter Russell has shown, the record of the Portuguese in this regard, both at Ceuta and in their Atlantic and sub-Saharan conquests, was actually negligible.[123] In this light it is all the more telling that in December 1434 Martin V's successor Eugenius IV took action that appeared to demonstrate a much less compliant response to Portuguese demands. Informed of pillaging carried out by a Portuguese expedition on Canarian islands which were in Christian hands, the pope, in the bull *Creator omnium rerum*, annulled the permission previously granted to the king of Portugal to conquer those islands which were still pagan.[124]

Creator omnium rerum is a highly revealing document. The complainant in 1434 was the bishop residing on the islands which had been settled, Fernando Calvetos, and the bull's detail about what had happened presumably originated with him. The argument of the bull was clear: conversion was proceeding smoothly but had recently become imperilled through enslavement and pillage. The description of this was detailed, stark, and unsparing, and it merits lengthy quotation.

We grieve to report that certain Christians, making use of various opportunities and fabricated excuses, have made armed incursions on these islands. There they have seized many people of both sexes, catching them unawares due to their naivety. Some of them were already baptized, while to others they promised that it was their desire to bring them to baptism. They behaved fraudulently and deceitfully, with promises of security which they made and did not keep. They brought them back to this side of the sea as captives, having treated their belongings as booty or turned them to their own uses and purposes. Some of these inhabitants and residents they subjected to perpetual slavery, and others they sold to third parties. They committed various other illicit and wicked acts against them. As a result many of the remaining inhabitants of the said islands, appalled at this slavery, remain sunk in their original errors and have abandoned their desire to receive baptism, which is a grave offence to the divine name, a danger to souls, and no small harm to the Christian religion.[125]

A few months previously, moreover, Eugenius IV had issued other bulls of a similar nature. *Etsi cunctis fidei* forbade the imposition of inordinately high dues on

---

[121] Ibid. 317, no. 157, and cf. n. 2. At other times Ceuta could itself be a *propugnaculum*: ibid. 357, no. 174. For Harfleur, coincidentally captured just a few weeks after Ceuta, as 'la principall Claeve de France', see *Rotuli parliamentorum*, iv. 94.
[122] Zurara, *Conquests*, 132.   [123] Russell, *Prince Henry*, 69, 318–19, 352.
[124] *MH* v. 118–23, no. 52.   [125] Ibid. 121–2, no. 52.

Canarian converts, and the pope issued safe conducts to make the missionary work easier.[126] The preambles to all these documents referred to the papal responsibility to spread the faith and to protect neophytes lest they desert their new-found faith. *Creator omnium rerum* is particularly revealing with its allusions to the common humanity of converters and converted, and the universal applicability of the economy of salvation.[127] As stated, the context was the Canaries, but it was not far from such a viewpoint to the negative comments made by one curialist on Portuguese requests for a Moroccan crusade, in the summer of 1436, to the effect that the pope's duty was to feed all his sheep, as enjoined on him in John 10: 16 and 21: 17. 'Peter's successor has the job of feeding and defending those [sheep], so he should not allow them to be attacked or harmed.'[128]

It was only two years later that the punitive veto imposed by *Creator omnium rerum* was lifted. Had the pope adhered to his initial sensitivity regarding the situation which had come about in the Canaries, and had it been adopted by his successors in the case of later discoveries, the history of European overseas discovery and conversion might have been very different. Instead the bulls of 1434 stand out as exceptional. When he revoked *Creator omnium rerum* in September 1436 Eugenius IV evidently accepted King Duarte's claim that it was only through force of arms that Christianity could be brought to the entire Canarian archipelago.[129] Nineteen years later Pope Nicholas V's definitive treatment of the discoveries, *Romanus pontifex*, took it for granted that the sheep could not be brought into the fold except through military conquest. The surgical sensitivity displayed in *Creator omnium rerum* was replaced by a tide of rhetoric, formula, and assertion.[130]

Why did Eugenius IV's successors fail to follow the lead which he set, albeit briefly, in 1434? The intellectual arguments for a more sophisticated response to non-believers overseas were undoubtedly to hand. In 1436 two Italian jurists, Antonio Minucci da Pratovecchio and Antonio de Rosellis, both professors at Bologna, produced formidably long *consulta* on the Portuguese proposal to attack Tangier which used arguments from both canon and civil law to throw the legality of that project into serious doubt. Of particular interest was Pratovecchio's citation of Pope Innocent IV's view that non-believers legitimately held *dominium* and therefore could not be attacked justly solely on the basis that they were infidels.[131] Such a belief underpinned the expansionist

---

[126] *MH* v. 84–93, nos. 36–8.   [127] Ibid. 119–20, no. 52.   [128] Ibid. 269, no. 132.

[129] Ibid. 254–8, 281–2, nos. 129, 137. For discussion see de Witte, 'Les Bulles pontificales', 48 (1953), 702–3; Muldoon, *Popes, Lawyers, and Infidels*, 119–24. There is a translation of Duarte's letter requesting the lifting of the ban in J. Muldoon (ed.), *The Expansion of Europe: The First Phase* (Philadelphia: University of Pennsylvania Press, 1977), 54–6.

[130] *MH* xii. 71–9, no. 36. See also J. Muldoon, 'Papal Responsibility for the Infidel: Another Look at Alexander VI's *Inter caetera*', *Catholic Historical Review*, 64 (1978), 168–84, at 180–1; J. O'Callaghan, 'Castile, Portugal, and the Canary Islands: Claims and Counterclaims, 1344–1479', *Viator*, 24 (1993), 287–309, at 305–6, 309.

[131] *MH* v. 285–343, nos. 140–1, and see the analysis in Russell, *Prince Henry*, 161–3.

thinking of Henry the Navigator just as it had many crusading enthusiasts before him. The destruction of this viewpoint on broad-based legal and theological grounds, conjoined with the sort of clinical detail contained in *Creator omnium rerum*, could have brought about a long-term dissociation of conquest and conversion.[132] It is apparent that most of the arguments which would be deployed by Francisco de Vitoria in his detailed critique of Spanish imperialism in the 1530s were already being advanced a century earlier, at a point when they might have made a difference.[133] Not surprisingly, therefore, historians have looked very closely at these years, and several explanations have been advanced as to why the popes chose to turn a blind eye to the issues which they knew very well, as individuals, beset any bland approval of overseas conquest as 'expanding the faith' (*dilatatio fidei*).

James Muldoon considered that the key consideration shaping their blunter approach towards the situation was their acceptance that a ban on raiding, enslavement, and colonization in the interests of promoting conversion was unrealistic: even if it held back governments and their agents, it would not curtail the activities of private groups. It was better to support state-directed conquest, which could at least be validated on the grounds that conversion would be incorporated. The desire to save souls could only be realized if based on political and economic reality.[134] More recently, Peter Russell has highlighted the political context in western Europe. The validation of conquest was an expression of papal supremacy, albeit a reactive one, in an age of conciliarist challenge to that supremacy. 'It was, after all, unlikely that any pope would find legal grounds for questioning the actions of a ruler who wholeheartedly espoused the doctrine of the universal sovereignty of the Holy See at a time when this doctrine was under severe attack from within the Church.'[135]

Charles-Martial de Witte drew a rather different conclusion from his study of the sixty-nine documents issued by the popes of the fifteenth century in relation to Portuguese overseas expansion. He argued that the dominant consideration in the minds of the popes was the promotion of the war against Islam, which featured in forty-seven of the bulls. It was essential to mobilize any strength which would assist that goal and to show good will towards any Christian government which was predisposed to help. Distinctions were not made between African Muslims and the Ottoman sultanate. Thus 'the scruples of Eugenius IV were swept aside'.[136] It is undeniable that the Portuguese attempted to conflate the

---

[132] Cf. Russell, *Prince Henry*, 163: 'a declaration that attacked the very core of Prince Henry's crusading ideology'.
[133] Francisco de Vitoria, 'On the American Indians', in *Political Writings*, ed. and trans. A. Pagden and J. Lawrance (Cambridge: Cambridge University Press, 1991), 231–92.
[134] Muldoon, *Popes, Lawyers, and Infidels*, 129–31; id., 'Papal Responsibility for the Infidel', 181–3; id., in *The Expansion of Europe*, 54.
[135] Russell, *Prince Henry*, 164, and cf. Muldoon, *Popes, Lawyers, and Infidels*, 105–6.
[136] De Witte, 'Les Bulles pontificales', 51 (1956), 428, and 53 (1958), 454–70, esp. 457.

Atlantic islands with Africa in their lobbying at the *curia*. The request made in August 1436 that the 1434 ban be revoked put forward as its second reason (after hopes for the conversion of the Canarians) the fact that 'the said islands [sc. the Canaries] lie in close proximity to Africa, as may be clearly seen through cosmography and marine charts, indeed they are really a part of Africa'.[137] The argument struck home, and the bulls issued in September constituted a wholesale accession to Portuguese demands both in relation to the remaining Canarian islands and in terms of the desired crusade in Morocco.[138]

This was even more evidently the case in Nicholas V's bull *Romanus pontifex*. The opening paragraph slides imperceptibly from an espousal of the papal duty to realize John 10: 16 into advocacy of the war against Islam. 'Defensio et augmentum fidei' were both to be achieved by the same sword, one wielded by the Catholic princes of Portugal 'as athletes and intrepid prize-fighters of the Christian faith'. This sleight of hand pervaded the rest of the bull, which viewed the capture of Ceuta, Prince Henry's southwards explorations, the search for Prester John, and the forced conversions of Negroes in Guinea as diverse elements in a single struggle. There was a clear precedent for this 'unifying' tendency at the *curia*, in so far as the popes had in the past yielded to the insistence of Iberian rulers that the *Reconquista* and the Palestine crusade could be brought into the same ideological pattern; what makes it jarring in this case is the disregard for earlier distinctions. It is hard not to believe that what lay at the root of such a wholesale blurring of reality was the anxiety created by the fall of Constantinople in 1453.[139]

These explanations are convergent rather than divergent, and at least one further one should be added. Joachites reacted with particular jubilation to the news of overseas discoveries and conquests. For Giles of Viterbo, Castile's victories in Granada and the Maghrib, the discovery of 'islands' in the western Atlantic, and the circumnavigation of the globe made up a clear and invigorating pattern. His sense of eschatological urgency overrode any concerns about the treatment of defeated pagans, and he welcomed Manuel of Portugal's policy of forced baptism. In the discourse which he delivered in St Peter's in December 1507 celebrating Portuguese victory in the Indian Ocean, Giles declared that while the reigns of recent popes had been characterized by the loss of entire Christian populations to Islam, Julius II was presiding over remarkable gains. It was true that the pagan enemies of the Portuguese were losing their lands, but they were saving their souls: 'Others lose their homeland (*patria*) when they are conquered; these would never find it unless they were conquered.'[140] All that was now needed to confirm Julius II's pontificate as the Age of Gold was the recovery of

---

[137] *MH* v. 257, no. 129.   [138] Ibid. 270–5, 281–2, nos. 133, 137.   [139] Ibid., xii. 71–9, no. 36.
[140] 'Fulfillment', 316. Cf. O'Malley, 'Discovery of America', 190–2. Predictably, the Protestant riposte was that pagans converted by Catholics lost both souls and lands. Williams, 'Erasmus and the Reformers', 356–7.

Jerusalem.[141] Giles was not the only contemporary to become excited about Manuel's successes in the seas south of India: others also saw them as a sign that the time was ripe to recover the Holy Land.[142] In such circumstances of heady expectation it was all too easy to ignore or gloss over the thorny question of how the newly discovered peoples might best be incorporated into the single flock of Christians.

A combination of pragmatism, fear of the Ottomans, Joachimist programmes (including the recovery of the Holy Land), and of course lobbying from powers with vested interests, thus meant that the crusade continued to be associated with discovery well into the sixteenth century.[143] Joachimism exerted a particularly important impact because of the extent to which the early Franciscan missionaries in the New World were infected by it. It was only gradually that the idea took root of an indigenous Indian church with its own identity and interests, uncoupled from the eschatological needs of Europe.[144] Only when that had occurred could some of the sophistication which had entered the discussion about Islamic–Christian relations penetrate the Indies. When this happened, however, it was subsumed by the much more compelling debate about the natural rights of the Indians, the treatment of the subject natives by the European settlers, and the overall validity of the Spanish presence in the Americas.[145]

To a large degree, the association of the early discoveries with crusading, especially 'chivalric crusading', had the effect of stifling almost all useful discussion of the precise relationship between conquest and conversion. Yet it would be unfair to criticize the papal court exclusively for its failure to be more discriminating in its grants or to take more frequently the kind of action which Eugenius IV adopted in 1434 over the Canaries. New situations are usually dealt with by adapting rather than discarding existing patterns of thought. So it can hardly be surprising that contemporaries assimilated discovery, and the conversion and enslavement which ensued, with well-embedded ideologies of crusade and chivalry. For all the wealth of their learning, Pratovecchio and de Rosellis were writing in 1436 as academic lawyers, and there is little evidence that their negative views on Portugal's African plans had broader resonance. Russell has

---

[141] 'Fulfillment', 326–7.

[142] F. M. Rogers, *The Travels of the Infante Dom Pedro of Portugal* (Cambridge: Cambridge University Press, 1961), 218–19.

[143] For the attitudes of the reformers, see Williams, 'Erasmus and the Reformers', *passim*.

[144] Phelan, *Millennial Kingdom*, *passim*; Lafaye, *Quetzalcóatl and Guadalupe*, *passim*; Housley, 'Holy Land or Holy Lands?', 245–7.

[145] e.g. the stridently hostile conclusion of Alonso de Espinosa on the Castilian conquest of Tenerife, written in the late 16th cent. but echoing earlier commentators on Christian–Islamic relations: 'It is an acknowledged fact, both as regards divine and human right, that the wars waged by the Spaniards against the natives of these islands, as well as against the Indians in the western regions, were unjust and without any reason to support them. For the natives had not taken the lands of Christians, nor had they gone beyond their own frontier to molest or invade their neighbours. If it is said that the Spaniards brought the Gospel, this should have been done by admonition and preaching—not by drum and banner; by persuasion, not by force.' Muldoon (ed.), *The Expansion of Europe*, 101.

pointed out that 'not until 1555 would anyone ever be heard in Portugal criticizing the country's involvement in the slave trade'.[146] It seems unlikely that any voice would have been raised either against the Avis dynasty's insistence on viewing its overseas conquests within the traditions of crusading. In fact, as Joan-Pau Rubiés has recently demonstrated, one of the most detailed and sophisticated analyses of Portuguese imperialism, that of João de Barros (1469–1570), 're-asserted the ideological principles of a medieval crusader king'.[147] As emphasized in Chapter 1, we have to appreciate the extent to which the exporting of chivalric modes of viewing the world facilitated the ready association of overseas conquest with religious approval.[148] Anthony Pagden put it well in the case of Cortés: 'true to the aspirations of the world in which he had been reared, [he] saw himself as the feudal vassal of a medieval monarch, and the instrument, as he never tired of repeating, of a God-directed enterprise.'[149] As late as 1583 the Spanish captain García de Palacio still took it as read that Christian princes could attack Muslims whenever and wherever they wished.[150] In this respect Jennifer Goodman was quite right to suggest that one of the most abiding legacies of humanist ideas might well be a condemnation of chivalric mores which most contemporaries simply would not have recognized.[151]

6.4 CONCLUSION

There was no consensus amongst those who criticized the practice of religious war, nor could there be. Separatists like Peter Chelčický and some of the early Anabaptists could condemn it out of hand, but for most others it was a matter of steering a difficult course between ideals and reality. For men like Nicholas of Pelhřimov and Erasmus, it was painful to entrust a holy cause to men who would certainly be woefully deficient as its agents. If Erasmus could not bring himself finally to do so because, as he put it, the remedy was worse than the disease, Nicholas imposed unrealistic demands upon Tabor's holy warriors:

Those who say that they are fighting for evangelical truth must see to it that they are as humble and patient as the lamb whose cause they are vindicating. They must see to it that

[146] Russell, *Prince Henry*, 246.

[147] J.-P. Rubiés, *Travel and Ethnology in the Renaissance: South India through European Eyes, 1250–1625* (Cambridge: Cambridge University Press, 2000), 177–81.

[148] Above, Ch. 1, at nn. 73–83.

[149] Pagden, 'Identity Formation', 52. See also Pagden, *Lords of All the World*, 74; S. B. Schwartz, 'New World Nobility: Social Aspirations and Mobility in the Conquest and Colonization of Spanish America', in M. U. Chrisman and O. Gründler (eds.), *Social Groups and Religious Ideas in the Sixteenth Century* (Kalamazoo: The Board of the Medieval Institute, Western Michigan University, 1978), 23–37, 154–8, at 34–5.

[150] D. García de Palacio, *Dialogos militares* (Mexico City: Pedro de Ocharte, 1583), 16ᵛ–17.

[151] Goodman, *Chivalry and Exploration*, 219. See also her 'European Chivalry in the 1490s', *Comparative Civilizations Review*, 26 (1992), 43–72.

they do not live in a bestial way, and that they contradict no truth. They must see to it that they are [personally] worthy of the cause for which they fight, communing in both kinds; that they have right intention; that they hear God's word willingly; that they hate all vices, both in themselves and in others; that they do no harm to any just and innocent lamb in the flock; that they all shun avarice and love the life of poverty which is Jesus Christ's. Without all this we shall never be able to resist our enemies, even if we summon all the world's armies to our assistance.[152]

More had not been demanded of the early Templars, and it is revealing that Erasmus could only contemplate a war against the Turks without distaste if the lifestyle of the combatants resembled the Bernardine prescription for the original members of the Order.[153] Others were even less straightforward in their positions: Nicholas of Cusa, for example, wanted to see religious dialogue but on at least one occasion applauded a crusading venture.[154]

If there was no chorus of disapproval, neither was there any lack of individuals and groups prepared to construct a position of reasoned rejection of war in the name of the faith, whichever context that war occurred in. The problem was that no authority, whether political or spiritual, was willing to play a role in encouraging these voices, co-ordinating their views, or providing the means for their arguments to reach a wider audience.[155] In the case of the papacy and overseas conquest, this was so even when a respectable intellectual tradition was at hand. Yet we must resist the temptation to view this as (literally) *trahison des clercs*, or to depict the battles of ideas which occurred as conflicts between vested interests and 'moral minorities'. It is true that Chelčickian or Erasmian pacifism stood little chance given the circumstances prevailing in Bohemia in the 1420s and in central Europe a century later. To adopt either would have been a form of suicide. But in the case of the debate which took place at the Avis court about Moroccan expansion in the 1430s, the situation was much less clear-cut. Perhaps the most telling of the several 'opinions' (*pareceres*) which were drawn up during this debate emanated from King Duarte's brother João. He cited at length the arguments against expansion, on legal as well as practical grounds, with such force that he seemed to be damning the idea totally. But he also accepted that the demands of chivalry were strongly in favour of such a war, no matter what the dangers for Portugal. Power politics were undoubtedly involved; but so too were ideological forces, in this case chivalry, in others apocalypticism or sectarian commitment, and their sheer impact should not be underestimated.[156]

[152] Bartoš, 'Táborské bratrstvo', 115.　[153] Erasmus, 'Utilissima consultatio', 68.
[154] Hankins, 'Renaissance Crusaders', 128 n. 49; Schwoebel, *The Shadow of the Crescent*, 56 n. 86.
[155] Cf. Johnson, *Holy War Idea*, 44–5, on Vitoria and Grotius.
[156] *MH* iv. 111–23, no. 23.

CHAPTER SEVEN

Conclusion: Perspectives

7.1 RELIGIOUS WARFARE, 1400–1536

Religious warfare was an important feature of European life in the fifteenth and early sixteenth centuries. All of the contexts described in Chapter 1 generated military activity which was characterized by the belief that God's will and purpose were directly and urgently present: frontiers, chivalric warfare, conflicts shaped by eschatological hopes, and wars between states based on national communities. This is far from saying that all such combat was sanctified, rather that it all possessed a potential which could be released, that a transformation could occur in terms of attitude and perception from a world-view in which God was only formally or distantly steering events, to one in which he was actively and purposefully engaged. Typical signs of this transformation were the various attributes examined in Chapter 4: an engagement with Scripture as a means of elucidating God's will in detail; the attempt to locate the roles of leaders within a programme which expressed that will; and a strong attachment to symbols, devotional practices, and ideas (such as the Elect People or the *antemurale Christianitatis*) which gave religious form to the sense of commonality existing amongst the belligerents. Often this process was accompanied by the demonization of the enemy (in this period typically their 'turkification'), and sometimes by the emergence of a critique stimulated precisely by the radical nature of the claims which were being advanced by protagonists.

But if the signs of transformation can be read, what brought it about? How was the potential released? It may be suggested that the religious wars we have examined were rooted in four patterns of thought and belief. First there was the crusade. As I emphasized at the outset, this book had its origins in the growing realization of how important crusading ideas and practices remained in this period, and of the way in which they were shaped by, *inter alia*, patriotic feelings, eschatological convictions, and chivalric aspirations.[1] In turn, it would be very surprising if religious warfare which did not assume the formal shape of a crusade failed to be influenced by the sheer weight of the institution, which made itself felt so constantly under the impact of the Turkish advance in the east. We have seen that this may have applied, albeit in an inverted sense, in the case of the

---

[1] e.g. Housley, *Later Crusades*, chs. 13–14 *passim*.

Hussites' defence of their cause: but that there are also strong arguments against such a view. It certainly did apply in the case of the Dózsa rebellion, which began life as a crusade and, I have argued, retained its crusading form', at least in the eyes of its participants, throughout its duration. The crusade exerted probably its most powerful impact on Castilian and Portuguese national messianism. Here of course the crusade itself was repeatedly preached: indulgences, cross-taking, and the privileges of the crusader were manifestly present, albeit operating most frequently within a financial context. More broadly it was filtered through hegemonic ideologies: the ongoing royal obligation of *Reconquista* in Castile and the remarkable persistence of chivalric values in Portugal.[2] At Senj, where the crusade does not appear to have been present as an institution, it nonetheless shaped the activities of the uskoks through their self-perception, in particular the claim which they advanced with vigour that they were manning a particularly important stretch of the *antemurale Christianitatis*. The crusade was a constant undercurrent in public life and its impact was registered in unexpected ways. Even Pope Alexander VI's call to crusade of June 1500, otherwise a lacklustre occasion, shaped Columbus' writing of what became his most important prophetic utterance, the *Libro de las profecias*.[3]

The second transforming force was sectarian apocalypticism, the belief nourished by a particular group that they were God's elect and, as part of that allotted role, possessed an inescapable mandate to wage holy war in terms of a programme of events which would culminate in the return of Christ. The two classic instances in our period were Tabor in 1419–20 and Anabaptist Münster in 1534–5. They differed in so far as Tabor cast off its apocalypticism (as well as its communism), evolving into a radical but stable community, whereas the Anabaptist regime at Münster perished, leaving no legacy except the negative one of a powerful backlash against its sanctified violence on the part of other Anabaptist groups. In these two communities we possess the strongest examples of warfare which was not just religious in conception and purpose but purgative, even celebratory, in nature. They come closest to the rather narrow definition of holy war espoused by Alphonse Dupront, who emphasized extremities of perception and behaviour in the pursuit of goals which were inherently world-changing.[4] It is to the worst excesses of early Taborite and Münsterite violence that we have to look to locate anything in this period which resembled the 'holy massacres' perpetrated during the Wars of Religion; and in the Münsterite case that violence was not just short-lived but also localized.

---

[2] T. F. Ruiz, 'Une royauté sans sacre: La Monarchie castillane du bas moyen âge', *Annales ESC* 39 (1984), 429–53; Russell, *Prince Henry*, 25–6, 346 *et passim*.

[3] Setton, *PL* ii. 527–34; Milhou, *Colón*, 444.

[4] A. Dupront, 'Guerre sainte et Chrétienté', and 'Croisade et eschatologie', in his *Du sacré: Croisades et pèlerinages. Images et langages* (Mayenne: Gallimard, 1987), 264–87, 288–312; D. Crouzet, *Les Guerriers de Dieu: La Violence au temps des troubles de religion vers 1525–vers 1610*, 2 vols. (Seyssel: Champ Vallon, 1990), i. 395–6.

I have argued elsewhere that sectarian messianism of the type espoused in these two communities was exciting but inherently volatile and short-lived, while national messianism, the vesting of divine missions in 'chosen peoples' possessing a settled ethnic identity and territorial base, was less effervescent but had greater staying power.[5] The former was little more than a lively firework while the latter became a powerful force in European history. But it has to be admitted that national messianism too was problematic. I have emphasized that the natural tendency to mobilize religious rhetoric in order to raise resources for a conflict has to be kept in mind; so too does the methodological difficulty of 'reading' public opinion at large on the basis of what always constitutes a limited range of evidence mainly emanating from elites. Having said that, there are some remarkable examples in this period of national messianism finding expression in the language of holy war. Some were eschatological: the growing importance of Joachimist prophecies in Castile and Aragon in the last decades of the fifteenth century cannot be denied, even if it is difficult to disentangle the resulting excitement from crusading or patriotic enthusiasm. The same was true, on a much smaller canvas, of Savonarola's yoking together of prophecy and *campanilismo* at Florence, a development which bore its richest fruit some time after the preacher's death, in the defence of Florence against the imperialist army in 1530.

That eschatological formulations were not essential to bestow dynamism and direction on national messianism is clear from events during the Anglo-French war in the early fifteenth century. There are good grounds for arguing that for a relatively short period of time, from Henry V's victory at Agincourt in 1415 through to Joan of Arc's triumphs in 1429, perceptions on both sides of the conflict brought God right to the heart of the conduct of military affairs. Pronouncements were so excited and claims so assertive that if this was not a religious war, it certainly looks very much like one.[6] The English were triumphalist, the French embattled, but in certain other respects they were similar: both were enmeshed in a war which was exerting the greatest of demands, and both possessed an ancient tradition of conceiving their identity in scriptural terms. In this light the situation which came into being in Switzerland not long afterwards is instructive. The *Eidgenossen* encountered an extremely hostile reception in terms of ideas as well as military resistance: their perception of themselves as a Chosen People enjoying victories bestowed by God was a triumphalist response to ideological vulnerability. It combined elements of the English and French positions, religious values and devotional practices being deployed in order to compensate for ideological weaknesses. And in the same way that Joan's claims met with an indignant response from the duke of Bedford,

---

[5] Housley, 'The Eschatological Imperative', 149–50.
[6] Cf. M. Vale, 'France at the End of the Hundred Years War (*c.*1420–1461)', in Allmand (ed.), *New Cambridge Medieval History*, vii. 392–407, at 396.

so those of the *Eidgenossen* were countered sharply by the Habsburg apologist Jakob Wimpfeling.

The fourth and last transforming force was the need to defend doctrinal truth against external assault. The outstanding example of this in our period is naturally the organization of the Hussite military coalition in the face of Sigismund's crusades. The shielding of the newly rediscovered 'God's Law' against attempts to suppress it by force was bound to encounter the central conundrum of using force to defend the teachings of the Prince of Peace. In the winter of 1419–20 the Hussites therefore experienced in highly condensed form a debate about the validity of using violence in defence of the faith which had occurred over entire generations in the early history of the church. But it was almost inevitable that once the decision to fight was made, the resulting war would be perceived as religious in nature. Human nature would look for God's active, and miraculous, intervention in any conflict waged on behalf of his faith, especially against an opposition declaring itself to be God's army; and this tendency was sharpened by the fact that the entire spectrum of the Hussite coalition was eschatologically minded. It is worth emphasizing, nonetheless, that far from bestowing a blanket seal of approval on the resulting operations, the sanctification of the conflict made the Hussites (and in particular the Taborites) more than normally scrupulous about how their troops fought.

Crusade, sectarian apocalypticism, national messianism, and the defence of a reformed faith: all but the first were present in the war waged by the Hussites, which is one reason for its enduring fascination. The years between the Jihlava Accord of 1436 and the outbreak of the Protestant Reformation do not display such a strong convergence of themes, with the possible exception of Iberia, where crusading interwove with both 'official' and 'subversive' Joachimism, bearing such remarkable fruits as the cluster of Fernandine prophecies and the short-lived reign of the *Encubierto* of Játiva in 1522. In other respects, though, these decades were rich in developments. The Atlantic voyages and overseas conquests carried out by the Portuguese and Castilians forced contemporaries to pose important questions relating to coercive conversion, in which arguments drawing on crusade and eschatological readings played key roles. These arguments did not go unchallenged, but the challenge was remarkably ineffective; so too were the writings of the north European humanists, especially Erasmus, who subjected the practice of religious war, in its various formats, to a searching critique. One important reason for the failure of all these critics to prevent the trend towards sanctifying conflict was the advance of the Ottoman Turks. This had several consequences. It sharpened the eschatological perspective; it emphasized the importance of crusade as a necessary response (irrespective of its structural deficiencies and recent legacy of failures) to an implacable foe; and it generated a range of new vocabulary and images for use in conceptualizing Christendom's internal fault lines.

This latter development was evident in the writings of Luther, and there can be no doubt that the subject of religious war acquires a particular interest in the first generation of the Reformation. This was in part because of the sectarian violence which was generated, and because of the difficulty of interpreting events with especially complex causality like the German Peasants' War and the Pilgrimage of Grace. It was also because the interaction between the Ottoman threat and the conflicts over reform produced one of the richest phases in the age-old debate about the dialectic of external threat and internal schism. Above all, it is because Luther's own voluminous writings enable us to see how he, like the Hussites before him, grappled with the issues raised by the defence of the reformed faith. Luther was fortunate: death spared him the anguish of sanctioning a defensive war against Charles V. Yet there are indications that had he done so, the early Protestants would have gone down a road not dissimilar to that trodden a century previously by the Hussites.

7.2 RELIGIOUS WARFARE AND THE WARS OF RELIGION

'If we failed to intervene now, all the Estates of Germany would be in danger of breaking with the faith . . . After considering this and considering it again, I decided to embark on war against Hesse and Saxony as transgressors of the peace against the Duke of Brunswick and his territory. And although this pretext will not long disguise the fact that it is a matter of religion, yet it serves for the present to divide the renegades.'[7] Charles V's words to his sister Mary at the outbreak of the Schmalkaldic War in June 1546 serve as a useful introduction to the range of issues opened up by the Wars of Religion. In an article on the origins of the Wars of Religion Konrad Repgen concluded that the Schmalkaldic War was the first occasion on which a religious war (*guerre de religion*, *Religionskrieg*) was waged on confessional issues. 'War . . . was no longer waged *and* justified as a crusade but as *Religionskrieg*, as the military solution to conflicts arising from the protection of confessional possessions or from confessional conquest.'[8] Repgen pointed to the significance of the Emperor's last sentence. It laid down an approach towards the suppression of internal confessional dissent which became standard Habsburg policy in the Empire under Charles V and later in the Low Countries: the desirability of presenting the war as a 'policing' matter rather than a religious one so that intervention by Protestants from other lands would become less likely.[9] But this politically inspired gambit should not disguise the fact that religious differences really lay at the heart of the conflict. So much is

---

[7] Quoted by K. Repgen, 'What is a "Religious War"?', in E. I. Kouri and T. Scott (eds.), *Politics and Society in Reformation Europe* (London: Macmillan, 1987), 311–28, at 319.

[8] Ibid. 323.

[9] L. Van der Essen, 'Croisade contre les hérétiques ou guerre contre des rebelles? La Psychologie des soldats et des officiers espagnols de l'armée de Flandre au XVIe siècle', *RHE* 51 (1956), 42–78, at 56–8.

clear not just from Charles V's letter but also from the Protestant response, which was to mobilize in defence of 'this our true Christian religion, which the pope calls heresy'.[10]

Once the decision had been made to use violence in this way, all the forces described above may be observed playing their part in giving the Wars of Religion their destructive vigour and personality; indeed it would have been surprising if they had not, given their conspicuous presence in so many parts of Europe on the very eve of combat. For the pragmatic and political reasons referred to in Charles V's letter, the crusade made no entry into the Schmalkaldic War, despite the ruling made by Giovanni del Monte in 1546 that 'una cruciata contra gl'heretici' would be canonically correct.[11] In different contexts, however, it did feature, perhaps most emphatically during the first three outbreaks of civil warfare in France (1562–70). A number of the associations and confraternities formed by the Catholics to combat Huguenot ambitions adopted crusading measures. Writing of the Confraternity of the Holy Ghost at Dijon, which was founded in 1567, Mack P. Holt commented that 'in essence, the confraternity was a crusade against the infidel Protestants, with the kingdom of France being the new Jerusalem infiltrated by God's enemies'.[12] A cluster of similar confraternities sprang up across Burgundy and in other provinces in 1567–8. In what was probably the most remarkable incident, the Catholics of Toulouse reacted to the Huguenot siege of the city in 1567 by defiantly wearing white crosses. 'It is held by all to be a most evident indication of a true Catholic Christian that he arms himself with the sign of the cross (*sil se munit du signe de la croix*). For this reason the lords and council had it proclaimed publicly through the sounding of silver trumpets that every inhabitant of the town was to put on a white cross, and wear it in a place both clear and visible on his person.' The practice received the enthusiastic support of Pope Pius V, who in March 1568 granted a plenary indulgence to 'all truly faithful and confessed people who enter this holy confraternity (*hoc sanctum sodalitium*), and, signed with the cross (*cruce signati*), take up pious and salutary arms for the defence of the Christian religion, the see [of Toulouse], and the king'. In September 1568 the Catholics laid down the various devotional conditions which were required of 'those who take the cross (*se croiseront*) to proceed to holy war for the faith'. These were elaborate: it was specified that the volunteers would assemble in the cathedral church of S. Étienne on 13 September where they would make a profession of faith, confess, and receive the sacraments. It was agreed that 'The motto of the holy militia is as follows: "Let us go forth and die with Christ." '[13]

The existence of this Toulousain *sodalitas* of cross-bearers shows the futility

---

[10] Repgen, ' "Religious War" ', 321. He terms this 'a preventive religious war'.   [11] Ibid. 322–3.
[12] Holt, *French Wars of Religion*, 68 and see too 74.
[13] C. de Vic, J. J. Vaissete, et al. (eds.), *Histoire générale de Languedoc*, 16 vols. (Toulouse: E. Privat, 1872–1905), xii, *Preuves*, cols. 873, 885–90.

of trying to compel historical events to fit into a simplistic pattern of 'continuity or change'. This was undoubtedly a crusading confraternity, and the people who took the cross at Toulouse were at least as much crusaders as those who fought the Turks at Lepanto three years later. Taking the cross to fight against heretics had particular resonance in the Toulouse region, a fact of which the Catholics were well aware: amongst the scriptural and historical exempla to which they appealed was that of the battle of Muret, where it was alleged that 800 men had miraculously defeated 60,000.[14] But when reading these documents one is constantly made aware of startlingly new currents of religious and cultural thought. In much the same way that the crusade evolved during the fifteenth century under the impact of developments such as humanism, so its revival during the Wars of Religion was conditioned, above all by the distinctive fervour of Counter-Reformation Catholicism.[15] The willingness of the Toulouse Catholics to die *with* Christ in 1568 rather than *for* him is a sign of this. The wearing of the cross had pointedly self-sacrificial connotations: death for the cross-bearers was described as a second baptism.[16] The point was emphasized by R. H. Harding in his specialized studies of the confraternities, both those of the 1560s and the second wave formed in the context of the Catholic League in the 1580s.[17] Thus the initial reason why the Catholics wore crosses was to defy their Huguenot enemies, because it was 'a sign which the enemy not only [fail to] venerate, but one which they hold in such horror that they are not afraid to pull down, destroy, break up, incinerate, and snap the crosses set up on the thoroughfares out of devotion, and to remind passers-by of the death of Our Lord Jesus Christ, who was hung for our sins on the wood of the cross; in so doing they seek to efface the memory, sign, and remembrance of our salvation'.[18] In the contest between the Sign and the Word which is now seen as residing at the heart of this confessional strife, the cross, like other traditional Catholic devotional foci such as the Five Wounds of Christ, the Rosary, and the Name of Jesus, thus acquired a significance greater even than in Hungary in 1514 or in England in 1536.[19] Denis Crouzet put it well: 'In the violent acts of the Catholics the crusade becomes reality. Even if it is not made explicit, it is experienced in the immediacy of the lurch into violence, because it was the only response which the faithful could make to this assault on their system of representation.'[20] If resort to the mechanisms of crusade was 'archaic', it was consciously and provocatively so: 'taking

[14] Vic et al. (eds.), *Histoire générale de Languedoc*, xii, *Preuves*, cols. 888–90.
[15] e.g. A. E. Barnes, 'Religious Anxiety and Devotional Change in Sixteenth-Century French Penitential Confraternities', *Sixteenth-Century Journal*, 19 (1988), 389–405.
[16] Cf. Diefendorf, *Beneath the Cross*, 139–42, for similar thinking on the Huguenot side.
[17] R. R. Harding, 'The Mobilization of Confraternities against the Reformation in France', *Sixteenth-Century Journal*, 11 (1980), 85–107; id., 'Revolution and Reform', *passim*.
[18] Vic et al. (eds.), *Histoire générale de Languedoc*, xii, *Preuves*, col. 873.
[19] Davis, 'Rites of Violence', esp. 88–9; E. Cameron, 'For Reasoned Faith or Embattled Creed? Religion for the People in Early Modern Europe', *TRHS* 6th ser. 8 (1998), 165–87.
[20] Crouzet, *Les Guerriers de Dieu*, i. 396.

the cross' was part of a whole system of belief which was under savage assault, so there could be no better reply to the assault than to rally to the defence of such formulae and rites.[21] This was revival, but occurring within a religious context which was changing even more radically than in the period which we have been studying.

Political circumstances too had altered in France. No application of the crusade to the situation which prevailed in the 1560s could be divorced from an acute awareness of the paralysis of royal government. Crusading associations like that at Toulouse were in essence a *faute de mieux*.[22] There was realism as well as tact in Pius V's comment in the bull of crusade which he dispatched to the Toulousain *sodalitas* that those who enrolled in its ranks would be fighting 'pro fide, pro patria, pro principe'.[23] The Toulousain cross-bearers emphasized their own loyalty to the king and, more broadly and pointedly, to the social order itself. Both at Toulouse and at Paris, the analogy between cathars and Huguenots was given a specifically political twist, in the form of unfavourable comparisons between the conciliatory stance of Catherine de' Medici and her chancellor Michel de l'Hôpital on the one hand, and the vigorous anti-heresy measures of the young King Louis IX on the other. The contrast was pointed out by Jean du Tillet, who as royal archivist had good reason to be aware of it; he drafted a remonstrance to Charles IX on behalf of the Paris *parlement*, which refused to ratify the edict of pacification of January 1562. A few months later du Tillet presented a manuscript history of the Albigensian Crusade to Catherine de' Medici, urging her to follow the example of Blanche of Castile, Louis IX's mother, who had acted with vigour to suppress baronial rebellion during the king's minority. Meanwhile Jean Gay, a member of the militantly Catholic *parlement* of Toulouse, took a very similar approach in a work published in 1561, the title of which aptly indicates his intention: 'Histoire des Scismes et Heresies des Albigeois conforme à celle du present: par laquelle appert que plusieurs grands princes, & seigneurs sont tombez en extremes desolations & ruynes, pour avoir favorisé aux heretiques'. Both du Tillet and Gay were engaging in much more than an academic exercise: certainly history taught by example, but it was also living tissue, proof of God's purpose which could be read like prophecy, only rather more easily. Charles IX and his mother could seal the fate of the Valois dynasty if they failed to honour the historic link between the monarchy and the Catholic faith; while the prince du Condé would bring ruin to his family if he insisted on imitating the comital house of Toulouse by favouring heresy.[24]

Continuity and change are evident too in the way the Toulousain Catholics

---

[21] This is clear from Barbara Diefendorf's brilliant study *Beneath the Cross.*

[22] Harding, 'Mobilization', 92.

[23] Vic et al. (eds.), *Histoire générale de Languedoc*, xii, *Preuves*, cols. 885–8.

[24] Crouzet, *Les Guerriers de Dieu*, i. 381–2; L. Racaut, 'The Polemical Use of the Albigensian Crusade during the French Wars of Religion', *French History*, 13 (1999), 261–79.

portrayed their Protestant enemies. The crimes of the Huguenots were comprehensively described in the call to arms issued on 12 September 1568. They had assaulted the church and faith in every imaginable way, through attacks on buildings, priests, symbols, and books. They defied Charles IX and threatened to restore Guyenne to English rule. They would make the streets of Toulouse run with Catholic blood. They were intent on destroying the social order itself. Their demonization was comprehensive, culminating in the sweeping assertion that they were 'these enemies of God and of the whole of human nature'.[25] It may be argued that this was only an intensification of the process of 'turkification' which we examined in Chapter 5; it comes as no surprise to find the Huguenots repeatedly condemned as the 'new Turks'.[26] But their labelling as 'enemies of human nature' is different: it is redolent of a systematic dehumanization which helps to explain the fearful atrocities so often practised during the French civil wars.[27] This was something new, an unenviable product of this second generation of confessional strife which has most satisfactorily been explained by Natalie Zemon Davis as purgative and purifying in nature.[28]

Much the same goes for the second transforming force, sectarian apocalypticism. There is no sign of its slackening as we move into the middle decades of the sixteenth century. Indeed, Denis Crouzet placed the concept of a Catholic *angoisse eschatologique* at the very heart of his overall explanation of the religious violence which was practised in France. For him, a deeply rooted belief in divine agency based on the world's rapidly approaching its appointed end was the only way to explain the extremity of the Catholic response to the Huguenots' attempt to 'desacralize' that world, including its movement through time. In one of many telling phrases, Crouzet wrote of the 'théâtre enchanté de la violence catholique', meaning that it bore a direct and crucial relationship to their belief in God's immanence and their inability to tolerate the Huguenots' aggressive denial of that immanence.[29] At their worst, the French Wars of Religion thus represented a nation-wide and recurrent affliction of the kind of holy war which in our period was restricted to Tabor and Münster, and to just a few months in each case. Because they were acting as 'God's warriors', Catholics who died while fighting for the Holy League were assured of salvation, without reference to the grant of indulgences.[30] Further east, it has been convincingly argued that apocalyptic patterns of thought persisted into the first decade of the Thirty Years War.[31]

---

[25] Vic et al. (eds.), *Histoire générale de Languedoc*, xii, *Preuves*, cols. 888–90.

[26] Crouzet, *Les Guerriers de Dieu*, i. 393; Davis, 'Rites of Violence', 77; P. Rousset, 'L'Idéologie de croisade dans les guerres de religion au XVIe siècle', *Schweizerische Zeitschrift für Geschichte*, 31 (1981), 174–84, at 182.

[27] e.g. Holt, *French Wars of Religion*, 86–7.

[28] Davis, 'Rites of Violence', *passim*. See also Scribner, 'Preconditions', esp. 45.

[29] Crouzet, *Les Guerriers de Dieu*, i. 493.   [30] Rousset, 'L'Idéologie de croisade', 176.

[31] R. B. Barnes, *Prophecy and Gnosis: Apocalypticism in the Wake of the Lutheran Reformation* (Stanford, Calif.: Stanford University Press, 1988), 249, 258, 265.

Continuity and change again then, but with the latter dominant as two systems of belief which were seemingly irreconcilable fashioned themselves into holy communities, each charged with the role of imposing God's will upon the other.

At first glance it looks as if national messianism was submerged by confessional messianism.[32] The second generation of the Reformation was a period in which confessional identities were formed. To a large degree this happened through the creation of a Protestant view of history which, in turn, elicited a Catholic response.[33] At the same time reformers like Bullinger fashioned a specifically Protestant eschatology to replace the eclectic version which had served Luther and Melanchthon. It thus became possible to conceive of an 'elect Protestant nation' with deep roots in the past and a specific role in God's plan for the future. Modelled on the Israelites, it crossed state boundaries and defended the gospel in a pattern of events which was certainly eschatological in character, if not explicitly apocalyptic. In the 1620s and 1630s a whole group of English preachers, notably William Gouge, Thomas Barnes, and Alexander Leighton, argued strenuously that the overall Protestant cause in Europe was a religious war, and that England had a duty to intervene on behalf of its embattled co-religionists. 'Such warres are Gods warres, the battels of the Lord, which he can and will prosper,' as Gouge put it in 1631.[34] Geoffrey Gates, a Puritan MP in the late sixteenth century, claimed that God was fighting for the Dutch rebels against the forces of Antichrist: 'And now let us father beholde with discretion what worke the Lord is entered into by Armes, in these last dayes of the worlde: And how martiall prowesse and industrie hath mightely served to advaunce the name and glorye of God, and so giue passage to his Gospell, where it lay prostrate and troden under the feete of Antichrist and his consorts.'[35] And of the Calvinist captain Henry Hexham it has been remarked that he 'considered the struggle against Spain as part of the great apocalyptic battle against Antichrist and saw himself as one of Christ's soldiers marching into battle for the Lord'.[36] For their part, Catholic communities continued to view their confessional antagonists in heretical terms, as a threat to their own hope of salvation and a plague afflicting society. Defence of the faith against them was manifestly God's work.[37]

[32] e.g., in the case of England, D. Loades, 'The Origins of English Protestant Nationalism', in Mews (ed.), *Religion and National Identity*, 297–307, at 303–4; A. Fletcher, 'The First Century of English Protestantism and the Growth of National Identity', ibid. 309–17, at 309–10.

[33] e.g. Racaut, 'Polemical Use', a good account of how this occurred in the case of the cathars.

[34] Johnson, *Ideology*, 118–29, with quote at 123. Also useful on these preachers is J. R. Hale, 'Incitement to Violence? English Divines on the Theme of War, 1578 to 1631', in J. G. Rowe and W. H. Stockdale (eds.), *Florilegium historiale: Essays Presented to Wallace K. Ferguson* (Toronto: University of Toronto Press, 1971), 369–99, repr. in J. R. Hale, *Renaissance War Studies* (London: Hambledon, 1983).

[35] Cunningham and Grell, *The Four Horsemen of the Apocalypse*, 165–7, with quote at 166.

[36] Ibid. 168.

[37] Cf. Diefendorf, *Beneath the Cross*, 178: 'At the popular level, the religious wars represented a crusade against heresy, a crusade that had to be won if civil society was to be preserved and salvation to be assured.'

However, the strongest expressions of religious war came into being when national messianism was not replaced by confessional identity but reinforced by it. The basic covenanting idea thereby gained massive extra impetus.[38] Of England, David Loades has commented that 'by the time of the Armada it was possible to assume . . . that protestantism and patriotism were the same thing'.[39] William Clarke could then celebrate England's condition in phrases which, doubtless without knowing it, virtually replicated those of Archbishop William Courtenay two centuries previously: 'He that smiteth our religion woundeth our commonwealth; because our blessed estate of policie standeth in defence of religion, and our most blessed religion laboureth in maintenance of the commonwealth. Religion and policie are, through God's singular blessings, preserved together in life as with one spirit; he that doth take away the life of the one doth procure the death of the other.'[40]

As Loades pointed out, in England the path towards this happy state of affairs was far from being an easy one.[41] In France, national loyalties, like everything else, became enmeshed in the confessional turmoil. We have already seen the Catholic *sodalitas* at Toulouse trying to appropriate the patriotic position. A central tenet of belief for militant French Catholics was that the *infidelitas* of the Huguenots was political as well as religious: their desertion of the church meant that even if they were not consciously disloyal, they acted to the detriment of the realm by bringing God's wrath down upon it. They imperilled the position of the Chosen People. For example, they were held responsible for France's serious defeat at the battle of Saint-Quentin in 1557.[42] This may sound extreme, but at the time the battle was fought Raoul Spifame was prepared to argue that 'it is the act of a true martyr, a bloody sacrifice, to die for the well-being of this state' (*mourir pour le bien d'icelle republicque*). In his view a full-scale martyrology should be compiled of all the men who had died in the service of the French crown since the time of Charlemagne, for reading in churches throughout France at terce, mirroring the reading of the church's existing martyrology which took place at prime.[43]

Two texts, one Protestant and the other Catholic, perhaps best illustrate the impact of the confessional divide on existing traditions of national messianism. The first text, which illustrates the Protestant perspective, is the manifesto issued by the under-officers and men in the English army in Scotland in August 1650. This document projects with considerable force the world-view of a group of men who saw their recent success in the English Civil War as the vindication both of Puritanism and of their nation's eschatological role. The manifesto of 1650 shows that the bellicose approach taken up by Puritan preachers a

---

[38] Johnson, *Ideology*, 110–13.   [39] Loades, 'The Origins', 307.
[40] Ibid. 297; above, Ch. 1, at n. 122.   [41] Loades, 'The Origins', esp. 307.
[42] Diefendorf, *Beneath the Cross*, 50–1.
[43] L. Rothkrug, *Religious Practices and Collective Perceptions: Hidden Homologies in the Renaissance and Reformation* (Waterloo: University of Waterloo, 1980), 33–4.

generation earlier in relation to England's relations with Catholic Spain was far from lacking resonance in the ranks of the parliamentary army as it emerged from the Civil War.[44] 'The Lord hath brought us hither by his providence, and upon him we shall with confidence depend till we see a glorious issue; which we humbly and heartily desire may be without the effusion of any more blood and (if it be the will of God) both speedy and comfortable to you and us, that we may return with joy into England, and leave Scotland rejoicing that an English army hath been amongst them.'[45] This remarkable triumphalism was born of the fusion of patriotic sentiment with proselytizing confessional conviction; yet the rhetoric had a clear ancestry in the post-Agincourt theme of England and France uniting under Henry V's proven leadership in the common cause of a crusade.[46]

The other text was written in Catholic Spain. In Chapter 3 it was noted in passing that Castilian national messianism reached its full flowering only in the reign of Philip II.[47] This was undoubtedly due in part to the way in which Counter-Reformation piety harmonized with a powerful existing sense of national destiny. No single document communicates this better than Pedro de Ribadeneyra's sermon to the soldiers who were embarking on the Spanish Armada in 1588.[48] The Jesuit began by remarking that the campaign held 'all the reasons that there could possibly be for a just and holy war', and that it was being waged in defence of the Catholic faith, the honour of Philip II and the Spanish nation, and the interests of all the realms belonging to Spain. He then pursued each of these three themes in turn. The threat to 'our sacred religion and our most holy Roman Catholic faith' resided in Elizabeth II's ruthless persecution of the English Catholics, and her unceasing promotion of the Protestant cause abroad, above all in the Low Countries. She was even sending ambassadors to Muscovy and trading with the Ottomans. By contrast, 'who has the job of defending the Catholic faith, if not the Catholic King?' Spain was the repository of the true Catholic faith. The defeat of England would rank with the evangelization of the Indies: 'It will be no less of an honour for Spain to chase the demon out of England (*echar el demonio de Inglaterra*), than to have driven it out of the Indies.' In addition (a particularly interesting argument), such an action would repay Spain's debt of gratitude to other nations for the help of their volunteers during the *Reconquista*, when knights from France, Flanders, Germany, and England had come to free Spanish Christians from Moorish oppression.[49]

---

[44] Cf. P. Rousset, 'La "Croisade" puritaine de Cromwell', *Schweizerische Zeitschrift für Geschichte*, 28 (1978), 15–28; G. Burgess, 'Was the English Civil War a War of Religion? The Evidence of Political Propaganda', *Huntingdon Library Quarterly*, 61 (2000), 173–201. I am grateful to Prof. Burgess for alerting me to this article.

[45] A. S. P. Woodhouse (ed.), *Puritanism and Liberty, Being the Army Debates (1647–9) from the Clarke Manuscripts with Supplementary Documents* (London: Dent & Sons, 1950), 474–8, at 478.

[46] *Gesta*, 180–1.   [47] Above, Ch. 3, at n. 100.

[48] *Patris Petri de Ribadeneira Societatis Jesu sacerdotis confessiones, epistolae aliaque scripta inedita*, 2 vols. (Madrid: La Editorial Ibérica, 1920–3), ii. 347–70.

[49] Ibid. 348–55.

Ribadeneyra was no less insistent on the need to defend Spain's reputation. His country's deeds were greater than those of the Assyrians, Medes, Persians, Greeks, *latinos* (Etruscans?), Carthaginians, and Romans, and Philip II was the greatest Christian monarch who had ever ruled, but 'the world is ruled by opinion', and if Elizabeth's machinations were not resisted, the revolt in the Low Countries would be just the prologue to the general collapse of the king's possessions. This was a matter of reputation, and 'things go down hill more frequently because of reputation than because of arms and armies'; but interests were also at stake because of England's support for the Dutch and its disruption of the Indies trade. In a peroration which was positively Bernardine in tone, Ribadeneyra asked what Christian would neglect the first cause, what Spaniard the second, and what living man the third. The war therefore was 'profitable for God, for his church, for his saints and for our nation', bringing together glory, honour, the faith, and justice.[50]

Only briefly, and towards the end of this speech, did Ribadeneyra mention the pope's deposition of Elizabeth I.[51] This sidelining of papal authority was wholly characteristic of Spanish messianism. What counted was the belief that history, national interests and honour, and the defence of the entire Catholic faith converged in the waging of Spain's many conflicts. She became, to use the remarkable language of Cervantes' second *canción* on the Armada, 'Mother of the heroes of the war, confidant [*sic*] of Catholic soldiers, crucible in which the love of God is purified, land where it is seen that Heaven buries those who to Heaven will be borne as defenders of the purest faith'.[52] Cervantes' last phrase is a reminder that many of Spain's wars, including the Armada, were formally supported with indulgences, but what is striking about his poem, and Ribadeneyra's sermon, is the commingling of religious and secular themes. In 1583, before the start of the battle of Steenbergen, Alexander Farnese reportedly encouraged his troops with the prediction that they would win 'a fair victory over the enemies of the Catholic religion, of your king and mine; this is the day on which Jesus Christ will make you all immortal and place you in the ranks of the chosen'.[53]

National messianism, Geoffrey Parker has recently argued, was unquestioned by Philip II and formed a central feature of his imperial ideology.[54] What is perhaps more surprising is the extent to which the Spanish military shared their king's outlook. Raffaele Puddu expressed it well, describing how 'a tension which was rooted in a fusion of religiosity and bellicosity energized the *tercios*, and their force seemed to reflect the discipline, internal coherence, and absence

---

[50] *Patris Petri de Ribadeneira Societatis Jesu sacerdotis confessiones, epistolae aliaque scripta inedita*, ii. 356–68.

[51] Ibid. 365.

[52] Quoted in F. Navarro Ledesma, *Cervantes: The Man and the Genius*, trans. D. and G. Bliss (New York: Charterhouse, 1973), 172.

[53] Quoted in Housley, '*Pro deo et patria mori*', 245.

[54] Parker, 'Tudor England'. Cf. Milhou's comments on Philip's kingship in *Colón*, 421, and 'Propaganda mesiánica', 58–9.

of political, confessional, and social conflicts of a people which followed in unity the guidance of pulpit and throne'.[55] This is probably taking things too far, but there is strong evidence that many Spanish fighting men did view their vocation as, amongst other things, a sacred task. Puddu's own investigation was based in part on a remarkable group of treatises written in Spain by veteran captains, mainly towards the end of Philip II's reign.[56] They strongly echoed the views expressed by Ribadeneyra and Cervantes. In his *Dialogos militares*, first published at Mexico City in 1583, D. García de Palacio advised captains to exhort their soldiers to remember 'the gratitude which they owe to God, and the obligation which they face as the church's sons, to defend both her and the Christian religion', together with their duties to country and prince. The soldiers should bear in mind that God supported all those who fought for his cause. This had applied to Moses, Gideon, Samson, Joshua, David, the Maccabees, and others in Old Testament times. God had similarly assisted Heraclius, Fernán González, Rodrigo Díaz (*El Cid*), Alfonso VII of Castile, Fernando III of Castile, and the Catholic Monarchs. Most recently he had shown his support for Charles V and Philip II, 'whose marvellous victories have been gained more by his sanctity and goodness, than by the virtue and strength of his armies'.[57] In a similar vein, in his *Avisos para soldados y gente de guerra* (1590), F. Antonio quoted St Bernard's *De laude novae militiae* as a fitting parallel to the contemporary situation.[58] Equally, there can have been few less rewarding locations to serve Spain than its North African *presidios*, which for the most part were isolated, remote, poorly supplied, and irregularly funded. Yet one historian has noted that members of their garrisons, demoralized though they often were, still perceived in their task a nobility which sprang from its connection with Spain's historic role: 'This was where the Spanish nation continued to wage war against the infidel, one of the most memorable activities in which a Christian knight could engage, above all if he belonged to the noble estate.'[59]

The chief problem with national messianism had always been the explanation of defeat, and a major feature of Ribadeneyra's argument in 1588 was that God revealed his favour through victory. To retain his support, the Armada's troops must behave appropriately while on campaign, 'living a Christian life, without scandal and without public offences to God'. Provided they did this, victory was certain, for (twisting history somewhat) 'over the course of the seventy years since Martin Luther's pestilential sect began, on every occasion that Catholics have fought heretics, they have beaten them, whether in Germany, Switzerland, France, Flanders and in England too, because God has always favoured his truth and his most holy religion'.[60] This was a commonplace, but it carried substantial

---

[55] Puddu, *Il soldato gentiluomo*, 9–10.　　[56] See too Van der Essen, 'Croisade', 77–8.
[57] García de Palacio, *Dialogos militares*, 60ᵛ–61ᵛ, 28ᵛ–29ᵛ.　　[58] Puddu, *Il soldato gentiluomo*, 248.
[59] M. A. de Bunes Ibarra, 'La vida en los presidios del Norte de Africa', in M. García-Arenal and M. J. Viguera (eds.), *Relaciones de la península ibérica con el Maghreb siglos XIII–XVI* (Madrid: Consejo Superior de Investigaciones Científicas, 1988), 561–90, at 570, and cf. 563–4.
[60] *Patris Petri de Ribadeneira . . . confessiones*, ii. 364–5, 370.

extra freight in the last quarter of the sixteenth century, as a series of Catholic apologists attempted to do battle with Machiavelli's detachment of successful statecraft from Christian morality. Their response included the compilation of roll calls of Catholic commanders who had been successful when fighting for God, a process which accentuated the formation of a specifically Catholic historical perspective even though it did not spring from the confessional divide. Naturally enough the Crusades loomed large in this roll call: in 1597, for instance, Ribadeneyra cited the First Crusade, the Albigensian Crusade, the victories of the *Reconquista*, and the battle of Lepanto in making the point.[61] The failure of the Armada was therefore a blow from which Ribadeneyra never really recovered: Breitenfeld played a similar role amongst supporters of the common Catholic cause in the Thirty Years War.[62] For the moment, however, there were many who would have agreed with the high-flown rhetoric of Marcelino Menéndez y Pelayo's verdict on Spanish history: 'Spain, the evangeliser of half the globe; Spain, the hammer of heretics; Spain, the sword of the Pope. This is our greatness and our glory: we have no other.'[63]

The European Wars of Religion did not simply develop from the accentuation of the confessional divide or even from the crystallization of the various groups into 'faith communities' nourishing separate and irreconcilable histories, identities, and agendas. They resulted also from the fact that these communities could draw, organically and with comparatively little effort, on a range of ideas, interpretations, leadership roles, and patterns of group behaviour which had evolved seamlessly from the late Middle Ages. There was a radicalization of thought and behaviour, much of it along disastrously barbaric paths, but it all took place in a context of continuity. This becomes clear when one reflects that in the background to the great conflicts of this century of Wars of Religion ($c.1546$–$c.1650$) there continued the other, less dramatic forms of religious war which we have traced through this study. On Christendom's frontiers, defensive measures against Ottoman expansion persisted. For example, the uskok community at Senj continued to wage its holy war against the Turks through to the end of the

---

[61] Pedro de Ribadeneyra, *Tratado de la religion y virtudes que deve tener el príncipe christiano, para governar y conservar sus estados* (Antwerp, 1597), 418–19. See also R. Bireley, *The Counter-Reformation Prince: Anti-Machiavellianism or Catholic Statecraft in Early Modern Europe* (Chapel Hill: University of North Carolina Press, 1990), 69–70, 111–35, 210.

[62] Bireley, *The Counter-Reformation Prince*, 142, 159–60, 213. For an attempt to assess the impact of the Armada's failure see P. Gallagher and D. W. Cruikshank, 'The Armada of 1588 Reflected in Serious and Popular Literature of the Period', in P. Gallagher and D. W. Cruikshank (eds.), *God's Obvious Design: Papers for the Spanish Armada Symposium, Sligo, 1988* (London: Tamesis Books Ltd., 1990), 167–83.

[63] Quoted by R. Fletcher, *The Quest for El Cid* (London: Hutchinson, 1989), 203. For balanced views see H. Koenigsberger, 'Spain', in O. Ranum (ed.), *National Consciousness, History, and Political Culture in Early-Modern Europe* (Baltimore: Johns Hopkins University Press, 1975), 144–72; I. A. A. Thompson, 'Castile, Spain and the Monarchy: The Political Community from *patria natural* to *patria nacional*', in R. L. Kagan and G. Parker (eds.), *Spain, Europe and the Atlantic World* (Cambridge: Cambridge University Press, 1995), 125–59; M. J. Rodríguez-Salgado, 'Christians, Civilized and Spanish: Multiple Identities in Sixteenth-Century Spain', *TRHS* 6th ser. 8 (1998), 233–51.

century, perhaps its most ambitious enterprise, an attempt to retake the fortress at Klis, occurring in 1596.[64] Volunteer nobles also continued the practice of travelling to take part in conflicts against the Turks both in the Mediterranean and in eastern Europe. Both in the old world and in the new, it would be a long time before men of noble birth and means with a disposition to fight ceased to place a special value on combat against non-Christians.[65] And to move to the opposite end of the spectrum of religious warfare, Alain Milhou showed that it was in the late sixteenth century that the subversive apocalyptic tradition attained its fullest expression in Iberia, coexisting with the 'official messianism' which naturally leaves more traces in the sources.[66]

Practising historians, and even more so those who study history at school and university, like to impose order on the past by periodizing it. The result is labels like 'The Crusades' and 'The Wars of Religion'. This is inevitable and, as emphasized in the opening chapter of this study, no bad thing. Tempting though it is, I am not about to conclude this study by proposing that there was a single 'Age of Religious War' which stretched all the way from the council of Clermont in 1095 to the Peace of Westphalia in 1648. It is certainly the case that the sheer volume of religious warfare which occurred during the fifteenth and early sixteenth centuries should firmly dislodge the notion that this was an age when any 'secularization' of warfare took place. What I am suggesting, however, is that this warfare manifested certain recurrent patterns of thinking and group behaviour which functioned as a bridge between the twelfth and thirteenth centuries, when crusading was at its height of popularity, and the Wars of Religion. These patterns are remarkable in themselves. Furthermore, they show that, given the way their ancestors had acted, the escalation of religious violence amongst Catholics and Protestants in Early Modern Europe becomes less bizarre, without becoming any less exceptional or indeed horrific. The conviction that human armies could literally fight God's war was not to be easily uprooted from the European consciousness.

---

[64] Bracewell, *Uskoks*, 161   [65] Goodman, *Chivalry and Exploration*, 198–9.
[66] Milhou, *Colón*, 316–18.

Bibliography

[When more than one place of publication is given only the first is cited here.]

I PRINTED SOURCES

ALBERI, E. (ed.), *Relazioni degli ambasciatori veneti al Senato*, ser. 2, vol. i (Florence: Società Editrice Fiorentina, 1839).

BATESON, M. (ed.), 'Aske's Examination', *EHR* 5 (1890), 550–73.

BAYLOR, M. G. (ed. and trans.), *The Radical Reformation* (Cambridge: Cambridge University Press, 1991).

BERGENROTH, G. A. (ed.), *Calendar of Letters, Despatches, and State Papers, Relating to the Negotiations between England and Spain*, ii: *Henry VIII, 1509–1525* (London: Longmans, 1866).

BESSARION, CARDINAL JOHN, 'Bessarions Instruktion für die Kreuzzugspredigt in Venedig (1463)', ed. L. Mohler, *Römische Quartalschrift*, 35 (1927), 337–49.

BREWER, J. S., et al. (eds.), *Letters and Papers, Foreign and Domestic, of the Reign of Henry VIII*, 21 vols. and addenda (Vaduz: Kraus Reprint, 1965).

BROWN, R. (ed.), *Calendar of State Papers and Manuscripts, Relating to English Affairs, Existing in the Archives and Collections of Venice, and in Other Libraries of Northern Italy*, ii: *1509–1519* (Nendeln: Kraus Reprint, 1970).

CHARTIER, ALAIN, *Le Quadrilogue invectif*, ed. E. Droz (Paris: Honoré Champion, 1923).

——*Les Œuvres latines d'Alain Chartier*, ed. P. Bourgain-Hemeryck (Paris: Éditions CNRS, 1977).

CHASTELLAIN, GEORGES, *Œuvres de Georges Chastellain*, ed. J. Kervyn de Lettenhove, 8 vols. (Brussels: F. Heussner, 1863–6).

CHELČICKÝ, PETER, 'On the Triple Division of Society', in Kaminsky, 'Peter Chelčický', 137–67.

CHRISTINE DE PISAN, *The Book of Fayttes of Armes and of Chyvalrye*, ed. A. T. P. Byles (London: Oxford University Press for Early English Text Society, 1932).

——*Ditié de Jehanne d'Arc*, ed. A. J. Kennedy and K. Varty (Oxford: Society for the Study of Mediaeval Languages and Literature, 1977).

Das Buch der Hundert Kapitel und der vierzig Statuten des sogenannten Oberrheinischen Revolutionärs, ed. A. Franke and G. Zschäbitz (Berlin: Deutscher Verlag der Wissenschaften, 1967).

ERASMUS, DESIDERIUS, 'Enchiridion militis christiani', trans. C. Fantazzi, ed. J. W. O'Malley, in *CWE* lxvi. 1–127.

——'Institutio principis christiani', trans. N. M. Cheshire and M. J. Heath, ed. A. H. T. Levi, in *CWE* xxvii. 199–288.

——'Moriae encomium', trans. B. Radice, ed. A. H. T. Levi, in *CWE* xxvii. 77–153.

——'Querela pacis', trans. B. Radice, ed. A. H. T. Levi, in *CWE* xxvii. 289–322.

——'Utilissima consultatio de bello Turcis inferendo', ed. A. G. Weiler, in *Opera omnia Desiderii Erasmi Roterodami* (Amsterdam: North-Holland, 1969–), v/iii. 1–82.

—— 'De vidua christiana', trans. J. T. Roberts, ed. J. W. O'Malley, in *CWE* lxvi. 177–257.

—— *Erasmus on his Times: A Shortened Version of the 'Adages' of Erasmus*, ed. and trans. M. Mann Phillips (Cambridge: Cambridge University Press, 1967).

—— *Opus epistolarum Des. Erasmi Roterodami*, ed. P. S. Allen et al., 11 vols. (Oxford: Oxford University Press, 1906–47).

—— *The Colloquies of Erasmus*, ed. and trans. C. R. Thompson (Chicago: University of Chicago Press, 1965).

—— *Guerre et paix dans la pensée d'Érasme*, ed. J.-C. Margolin (Paris: Aubier Montaigne, 1973).

ERSIL, J. (ed.), *Acta summorum pontificum res gestas Bohemicas aevi praehussitici et hussitici illustrantia*, 2 vols. (Prague: Academia h.e. in Aedibus Academiae Scientiarum Bohemoslovacae, 1980).

FEKETE NAGY, A., et al. (eds.), *Monumenta rusticorum in Hungaria rebellium anno MDXIV* (Budapest: Akadémiai Kiadó, 1979).

FRANCISCO DE VITORIA, 'On the American Indians', in *Political Writings*, ed. and trans. A. Pagden and J. Lawrance (Cambridge: Cambridge University Press, 1991), 231–92.

—— 'On the Law of War', in *Political Writings*, ed. and trans. A. Pagden and J. Lawrance (Cambridge: Cambridge University Press, 1991), 293–327.

FRANZ, G. (ed.), *Quellen zur Geschichte des Bauernkrieges* (Darmstadt: Wissenschaftliche Buchgesellschaft, 1963).

GARCÍA DE PALACIO, D., *Dialogos militares* (Mexico City: Pedro de Ocharte, 1583).

GAYANGOS, P. DE (ed.), *Calendar of Letters, Despatches, and State Papers, Relating to the Negotiations between England and Spain*, iv. 2: *Henry VIII, 1531–1533* (London: Longmans, 1882).

Gesta Henrici Quinti, ed. and trans. F. Taylor and J. S. Roskell (Oxford: Oxford University Press, 1975).

GILES OF VITERBO, 'Fulfillment of the Christian Golden Age under Pope Julius II: Text of a Discourse of Giles of Viterbo, 1507', ed. J. W. O'Malley, *Traditio*, 25 (1969), 265–338, repr. in *Rome and the Renaissance: Studies in Culture and Religion* (London: Variorum, 1981), study V.

—— *Scechina e libellus de litteris Hebraicis*, ed. F. Secret, 2 vols. (Rome: Centro Internazionale di Studi Umanistici, 1959).

GIOVANNI DA TAGLIACOZZO, 'Relatio de victoria Belgradensi', in *Annales Minorum*, 3rd edn. by J. M. Fonseca (Quaracchi: Tipografia Barbèra-Alfani e Venturi, 1931–), xii. 750–96.

Hechos del condestable don Miguel Lucas de Iranzo (Crónica del siglo XV), ed. J. de M. Carriazo (Madrid: Espasa-Calpe, 1940).

HÖFLER, K. (ed.), *Geschichtschreiber der husitischen Bewegung in Böhmen*, 2 vols. (Vienna: Kaiserl. Königl. Hof- und Staatsdruckerei, 1856–65).

JACOBUS DE VORAGINE, *Legenda aurea*, ed. T. Graesse (repr. Osnabrück: Otto Zeller, 1965).

JOHANNES DE RUPESCISSA, *Liber secretorum eventuum*, ed. C. Morerod-Fattebert with an introduction by R. E. Lerner (Fribourg: Éditions Universitaires Fribourg Suisse, 1994).

KAMINSKY, H. (ed.), 'The Treatises of MS o 13 on Adventism, Chiliasm and Warfare', in H. Kaminsky, *A History of the Hussite Revolution* (Berkeley and Los Angeles: University of California Press, 1967), 517–50.

KERSSENBRÜCK, HERMAN, *Hermanni A. Kerssenbroch Anabaptistici Furoris Monasterium inclitam Westphaliae metropolim evertentis historica narratio*, ed. H. Detmer (Münster: Theissing, 1899).

KLAASSEN, W. (ed.), *Anabaptism in Outline: Selected Primary Sources* (Kitchener: Herald Press, 1981).

LAIGLESIA, F. DE (ed.), *Estudios históricos (1515–19)*, 3 vols. (Madrid: Imprenta Clásica Española, 1918–19).

LANÉRY D'ARC, P. (ed.), *Mémoires et consultations en faveur de Jeanne d'Arc* (Paris: Alphonse Picard, 1889).

LATIMER, HUGH, *Sermons by Hugh Latimer Sometime Bishop of Worcester*, ed. Canon Beeching (London: J. M. Dent & Co., 1906).

LAWRENCE of BŘEZOVÁ, 'Carmen insignis corone Boemie', in Höfler (ed.), *Geschichtschreiber*, i. 596–620.

——'De gestis et variis accidentibus regni Boemiae 1414–1422', in Höfler (ed.), *Geschichtschreiber*, i. 321–527.

Le Livre des fais du bon messire Jehan le Maingre, dit Bouciquaut, mareschal de France et gouverneur de Jennes, ed. D. Lalande (Geneva: Droz, 1985).

LILIENCRON, R. VON (ed.), *Die historischen Volkslieder der Deutschen vom 13. bis 16. Jahrhundert*, 4 vols. (Leipzig: Königliche Akademie der Wissenschaften, 1865–9; repr. Hildesheim, 1966).

'Litera de civitate Pragensi continens lamentationes de actis et factis quondam ab haereticis ibidem commissis', in Höfler (ed.), *Geschichtschreiber*, ii. 311–19.

LUTHER, MARTIN, 'Against the Robbing and Murdering Hordes of Peasants', trans. C. M. Jacobs, in *LW* xlvi. 45–55.

——'An Open Letter on the Harsh Book against the Peasants', trans. C. M. Jacobs, in *LW* xlvi. 57–85.

——'Dr Martin Luther's Warning to his Dear German People, 1531', trans. M. H. Bertram, in *LW* xlvii. 3–55.

——'Letters', ed. and trans. G. G. Krödel and H. T. Lehmann, *LW* xlviii–l.

——'On War against the Turk', trans. C. M. Jacobs in *LW* xlvi. 155–205.

——'To the Christian Nobility of the German Nation', trans. C. M. Jacobs, in *LW* xliv. 115–217.

——'Treatise on Good Works', trans. W. A. Lambert, in *LW* xliv. 15–114.

——'Whether Soldiers, Too, Can Be Saved', trans. C. M. Jacobs, in *LW* xlvi. 87–137.

MACHIAVELLI, NICCOLÒ, *The Prince*, ed. and trans. Q. Skinner and R. Price (Cambridge: Cambridge University Press, 1988).

McGINN, B. (ed.), *Visions of the End: Apocalyptic Traditions in the Middle Ages* (New York: Columbia University Press, 1998).

Monumenta conciliorum generalium seculi decimi quinti, 3 vols. (Vienna: Österreichische Akademie der Wissenschaften, 1857–86).

Monumenta Henricina, 15 vols. (Coimbra: Comissão Executiva das Comemorações do Quinto Aniversário da Morte do Infante D. Henrique, 1960–74).

MORE, THOMAS, 'The Apology', ed. J. B. Trapp, *CWSTM* ix.

——'The Debellation of Salem and Bizance', ed. J. Guy et al., *CWSTM* x.

——'A Dialogue Concerning Heresies', ed. T. M. C. Lawler et al., *CWSTM* vi.

——'A Dialogue of Comfort against Tribulation', ed. L. I. Martz and F. Manley, *CWSTM* xii.

——'Responsio ad Lutherum', ed. J. M. Headley, *CWSTM* v.

MULDOON, J. (ed.), *The Expansion of Europe: The First Phase* (Philadelphia: University of Pennsylvania Press, 1977).

MÜNTZER, THOMAS, *The Collected Works of Thomas Müntzer*, ed. and trans. P. Matheson (Edinburgh: T. & T. Clark, 1988).

NICHOLAS OF PELHŘIMOV, *Confessio Taboritarum*, ed. A. Molnár and R. Cegna (Rome: Istituto Storico Italiano per il Medio Evo, 1983).

——and JOHN of LUKAVECZ, 'Chronicon Taboritarum', in Höfler (ed.), *Geschichtschreiber*, ii. 475–820.

NICOLAUS CUSANUS, *De pace fidei*, ed. R. Klibansky and H. Bascour (London: Warburg Institute, 1956).

PALACKÝ, F. (ed.), *Urkundliche Beiträge zur Geschichte des Hussitenkrieges in den Jahren 1419–1436*, 2 vols. (Prague: Friedrich Tempsky, 1873).

PICCOLOMINI, AENEAS SYLVIUS, *Historia bohemica* (Frankfurt: Christophorus Olffen, 1687).

PIUS II, *Commentaries*, trans. F. A. Gragg, in *Smith College Studies in History*, 22 (1936–7), 25 (1939–40), 30 (1947), 35 (1951), 43 (1957), 5 vols. (Northampton, Mass., 1936–57).

——*Epistola ad Mahomatem II*, ed. and trans. A. R. Baca (New York: Peter Lang, 1990).

QUICHERAT, J. (ed.), *Procès de condamnation et de réhabilitation de Jeanne d'Arc dite la Pucelle*, 5 vols. (Paris: Jules Renouard, 1841–9).

RIBADENEYRA, P. DE, *Tratado de la religion y virtudes que deve tener el príncipe christiano, para governar y conservar sus estados* (Antwerp, 1597).

——*Patris Petri de Ribadeneira Societatis Jesu sacerdotis confessiones, epistolae aliaque scripta inedita*, 2 vols. (Madrid: La Editorial Ibérica, 1920–3).

ROSA, L. G., et al. (eds.), *Gli umanisti e la guerra otrantina: Testi dei secoli XV e XVI* (Bari: Dedalo, 1982).

ROTHMANN, BERNHARD, *Die Schriften Bernhard Rothmanns*, ed. R. Stupperich (Münster: Aschendorffsche Verlagsbuchhandlung, 1970).

Rotuli parliamentorum, 6 vols. (London, 1767–77).

ST GERMAN, CHRISTOPHER, 'Salem and Bizance', in *CWSTM* x, ed. J. Guy et al. (New Haven: Yale University Press, 1987), 323–92.

SANUTO, MARINO, *I diarii di Marino Sanuto*, ed. R. Fulin et al., 58 vols. (Venice: Commercio di Marco Visentini, 1879–1903).

SAVONAROLA, FRA GIROLAMO, *Lettere e scritti apologetici*, ed. R. Ridolfi et al. (Rome: Angelo Belardetti Editore, n.d.).

——*Prediche italiane ai Fiorentini*, ed. F. Cognasso and R. Palmarocchi, 4 vols. (Perugia: 'La Nuova Italia' Editrice, 1930–5).

——*Prediche sopra Aggeo*, ed. L. Firpo (Rome, 1965).

SCOTT, T., and SCRIBNER, B. (eds. and trans.), *The German Peasants' War: A History in Documents* (Atlantic Highlands, NJ: Humanities Press International, 1991).

SIEBER-LEHMANN, C., and WILHELMI, T. (eds.), *In Helvetios – Wider die Kuhschweizer. Fremd- und Feindbilder von den Schweizern in antieidgenössischen Texten aus der Zeit von 1386 bis 1532* (Bern: Verlag Paul Haupt, 1998).

STRAUSS, G. (ed.), *Manifestations of Discontent in Germany on the Eve of the Reformation* (Bloomington: Indiana University Press, 1971).

SZERÉMI, GYÖRGY, 'Epistola de perdicione regni Hungarorum', in G. Wenzel (ed.), *Monumenta Hungariae historica*, vol. i (Pest: Magyar Tudományos Akadémia, 1857).

THALLÓCZY, L., and ANTAL, H., *Codex diplomaticus partium regno Hungariae adnexarum II* (Budapest: Magyar Tudományos Akadémia, 1907).

UNREST, JAKOB, *Österreichische Chronik*, ed. K. Grossmann, Monumenta Germaniae Historica, Scriptores rerum germanicarum, NS 11 (Weimar: Hermann Böhlaus Nachfolger, 1957).

VARCHI, BENEDETTO, *Storia fiorentina* (Cologne: Pietro Martello, 1721).

'The Very Pretty Chronicle of John Žižka', trans. F. G. Heymann, in his *John Žižka and the Hussite Revolution* (Princeton: Princeton University Press, 1955), 3–10.

VIC, C. DE, VAISSETE, J. J., et al. (eds.), *Histoire générale de Languedoc*, 16 vols. (Toulouse: E. Privat, 1872–1905).

WALSINGHAM, THOMAS, *Historia anglicana*, ed. H. T. Riley, 2 vols. (London: Rolls Series, 1863–4).

WOODHOUSE, A. S. P. (ed.), *Puritanism and Liberty, Being the Army Debates (1647–9) from the Clarke Manuscripts with Supplementary Documents* (London: Dent & Sons, 1950).

WYCLIF, JOHN, 'Cruciata', in *John Wyclif's Polemical Works in Latin*, ed. R. Buddensieg, 2 vols. (London: Trübner & Co., 1883), ii. 577–632.

'Z bratislavské schůzky krále Zikmunda s husitskými vůdci r. 1429', ed. F. M. Bartoš, *Časopis matice Moravské*, 49 (1925), 171–95.

ZURARA, GOMES EANNES DE, *Conquests and Discoveries of Henry the Navigator*, ed. V. de Castro e Almeida, trans. B. Miall (London: Allen & Unwin, 1936).

ZWINGLI, ULRICH, 'Eine göttliche Vermahnung an die Eidgenossen zu Schwyz', in *Huldreich Zwinglis sämtliche Werke*, vol. i (Munich: Kraus reprint, 1981), 155–88.

2 SECONDARY WORKS

ACKROYD, P., *The Life of Thomas More* (London: Chatto & Windus, 1998).

ADAMS, R. P., *The Better Part of Valor: More, Erasmus, Colet and Vives on Humanism, War, and Peace, 1496–1535* (Seattle: University of Washington Press, 1962).

AKENSON, D. H., *God's Peoples: Covenant and Land in South Africa, Israel, and Ulster* (Ithaca, NY: Cornell University Press, 1992).

ALLMAND, C., *Henry V* (London: Methuen, 1992).

——(ed.), *The New Cambridge Medieval History*, vii: *c.1415–c.1500* (Cambridge: Cambridge University Press, 1998).

ANDERMANN, U., 'Geschichtsdeutung und Prophetie. Krisenerfahrung und -bewältigung am Beispiel der osmanischen Expansion im Spätmittelalter und in der Reformationszeit', in Guthmüller and Kühlmann (eds.), *Europa und die Türken*, 29–54.

ARNOLD, K., *Niklashausen 1476: Quellen und Untersuchungen zur sozialreligiösen Bewegung des Hans Behem und zur Agrarstruktur eines spätmittelalterlichen Dorfes* (Baden-Baden: Verlag Valentin Koerner, 1980).

AROSIO, M., 'Bartolomeo da Colle (1421–1484): Predicatore dell'Osservanza francescana e dantista minore', in *Gli ordini mendicanti in Val d'Elsa* (Castelfiorentino: Società Storica della Valdelsa, 1999), 73–189.

ARTHUR, A., *The Tailor-King: The Rise and Fall of the Anabaptist Kingdom of Münster* (New York: St Martin's Press, 1999).

AURELL, M., 'Prophétie et messianisme politique: La Péninsule ibérique au miroir du *Liber Ostensor* de Jean de Roquetaillade', in A. Vauchez (ed.), *Les Textes prophétiques et la prophétie en Occident (XIIe–XVIe siècle)*, Mélanges de l'École Française de Rome 102 (Rome: École Française de Rome, 1990), 317–61.

—— 'Eschatologie, spiritualité et politique dans la confédération catalano-aragonaise (1282–1412)', in *Fin du monde et signes des temps: Visionnaires et prophètes en France méridionale (fin XIIIe–début XVe siècle)*, Cahiers de Fanjeaux 27 (Toulouse: Privat, 1992), 191–235.

BAILEY, R., 'The Sixteenth Century's Apocalyptic Heritage and Thomas Müntzer', *Mennonite Quarterly Review*, 57 (1983), 27–44.

BAK, J. M., 'Politics, Society and Defense in Medieval and Early Modern Hungary', in Bak and Király (eds.), *From Hunyadi to Rákóczi*, 1–22.

—— 'Delinquent Lords and Forsaken Serfs: Thoughts on War and Society during the Crisis of Feudalism', in S. B. Vardy (ed.), *Society in Change: Studies in Honour of Bela K. Király* (Boulder, Colo.: East European Monographs, 1983), 291–304.

—— 'The Price of War and Peace in Late Medieval Hungary', in B. P. McGuire (ed.), *War and Peace in the Middle Ages* (Copenhagen: Reitzels, 1987), 161–78.

—— and KIRÁLY, B. K. (eds.), *From Hunyadi to Rákóczi: War and Society in Late Medieval and Early Modern Hungary* (New York: Brooklyn College Press, 1982).

BARNES, A. E., 'Religious Anxiety and Devotional Change in Sixteenth-Century French Penitential Confraternities', *Sixteenth-Century Journal*, 19 (1988), 389–405.

BARNES, R. B., *Prophecy and Gnosis: Apocalypticism in the Wake of the Lutheran Reformation* (Stanford, Calif.: Stanford University Press, 1988).

BARTA, G., 'Der ungarische Bauernkrieg vom Jahre 1514', in Heckenast (ed.), *Aus der Geschichte*, 63–9.

BARTOŠ, F. M., 'Táborské bratrstvo let 1425–1426 na soudě svého biskupa Mikuláše z Pelhřimova', *Časopis Společnosti přátel starožitností českých v Praze*, 29 (1921), 102–22.

—— *The Hussite Revolution 1424–1437*, Engl. edn. by J. M. Klassen (Boulder, Colo.: East European Monographs, 1986).

BEAN, R., 'War and the Birth of the Nation State', *Journal of Economic History*, 33 (1973), 203–21.

BEAUNE, C., *The Birth of an Ideology: Myths and Symbols of Nation in Late-Medieval France*, trans. S. R. Huston, ed. F. L. Cheyette (Berkeley and Los Angeles: University of California Press, 1991).

BENITO RUANO, E., 'Granada o Constantinopla', *Hispania*, 60 (1960), 267–314.

BENSE, W. F., 'Paris Theologians on War and Peace, 1521–1529', *Church History*, 41 (1972), 168–85.

BIECHLER, J. E., 'A New Face toward Islam: Nicholas of Cusa and John of Segovia', in Christianson and Izbicki (eds.), *Nicholas of Cusa*, 185–202.

BIRELEY, R., *The Counter-Reformation Prince: Anti-Machiavellianism or Catholic Statecraft in Early Modern Europe* (Chapel Hill: University of North Carolina Press, 1990).

BIRNBAUM, M. D., 'A Mock Calvary in 1514? The Dózsa-Passion', in G. E. Szönyi (ed.), *European Iconography East and West* (Leiden: Brill, 1996), 91–108.

BISAHA, N., '"New Barbarian" or Worthy Adversary? Humanist Constructs of the

Ottoman Turks in Fifteenth-Century Italy', in D. R. Blanks and M. Frassetto (eds.), *Western Views of Islam in Medieval and Early Modern Europe: Perception of Other* (Basingstoke: Macmillan, 1999), 185–205.

BLICKLE, P. (ed.), *Revolte und Revolution in Europa*, HZ NS 4 (Munich: Oldenbourg, 1975).

—— 'Peasant Revolts in the German Empire in the Late Middle Ages', *Social History*, 4 (1979), 223–39.

—— 'Social Protest and Reformation Theology', in K. von Greyerz (ed.), *Religion, Politics and Social Protest: Three Studies on Early Modern Germany* (London: George Allen & Unwin, 1984), 1–23.

—— *The Revolution of 1525: The German Peasants' War from a New Perspective*, trans. T. A. Brady Jr. and H. C. E. Midelfort, 2nd edn. (Baltimore: Johns Hopkins University Press, 1985).

BOHNSTEDT, J. W., 'The Infidel Scourge of God: The Turkish Menace as Seen by German Pamphleteers of the Reformation Era', *Transactions of the American Philosophical Society*, NS 58 (1968), 1–58.

BRACEWELL, C. W., *The Uskoks of Senj: Piracy, Banditry, and Holy War in the Sixteenth-Century Adriatic* (Ithaca, NY: Cornell University Press, 1992).

BRACHIN, P., '*Vox clamantis in deserto*: Réflexions sur le pacifisme d'Érasme', in J.-C. Margolin (ed.), *Colloquia erasmiana turonensia: douzième stage international d'études humanistes, Tours 1969*, 2 vols. (Toronto: University of Toronto Press, 1972), i. 247–75.

BRADY, T. A., et al. (eds.), *Handbook of European History, 1400–1600*, 2 vols. (Grand Rapids, Mich.: William B. Eerdsmans, 1996).

BRECHT, M., 'Die Theologie Bernhard Rothmanns', *Jahrbuch für Westfälische Kirchengeschichte*, 78 (1985), 49–82.

—— 'Luther und die Türken', in Guthmüller and Kühlmann (eds.), *Europa und die Türken*, 9–27.

BREMER, T., 'Religiöse Motive im jugoslawischen Konflikt der Gegenwart', in Herrmann (ed.), *Glaubenskriege*, 139–51.

BROCK, P., *The Political and Social Doctrines of the Unity of Czech Brethren in the Fifteenth and Early Sixteenth Centuries* (The Hague: Mouton & Co., 1957).

BRUNETTI, M., 'Alla vigilia di Cambrai: La legazione di Vincenzo Querini all'imperatore Massimiliano (1507)', *Archivio veneto*, 10 (1926), 1–108.

BUNES IBARRA, M. A. DE, 'La vida en los presidios del Norte de Africa', in M. García-Arenal and M. J. Viguera (eds.), *Relaciones de la península ibérica con el Maghreb siglos XIII–XVI* (Madrid: Consejo Superior de Investigaciones Científicas, 1988), 561–90.

BURGESS, G., 'Was the English Civil War a War of Religion? The Evidence of Political Propaganda', *Huntingdon Library Quarterly*, 61 (2000), 173–201.

BUSH, M., *The Pilgrimage of Grace: A Study of the Rebel Armies of October 1536* (Manchester: Manchester University Press, 1996).

—— 'The Risings of the Commons in England, 1381–1549', in J. Denton (ed.), *Orders and Hierarchies in Late Medieval and Renaissance Europe* (Manchester: Manchester University Press, 1999), 109–25.

BYLINA, S., 'Le Mouvement hussite devant les problèmes nationaux', in D. Loades and

K. Walsh (eds.), *Faith and Identity: Christian Political Experience*, SCH, Subsidia 6 (Oxford: Blackwell, 1990), 57–67.

CABANELAS RODRÍGUEZ, D., *Juan de Segovia y el problema islámico* (Madrid: Universidad de Madrid, 1952).

CAMERON, E., 'For Reasoned Faith or Embattled Creed? Religion for the People in Early Modern Europe', *TRHS* 6th ser. 8 (1998), 165–87.

CARRASCO MANCHADO, A. I., 'Propaganda política en los panegíricos poéticos de los reyes católicos: una aproximación', *Anuario de estudios medievales*, 25 (1995), 517–43.

CÁTEDRA, P. M., *La historiografía en verso en la época de los reyes católicos: Juan Barba y su Consolatoria de Castilla* (Salamanca: University of Salamanca, 1989).

CHRISTIANSON, G., and Izbicki, T. M. (eds.), *Nicholas of Cusa in Search of God and Wisdom* (Leiden: Brill, 1991).

COHN, H. J., 'Anticlericalism in the German Peasants' War 1525', *Past and Present*, 83 (1979), 3–31.

COHN, N., *The Pursuit of the Millennium: Revolutionary Millenarians and Mystical Anarchists of the Middle Ages*, rev. and expanded edn. (New York: Oxford University Press, 1970).

CROUZET, D., *Les Guerriers de Dieu: La Violence au temps des troubles de religion vers 1525–vers 1610*, 2 vols. (Seyssel: Champ Vallon, 1990).

CUNNINGHAM, A., and GRELL, O. P., *The Four Horsemen of the Apocalypse: Religion, War, Famine and Death in Reformation Europe* (Cambridge: Cambridge University Press, 2000).

DAVIES, C. S. L., 'The Pilgrimage of Grace Reconsidered', *Past and Present*, 41 (1968), 54–75.

—— 'Popular Religion and the Pilgrimage of Grace', in A. Fletcher and J. Stevenson (eds.), *Order and Disorder in Early Modern England* (Cambridge: Cambridge University Press, 1985), 58–91.

DAVIS, N. Z., 'The Rites of Violence: Religious Riot in Sixteenth-Century France', *Past and Present*, 59 (1973), 51–91.

DE CHERRIER, C., *Histoire de Charles VIII roi de France*, 2 vols. (Paris: Didier, 1868).

DENIS, A., *Charles VIII et les Italiens: histoire et mythe* (Geneva: Droz, 1979).

DENNIS, G. T., 'Defenders of the Christian People: Holy War in Byzantium', in A. E. Laiou and R. P. Mottahedeh (eds.), *The Crusades from the Perspective of Byzantium and the Muslim World* (Washington: Dumbarton Oaks Research Library and Collection, 2001), 31–9.

DEPPERMANN, K., *Melchior Hoffman: Social Unrest and Apocalyptic Visions in the Age of Reformation*, trans. M. Wren, ed. B. Drewery (Edinburgh: T. & T. Clark, 1987).

DESSI, R. M., 'Entre prédication et réception: Les Thèmes eschatologiques dans les "reportationes" des sermons de Michele Carcano de Milan (Florence, 1461–1466)', in A. Vauchez (ed.), *Les Textes prophétiques et la prophétie en Occident (XIIe–XVIe siècle)* (Rome: École Française de Rome, 1990), 457–79.

DE WITTE, C.-M., 'Les Bulles pontificales et l'expansion portugaise au XVe siècle', *RHE* 48 (1953), 683–718, 49 (1954), 438–61, 51 (1956), 413–53, 809–36, 53 (1958), 5–46, 443–71.

DICKSON, G., 'Revivalism as a Medieval Religious Genre', *JEH* 51 (2000), 473–96.

DIEFENDORF, B., *Beneath the Cross: Catholics and Huguenots in Sixteenth-Century Paris* (New York: Oxford University Press, 1991).

Dizionario biografico degli Italiani (Rome: Istituto della Enciclopedia Italiana, 1960 ff.).

DOUSSINAGUE, J. M., *La política internacional de Fernando el Católico* (Madrid: Espasa-Calpe, 1944).

DROBNÁ, Z., *The Jena Codex: Hussite Pictorial Satire from the End of the Middle Ages*, trans. E. Wheeler (Prague: Odeon, 1970).

DUCHHARDT, H., 'Das Tunisunternehmen Karls V. 1535', *Mitteilungen des österreichischen Staatsarchivs*, 37 (1984), 35–72.

DUPRONT, A., 'Guerre sainte et Chrétienté', in his *Du sacré*, 264–87.

——'Croisade et eschatologie', in his *Du sacré*, 288–312.

——*Du sacré: Croisades et pèlerinages. Images et langages* (Mayenne: Gallimard, 1987).

DURDÍK, J., *Hussitisches Heerwesen* (Berlin: Deutscher Militärverlag, 1961).

ECHEVARRIA, A., *The Fortress of Faith: The Attitude towards Muslims in Fifteenth-Century Spain* (Leiden: Brill, 1999).

ELLIOTT, J. H., *Imperial Spain 1469–1716* (London: Edward Arnold, 1963).

EMMERSON, R. K., *Antichrist in the Middle Ages: A Study in Medieval Apocalypticism, Art, and Literature* (Seattle: University of Washington Press, 1981).

——and McGINN, B. (eds.), *The Apocalypse in the Middle Ages* (Ithaca, NY: Cornell University Press, 1992).

ENGEL, P., *The Realm of St Stephen: A History of Medieval Hungary, 895–1526*, trans. T. Pálosfalvi, ed. A. Ayton (London: I. B. Tauris, 2001).

ERDMANN, C., 'Der Kreuzzugsgedanke in Portugal', *HZ* 141 (1930), 23–53.

ERKENS, F.-R., 'Einleitung', in Erkens (ed.), *Europa und die osmanische Expansion*, 7–12.

——(ed.), *Europa und die osmanische Expansion im ausgehenden Mittelalter* (*Zeitschrift für historische Forschung*, 20) (Berlin: Duncker & Humblot, 1997).

FAUTH, D., 'Das Türkenbild bei Thomas Müntzer', *Berliner theologische Zeitschrift*, 11 (1994), 2–12.

FERNÁNDEZ, J. A., 'Erasmus on the Just War', *Journal of the History of Ideas*, 34 (1973), 209–26.

FERNÁNDEZ-ARMESTO, F., *Millennium* (London: Bantam, 1995).

FISCHER-GALATI, S. A., *Ottoman Imperialism and German Protestantism 1521–1555* (Cambridge, Mass.: Harvard University Press, 1959).

FLETCHER, A., 'The First Century of English Protestantism and the Growth of National Identity', in Mews (ed.), *Religion and National Identity*, 309–17.

FLETCHER, R., *The Quest for El Cid* (London: Hutchinson, 1989).

FOX, A., *Thomas More: History and Providence* (Oxford: Blackwell, 1982).

——'Prophecies and Politics in the Reign of Henry VIII', in A. Fox and J. Guy (eds.), *Reassessing the Henrician Age: Humanism, Politics and Reform 1500–1550* (Oxford: Blackwell, 1986), 77–94.

FRAIOLI, D. A., *Joan of Arc: The Early Debate* (Woodbridge: Boydell, 2000).

FRANZ, G., 'Zur Geschichte des Bundschuhs', *Zeitschrift für die Geschichte des Oberrheins*, NS 47 (1934), 1–23.

——*Der deutsche Bauernkrieg*, 10th edn. (Darmstadt: Wissenschaftliche Buchgesellschaft, 1975).

FREEDMAN, P., 'The German and Catalan Peasant Revolts', *AHR* 98 (1993), 39–54.

—— 'The Hungarian Peasant Revolt of 1514', in V. Rajsp (ed.), *Grafenauerjev Zbornik* (Ljubljana: Znanstvenoraziaskovalni Center SAZU, 1996), 433–46.

—— *Images of the Medieval Peasant* (Stanford, Calif.: Stanford University Press, 1999).

FUDGE, T. A., 'The State of Hussite Historiography', *Mediaevistik*, 7 (1994), 93–117.

—— 'The Night of Antichrist: Popular Culture, Judgment and Revolution in Fifteenth-Century Bohemia', *Communio viatorum*, 37 (1995), 33–45.

—— *The Magnificent Ride: The First Reformation in Hussite Bohemia* (Aldershot: Ashgate, 1998).

—— '"Neither Mine nor Thine": Communist Experiments in Hussite Bohemia', *Canadian Journal of History*, 33 (1998), 26–47.

FÜGEDI, E., 'Two Kinds of Enemies—Two Kinds of Ideology: The Hungarian–Turkish Wars in the Fifteenth Century', in B. P. McGuire (ed.), *War and Peace in the Middle Ages* (Copenhagen: C. A. Reitzels Forlag, 1987), 146–60.

GALLAGHER, P., and CRUIKSHANK, D. W., 'The Armada of 1588 Reflected in Serious and Popular Literature of the Period', in P. Gallagher and D. W. Cruikshank (eds.), *God's Obvious Design: Papers for the Spanish Armada Symposium, Sligo, 1988* (London: Tamesis Books Ltd., 1990), 167–83.

GARCÍA CÁRCEL, R., *Las Germanías de Valencia* (Barcelona: Ediciones Península, 1975).

GOERTZ, H.-J., 'The Mystic with the Hammer: Thomas Müntzer's Theological Basis for Revolution', in Stayer and Packull (eds.), *The Anabaptists and Thomas Müntzer*, 118–32.

—— 'A Common Future Conversation: A Revisionist Interpretation of the September 1524 Grebel Letters to Thomas Müntzer', in W. O. Packull and G. L. Dipple (eds.), *Radical Reformation Studies: Essays Presented to James M. Stayer* (Aldershot: Ashgate, 1999), 73–90.

GÖLLNER, C., *Turcica*, 3 vols. (Bucharest: Editura Academiei Republicii Socialiste România, 1961–78).

—— 'Zur Problematik der Kreuzzüge und der Türkenkriege im 16. Jahrhundert', *Revue des études sud-est européennes*, 12 (1975), 97–115.

GOÑI GAZTAMBIDE, J., *Historia de la Bula de la cruzada en España* (Vitoria: Editorial del Seminario, 1958).

GOODMAN, J. R., 'European Chivalry in the 1490s', *Comparative Civilizations Review*, 26 (1992), 43–72.

—— *Chivalry and Exploration 1298–1630* (Woodbridge: Boydell, 1998).

GUENÉE, B., 'État et nation en France au moyen âge', *Revue historique*, 237 (1967), 17–30.

GUNN, S., 'The French Wars of Henry VIII', in J. Black (ed.), *The Origins of War in Early Modern Europe* (Edinburgh: John Donald Publishers Ltd., 1987), 28–51.

GUNST, P., 'Der ungarische Bauernaufstand von 1514', in Blickle (ed.), *Revolte und Revolution*, 62–83.

GUTHMÜLLER, B., and KÜHLMANN, W. (eds.), *Europa und die Türken in der Renaissance* (Tübingen: Max Niemeyer, 2000).

GUY, J., 'The Later Career of Christopher St German (1534–1541)', app. C in *CWSTM* x. 393–417.

HALE, J. R., 'Incitement to Violence? English Divines on the Theme of War, 1578 to 1631', in J. G. Rowe and W. H. Stockdale (eds.), *Florilegium historiale: Essays Presented to Wallace K. Ferguson* (Toronto: University of Toronto Press, 1971), 369–99, repr. in J. R. Hale, *Renaissance War Studies* (London: Hambledon, 1983).

HALE, J. R., *The Civilization of Europe in the Renaissance* (London: Fontana, 1993).

HALKIN, L.-E., 'Érasme, la guerre et la paix', in *Krieg und Frieden im Horizont des Renaissancehumanismus* (Weinheim: Acta Humaniora, 1986), 13–44, repr. in his *Érasme: Sa pensée et son comportement*, study XV.

—— *Érasme: Sa pensée et son comportement* (London: Variorum, 1988).

HANKINS, J., 'Renaissance Crusaders: Humanist Crusade Literature in the Age of Mehmed II', *Dumbarton Oaks Papers*, 49 (1995), 111–207.

HARDING, R. R., 'The Mobilization of Confraternities against the Reformation in France', *Sixteenth-Century Journal*, 11 (1980), 85–107.

—— 'Revolution and Reform in the Holy League: Angers, Rennes, Nantes', *Journal of Modern History*, 53 (1981), 379–416.

HASTINGS, A., *The Construction of Nationhood: Ethnicity, Religion and Nationalism* (Cambridge: Cambridge University Press, 1997).

HEADLEY, J. M., 'Rhetoric and Reality: Messianic, Humanist, and Civilian Themes in the Imperial Ethos of Gattinara', in Reeves (ed.), *Prophetic Rome*, 241–69.

HEATH, M. J., *Crusading Commonplaces: La Noue, Lucinge and Rhetoric against the Turks* (Geneva: Droz, 1986).

HECKENAST, G. (ed.), *Aus der Geschichte der ostmitteleuropäischen Bauernbewegungen im 16.–17. Jahrhundert* (Budapest: Akadémiai Kiadó, 1977).

HEHL, E.-D., 'Was ist eigentlich ein Kreuzzug?', *HZ* 259 (1994), 297–336.

HELD, J., 'Peasants in Arms, 1437–1438 & 1456', in Bak and Király (eds.), *From Hunyadi to Rákóczi*, 81–101.

—— *Hunyadi: Legend and Reality* (Boulder, Colo.: East European Manographs, 1985).

HELMRATH, J., 'Pius II und die Türken', in Guthmüller and Kühlmann (eds.), *Europa und die Türken*, 79–137.

HERRMANN, P. (ed.), *Glaubenskriege in Vergangenheit und Gegenwart* (Göttingen: Vandenhoeck & Ruprecht, 1996).

HEYMANN, F. G., *John Žižka and the Hussite Revolution* (Princeton: Princeton University Press, 1955).

—— 'The Hussite Revolution and the German Peasants' War: An Historical Comparison', *Medievalia et humanistica*, NS 1 (1970), 141–59.

—— 'The Crusades against the Hussites', in K. M. Setton (gen. ed.), *A History of the Crusades*, 2nd edn., 6 vols. (Madison: University of Wisconsin Press, 1969–90), iii. 586–646.

HEYWOOD, C., 'The Frontier in Ottoman History: Old Ideas and New Myths', in D. Power and N. Standen (eds.), *Frontiers in Question: Eurasian Borderlands, 700–1700* (Basingstoke: Macmillan, 1999), 228–50.

HILLERBRAND, H. J. (ed.), *Radical Tendencies in the Reformation: Divergent Perspectives* (Kirksville, Mo.: Sixteenth Century Journal Publishers, 1988).

HOFER, J., 'Der Sieger von Belgrad 1456', *Historisches Jahrbuch*, 51 (1931), 163–212.

HOFFMANN, R. C., 'Warfare, Weather, and a Rural Economy: The Duchy of Wroclaw in the Mid-Fifteenth Century', *Viator*, 4 (1973), 273–305.

HOGG, M. A., and VAUGHAN, G. M., *Social Psychology*, 2nd edn. (Hemel Hempstead: Prentice Hall, 1998).

HOLMES, G., 'Cardinal Beaufort and the Crusade against the Hussites', *EHR* 349 (1973), 721–50.

HOLT, M. P., 'Putting Religion back into the French Wars of Religion', *French Historical Studies*, 18 (1993), 524–51.

—— *The French Wars of Religion, 1562–1629* (Cambridge: Cambridge University Press, 1995).

HOUSLEY, N., 'France, England, and the "National Crusade", 1302–1386', in G. Jondorf and D. N. Dumville (eds.), *France and the British Isles in the Middle Ages and Renaissance* (Woodbridge: Boydell, 1991), 183–201, repr. in *CWMRE*, study VII.

—— *The Later Crusades, 1274–1580: From Lyons to Alcazar* (Oxford: Oxford University Press, 1992).

—— 'Frontier Societies and Crusading in the Late Middle Ages', *Mediterranean Historical Review*, 10 (1995), 104–19, repr. in *CWMRE*, study V.

—— 'The Eschatological Imperative: Messianism and Holy War in Europe, 1260–1556', in Schäfer and Cohen (eds.), *Toward the Millennium*, 123–50, repr. in *CWMRE*, study III.

—— 'Crusading as Social Revolt: The Hungarian Peasant Uprising of 1514', *JEH* 49 (1998), 1–28, repr. in *CWMRE*, study XVII.

—— 'A Necessary Evil? Erasmus, the Crusade, and War against the Turks', in J. France and W. G. Zajac (eds.), *The Crusades and their Sources: Essays Presented to Bernard Hamilton* (Aldershot: Ashgate, 1998), 259–79, repr. in *CWMRE*, study XVIII.

—— 'Insurrection as Religious War, 1400–1536', *JMH* 25 (1999), 141–54, repr. in *CWMRE*, study VIII.

—— 'Holy Land or Holy Lands? Palestine and the Catholic West in the Late Middle Ages and Renaissance', in R. N. Swanson (ed.), *The Holy Land, Holy Lands, and Christian History*, SCH 36 (Woodbridge: Boydell, 2000), 228–49.

—— '*Pro deo et patria mori*: Sanctified Patriotism in Europe, 1400–1600', in P. Contamine (ed.), *War and Competition between States* (Oxford: Oxford University Press, 2000), 221–48.

—— 'Explaining Defeat: Andrew of Regensburg and the Hussite Crusades', in M. Balard et al. (eds.), *Dei gesta per Francos: Études sur les croisades dédiées à Jean Richard* (Aldershot: Ashgate, 2001), 87–95.

HRUZA, K., 'Die hussitischen Manifeste vom April 1420', *Deutsches Archiv für Erforschung des Mittelalters*, 53 (1997), 119–77.

HSIA, R. PO-CHIA, 'Münster and the Anabaptists', in R. Po-chia Hsia (ed.), *The German People and the Reformation* (Ithaca, NY: Cornell University Press, 1988), 51–69.

IGLESIAS, C., et al. (eds.), *Homenaje a José Antonio Maravall*, 3 vols. (Madrid: Centro de Investigaciones Sociológicas, 1985).

IMBER, C., *The Ottoman Empire 1300–1481* (Istanbul: Isis, 1990).

IWAŃCZAK, W., 'Between Pacifism and Anarchy: Peter Chelčický's Teaching about Society', *JMH* 23 (1997), 271–83.

IZBICKI, T. M., 'The Possibility of Dialogue with Islam in the Fifteenth Century', in Christianson and Izbicki (eds.), *Nicholas of Cusa*, 175–83.

JANKOVICS, J., 'The Image of the Turks in Hungarian Renaissance Literature', in Guthmüller and Kühlmann (eds.), *Europa und die Türken*, 267–73.

JOHNSON, J. T., *Ideology, Reason and the Limitation of War: Religious and Secular Concepts 1200–1740* (Princeton: Princeton University Press, 1975).

—— *The Holy War Idea in Western and Islamic Traditions* (University Park: Pennsylvania State University Press, 1997).

JOLSTAD, A., and LUNDE, M. (eds.), *Proceedings, 19th International Congress of Historical Sciences* (Oslo: University of Oslo, 2000).

JONES, M. (ed.), *The New Cambridge Medieval History*, vi: *c.1300–c.1415* (Cambridge: Cambridge University Press, 2000).

KAMINSKY, H., 'Chiliasm and the Hussite Revolution', *Church History*, 26 (1957), 43–71.

——'Peter Chelčický: Treatises on Christianity and the Social Order', *Studies in Medieval and Renaissance History*, 1 (1964), 105–79.

——*A History of the Hussite Revolution* (Berkeley and Los Angeles: University of California Press, 1967).

——'Nicholas of Pelhřimov's Tabor: An Adventure into the Eschaton', in Patschovsky and Šmahel (eds.), *Eschatologie und Hussitismus*, 139–67.

KANTOROWICZ, E. H., '*Pro patria mori* in Medieval Political Thought', *AHR* 56 (1951), 472–92.

KEEN, M., 'Huizinga, Kilgour and the Decline of Chivalry', *Medievalia et humanistica*, NS 8 (1977), 1–20.

KEJŘ, J., *The Hussite Revolution*, trans. T. Gottheinerová (Prague: Orbis Press Agency, 1988).

KEMPERS, B., 'Icons, Altarpieces, and Civic Ritual in Siena Cathedral, 1100–1530', in B. A. Hanawalt and K. L. Reyerson (eds.), *City and Spectacle in Medieval Europe* (Minneapolis: University of Minnesota Press, 1994), 89–136.

KLAASSEN, W., *Michael Gaismair Revolutionary and Reformer* (Leiden: Brill, 1978).

KLASSEN, J., 'The Disadvantaged and the Hussite Revolution', *International Review of Social History*, 35 (1990), 249–72.

——'Hus, the Hussites and Bohemia', in Allmand (ed.), *New Cambridge Medieval History*, vii. 367–91.

KNOLL, P., 'Poland as *Antemurale Christianitatis* in the Late Middle Ages', *Catholic Historical Review*, 60 (1974), 381–401.

KOENIGSBERGER, H., 'Spain', in O. Ranum (ed.), *National Consciousness, History, and Political Culture in Early-Modern Europe* (Baltimore: Johns Hopkins University Press, 1975), 144–72.

KOLB, R., 'The Theologians and the Peasants: Conservative Evangelical Reactions to the German Peasants' Revolt', *Archiv für Reformationsgeschichte*, 69 (1978), 103–31.

KRYNEN, J., *L'Empire du roi: Idées et croyances politiques en France XIIIe–Xve siècle* (Paris: Gallimard, 1993).

LABANDE-MAILFERT, Y., *Charles VIII et son milieu (1470–1498): La Jeunesse au pouvoir* (Paris: Klincksieck, 1975).

LAFAYE, J., *Quetzalcóatl and Guadalupe: The Formation of Mexican National Consciousness 1531–1813*, trans. B. Keen (Chicago: University of Chicago Press, 1976).

LAMBERT, M., *Medieval Heresy: Popular Movements from the Gregorian Reform to the Reformation*, 2nd edn. (Oxford: Blackwell, 1992).

LERNER, R. E., *The Powers of Prophecy: The Cedar of Lebanon Vision from the Mongol Onslaught to the Dawn of the Enlightenment* (Berkeley and Los Angeles: University of California Press, 1983).

——'The Medieval Return to the Thousand-Year Sabbath', in Emmerson and McGinn (eds.), *Apocalypse*, 51–71.

——'"Popular Justice": Rupescissa in Hussite Bohemia', in Patschovsky and Šmahel (eds.), *Eschatologie und Hussitismus*, 39–51.

LINEHAN, P., 'Religion, Nationalism and National Identity in Medieval Spain and Portugal', in Mews (ed.), *Religion and National Identity*, 161–99.

LLOYD, H. A., 'Josse Clichtove and the Just War', in A. Ayton and J. L. Price (eds.), *The Medieval Military Revolution: State, Society and Military Change in Medieval and Early Modern Europe* (London: I. B. Tauris, 1995), 145–62.

LOADES, D., 'The Origins of English Protestant Nationalism', in Mews (ed.), *Religion and National Identity*, 297–307.

LONGWORTH, P., 'The Senj Uskoks Reconsidered', *Slavonic and East European Review*, 57 (1979), 348–68.

LOWE, B., *Imagining Peace: A History of Early English Pacifist Ideas, 1340–1560* (University Park: Pennsylvania State University Press, 1997).

LUTTRELL, A., 'The Military Orders, 1312–1798', in J. Riley-Smith, *The Oxford Illustrated History of the Crusades* (Oxford: Oxford University Press, 1995), 326–64.

McGINN, B., 'Angel Pope and Papal Antichrist', *Church History*, 47 (1978), 155–73.

MACHILEK, F., 'Heilserwartung und Revolution der Täboriten 1419/21', in K. Schnith (ed.), *Festiva Lanx: Studien zum mittelalterlichen Geistesleben Johannes Spörl darge-bracht aus Anlass seines sechzigsten Geburtstages* (Munich: Salesianische Offizin, 1966), 67–94.

MACKAY, A., 'The Ballad and the Frontier in Late Mediaeval Spain', *Bulletin of Hispanic Studies*, 53 (1976), 15–33.

—— 'Religion, Culture, and Ideology on the Late Medieval Castilian–Granadan Frontier', in R. Bartlett and A. MacKay (eds.), *Medieval Frontier Societies* (Oxford: Oxford University Press, 1989), 217–43.

McKENNA, J. W., 'How God Became an Englishman', in D. J. Guth and J. W. McKenna (eds.), *Tudor Rule and Revolution: Essays for G. R. Elton from his American Friends* (Cambridge: Cambridge University Press, 1982), 25–43.

MAIER, C. T., 'Crisis, Liturgy and the Crusade in the Twelfth and Thirteenth Centuries', *JEH* 48 (1997), 628–57.

MARCHAL, G. P., 'Bellum justum contra judicium belli. Zur Interpretation von Jakob Wimpfelings antieidgenössischer Streitschrift "Soliloquium pro Pace Christianorum et pro Helvetiis ut resipiscant . . ." (1505)', in N. Bernard and Q. Reichen (eds.), *Gesellschaft und Gesellschaften. Festschrift Ulrich Im Hof* (Bern: Wyss Verlag, 1982), 114–37.

—— 'Die Antwort der Bauern: Elemente und Schichtungen des eidgenössischen Geschichtsbewusstseins am Ausgang des Mittelalters', in H. Patze (ed.), *Geschichts-schreibung und Geschichtsbewusstsein im späten Mittelalter* (Sigmaringen: Jan Thorbecke, 1987), 757–90.

—— 'De la "Passion du Christ" à la "Croix Suisse": Quelques réflexions sur une enseigne suisse', in M. Comina (ed.), *Histoire et belles histoires de la Suisse: Guillaume Tell, Nicolas de Flüe et les autres, des chroniques au cinéma* (Basle: Schwabe, 1989), 107–31.

—— 'Stigmatisierungskonzept und Semiotik: Annäherungen an die eidgenössische Selbstpräsentation um 1500', in *Schwaben-oder Schweizerkrieg. Ereignis und kollektive Identität*, forthcoming.

MARGOLIN, J.-C., 'Érasme et la guerre contre les Turcs', *Il pensiero politico*, 13 (1980), 3–38.

MARSCH, E., *Biblische Prophetie und chronographische Dichtung. Stoff- und Wirkungs-*

geschichte der Vision des Propheten Daniel nach Dan. VII (Berlin: Erich Schmidt Verlag, 1972).

MARTIN, D., Does Christianity Cause War? (Oxford: Oxford University Press, 1997).

MAU, R., 'Luthers Stellung zu den Türken', in H. Junghans (ed.), Leben und Werk Martin Luthers von 1526 bis 1546, 2 vols. (Göttingen: Vandenhoeck & Ruprecht, 1983), i. 647–62, ii. 956–66.

MAŽEIKA, R., 'Of Cabbages and Knights: Trade and Trade Treaties with the Infidel on the Northern Frontier', JMH 20 (1994), 63–76.

Memory and Reconciliation: The Church and the Faults of the Past (London: Catholic Truth Society, 2000).

MERTENS, D., 'Europäische Friede und Türkenkrieg im Spätmittelalter', in H. Duchhardt (ed.), Zwischenstaatliche Friedenswahrung in Mittelalter und Früher Neuzeit (Cologne: Böhlau, 1991), 45–90.

—— ' "Europa, id est patria, domus propria, sedes nostra . . .". Zu Funktionen und Uberlieferung lateinischer Türkenreden im 15. Jahrhundert', in Erkens (ed.), Europa und die osmanische Expansion, 39–57.

MESERVE, M., 'Medieval Sources for Renaissance Theories on the Origins of the Ottoman Turks', in Guthmüller and Kühlmann (eds.), Europa und die Türken, 409–36.

MEUTHEN, E., 'Der Fall von Konstantinopel und der lateinische Westen', HZ 237 (1983), 1–35.

MEWS, S. (ed.), Religion and National Identity, SCH 18 (Oxford: Blackwell, 1982).

MEYUHAS GINIO, A., 'Rêves de croisade contre les Sarrasins dans la Castile du XVe siècle (Alonso de Espina, Fortalitium fidei)', Revue de l'histoire des religions, 212 (1995), 145–74.

MICHAUD-FRÉJAVILLE, F., 'Jeanne d'Arc, dux, chef de guerre: Les Points de vue des traités en faveur de la Pucelle', in J. Paviot and J. Verger (eds.), Guerre, pouvoir et noblesse au moyen âge. Mélanges en l'honneur de Philippe Contamine (Paris: Presses de l'Université de Paris-Sorbonne, 2000), 523–31.

MILHOU, A., 'La Chauve-souris, le Nouveau David et le roi caché (trois images de l'empereur des derniers temps dans le monde ibérique: XIIIe–XVIIe s.)', Mélanges de la Casa de Velásquez, 18 (1982), 61–78.

—— Colón y su mentalidad mesiánica en el ambiente franciscanista español (Valladolid: Casa-Museo de Colón Seminario Americanista de la Universidad de Valladolid, 1983).

—— 'Propaganda mesiánica y opinión pública: Las reacciones de las ciudades del reino de Castilla frente al proyecto fernandino de cruzada (1510–11)', in Iglesias et al. (eds.), Homenaje a José Antonio Maravall, iii. 51–62.

MILLWARD, L., 'Social Psychology 2', in M. Eysenck (ed.), Psychology: An Integrated Approach (Harlow: Addison Wesley Longman, 1998), 356–406.

MINNICH, N. H., 'The Role of Prophecy in the Career of the Enigmatic Bernardino López de Carvajal', in Reeves (ed.), Prophetic Rome, 111–20.

MOLNÁR, A., 'L'Évolution de la théologie hussite', Revue d'histoire et de philosophie religieuses, 43 (1963), 133–71.

—— 'Non-violence et théologie de la révolution chez les Hussites du XVème siècle', Lumière et vie, 91 (1969), 33–46.

—— 'Réformation et révolution: Le Cas du senior taborite Nicolas Biskupec de Pelhřimov', Communio viatorum, 13 (1970), 137–70.

MULDOON, J., 'Papal Responsibility for the Infidel: Another Look at Alexander VI's *Inter caetera*', *Catholic Historical Review*, 64 (1978), 168–84.

—— *Popes, Lawyers, and Infidels: The Church and the Non-Christian World 1250–1550* (Liverpool: Liverpool University Press, 1979).

MÜLLER, U., 'Ein Zürich-Habsburgisches Kreuzlied gegen die Eidgenossen. Beobachtungen zur Kreuzzugslyrik des späten Mittelalters', in H. Wenzel (ed.), *Adelsherrschaft und Literatur* (Bern: Peter Lang, 1980), 259–86.

MUSTO, R. G., 'Just Wars and Evil Empires: Erasmus and the Turks', in J. Monfasani and R. G. Musto (eds.), *Renaissance Society and Culture: Essays in Honor of Eugene F. Rice, Jr.* (New York: Italica Press, 1991), 197–216.

NALLE, S. T., 'The Millennial Moment: Revolution and Radical Religion in Sixteenth-Century Spain', in Schäfer and Cohen (eds.), *Toward the Millennium*, 151–71.

NAVARRO LEDESMA, F., *Cervantes: The Man and the Genius*, trans. D. and G. Bliss (New York: Charterhouse, 1973).

NICCOLI, O., *Prophecy and People in Renaissance Italy*, trans. L. G. Cochrane (Princeton: Princeton University Press, 1990).

—— 'High and Low Prophetic Culture in Rome at the Beginning of the Sixteenth Century', in Reeves (ed.), *Prophetic Rome*, 203–22.

NIPPERDEY, T., 'Theology and Revolution in Thomas Müntzer', in Stayer and Packull (eds.), *The Anabaptists and Thomas Müntzer*, 105–17.

OBERMAN, H. A., 'The Gospel of Social Unrest: 450 Years after the So-Called "German Peasants' War" of 1525', *Harvard Theological Review*, 69 (1976), 103–29.

O'CALLAGHAN, J., 'Castile, Portugal, and the Canary Islands: Claims and Counterclaims, 1344–1479', *Viator*, 24 (1993), 287–309.

OCHSENBEIN, P., 'Beten "mit zertanen armen": Ein alteidgenössischer Brauch', *Schweizerisches Archiv für Volkskunde*, 75 (1979), 129–72.

—— 'Jakob Wimpfelings literarische Fehde mit den Baslern und Eidgenossen', *Basler Zeitschrift für Geschichte und Altertumskunde*, 79 (1979), 37–65.

O'MALLEY, J. W., *Giles of Viterbo on Church and Reform: A Study in Renaissance Thought* (Leiden: Brill, 1968).

—— 'The Discovery of America and Reform Thought at the Papal Court in the Early Cinquecento', in F. Chiappelli et al. (eds.), *First Images of America: The Impact of the New World on the Old*, 2 vols. (Berkeley and Los Angeles: University of California Press, 1976), i. 185–200.

—— *Praise and Blame in Renaissance Rome: Rhetoric, Doctrine and Reform in the Sacred Orators of the Papal Court, c.1450–1521* (Durham, NC: Duke University Press, 1979).

PAGDEN, A., 'Identity Formation in Spanish America', in N. Canny and A. Pagden (eds.), *Colonial Identity in the Atlantic World, 1500–1800* (Princeton: Princeton University Press, 1987), 51–93.

—— *Lords of All the World: Ideologies of Empire in Spain, Britain and France c.1500–c.1800* (New Haven: Yale University Press, 1995).

PARAVICINI, W., *Die Preussenreisen des europäischen Adels*, 3 vols. (Sigmaringen: Jan Thorbecke, 1989 ff.).

PARKER, G., *Philip II* (London: Hutchinson, 1979).

—— 'Tudor England in the Messianic Vision of Philip II of Spain', *TRHS* forthcoming.

PARTNER, P., *God of Battles: Holy Wars of Christianity and Islam* (London: Harper Collins, 1997).

PATSCHOVSKY, A., and ŠMAHEL, F. (eds.), *Eschatologie und Hussitismus* (Prague: Historisches Institut, 1996).

PETERSEN, R. L., *Preaching in the Last Days: The Theme of 'Two Witnesses' in the Sixteenth and Seventeenth Centuries* (New York: Oxford University Press, 1993).

PHELAN, J. L., *The Millennial Kingdom of the Franciscans in the New World*, 2nd edn. (Berkeley and Los Angeles: University of California Press, 1970).

POLIZZOTTO, L., 'Prophecy, Politics and History in Early Sixteenth-Century Florence: The Admonitory Letters of Francesco d'Antonio de' Ricci', in P. Denley and C. Edam (eds.), *Florence and Italy: Renaissance Studies in Honour of Nicolai Rubinstein* (London: Committee for Medieval Studies, Westfield College, 1988), 107–31.

——— *The Elect Nation: The Savonarolan Movement in Florence 1494–1545* (Oxford: Oxford University Press, 1994).

PRETO, P., *Venezia e i Turci* (Florence: Sansoni, 1975).

PROCHNO, J., 'Terra Bohemiae, Regnum Bohemiae, Corona Bohemiae', in M. Hellmann (ed.), *Corona Regni: Studien über die Krone als Symbol des Staates im späteren Mittelalter* (Weimar: Hermann Böhlaus Nachfolger, 1961), 198–224.

PROKEŠ, J., 'Táborské manifesty z r. 1430 a 1431. Příspěvek k politice Prokopa Velikého', *Časopis matice Moravské*, 52 (1928).

PUDDU, R., *Il soldato gentiluomo: Autoritratto d'una società guerriera: La Spagna del Cinquecento* (Bologna: Società Editrice il Mulino, 1982).

RABB, T. K., and SEIGEL, J. E. (eds.), *Action and Conviction in Early Modern Europe: Essays in Memory of E. H. Harbison* (Princeton: Princeton University Press, 1969).

RACAUT, L., 'The Polemical Use of the Albigensian Crusade during the French Wars of Religion', *French History*, 13 (1999), 261–79.

REDONDO, A., 'Mesianismo y reformismo en Castilla a raíz de la batalla de Pavía: el *Memorial* de don Beltrán de Guevara dirigido a Carlos V (1525)', in Iglesias et al. (eds.), *Homenaje a José Antonio Maravall*, iii. 237–57.

REEVES, M., *The Influence of Prophecy in the Later Middle Ages: A Study in Joachimism* (Oxford: Oxford University Press, 1969).

——— 'The Originality and Influence of Joachim of Fiore', *Traditio*, 36 (1980), 269–316.

——— (ed.), *Prophetic Rome in the High Renaissance Period* (Oxford: Oxford University Press, 1992).

REPGEN, K., 'What is a "Religious War"?', in E. I. Kouri and T. Scott (eds.), *Politics and Society in Reformation Europe* (London: Macmillan, 1987), 311–28.

RICHES, S., *St George: Hero, Martyr and Myth* (Stroud: Sutton, 2000).

RILEY-SMITH, J., *What Were the Crusades?* (London: Macmillan, 1977).

RODRÍGUEZ-SALGADO, M. J., 'Christians, Civilized and Spanish: Multiple Identities in Sixteenth-Century Spain', *TRHS* 6th ser. 8 (1998), 233–51.

ROGERS, F. M., *The Travels of the Infante Dom Pedro of Portugal* (Cambridge: Cambridge University Press, 1961).

ROTH, C., *The Last Florentine Republic* (London: Methuen, 1925).

ROTHKRUG, L., *Religious Practices and Collective Perceptions: Hidden Homologies in the Renaissance and Reformation* (Waterloo: University of Waterloo, 1980).

ROUSSET, P., *Les Origines et les caractères de la Première Croisade* (Neuchâtel: Baconnière, 1945).

——— 'La "Croisade" puritaine de Cromwell', *Schweizerische Zeitschrift für Geschichte*, 28 (1978), 15–28.

—— 'L'Idéologie de croisade dans les guerres de religion au XVIe siècle', *Schweizerische Zeitschrift für Geschichte*, 31 (1981), 174–84.

ROWELL, S. C., *Lithuania Ascending: A Pagan Empire within East-Central Europe, 1295–1345* (Cambridge: Cambridge University Press, 1994).

—— 'Unexpected Contacts: Lithuanians at Western Courts, *c*.1316–*c*.1400', *EHR* 101 (1996), 557–77.

—— 'Baltic Europe', in Jones (ed.), *New Cambridge Medieval History*, vi. 699–734.

RUBIÉS, J.-P., *Travel and Ethnology in the Renaissance: South India through European Eyes, 1250–1625* (Cambridge: Cambridge University Press, 2000).

RUIZ, T. F., 'Une royauté sans sacre: La Monarchie castillane du bas moyen âge', *Annales ESC* 39 (1984), 429–53.

—— 'Elite and Popular Culture in Late Fifteenth-Century Castilian Festivals: The Case of Jaen', in B. A. Hanawalt and K. L. Reyerson (eds.), *City and Spectacle in Medieval Europe* (Minneapolis: University of Minnesota Press, 1994), 296–318.

—— *Spanish Society, 1400–1600* (Harlow: Longman, 2001).

RUSCONI, R., 'L'escatologia negli ultimi secoli del Medioevo', in Patschovsky and Šmahel (eds.), *Eschatologie und Hussitismus*, 7–24.

RUSSELL, F. H., 'Paulus Vladimiri's Attack on the Just War: A Case Study in Legal Polemics', in B. Tierney and P. Linehan (eds.), *Authority and Power: Studies on Medieval Law and Government Presented to Walter Ullmann on his Seventieth Birthday* (Cambridge: Cambridge University Press, 1980), 237–54.

RUSSELL, P., *Prince Henry 'the Navigator': A Life* (New Haven: Yale University Press, 2000).

SÁNCHEZ MONTES, J., *Franceses, Protestantes, Turcos: Los Españoles ante la política internacional de Carlos V* (Madrid: Consejo Superior de Investigaciones Científicas, 1951).

SCHÄFER, P., and COHEN, M. R. (eds.), *Toward the Millennium: Messianic Expectations from the Bible to Waco* (Leiden: Brill, 1998).

SCHEIN, S., 'Philip IV and the Crusade: A Reconsideration', in P. W. Edbury (ed.), *Crusade and Settlement* (Cardiff: University College Cardiff Press, 1985), 121–6.

SCHOECK, R. J., 'Thomas More's "Dialogue of Comfort" and the Problem of the Real Grand Turk', *English Miscellany*, 20 (1969), 23–37.

SCHOTTENLOHER, O., 'Erasmus und die Respublica Christiana', *HZ* 210 (1970), 295–323.

SCHWARTZ, S. B., 'New World Nobility: Social Aspirations and Mobility in the Conquest and Colonization of Spanish America', in M. U. Chrisman and O. Gründler (eds.), *Social Groups and Religious Ideas in the Sixteenth Century* (Kalamazoo: The Board of the Medieval Institute, Western Michigan University, 1978), 23–37, 154–8.

SCHWOEBEL, R., *The Shadow of the Crescent: The Renaissance Image of the Turk (1453–1517)* (Nieuwkoop: B. de Graaf, 1967).

SCOTT, T., 'Reformation and Peasants' War in Waldshut and Environs: A Structural Analysis', *Archiv für Reformationsgeschichte*, 69 (1978), 82–102, 70 (1979), 140–68.

—— 'The Peasants' War: A Historiographical Review', *Historical Journal*, 22 (1979), 693–720, 953–74.

—— 'From Polemic to Sobriety: Thomas Müntzer in Recent Research', *JEH* 39 (1988), 557–72.

—— *Thomas Müntzer: Theology and Revolution in the German Reformation* (Basingstoke: Macmillan, 1989).

SCRIBNER, B., 'Communities and the Nature of Power', in B. Scribner (ed.), *Germany: A New Social and Economic History*, i: *1450–1630* (London: Arnold, 1996), 291–325.
—— 'Preconditions of Tolerance and Intolerance in Sixteenth-Century Germany', in O. P. Grell and B. Scribner (eds.), *Tolerance and Intolerance in the European Reformation* (Cambridge: Cambridge University Press, 1996), 32–47.
SEIBT, F., 'Communitas primogenita. Zur Prager Hegemonialpolitik in der hussitischen Revolution', *Historisches Jahrbuch*, 81 (1962), 80–100, repr. in Seibt, *Hussitenstudien*, 61–77.
—— *Hussitica: Zur Struktur einer Revolution* (Cologne: Böhlau, 1965).
—— 'Revolution und Hussitenkriege 1419–1436', in K. Bosl (ed.), *Handbuch der Geschichte der böhmischen Länder*, 4 vols. (Stuttgart, 1966–74), i. 444–536.
—— 'Tabor und die europäischen Revolutionen', *Bohemia: Jahrbuch des Collegium Carolinum*, 14 (1973), 33–42, repr. in Seibt, *Hussitenstudien*, 175–84.
—— 'Vom Vítkov bis zum Vyšehrad. Der Kampf um die böhmische Krone 1420 im Licht der Prager Propaganda', *Historisches Jahrbuch*, 94 (1974), 89–117, repr. in Seibt, *Hussitenstudien*, 185–207.
—— 'Peter Chelčický', in K. Bosl (ed.), *Lebensbilder zur Geschichte der böhmischen Länder*, vol. i (Munich: Oldenbourg, 1974), 49–61, repr. in Seibt, *Hussitenstudien*, 209–16.
—— 'Die hussitische Revolution und der Deutsche Bauernkrieg', in Blickle (ed.), *Revolte und Revolution*, 47–61, repr. in Seibt, *Hussitenstudien*, 217–28.
—— *Hussitenstudien: Personen, Ereignisse, Ideen einer frühen Revolution* (Munich: Oldenbourg, 1987).
SETTON, K. M., 'Pope Leo X and the Turkish Peril', *Proceedings of the American Philosophical Society*, 113 (1969), 367–424.
—— *The Papacy and the Levant (1204–1571)*, 4 vols. (Philadelphia: American Philosophical Society, 1976–84).
SHEILS, W. J. (ed.), *The Church and War*, SCH 20 (Oxford: Blackwell, 1983).
SIEBER-LEHMANN, C., ' "Teutsche Nation" und Eidgenossenschaft. Der Zusammenhang zwischen Türkenkrieg und Burgunderkriegen', *HZ* 253 (1991), 561–602.
—— 'Der türkische Sultan Mehmed II. und Karl der Kühne, der "Türk im Occident" ', in Erkens (ed.), *Europa und die osmanische Expansion*, 13–38.
SKINNER, Q., *The Foundations of Modern Political Thought*, 2 vols. (Cambridge: Cambridge University Press, 1978).
ŠMAHEL, F., 'The Idea of the "Nation" in Hussite Bohemia', *Historica*, 16 (1969), 143–247, 17 (1969), 93–197.
—— ' "Doctor evangelicus super omnes evangelistas": Wyclif's Fortune in Hussite Bohemia', *Bulletin of the Institute of Historical Research*, 43 (1970), 16–34.
—— *La Révolution hussite: une anomalie historique* (Paris: Presses Universitaires de France, 1985).
—— 'Reformatio und Receptio: Publikum, Massenmedien und Kommunikationshindernisse zu Beginn der hussitischen Reformbewegung', in J. Miethke (ed.), *Das Publikum politischer Theorie im 14. Jahrhundert* (Munich: Oldenbourg, 1992), 255–68.
SOUTHERN, R. W., *Western Views of Islam in the Middle Ages* (Cambridge, Mass.: Harvard University Press, 1962).
SPOTTS, F., *Bayreuth: A History of the Wagner Festival* (New Haven: Yale University Press, 1994).

STAYER, J. M., 'The Münsterite Rationalization of Bernhard Rothmann', *Journal of the History of Ideas*, 28 (1967), 179–92.

—— 'Melchior Hoffman and the Sword', *Mennonite Quarterly Review*, 45 (1971), 265–77.

—— *Anabaptists and the Sword* (Lawrence, Kan.: Coronado Press, 1972).

—— 'Christianity in One City: Anabaptist Münster, 1534–35', in Hillerbrand (ed.), *Radical Tendencies in the Reformation*, 117–34.

—— *The German Peasants' War and Anabaptist Community of Goods* (Montreal: McGill-Queen's University Press, 1991).

—— and PACKULL, W. O. (eds.), *The Anabaptists and Thomas Müntzer* (Dubuque, Ia.: Kendall/Hunt Publishing Co., 1980).

STEPHENS, J. N., *The Fall of the Florentine Republic 1512–1530* (Oxford: Oxford University Press, 1983).

STRAYER, J., 'France: The Holy Land, the Chosen People, and the Most Christian King', in Rabb and Seigel (eds.), *Action and Conviction in Early Modern Europe*, 3–16.

SUÁREZ FERNÁNDEZ, L., *Juan II y la frontera de Granada* (Valladolid: Universidad de Valladolid, Consejo Superior de Investigaciones Científicas, 1954).

SZAKÁLY, F., 'Das Bauerntum und die Kämpfe gegen die Türken bzw. gegen Habsburg in Ungarn im 16.–17. Jahrhundert', in Heckenast (ed.), *Aus der Geschichte*, 251–66.

SZŰCS, J., 'Die Nation in historischer Sicht und der nationale Aspekt der Geschichte', in his *Nation und Geschichte. Studien*, trans. J. Kerekes et al. (Gyoma: Corvina Kiadó, 1981), 11–160.

—— '"Nationalität" und "Nationalbewusstsein" in Mittelalter', in his *Nation und Geschichte. Studien*, trans. J. Kerekes et al. (Gyoma: Corvina Kiadó, 1981), 161–243.

—— 'Die Ideologie des Bauernkrieges', in his *Nation und Geschichte. Studien*, trans. J. Kerekes et al. (Gyoma: Corvina Kiadó, 1981), 329–78.

TAMBORRA, A., 'Problema turco e avamposto polacco fra Quattrocento e Cinquecento', in V. Branca and S. Graciotti (eds.), *Italia, Venezia e Polonia tra medio evo e età moderna* (Florence: Olschki, 1980), 531–49.

TANNER, M., *The Last Descendant of Aeneas: The Hapsburgs and the Mythic Image of the Emperor* (New Haven: Yale University Press, 1993).

TATEO, F., 'Letterati e guerrieri di fronte al pericolo turco', in his *Chierici e feudatari del Mezzogiorno* (Bari: Laterza, 1984), 21–68.

TERRY, A., 'War and Literature in Sixteenth-Century Spain', in J. R. Mulryne and M. Shewring (eds.), *War, Literature and the Arts in Sixteenth-Century Europe* (Basingstoke: Macmillan, 1989), 101–18.

THOMPSON, I. A. A., 'Castile, Spain and the Monarchy: The Political Community from *patria natural* to *patria nacional*', in R. L. Kagan and G. Parker (eds.), *Spain, Europe and the Atlantic World* (Cambridge: Cambridge University Press, 1995), 125–59.

THUMSER, M., 'Türkenfrage und öffentliche Meinung. Zeitgenössische Zeugnisse nach dem Fall von Konstantinopel (1453)', in Erkens (ed.), *Europa und die osmanische Expansion*, 59–78.

TRAME, R. H., *Rodrigo Sánchez de Arévalo 1404–1470: Spanish Diplomat and Champion of the Papacy* (Washington: Catholic University of America Press, 1958).

TYERMAN, C., *England and the Crusades 1095–1588* (Chicago: University of Chicago Press, 1988).

—— *The Invention of the Crusades* (Basingstoke: Macmillan, 1998).

VALE, M. G. A., *Charles VII* (London: Eyre Methuen, 1974).
—— 'France at the End of the Hundred Years War (*c.*1420–1461)', in Allmand (ed.), *New Cambridge Medieval History*, vii. 392–407.
VALOIS, N., 'Conseils et prédictions adressés à Charles VII, en 1445 par un certain Jean du Bois', *Annuaire-Bulletin de la Société de l'Histoire de France*, 46 (1909), 201–38.
VAN DER ESSEN, L., 'Croisade contre les hérétiques ou guerre contre des rebelles? La Psychologie des soldats et des officiers espagnols de l'armée de Flandre au XVIe siècle', *RHE* 51 (1956), 42–78.
VARGA, J. J., 'Europa und "Die Vormauer des Christentums". Die Entwicklungsgeschichte eines geflügelten Wortes', in Guthmüller and Kühlmann (eds.), *Europa und die Türken*, 55–63.
VIORA, M., 'Angelo Carletti da Chivasso e la crociata contro i Turchi del 1480–81', *Studi francescani*, NS 22 (1925), 319–40.
VOGLER, G., 'The Anabaptist Kingdom of Münster in the Tension between Anabaptist and Imperial Policy', in Hillerbrand (ed.), *Radical Tendencies in the Reformation*, 99–116.
VOGTHERR, T., '"Wenn hinten, weit, in der Türkei . . .". Die Türken in der spätmittelalterlichen Stadtchronistik Norddeutschlands', in Erkens (ed.), *Europa und die osmanische Expansion*, 103–25.
WAGNER, M. L., *Petr Chelčický: A Radical Separatist in Hussite Bohemia* (Scottdale, Pa.: Herald Press, 1983).
WALZER, M., 'Exodus 32 and the Theory of Holy War: The History of a Citation', *Harvard Theological Review*, 61 (1968), 1–14.
WEINSTEIN, D., *Savonarola and Florence: Prophecy and Patriotism in the Renaissance* (Princeton: Princeton University Press, 1970).
WILKS, M., 'Royal Patronage and Anti-Papalism from Ockham to Wyclif', in A. Hudson and M. Wilks (eds.), *From Ockham to Wyclif*, SCH Subsidia 5 (Oxford: Blackwell, 1987), 135–63.
WILLIAMS, G. H., 'Erasmus and the Reformers on Non-Christian Religions and *Salus extra Ecclesiam*', in Rabb and Seigel (eds.), *Action and Conviction in Early Modern Europe*, 319–70.
WINTER, J., *Sites of Memory, Sites of Mourning: The Great War in European Cultural History* (Cambridge: Cambridge University Press, 1995).
ZACHARIADOU, E. A., 'Holy War in the Aegean during the Fourteenth Century', in B. Arbel, B. Hamilton, and D. Jacoby (eds.), *Latins and Greeks in the Eastern Mediterranean after 1204* (London: Frank Cass, 1989), 212–25.

Index

The following abbreviations are used: a = archbishop [of]; b = bishop [of]; k = king [of]; NT = New Testament; OT = Old Testament; q = queen [of]

All individuals except rulers are listed under their last name. Entries are given letter by letter.

Index of Scriptural References